75 Readings:
A Freshman Anthology

D0161929

75 Readings:
A Freshman Anthology

McGraw-Hill Book Company

New York   St. Louis   San Francisco   Auckland   Bogotá   Hamburg   Johannesburg
London   Madrid   Mexico   Milan   Montreal   New Delhi   Panama
Paris   São Paulo   Singapore   Sydney   Tokyo   Toronto

**In special appreciation
Santi Buscemi
Middlesex County College**

This book was set in Times Roman by J. M. Post Graphics, Corp.
The editor was Emily G. Barrosse;
the cover was designed by Jane Moorman;
the production supervisor was Diane Renda.
Project supervision was done by The Total Book.
Arcata Graphics/Fairfield was printer and binder.

**75 READINGS:
A FRESHMAN ANTHOLOGY**

Copyright © 1987 by McGraw-Hill, Inc. All rights reserved. Printed in the
United States of America. Except as permitted under the United States Copyright Act of 1976, no part of this publication may be reproduced or distributed
in any form or by any means, or stored in a data base or retrieval system,
without the prior written permission of the publisher.

1 2 3 4 5 6 7 8 9 0 FGRFGR 8 9 4 3 2 1 0 9 8 7 6

ISBN 0-07-011816-7

Library of Congress Cataloging-in-Publication Data

75 readings.

    1. College readers.   2. English language—Rhetoric.
I. Title: Seventy-five readings.
PE1417.A13   1987   808′.0427   86-15189
ISBN 0-07-011816-7

Contents

2

DESCRIPTION

3

PROCESS

5
DIVISION AND CLASSIFICATION

6
COMPARISON AND CONTRAST

7

EXAMPLE AND ILLUSTRATION

8

CAUSE AND EFFECT

9

ANALOGY

10
ARGUMENT

Rhetorical Contents

GROWING UP/GROWING OLD

LAW, GOVERNMENT, AND
HUMAN RIGHTS

PROBLEMS, SOLUTIONS, AND CONSEQUENCES

TERRITORY AND COMPETITION

CULTURAL BY-PRODUCTS

ON LANGUAGE

ON WRITING

ON MEDIA

Preface

75 Readings: A Freshman Anthology is strategically designed to introduce students to a broad variety of both traditional and contemporary essays. This rhetorically organized collection—comprised of a total of 75 essays—includes classic selections as well as very topical pieces representing international, ethnic, and women writers. The primary aim has been to expose students to a range of styles while retaining maximum pedagogical flexibility for the instructor. Comprehensive apparatus, prepared by Professor Santi Buscemi of Middlesex County College, is provided separately in the Instructor's Manual to allow teachers greater flexibility in reading and writing assignments. Developed for each essay, the apparatus includes: Author's Biography, Vocabulary, Questions for Discussion, and Suggestions for Writing. The apparatus is also available on Ditto Masters.

Special thanks are due to those instructors who reviewed the anthology and pedagogical apparatus: Rosalie Hewitt, Northern Illinois University; Michael G. Moran, Clemson University; Leland Chambers, University of Denver; Robert Ochsner, University of Maryland—Baltimore County; Marion Linehan, Tarrant County Junior College—NE; and Timothy Terry Miller, Indian River Community College.

In addition, Kate Scheinman, Charlotte Smith, and the following people at McGraw-Hill helped to bring this project to fruition: Emily Barrosse, Phillip A. Butcher, Keith Herrmann, Alison Meerschaert, and Sheila Sponauer.

75 Readings:
A Freshman Anthology

Chapter One

Narration

Shooting an Elephant

George Orwell

1   In Moulmein, in lower Burma, I was hated by large numbers of people—the only time in my life that I have been important enough for this to happen to me. I was subdivisional police officer of the town, and in an aimless, petty kind of way anti-European feeling was very bitter. No one had the guts to raise a riot, but if a European woman went through the bazaars alone somebody would probably spit betel juice over her dress. As a police officer I was an obvious target and was baited whenever it seemed safe to do so. When a nimble Burman tripped me up on the football field and the referee (another Burman) looked the other way, the crowd yelled with hideous laughter. This happened more than once. In the end the sneering yellow faces of young men that met me everywhere, the insults hooted after me when I was at a safe distance, got badly on my nerves. The young Buddhist priests were the worst of all. There were several thousands of them in the town and none of them seemed to have anything to do except stand on street corners and jeer at Europeans.

2   All this was perplexing and upsetting. For at that time I had already made up my mind that imperialism was an evil thing and the sooner I chucked up my job and got out of it the better. Theoretically—and secretly, of course—I was all for the Burmese and all against their oppressors, the British. As for the job I was doing, I hated it more bitterly than I can perhaps make clear. In a job like that you see the dirty work of Empire at close quarters. The wretched prisoners huddling in the stinking cages of the lock-ups, the gray, cowed faces of the long-term convicts, the scarred buttocks of the men who had been flogged with bamboos—all these oppressed me with an intolerable sense of guilt. But I could get nothing into perspective. I was young and ill educated and I had had to think out my problems in the utter silence that is imposed on every Englishman in the East. I did not even know

that the British Empire is dying, still less did I know that it is a great deal better than the younger empires that are going to supplant it. All I knew was that I was stuck between my hatred of the empire I served and my rage against the evil-spirited little beasts who tried to make my job impossible. With one part of my mind I thought of the British Raj as an unbreakable tyranny, as something clamped down, in *saecula saeculorum,* upon the will of prostrate peoples; with another part I thought that the greatest joy in the world would be to drive a bayonet into a Buddhist priest's guts. Feelings like these are the normal by-products of imperialism; ask any Anglo-Indian official, if you can catch him off duty.

3   One day something happened which in a roundabout way was enlightening. It was a tiny incident in itself; but it gave me a better glimpse than I had had before of the real nature of imperialism—the real motives for which despotic governments act. Early one morning the sub-inspector at a police station the other end of the town rang me up on the 'phone and said that an elephant was ravaging the bazaar. Would I please come and do something about it? I did not know what I could do, but I wanted to see what was happening and I got on to a pony and started out. I took my rifle, an old .44 Winchester and much too small to kill an elephant, but I thought the noise might be useful *in terrorem.* Various Burmans stopped me on the way and told me about the elephant's doings. It was not, of course, a wild elephant, but a tame one which had gone "must." It had been chained up, as tame elephants always are when their attack of "must" is due, but on the previous night it had broken its chain and escaped. Its mahout, the only person who could manage it when it was in that state, had set out in pursuit, but had taken the wrong direction and was now twelve hours' journey away, and in the morning the elephant had suddenly reappeared in the town. The Burmese population had no weapons and were quite helpless against it. It had already destroyed somebody's bamboo hut, killed a cow and raided some fruit-stalls and devoured the stock; also it had met the municipal rubbish van and, when the driver jumped out and took to his heels, had turned the van over and inflicted violences upon it.

4   The Burmese sub-inspector and some Indian constables were wait-ing for me in the quarter where the elephant had been seen. It was a very poor quarter, a labyrinth of squalid bamboo huts, thatched with

palm-leaf, winding all over a steep hillside. I remember that it was a cloudy, stuffy morning at the beginning of the rains. We began questioning the people as to where the elephant had gone and, as usual, failed to get any definite information. That is invariably the case in the East; a story always sounds clear enough at a distance, but the nearer you get to the scene of events the vaguer it becomes. Some of the people said that the elephant had gone in one direction, some said that he had gone in another, some professed not even to have heard of any elephant. I had almost made up my mind that the whole story was a pack of lies, when we heard yells a little distance away. There was a loud, scandalized cry of "Go away, child! Go away this instant!" and an old woman with a switch in her hand came round the corner of a hut, violently shooing away a crowd of naked children. Some more women followed, clicking their tongues and exclaiming; evidently there was something that the children ought not to have seen. I rounded the hut and saw a man's dead body sprawling in the mud. He was an Indian, a black Dravidian coolie, almost naked, and he could not have been dead many minutes. The people said that the elephant had come suddenly upon him round the corner of the hut, caught him with its trunk, put its foot on his back and ground him into the earth. This was the rainy season and the ground was soft, and his face had scored a trench a foot deep and a couple of yards long. He was lying on his belly with arms crucified and head sharply twisted to one side. His face was coated with mud, the eyes wide open, the teeth bared and grinning with an expression of unendurable agony. (Never tell me, by the way, that the dead look peaceful. Most of the corpses I have seen looked devilish.) The friction of the great beast's foot had stripped the skin from his back as neatly as one skins a rabbit. As soon as I saw the dead man I sent an orderly to a friend's house nearby to borrow an elephant rifle. I had already sent back the pony, not wanting it to go mad with fright and throw me if it smelt the elephant.

5   The orderly came back in a few minutes with a rifle and five cartridges, and meanwhile some Burmans had arrived and told us that the elephant was in the paddy fields below, only a few hundred yards away. As I started forward practically the whole population of the quarter flocked out of the houses and followed me. They had seen the rifle and were all shouting excitedly that I was going to shoot the

elephant. They had not shown much interest in the elephant when he was merely ravaging their homes, but it was different now that he was going to be shot. It was a bit of fun to them, as it would be to an English crowd; besides they wanted the meat. It made me vaguely uneasy. I had no intention of shooting the elephant—I had merely sent for the rifle to defend myself if necessary—and it is always unnerving to have a crowd following you. I marched down the hill, looking and feeling a fool, with the rifle over my shoulder and an ever-growing army of people jostling at my heels. At the bottom, when you got away from the huts, there was a metalled road and beyond that a miry waste of paddy fields a thousand yards across, not yet ploughed but soggy from the first rains and dotted with coarse grass. The elephant was standing eight yards from the road, his left side toward us. He took not the slightest notice of the crowd's approach. He was tearing up bunches of grass, beating them against his knees to clean them, and stuffing them into his mouth.

6   I had halted on the road. As soon as I saw the elephant I knew with perfect certainty that I ought not to shoot him. It is a serious matter to shoot a working elephant—it is comparable to destroying a huge and costly piece of machinery—and obviously one ought not to do it if it can possibly be avoided. And at that distance, peacefully eating, the elephant looked no more dangerous than a cow. I thought then and I think now that his attack of "must" was already passing off; in which case he would merely wander harmlessly about until the mahout came back and caught him. Moreover, I did not in the least want to shoot him. I decided that I would watch him for a little while to make sure that he did not turn savage again, and then go home.

7   But at that moment I glanced round at the crowd that had followed me. It was an immense crowd, two thousand at the least and growing every minute. It blocked the road for a long distance on either side. I looked at the sea of yellow faces above the garish clothes—faces all happy and excited over this bit of fun, all certain that the elephant was going to be shot. They were watching me as they would watch a conjurer about to perform a trick. They did not like me, but with the magical rifle in my hands I was momentarily worth watching. And suddenly I realized that I should have to shoot the elephant after all. The people expected it of me and I had got to do it; I could feel their two thousand wills pressing me forward, irresistibly. And it was at this moment, as

I stood there with the rifle in my hands, that I first grasped the hollow-ness, the futility of the white man's dominion in the East. Here was I, the white man with his gun, standing in front of the unarmed native crowd—seemingly the leading actor of the piece; but in reality I was only an absurd puppet pushed to and fro by the will of those yellow faces behind. I perceived in this moment that when the white man turns tyrant it is his own freedom that he destroys. He becomes a sort of hollow, posing dummy, the conventionalized figure of a sahib. For it is the condition of his rule that he shall spend his life in trying to impress the "natives," and so in every crisis he has got to do what the "natives" expect of him. He wears a mask, and his face grows to fit it. I had got to shoot the elephant. I had committed myself to doing it when I sent for the rifle. A sahib has got to act like a sahib; he has got to appear resolute, to know his own mind and do definite things. To come all that way, rifle in hand, with two thousand people marching at my heels, and then to trail feebly away, having done nothing—no, that was im-possible. The crowd would laugh at me. And my whole life, every white man's life in the East, was one long struggle not to be laughed at.

8   But I did not want to shoot the elephant. I watched him beating his bunch of grass against his knees with that preoccupied grandmotherly air that elephants have. It seemed to me that it would be murder to shoot him. At that age I was not squeamish about killing animals, but I had never shot an elephant and never wanted to. (Somehow it always seems worse to kill a *large* animal.) Besides, there was the beast's owner to be considered. Alive, the elephant was worth at least a hundred pounds; dead, he would only be worth the value of his tusks, five pounds, possibly. But I had got to act quickly. I turned to some experienced-looking Burmans who had been there when we arrived, and asked them how the elephant had been behaving. They all said the same thing: he took no notice of you if you left him alone, but he might charge if you went too close to him.

9   It was perfectly clear to me what I ought to do. I ought to walk up to within, say, twenty-five yards of the elephant and test his behavior. If he charged, I could shoot; if he took no notice of me, it would be safe to leave him until the mahout came back. But also I knew that I was going to do no such thing. I was a poor shot with a rifle and the ground was soft mud into which one would sink at every step. If the

elephant charged and I missed him, I should have about as much chance as a toad under a steam-roller. But even then I was not thinking particularly of my own skin, only of the watchful yellow faces behind. For at that moment, with the crowd watching me, I was not afraid in the ordinary sense, as I would have been if I had been alone. A white man mustn't be frightened in front of "natives"; and so, in general, he isn't frightened. The sole thought in my mind was that if anything went wrong those two thousand Burmans would see me pursued, caught, trampled on, and reduced to a grinning corpse like that Indian up the hill. And if that happened it was quite probable that some of them would laugh. That would never do. There was only one alternative. I shoved the cartridges into the magazine and lay down on the road to get a better aim.

10   The crowd grew very still, and a deep, low, happy sigh, as of people who see the theater curtain go up at last, breathed from innumerable throats. They were going to have their bit of fun after all. The rifle was a beautiful German thing with cross-hair sights. I did not then know that in shooting an elephant one would shoot to cut an imaginary bar running from ear-hole to ear-hole. I ought, therefore, as the elephant was sideways on, to have aimed straight at his ear-hole; actually I aimed several inches in front of this, thinking the brain would be further forward.

11   When I pulled the trigger I did not hear the bang or feel the kick— one never does when a shot goes home—but I heard the devillish roar of glee that went up from the crowd. In that instant, in too short a time, one would have thought, even for the bullet to get there, a mysterious, terrible change had come over the elephant. He neither stirred, nor fell, but every line of his body had altered. He looked suddenly stricken, shrunken, immensely old, as though the frightful impact of the bullet had paralyzed him without knocking him down. At last, after what seemed a long time—it might have been five seconds, I dare say—he sagged flabbily to his knees. His mouth slobbered. An enormous senility seemed to have settled upon him. One could have imagined him thousands of years old. I fired again into the same spot. At the second shot he did not collapse but climbed with desperate slowness to his feet and stood weakly upright, with legs sagging and head drooping. I fired a third time. That was the shot that did for him. You could see the agony of it jolt his whole body and knock the last remnant of strength from his legs. But in falling he seemed for a moment to rise, for as his hind

legs collapsed beneath him he seemed to tower upward like a huge rock toppling, his trunk reaching skyward like a tree. He trumpeted, for the first and only time. And then down he came, his belly toward me, with a crash that seemed to shake the ground even where I lay.

12   I got up. The Burmans were already racing past me across the mud. It was obvious that the elephant would never rise again, but he was not dead. He was breathing very rhythmically with long rattling gasps, his great mound of a side painfully rising and falling. His mouth was wide open—I could see far down into caverns of pale pink throat. I waited a long time for him to die, but his breathing did not weaken. Finally I fired my two remaining shots into the spot where I thought his heart must be. The thick blood welled out of him like red velvet, but still he did not die. His body did not even jerk when the shots hit him, the tortured breathing continued without a pause. He was dying, very slowly and in great agony, but in some world remote from me where not even a bullet could damage him further. I felt that I had got to put an end to that dreadful noise. It seemed dreadful to see the great beast lying there, powerless to move and yet powerless to die, and not even to be able to finish him. I sent back for my small rifle and poured shot after shot into his heart and down his throat. They seemed to make no impression. The tortured gasps continued as steadily as the ticking of a clock.

13   In the end I could not stand it any longer and went away. I heard later that it took him half an hour to die. Burmans were bringing dahs and baskets even before I left, and I was told they had stripped his body almost to the bones by the afternoon.

14   Afterward, of course, there were endless discussions about the shooting of the elephant. The owner was furious, but he was only an Indian and could do nothing. Besides, legally I had done the right thing, for a mad elephant has to be killed, like a mad dog, if its owner fails to control it. Among the Europeans opinion was divided. The older men said I was right, the younger men said it was a damn shame to shoot an elephant for killing a coolie, because an elephant was worth more than any damn Coringhee coolie. And afterward I was very glad that the coolie had been killed; it put me legally in the right and it gave me a sufficient pretext for shooting the elephant. I often wondered whether any of the others grasped that I had done it solely to avoid looking a fool.

Salvation

Langston Hughes

1   I was saved from sin when I was going on thirteen. But not really saved. It happened like this. There was a big revival at my Auntie Reed's church. Every night for weeks there had been much preaching, singing, praying, and shouting, and some very hardened sinners had been brought to Christ, and the membership of the church had grown by leaps and bounds. Then just before the revival ended, they held a special meeting for children, "to bring the young lambs to the fold." My aunt spoke of it for days ahead. That night I was escorted to the front row and placed on the mourners' bench with all the other young sinners, who had not yet been brought to Jesus.

2   My aunt told me that when you were saved you saw a light, and something happened to you inside! And Jesus came into your life! And God was with you from then on! She said you could see and hear and feel Jesus in your soul. I believed her. I had heard a great many old people say the same thing and it seemed to me they ought to know. So I sat there calmly in the hot, crowded church, waiting for Jesus to come to me.

3   The preacher preached a wonderful rhythmical sermon, all moans and shouts and lonely cries and dire pictures of hell, and then he sang a song about the ninety and nine safe in the fold, but one little lamb was left out in the cold. Then he said: "Won't you come? Won't you come to Jesus? Young lambs, won't you come?" And he held out his arms to all us young sinners there on the mourners' bench. And the little girls cried. And some of them jumped up and went to Jesus right away. But most of us just sat there.

4   A great many old people came and knelt around us and prayed, old women with jet-black faces and braided hair, old men with work-gnarled hands. And the church sang a song about the lower lights are burning, some poor sinners to be saved. And the whole building rocked with prayer and song.

5   Still I kept waiting to *see* Jesus.

6   Finally all the young people had gone to the altar and were saved, but one boy and me. He was a rounder's son named Westley. Westley and I were surrounded by sisters and deacons praying. It was very hot in the church, and getting late now. Finally Westley said to me in a whisper: "God damn! I'm tired o' sitting here. Let's get up and be saved." So he got up and was saved.

7   Then I was left all alone on the mourners' bench. My aunt came and knelt at my knees and cried, while prayers and songs swirled all around me in the little church. The whole congregation prayed for me alone, in a mighty wail of moans and voices. And I kept waiting serenely for Jesus, waiting, waiting—but he didn't come. I wanted to see him, but nothing happened to me. Nothing! I wanted something to happen to me, but nothing happened.

8   I heard the songs and the minister saying: "Why don't you come? My dear child, why don't you come to Jesus? Jesus is waiting for you. He wants you. Why don't you come? Sister Reed, what is this child's name?"

9   "Langston," my aunt sobbed.

10   "Langston, why don't you come? Why don't you come and be saved? Oh, Lamb of God! Why don't you come?"

11   Now it was really getting late. I began to be ashamed of myself, holding everything up so long. I began to wonder what God thought about Westley, who certainly hadn't seen Jesus either, but who was now sitting proudly on the platform, swinging his knickerbockered legs and grinning down at me, surrounded by deacons and old women on their knees praying. God had not struck Westley dead for taking his name in vain or for lying in the temple. So I decided that maybe to save further trouble, I'd better lie, too, and say that Jesus had come, and get up and be saved.

12   So I got up.

13   Suddenly the whole room broke into a sea of shouting, as they saw me rise. Waves of rejoicing swept the place. Women leaped in the air. My aunt threw her arms around me. The minister took me by the hand and led me to the platform.

14   When things quieted down, in a hushed silence, punctuated by a few ecstatic "Amens," all the new young lambs were blessed in the name of God. Then joyous singing filled the room.

15　　That night, for the last time in my life but one—for I was a big boy twelve years old—I cried. I cried, in bed alone, and couldn't stop. I buried my head under the quilts, but my aunt heard me. She woke up and told my uncle I was crying because the Holy Ghost had come into my life, and because I had seen Jesus. But I was really crying because I couldn't bear to tell her that I had lied, that I had deceived everybody in the church, that I hadn't seen Jesus, and that now I didn't believe there was a Jesus any more, since he didn't come to help me.

Grandmother's Victory

Maya Angelou

1   "Thou shall not be dirty" and "Thou shall not be impudent" were the two commandments of Grandmother Henderson upon which hung our total salvation.

2   Each night in the bitterest winter we were forced to wash faces, arms, necks, legs and feet before going to bed. She used to add, with a smirk that unprofane people can't control when venturing into profanity, "and wash as far as possible, then wash possible."

3   We would go to the well and wash in the ice-cold, clear water, grease our legs with the equally cold stiff Vaseline, then tiptoe into the house. We wiped the dust from our toes and settled down for schoolwork, cornbread, clabbered milk, prayers and bed, always in that order. Momma was famous for pulling the quilts off after we had fallen asleep to examine our feet. If they weren't clean enough for her, she took the switch (she kept one behind the bedroom door for emergencies) and woke up the offender with a few aptly placed burning reminders.

4   The area around the well at night was dark and slick, and boys told about how snakes love water, so that anyone who had to draw water at night and then stand there alone and wash knew that moccasins and rattlers, puff adders and boa constrictors were winding their way to the well and would arrive just as the person washing got soap in her eyes. But Momma convinced us that not only was cleanliness next to Godliness, dirtiness was the inventor of misery.

5   The impudent child was detested by God and a shame to its parents and could bring destruction to its house and line. All adults had to be addressed as Mister, Missus, Miss, Auntie, Cousin, Unk, Uncle, Buhbah, Sister, Brother and a thousand other appellations indicating familial relationship and the lowliness of the addressor.

6   Everyone I knew respected these customary laws, except for the powhitetrash children.

7   Some families of powhitetrash lived on Momma's farm land be-

hind the school. Sometimes a gaggle of them came to the Store, filling the whole room, chasing out the air and even changing the well-known scents. The children crawled over the shelves and into the potato and onion bins, twanging all the time in their sharp voices like cigar-box guitars. They took liberties in my Store that I would never dare. Since Momma told us that the less you say to white-folks (or even powhite-trash) the better, Bailey and I would stand, solemn, quiet, in tne displaced air. But if one of the playful apparitions got close to us, I pinched it. Partly out of angry frustration and partly because I didn't believe in its flesh reality.

8   They called my uncle by his first name and ordered him around the Store. He, to my crying shame, obeyed them in his limping dip-straight-dip fashion.

9   My grandmother, too, followed their orders, except that she didn't seem to be servile because she anticipated their needs.

10   "Here's sugar, Miz Potter, and here's baking powder. You didn't buy soda last month, you'll probably be needing some."

11   Momma always directed her statements to the adults, but some-times, Oh painful sometimes, the grimy, snotty-nosed girls would an-swer her.

12   "Naw, Annie . . ."—to Momma? Who owned the land they lived on? Who forgot more than they would ever learn? If there was any justice in the world, God should strike them dumb at once!—"Just give us some extra sody crackers, and some more mackerel."

13   At least they never looked in her face, or I never caught them doing so. Nobody with a smidgen of training, not even the worst roust-about, would look right in a grown person's face. It meant the person was trying to take the words out before they were formed. The dirty little children didn't do that, but they threw their orders around the Store like lashes from a cat-o'-nine-tails.

14   When I was around ten years old, those scruffy children caused me the most painful and confusing experience I had ever had with my grandmother.

15   One summer morning, after I had swept the dirt yard of leaves, spearmint-gum wrappers and Vienna-sausage labels, I raked the yellow-red dirt, and made half-moons carefully, so that the design stood out clearly and mask-like. I put the rake behind the Store and came through the back of the house to find Grandmother on the front porch in her

big, wide white apron. The apron was so stiff by virtue of the starch that it could have stood alone. Momma was admiring the yard, so I joined her. It truly looked like a flat redhead that had been raked with a big-toothed comb. Momma didn't say anything but I knew she liked it. She looked over toward the school principal's house and to the right at Mr. McElroy's. She was hoping one of those community pillars would see the design before the day's business wiped it out. Then she looked upward to the school. My head had swung with hers, so at just about the same time we saw a troop of the powhitetrash kids marching over the hill and down by the side of the school.

16   I looked to Momma for direction. She did an excellent job of sagging from her waist down, but from the waist up she seemed to be pulling for the top of the oak tree across the road. Then she began to moan a hymn. Maybe not to moan, but the tune was so slow and the meter so strange that she could have been moaning. She didn't look at me again. When the children reached halfway down the hill, halfway to the Store, she said without turning, "Sister, go on inside."

17   I wanted to beg her, "Momma, don't wait for them. Come on inside with me. If they come in the Store, you go to the bedroom and let me wait on them. They only frighten me if you're around. Alone I know how to handle them." But of course I couldn't say anything, so I went in and stood behind the screen door.

18   Before the girls got to the porch I heard their laughter crackling and popping like pine logs in a cooking stove. I suppose my lifelong paranoia was born in those cold, molasses-slow minutes. They came finally to stand on the ground in front of Momma. At first they pretended seriousness. Then one of them wrapped her right arm in the crook of her left, pushed out her mouth and started to hum. I realized that she was aping my grandmother. Another said, "Naw, Helen, you ain't standing like her. This here's it." Then she lifted her chest, folded her arms and mocked that strange carriage that was Annie Henderson. Another laughed, "Naw, you can't do it. Your mouth ain't pooched out enough. It's like this."

19   I thought about the rifle behind the door, but I knew I'd never be able to hold it straight, and the .410, our sawed-off shotgun, which stayed loaded and was fired every New Year's night, was locked in the trunk and Uncle Willie had the key on his chain. Through the fly-specked screen-door, I could see that the arms of Momma's apron

jiggled from the vibrations of her humming. But her knees seemed to have locked as if they would never bend again.

20   She sang on. No louder than before, but no softer either. No slower or faster.

21   The dirt of the girls' cotton dresses continued on their legs, feet, arms and faces to make them all of a piece. Their greasy uncolored hair hung down, uncombed, with a grim finality. I knelt to see them better, to remember them for all time. The tears that had slipped down my dress left unsurprising dark spots, and made the front yard blurry and even more unreal. The world had taken a deep breath and was having doubts about continuing to revolve.

22   The girls had tired of mocking Momma and turned to other means of agitation. One crossed her eyes, stuck her thumbs in both sides of her mouth and said, "Look here, Annie." Grandmother hummed on and the apron strings trembled. I wanted to throw a handful of black pepper in their faces, to throw lye on them, to scream that they were dirty, scummy peckerwoods, but I knew I was as clearly imprisoned behind the scene as the actors outside were confined to their roles.

23   One of the smaller girls did a kind of puppet dance while her fellow clowns laughed at her. But the tall one, who was almost a woman, said something very quietly, which I couldn't hear. They all moved backward from the porch, still watching Momma. For an awful second I thought they were going to throw a rock at Momma, who seemed (except for the apron strings) to have turned into stone herself. But the big girl turned her back, bent down and put her hands flat on the ground—she didn't pick up anything. She simply shifted her weight and did a hand stand.

24   Her dirty bare feet and long legs went straight for the sky. Her dress fell down around her shoulders, and she had on no drawers. The slick pubic hair made a brown triangle where her legs came together. She hung in the vacuum of that lifeless morning for only a few seconds, then wavered and tumbled. The other girls clapped her on the back and slapped their hands.

25   Momma changed her song to "Bread of Heaven, bread of Heaven, feed me till I want no more."

26   I found that I was praying too. How long could Momma hold out? What new indignity would they think of to subject her to? Would I be able to stay out of it? What would Momma really like me to do?

27   Then they were moving out of the yard, on their way to town. They bobbed their heads and shook their slack behinds and turned, one at a time:

28   " 'Bye, Annie."

29   " 'Bye, Annie."

30   " 'Bye, Annie."

31   Momma never turned her head or unfolded her arms, but she stoped singing and said, " 'Bye, Miz Helen, 'bye, Miz Ruth, 'bye, Miz Eloise."

32   I burst. A firecracker July-the-Fourth burst. How could Momma call them Miz? The mean nasty things. Why couldn't she have come inside the sweet, cool store when we saw them breasting the hill? What did she prove? And then if they were dirty, mean and impudent, why did Momma have to call them Miz?

33   She stood another whole song through and then opened the screen door to look down on me crying in rage. She looked until I looked up. Her face was a brown moon that shone on me. She was beautiful. Something had happened out there, which I couldn't completely understand, but I could see that she was happy. Then she bent down and touched me as mothers of the church "lay hands on the sick and afflicted" and I quieted.

34   "Go wash your face, Sister." And she went behind the candy counter and hummed, "Glory, glory, hallelujah, when I lay my burden down."

35   I threw the well water on my face and used the weekday handkerchief to blow my nose. Whatever the contest had been out front, I knew Momma had won.

36   I took the rake back to the front yard. The smudged footprints were easy to erase. I worked for a long time on my new design and laid the rake behind the wash pot. When I came back in the Store, I took Momma's hand and we both walked outside to look at the pattern.

37   It was a large heart with lots of hearts growing smaller inside, and piercing from the outside rim to the smallest heart was an arrow. Momma said, "Sister, that's right pretty." Then she turned back to the Store and resumed, "Glory, glory, hallelujah, when I lay my burden down."

University Days

James Thurber

1   I passed all the other courses that I took at my university, but I could never pass botany. This was because all botany students had to spend several hours a week in a laboratory looking through a microscope at plant cells, and I could never see through a microscope. I never once saw a cell through a microscope. This used to enrage my instructor. He would wander around the laboratory pleased with the progress all the students were making in drawing the involved and, so I am told, interesting structure of flower cells, until he came to me. I would just be standing there. "I can't see anything," I would say. He would begin patiently enough, explaining how anybody can see through a microscope, but he would always end up in a fury, claiming that I could *too* see through a microscope but just pretended that I couldn't. "It takes away from the beauty of flowers anyway," I used to tell him. "We are not concerned with beauty in this course," he would say. "We are concerned solely with what I may call the *mechanics* of flars." "Well," I'd say, "I can't see anything." "Try it just once again," he'd say, and I would put my eye to the microscope and see nothing at all, except now and again a nebulous milky substance—a phenomenon of maladjustment. You were supposed to see a vivid, restless clockwork of sharply defined plant cells. "I see what looks like a lot of milk," I would tell him. This, he claimed, was the result of my not having adjusted the microscope properly, so he would readjust it for me, or rather, for himself. And I would look again and see milk.

2   I finally took a deferred pass, as they called it, and waited a year and tried again. (You had to pass one of the biological sciences or you couldn't graduate.) The professor had come back from vacation brown as a berry, bright-eyed, and eager to explain cell-structure again to his classes. "Well," he said to me, cheerily, when we met in the first laboratory hour of the semester, "we're going to see cells this time, aren't we?" "Yes, sir," I said. Students to right of me and to left of me

and in front of me were seeing cells; what's more, they were quietly drawing pictures of them in their notebooks. Of course, I didn't see anything.

3   "We'll try it," the professor said to me, grimly, "with every adjustment of the microscope known to man. As God is my witness, I'll arrange this glass so that you see cells through it or I'll give up teaching. In twenty-two years of botany, I—" He cut off abruptly for he was beginning to quiver all over, like Lionel Barrymore, and he genuinely wished to hold onto his temper; his scenes with me had taken a great deal out of him.

4   So we tried it with every adjustment of the microscope known to man. With only one of them did I see anything but blackness or the familiar lacteal opacity, and that time I saw, to my pleasure and amazement, a variegated constellation of flecks, specks, and dots. These I hastily drew. The instructor, noting my activity, came back from an adjoining desk, a smile on his lips and his eyebrows high in hope. He looked at my cell drawing. "What's that?" he demanded, with a hint of a squeal in his voice. "That's what I saw," I said. "You didn't, you didn't, you *didn't!*" he screamed, losing control of his temper instantly, and he bent over and squinted into the microscope. His head snapped up. "That's your eye!" he shouted. "You've fixed the lens so that it reflects! You've drawn your eye!"

5   Another course that I didn't like, but somehow managed to pass, was economics. I went to that class straight from the botany class, which didn't help me any in understanding either subject. I used to get them mixed up. But not as mixed up as another student in my economics class who came there direct from a physics laboratory. He was a tackle on the football team, named Bolenciecwcz. At that time Ohio State University had one of the best football teams in the country, and Bolenciecwcz was one of its outstanding stars. In order to be eligible to play it was necessary for him to keep up in his studies, a very difficult matter, for while he was not dumber than an ox he was not any smarter. Most of his professors were lenient and helped him along. None gave him more hints in answering questions or asked him simpler ones than the economics professor, a thin, timid man named Bassum. One day when we were on the subject of transportation and distribution, it came Bolenciecwcz's turn to answer a question. "Name one means of transportation," the professor said to him. No light came into the big tackle's

eyes. "Just any means of transportation," said the professor. Bolenciecwcz sat staring at him. "That is," pursued the professor, "any medium, agency, or method of going from one place to another." Bolenciecwcz had the look of a man who is being led into a trap. "You may choose among steam, horse-drawn, or electrically propelled vehicles," said the instructor. "I might suggest the one which we commonly take in making long journeys across land." There was a profound silence in which everybody stirred uneasily, including Bolenciecwcz and Mr. Bassum. Mr. Bassum abruptly broke this silence in an amazing manner. "Choo-choo-choo," he said, in a low voice, and turned instantly scarlet. He glanced appealingly around the room. All of us, of course, shared Mr. Bassum's desire that Bolenciecwcz should stay abreast of the class in economics, for the Illinois game, one of the hardest and most important of the season, was only a week off. "Toot, toot, tootoooooot!" some student with a deep voice moaned, and we all looked encouragingly at Bolenciecwcz. Somebody else gave a fine imitation of a locomotive letting off steam. Mr. Bassum himself rounded off the little show. "Ding, dong, ding, dong," he said, hopefully. Bolenciecwcz was staring at the floor now, trying to think, his great brow furrowed, his huge hands rubbing together, his face red.

6   "How did you come to college this year, Mr. Bolenciecwcz?" asked the professor. "*Chuffa* chuffa, *chuffa* chuffa."

7   "M'father sent me," said the football player.

8   "What on?" asked Bassum.

9   "I git an 'lowance," said the tackle, in a low, husky voice, obviously embarrassed.

10   "No, no," said Bassum. "Name a means of transportation. What did you *ride* here on?"

11   "Train," said Bolenciecwcz.

12   "Quite right," said the professor. "Now, Mr. Nugent, will you tell us—"

13   If I went through anguish in botany and economics—for different reasons—gymnasium work was even worse. I don't even like to think about it. They wouldn't let you play games or join in the exercises with your glasses on and I couldn't see with mine off. I bumped into professors, horizontal bars, agricultural students, and swinging iron rings. Not being able to see, I could take it but I couldn't dish it out. Also, in order to pass gymnasium (and you had to pass it to graduate) you

had to learn to swim if you didn't know how. I didn't like the swimming pool, I didn't like swimming, and I didn't like the swimming instructor, and after all these years I still don't. I never swam but I passed my gym work anyway, by having another student give my gymnasium number (978) and swim across the pool in my place. He was a quiet, amiable blond youth, number 473, and he would have seen through a microscope for me if we could have got away with it, but we couldn't get away with it. Another thing I didn't like about gymnasium work was that they made you strip the day you registered. It is impossible for me to be happy when I am stripped and being asked a lot of questions. Still, I did better than a lanky agricultural student who was cross-examined just before I was. They asked each student what college he was in—that is, whether Arts, Engineering, Commerce, or Agriculture. "What college are you in?" the instructor snapped at the youth in front of me. "Ohio State University," he said promptly.

14   It wasn't that agricultural student but it was another a whole lot like him who decided to take up journalism, possibly on the ground that when farming went to hell he could fall back on newspaper work. He didn't realize, of course, that that would be very much like falling back full-length on a kit of carpenter's tools. Haskins didn't seem cut out for journalism, being too embarrassed to talk to anybody and unable to use a typewriter, but the editor of the college paper assigned him to the cow barns, the sheep house, the horse pavilion, and the animal husbandry department generally. This was a genuinely big "beat," for it took up five times as much ground and got ten times as great a legislative appropriation as the College of Liberal Arts. The agricultural student knew animals, but nevertheless his stories were dull and colorlessly written. He took all afternoon on each of them, on account of having to hunt for each letter on the typewriter. Once in a while he had to ask somebody to help him hunt. "C" and "L," in particular, were hard letters for him to find. His editor finally got pretty much annoyed at the farmer-journalist because his pieces were so uninteresting. "See here, Haskins," he snapped at him one day, "why is it we never have anything hot from you on the horse pavilion? Here we have two hundred head of horses on this campus—more than any other university in the Western Conference except Purdue—and yet you never get any real lowdown on them. Now shoot over to the horse barns and dig up something lively." Haskins shambled out and came back in about an

hour; he said he had something. "Well, start it off snappily," said the editor. "Something people will read." Haskins set to work and in a couple of hours brought a sheet of typewritten paper to the desk; it was a two-hundred-word story about some disease that had broken out among the horses. Its opening sentence was simple but arresting. It read: "Who has noticed the sores on the tops of the horses in the animal husbandry building?"

15   Ohio State was a land grant university and therefore two years of military drill was compulsory. We drilled with old Springfield rifles and studied the tactics of the Civil War even though the World War was going on at the time. At 11 o'clock each morning thousands of freshmen and sophomores used to deploy over the campus, moodily creeping up on the old chemistry building. It was good training for the kind of warfare that was waged at Shiloh but it had no connection with what was going on in Europe. Some people used to think there was German money behind it, but they didn't dare say so or they would have been thrown in jail as German spies. It was a period of muddy thought and marked, I believe, the decline of higher education in the Middle West.

16   As a soldier I was never any good at all. Most of the cadets were glumly indifferent soldiers, but I was no good at all. Once General Littlefield, who was commandant of the cadet corps, popped up in front of me during regimental drill and snapped, "You are the main trouble with this university!" I think he meant that my type was the main trouble with the university but he may have meant me individually. I was mediocre at drill, certainly—that is, until my senior year. By that time I had drilled longer than anybody else in the Western Conference, having failed at military at the end of each preceding year so that I had to do it all over again. I was the only senior still in uniform. The uniform which, when new, had made me look like an interurban railway conductor, now that it had become faded and too tight made me look like Bert Williams in his bellboy act. This had a definitely bad effect on my morale. Even so, I had become by sheer practice little short of wonderful at squad maneuvers.

17   One day General Littlefield picked our company out of the whole regiment and tried to get it mixed up by putting it through one movement after another as fast as we could execute them: squads right, squads left, squads on right into line, squads right about, squads left front into

line, etc. In about three minutes one hundred and nine men were marching in one direction and I was marching away from them at an angle of forty degrees, all alone. "Company, halt!" shouted General Littlefield. "That man is the only man who has it right!" I was made a corporal for my achievement.

18   The next day General Littlefield summoned me to his office. He was swatting flies when I went in. I was silent and he was silent too, for a long time. I don't think he remembered me or why he had sent for me, but he didn't want to admit it. He swatted some more flies, keeping his eyes on them narrowly before he let go with the swatter. "Button up your coat!" he snapped. Looking back on it now I can see that he meant me although he was looking at a fly, but I just stood there. Another fly came to rest on a paper in front of the general and began rubbing its hind legs together. The general lifted the swatter cautiously. I moved restlessly and the fly flew away. "You startled him!" barked General Littlefield, looking at me severely. I said I was sorry. "That won't help the situation!" snapped the General, with cold military logic. I didn't see what I could do except offer to chase some more flies toward his desk, but I didn't say anything. He stared out the window at the faraway figures of co-eds crossing the campus toward the library. Finally, he told me I could go. So I went. He either didn't know which cadet I was or else he forgot what he wanted to see me about. It may have been that he wished to apologize for having called me the main trouble with the university; or maybe he had decided to compliment me on my brilliant drilling of the day before and then at the last minute decided not to. I don't know. I don't think about it much any more.

The Transaction

William Zinsser

1   Five or six years ago a school in Connecticut held "a day devoted to the arts," and I was asked if I would come and talk about writing as a vocation. When I arrived I found that a second speaker had been invited—Dr. Brock (as I'll call him), a surgeon who had recently begun to write and had sold some stories to national magazines. He was going to talk about writing as an avocation. That made us a panel, and we sat down to face a crowd of student newspaper editors and reporters, English teachers and parents, all eager to learn the secrets of our glamorous work.

2   Dr. Brock was dressed in a bright red jacket, looking vaguely Bohemian, as authors are supposed to look, and the first question went to him. What was it like to be a writer?

3   He said it was tremendous fun. Coming home from an arduous day at the hospital, he would go straight to his yellow pad and write his tensions away. The words just flowed. It was easy.

4   I then said that writing wasn't easy and it wasn't fun. It was hard and lonely, and the words seldom just flowed.

5   Next Dr. Brock was asked if it was important to rewrite. Absolutely not, he said. "Let it all hang out," and whatever form the sentences take will reflect the writer at his most natural.

6   I then said that rewriting is the essence of writing. I pointed out that professional writers rewrite their sentences repeatedly and then rewrite what they have rewritten. I mentioned that E. B. White and James Thurber were known to rewrite their pieces eight or nine times.

7   "What do you do on days when it isn't going well?" Dr. Brock was asked. He said he just stopped writing and put the work aside for a day when it would go better.

8   I then said that the professional writer must establish a daily schedule and stick to it. I said that writing is a craft, not an art, and

that the man who runs away from his craft because he lacks inspiration is fooling himself. He is also going broke.

9 "What if you're feeling depressed or unhappy?" a student asked. "Won't that affect your writing?"

10 Probably it will, Dr. Brock replied. Go fishing. Take a walk.

11 Probably it won't, I said. If your job is to write every day, you learn to do it like any other job.

12 A student asked if we found it useful to circulate in the literary world. Dr. Brock said that he was greatly enjoying his new life as a man of letters, and he told several lavish stories of being taken to lunch by his publisher and his agent at Manhattan restaurants where writers and editors gather. I said that professional writers are solitary drudges who seldom see other writers.

13 "Do you put symbolism in your writing?" a student asked me.

14 "Not if I can help it," I replied. I have an unbroken record of missing the deeper meaning in any story, play or movie, and as for dance and mime, I have never had even a remote notion of what is being conveyed.

15 "I *love* symbols!" Dr. Brock exclaimed, and he described with gusto the joys of weaving them through his work.

16 So the morning went, and it was a revelation to all of us. At the end Dr. Brock told me he was enormously interested in my answers—it had never occurred to him that writing could be hard. I told him I was just as interested in *his* answers—it had never occurred to me that writing could be easy. (Maybe I should take up surgery on the side.)

17 As for the students, anyone might think that we left them bewildered. But in fact we probably gave them a broader glimpse of the writing process than if only one of us had talked. For of course there isn't any "right" way to do such intensely personal work. There are all kinds of writers and all kinds of methods, and any method that helps somebody to say what he wants to say is the right method for him.

18 Some people write by day, others by night. Some people need silence, others turn on the radio. Some write by hand, some by typewriter, some by talking into a tape recorder. Some people write their first draft in one long burst and then revise; others can't write the second paragraph until they have fiddled endlessly with the first.

19 But all of them are vulnerable and all of them are tense. They

are driven by a compulsion to put some part of themselves on paper, and yet they don't just write what comes naturally. They sit down to commit an act of literature, and the self who emerges on paper is a far stiffer person than the one who sat down. The problem is to find the real man or woman behind all the tension.

20   For ultimately the product that any writer has to sell is not his subject, but who he is. I often find myself reading with interest about a topic that I never thought would interest me—some unusual scientific quest, for instance. What holds me is the enthusiasm of the writer for his field. How was he drawn into it? What emotional baggage did he bring along? How did it change his life? It is not necessary to want to spend a year alone at Walden Pond to become deeply involved with a man who did.

21   This is the personal transaction that is at the heart of good nonfiction writing. Out of it come two of the most important qualities that this book will go in search of: humanity and warmth. Good writing has an aliveness that keeps the reader reading from one paragraph to the next, and it's not a question of gimmicks to "personalize" the author. It's a question of using the English language in a way that will achieve the greatest strength and the least clutter.

22   Can such principles be taught? Maybe not. But most of them can be learned.

Hemingway and Fitzgerald

Morley Callaghan

1   A week later, a little after three, I was at home doing some work on a new novel. My wife was puttering around. Later on I was to call for Ernest. A knock came on the door. And there were Scott and Ernest. The two old friends seemed to be in the best of humor. I could hardly conceal my pleasure. When I had come to Paris I had wanted to enjoy the company of these two men. Now they were together and they had come to my place—my friends. They had had lunch, Ernest said, and had decided to pick me up rather than wait for me. And Scott now was having his way. Ernest was carrying the bag that held the gloves. While I was getting ready, Scott talked to Loretto. But Ernest, having spotted a copy of *The New York Times* Book Review on top of our trunk, began to go through it carefully. I can still see him standing by the window, slowly turning the pages. I can see us waiting at the door until he had finished reading a review.

2   On the way to the American Club in the taxi, it seemed to me that Scott and Ernest were at ease with each other. There was no sense of strain and Scott looked alert and happy. We joked a bit. At the club— I remember the scene so vividly—I remember how Scott, there for the first time, looked around in surprise. The floor had no mat. Through the doorway opening into the next room, he could see two young fellows playing billiards. Scott sat down on the bench by the wall, while Ernest and I stripped. Then Ernest had him take out his watch and gave him his instructions. A round was to be three minutes, then a minute for a rest. As he took these instructions, listening carefully, Scott had none of Míro's air of high professionalism. He was too enchanted at being there with us. Moving off the bench, he squatted down, a little smile on his face. "Time," he called.

3   Our first round was like most of the rounds we had fought that summer, with me shuffling around, and Ernest, familiar with my style, leading and chasing after me. No longer did he rush in with his old

brisk confidence. Now he kept an eye on my left and he was harder to hit. As I shuffled around I could hear the sound of clicking billiard balls from the adjoining room.

4   "Time," Scott called promptly. When we sat down beside him, he was rather quiet, meditative, and I could tell by the expression on his face that he was mystified. He must have come there with some kind of a picture of Ernest, the fighter, in his head. For Ernest and me it was just like any other day. We chatted and laughed. And it didn't seem to be important to us that Scott was there. He had made no comment that could bother us. He seemed to be content that he was there concentrating on the minute hand of his watch. "Time," he called.

5   Right at the beginning of that round Ernest got careless; he came in too fast, his left down, and he got smacked on the mouth. His lip began to bleed. It had often happened. It should have meant nothing to him. Hadn't he joked with Jimmy, the bartender, about always having me for a friend while I could make his lip bleed? Out of the corner of his eye he may have seen the shocked expression on Scott's face. Or the taste of blood in his mouth may have made him want to fight more savagely. He came lunging in, swinging more recklessly. As I circled around him, I kept jabbing at his bleeding mouth. I had to forget all about Scott, for Ernest had become rougher, his punching a little wilder than usual. His heavy punches, if they had landed, would have stunned me. I had to punch faster and harder myself to keep away from him. It bothered me that he was taking the punches on the face like a man telling himself he only needed to land one big punch himself.

6   Out of the corner of my eye, as I bobbed and weaved, I could see one of the young fellows who had been playing billiards come to the door and stand there, watching. He was in his shirt sleeves, but he was wearing a vest. He held his cue in his hand like a staff. I could see Scott on the bench. I was wondering why I was tiring, for I hadn't been hit solidly. Then Ernest, wiping the blood from his mouth with his glove, and probably made careless with exasperation and embarrassment from having Scott there, came leaping in at me. Stepping in, I beat him to the punch. The timing must have been just right. I caught him on the jaw; spinning around he went down, sprawled out on his back.

7   If Ernest and I had been there alone I would have laughed. I was sure of my boxing friendship with him; in a sense I was sure of him,

too. Ridiculous things had happened in that room. Hadn't he spat in my face? And I felt no surprise seeing him flat on his back. Shaking his head a little to clear it, he rested a moment on his back. As he rose slowly, I expected him to curse, then laugh.

8   "Oh, my God!" Scott cried suddenly. When I looked at him, alarmed, he was shaking his head helplessly. "I let the round go four minutes," he said.

9   "Christ!" Ernest yelled. He got up. He was silent for a few seconds. Scott, staring at his watch, was mute and wondering. I wished I were miles away. "All right, Scott," Ernest said savagely, "If you want to see me getting the shit knocked out of me, just say so. Only don't say you made a mistake," and he stomped off to the shower room to wipe the blood from his mouth.

10   As I tried to grasp the meaning behind his fierce words I felt helpless with wonder, and nervous too; I seemed to be on the edge of some dark pit, and I could only stare blankly at Scott, who, as his eyes met mine, looked sick. Ernest had told me he had been avoiding Scott because Scott was a drunk and a nuisance and he didn't want to be bothered with him. It was plain now it wasn't the whole story. Lashing out with those bitter angry words, Ernest had practically shouted that he was aware Scott had some deep hidden animosity toward him. Shaken as I was, it flashed through my mind, Is the animosity in Scott, or is it really in Ernest? And why should it be in Ernest? Did Scott do something for him once? Is it that Scott helped him along and for months and months he's wanted to be free of him? Or does he think he knows something—knows Scott has to resent him? What is it? Not just that Scott's a drunk. I knew there was something else.

11   Then Scott came over to me, his face ashen, and he whispered, "Don't you see I got fascinated watching? I forgot all about the watch. My God, he thinks I did it on purpose. Why would I do it on purpose?"

12   "You wouldn't," I said, deeply moved, for he looked so stricken. For weeks he had been heaping his admiration of Ernest on me, his hero worship, and I knew of his eagerness for the companionship. Anyone who could say that he was under some secret and malevolent compulsion to let the round go on would have to say, too, that all men are twisted and no man knows what is in his heart. All I knew was that for weeks he had wanted to be here with us, and now that he was here it had brought him this.

13   "Look, Scott," I whispered. "If you did it on purpose you wouldn't have suddenly cried out that you had let the round go on. You didn't need to. You would have kept quiet. Ernest will see it himself." But Scott didn't answer. He looked as lonely and as desperate as he had looked that night when he had insisted on coming to the Deux Magots with Loretto and me. The anguish in his face was the anguish of a man who felt that everything he had stood for when he had been at his best, had been belittled.

14   "Come on, Scott," I whispered. "Ernest didn't mean it. It's a thing I might have said myself. A guy gets sore and blurts out the first crazy thing that comes into his head."

15   "No, you heard him. He believes I did it on purpose," he whispered bitterly. "What can I do, Morley?"

16   "Don't do anything," I whispered. "Forget the whole thing. He'll want to forget it himself. You'll see."

17   He moved away from me as Ernest returned from the shower room. With his face washed, Ernest looked much calmer. He had probably done a lot of thinking, too. Yet he offered no retraction. For my part, I tried to ignore the whole incident. Since we had had a good two or three minutes' rest to make up for the long round, why couldn't we go on now? I asked. It gave us something to do. Ernest and I squared off.

18   Scott, appearing alert and efficient, and hiding his terrible sense of insult and bitterness, called "Time." As I look back now I wonder why it didn't occur to me, as we began the round, that Ernest might try to kill me. But between us there was no hostility. The fact that I had been popping him, and then had clipped him and knocked him down, was part of our boxing. We went a good brisk round, both keeping out of trouble. When we clinched, my eye would wander to Scott, sitting there so white-faced. Poor Scott. Then suddenly he made it worse. The corner of a wrestling mat stuck out from under the parallel bars, and when I half tripped on it and went down on one knee, Scott, to mollify Ernest, called out foolishly, but eagerly, "One knockdown to Ernest, one to Morley," and if I had been Ernest, I think I would have snarled at him, no matter how good his intentions were.

19   But it was to continue to be a terrible and ridiculous afternoon for Ernest. It is a wonder he didn't go a little mad.

20   As soon as we had finished the round, that slender young fellow

who had been playing billiards, the one wearing the vest, who had been standing watching, his cue in his hand, came over to us. He might have been an inch taller than me, but he was very slender; he couldn't have weighed more than a hundred and thirty-five pounds. A student probably. "Excuse me," he said to Ernest in an English accent. "I've been watching. Do you mind me saying something? Well, in boxing it isn't enough to be aggressive and always punching. If you don't mind me saying so, the real science of boxing is in defense, in not getting hit."

21   It was incredible. The student was prepared to tell Ernest how to box. I was shocked and fearful. Both Scott and I, gaping at the student, must have been sharing the same sense of dread. What would Ernest do? A man can stand only so many mortifications in a single afternoon. If Ernest had grabbed the presumptuous fellow's billiard cue and broken it over his head, I wouldn't have been surprised.

22   Yet Ernest, after waiting a moment, the moment of astonishment, asked quietly, "Do you think you could show me?"

23   "Well, I could try," the young fellow said modestly.

24   "Good," said Ernest. "No, wait. Don't show me. Show him," and he pointed at me. "I'll watch."

25   Now I, in my turn, felt a twinge of resentment against Ernest. The student didn't want to show me how to box; he wanted to show Ernest, didn't he? I was to be used as a tuning fork. And who could tell whether or not this slender fellow was an English lightweight champion? Scott hadn't said a word. Nor did he speak as he removed Ernest's gloves and laced them on the intruder. Squaring off with him, I was ready to cover up like a turtle. As we circled around each other, I tried warily to make him lead at me. A feeble left did come at me, but it seemed to be only a feint. This boy was obviously a counterpuncher. Sooner or later I would have to lead at him. He had probably worked with pros. He was probably a hooker; I had always been rattled by a good hooker. I would lead now, then he would blow my head off. But gradually I was forcing him into a corner. Suddenly I caught a familiar expression in his eyes. I could see he was more scared of me than I was of him. As I began to flail away happily at the young fellow's head, Ernest suddenly shouted, "Stop!"

26   Now Ernest had a very good moment. In a beautiful bit of acting, not a trace of mockery in his tone, he said to the student, "I think I understand what you meant. Now show me." Ernest now unlaced my

gloves. I in turn laced them on him. The student looked pale and worried. Against me he had been inept and he knew it, and he knew, too, that he had in effect invited Ernest to knock his block off. Then he caught the derision in Ernest's eyes. Shaking his head apologetically, he would have withdrawn. "No, come on. You've got to show me," Ernest insisted.

27 The student still believed, no doubt, that Ernest was wide open. As he faced him he crouched a little, his hands high, ready to demonstrate his defense. Smiling faintly, Ernest spread his legs, stood rooted there like a great stiff tree trunk, and simply stuck his long left arm straight out like a pole and put his right glove on his hip, contemptuously. He refused to move. It was a splendid dramatic gesture of complete disdain. In fairness to him, he didn't try to clobber the boy, didn't try to strike a single blow. As the student circled around him, he, himself, turned slowly like a gate, the hand still on his hip, the great pole of an arm thrust out stiffly.

28 The student grew humiliated. Without hitting a blow or being hit, he quit. "I'm sorry," he said. "I really haven't done much boxing. I've read a lot about it. It looked much easier than it is," and he held out his gloves to me and let me unlace them. I didn't feel sorry for him. He went back quickly to his billiard table.

29 The student's absurd intervention, adding to the general sense of humiliation, must have put Scott more on edge. He must have felt bewildered. Yet now my two friends began to behave splendidly. Not a word was said about the student. We were all suddenly polite, agreeable, friendly and talkative. I knew how Scott felt; he had told me. He felt bitter, insulted, disillusioned in the sense that he had been made saved him for Ernest. An apology. A restoration of respect, a lifting of the accusation. But Ernest had no intention of apologizing. He obviously saw no reason why he should. So we all behaved splendidly. We struck up a graceful camaraderie. Ernest was jovial with Scott. We were all jovial. We went out and walked up to the Falstaff. And no one watching us sitting at the bar could have imagined that Scott's pride had been shattered.

30 Yet he had some class, some real style there at the bar. I told Ernest that Scott agreed with me that the chapters of a novel I had started ought to be abandoned. I remember Ernest saying, "There are two ways of looking at it. You can think of a career, and would it help

your career to have it published? Or you can say to hell with a career and publish it anyway." Scott said he was glad I wasn't going on with the book. As we exchanged opinions I noticed that two of the patrons, two young fellows at a nearby table, were craning their necks, listening and watching. And I laughed and said that by tomorrow word would go around the café that I, shamefully, was letting Fitzgerald and Hemingway tell me what to do about a book. Ernest said, "What do you care? We're professionals. We only care whether the thing is as good as it should be." And again, as I say, anyone watching would have believed that we were three writers talking about a literary problem. No one could have imagined anything had happened that could be heartbreaking. Well, I had come a long way to have my two friends get together with me, and here they were.

The Wild Man of the Green Swamp

Maxine Hong Kingston

1   For eight months in 1975, residents on the edge of Green Swamp, Florida, had been reporting to the police that they had seen a Wild Man. When they stepped toward him, he made strange noises as in a foreign language and ran back into the saw grass. At first, authorities said the Wild Man was a mass hallucination. Man-eating animals lived in the swamp, and a human being could hardly find a place to rest without sinking. Perhaps it was some kind of a bear the children had seen.

2   In October, a game officer saw a man crouched over a small fire, but as he approached, the figure ran away. It couldn't have been a bear because the Wild Man dragged a burlap bag after him. Also, the fire was obviously man-made.

3   The fish-and-game wardens and the sheriff's deputies entered the swamp with dogs but did not search for long; no one could live in the swamp. The mosquitoes alone would drive him out.

4   The Wild Man made forays out of the swamp. Farmers encountered him taking fruit and corn from the turkeys. He broke into a house trailer, but the occupant came back, and the Wild Man escaped out a window. The occupant said that a bad smell came off the Wild Man. Usually, the only evidence of him were his abandoned campsites. At one he left the remains of a four-foot-long alligator, of which he had eaten the feet and tail.

5   In May a posse made an air and land search; the plane signaled down to the hunters on the ground, who circled the Wild Man. A fish-and-game warden "brought him down with a tackle," according to the news. The Wild Man fought, but they took him to jail. He looked Chinese, so they found a Chinese in town to come translate.

6   The Wild Man talked a lot to the translator. He told him his name. He said he was thirty-nine years old, the father of seven children, who were in Taiwan. To support them, he had shipped out on a Liberian freighter. He had gotten very homesick and asked everyone if he could

leave the ship and go home. But the officers would not let him off. They sent messages to China to find out about him. When the ship landed, they took him to the airport and tried to put him on an airplane to some foreign place. Then, he said, the white demons took him to Tampa Hospital, which is for insane people, but he escaped, just walked out and went into the swamp.

7   The interpreter asked how he lived in the swamp. He said he ate snakes, turtles, armadillos, and alligators. The captors could tell how he lived when they opened up his bag, which was not burlap but a pair of pants with the legs knotted. Inside, he had carried a pot, a piece of sharpened tin, and a small club, which he had made by sticking a railroad spike into a section of aluminum tubing.

8   The sheriff found the Liberian freighter that the Wild Man had been on. The ship's officers said that they had not tried to stop him from going home. His shipmates had decided that there was something wrong with his mind. They had bought him a plane ticket and arranged his passport to send him back to China. They had driven him to the airport, but there he began screaming and weeping and would not get on the plane. So they had found him a doctor, who sent him to Tampa Hospital.

9   Now the doctors at the jail gave him medicine for the mosquito bites, which covered his entire body, and medicine for his stomachache. He was getting better, but after he'd been in jail for three days, the U.S. Border Patrol told him they were sending him back. He became hysterical. That night, he fastened his belt to the bars, wrapped it around his neck, and hung himself.

10   In the newspaper picture he did not look very wild, being led by the posse out of the swamp. He did not look dirty, either. He wore a checkered shirt unbuttoned at the neck, where his white undershirt showed; his shirt was tucked into his pants; his hair was short. He was surrounded by men in cowboy hats. His fingers stretching open, his wrists pulling apart to the extent of the handcuffs, he lifted his head, his eyes screwed shut, and cried out.

11   There was a Wild Man in our slough too, only he was a black man. He wore a shirt and no pants, and some mornings when we walked to school, we saw him asleep under the bridge. The police came and took him away. The newspaper said he was crazy; it said the police had been on the lookout for him for a long time, but we had seen him every day.

The Discus Thrower

Richard Selzer

1   I spy on my patients. Ought not a doctor to observe his patients by any means and from any stance, that he might the more fully assemble evidence? So I stand in the doorways of hospital rooms and gaze. Oh, it is not all that furtive an act. Those in bed need only look up to discover me. But they never do.

2   From the doorway of Room 542 the man in the bed seems deeply tanned. Blue eyes and close-cropped white hair give him the appearance of vigor and good health. But I know that his skin is not brown from the sun. It is rusted, rather, in the last stage of containing the vile repose within. And the blue eyes are frosted, looking inward like the windows of a snowbound cottage. This man is blind. This man is also legless—the right leg missing from midthigh down, the left from just below the knee. It gives him the look of a bonsai, roots and branches pruned into the dwarfed facsimile of a great tree.

3   Propped on pillows, he cups his right thigh in both hands. Now and then he shakes his head as though acknowledging the intensity of his suffering. In all of this he makes no sound. Is he mute as well as blind?

4   The room in which he dwells is empty of all possessions—no get-well cards, small, private caches of food, day-old flowers, slippers, all the usual kickshaws of the sickroom. There is only the bed, a chair, a nightstand, and a tray on wheels that can be swung across his lap for meals.

5   "What time is it?" he asks.

6   "Three o'clock."

7   "Morning or afternoon?"

8   "Afternoon."

9   He is silent. There is nothing else he wants to know.

10   "How are you?" I say.

11   "Who is it?" he asks.

12   "It's the doctor. How do you feel?"

13   He does not answer right away.

14   "Feel?" he says.

15   "I hope you feel better," I say.

16   I press the button at the side of the bed.

17   "Down you go," I say.

18   "Yes, down," he says.

19   He falls back upon the bed awkwardly. His stumps, unweighted by legs and feet, rise in the air, presenting themselves. I unwrap the bandages from the stumps, and begin to cut away the black scabs and the dead, glazed fat with scissors and forceps. A shard of white bone comes loose. I pick it away. I wash the wounds with disinfectant and redress the stumps. All this while, he does not speak. What is he thinking behind those lids that do not blink? Is he remembering a time when he was whole? Does he dream of feet? Of when his body was not a rotting log?

20   He lies solid and inert. In spite of everything, he remains impressive, as though he were a sailor standing athwart a slanting deck.

21   "Anything more I can do for you?" I ask.

22   For a long moment he is silent.

23   "Yes," he says at last and without the least irony. "You can bring me a pair of shoes."

24   In the corridor, the head nurse is waiting for me.

25   "We have to do something about him," she says. "Every morning he orders scrambled eggs for breakfast, and, instead of eating them, he picks up the plate and throws it against the wall."

26   "Throws his plate?"

27   "Nasty. That's what he is. No wonder his family doesn't come to visit. They probably can't stand him any more than we can."

28   She is waiting for me to do something.

29   "Well?"

30   "We'll see," I say.

31   The next morning I am waiting in the corridor when the kitchen delivers his breakfast. I watch the aide place the tray on the stand and swing it across his lap. She presses the button to raise the head of the bed. Then she leaves.

32   In time the man reaches to find the rim of the tray, then on to find the dome of the covered dish. He lifts off the cover and places it on the stand. He fingers across the plate until he probes the eggs. He lifts the plate in both hands, sets it on the palm of his right hand, centers it, balances it. He hefts it up and down slightly, getting the feel of it. Abruptly, he draws back his right arm as far as he can.

33   There is the crack of the plate breaking against the wall at the foot of his bed and the small wet sound of the scrambled eggs dropping to the floor.

34   And then he laughs. It is a sound you have never heard. It is something new under the sun. It could cure cancer.

35   Out in the corridor, the eyes of the head nurse narrow.

36   "Laughed, did he?"

37   She writes something down on her clipboard.

38   A second aide arrives, brings a second breakfast tray, puts it on the nightstand, out of his reach. She looks over at me shaking her head and making her mouth go. I see that we are to be accomplices.

39   "I've got to feed you," she says to the man.

40   "Oh, no you don't," the man says.

41   "Oh, yes I do," the aide says, "after the way you just did. Nurse says so."

42   "Get me my shoes," the man says.

43   "Here's oatmeal," the aide says. "Open." And she touches the spoon to his lower lip.

44   "I ordered scrambled eggs," says the man.

45   "That's right," the aide says."

46   I step forward.

47   "Is there anything I can do?" I say.

48   "Who are you?" the man asks.

49   In the evening I go once more to that ward to make my rounds. The head nurse reports to me that Room 542 is deceased. She has discovered this quite by accident, she says. No, there had been no sound. Nothing. It's a blessing, she says.

50   I go into his room, a spy looking for secrets. He is still there in his bed. His face is relaxed, grave, dignified. After a while, I turn to leave. My gaze sweeps the wall at the foot of the bed, and I see the place where it has been repeatedly washed, where the wall looks very clean and very white.

Chapter Two

Description

Where the World Began

Margaret Laurence

1   A strange place it was, that place where the world began. A place of incredible happenings, splendors and revelations, despairs like multitudinous pits of isolated hells. A place of shadow-spookiness, inhabited by the unknowable dead. A place of jubilation and of mourning, horrible and beautiful.

2   It was, in fact, a small prairie town.

3   Because that settlement and that land were my first and for many years my only real knowledge of this planet, in some profound way they remain my world, my way of viewing. My eyes were formed there. Towns like ours, set in a sea of land, have been described thousands of times as dull, bleak, flat, uninteresting. I have had it said to me that the railway trip across Canada is spectacular, except for the prairies, when it would be desirable to go to sleep for several days, until the ordeal is over. I am always unable to argue this point effectively. All I can say is—well, you really have to live there to know that country. The town of my childhood could be called bizarre, agonizingly repressive or cruel at times, and the land in which it grew could be called harsh in the violence of its seasonal changes. But never merely flat or uninteresting. Never dull.

4   In winter, we used to hitch rides on the back of the milk sleigh, our moccasins squeaking and slithering on the hard rutted snow of the roads, our hands in ice-bubbled mitts hanging onto the box edge of the sleigh for dear life, while Bert grinned at us through his great frosted mustache and shouted the horse into speed, daring us to stay put. Those mornings, rising, there would be the perpetual fascination of the frost feathers on windows, the ferns and flowers and eerie faces traced there during the night by unseen artists of the wind. Evenings, coming back from skating, the sky would be black but not dark, for you could see a cold glitter of stars from one side of the earth's rim to the other. And then the sometime astonishment when you saw the Northern Lights

flaring across the sky, like the scrawled signature of God. After a blizzard, when the snowplow hadn't yet got through, school would be closed for the day, the assumption being that the town's young could not possibly flounder through five feet of snow in the pursuit of education. We would then gaily don snowshoes and flounder for miles out into the white dazzling deserts, in pursuit of a different kind of knowing. If you came back too close to night, through the woods at the foot of the town hill, the thin black branches of poplar and chokecherry now meringued with frost, sometimes you heard coyotes. Or maybe the banshee wolf-voices were really only inside your head.

5   Summers were scorching, and when no rain came and the wheat became bleached and dried before it headed, the faces of farmers and townsfolk would not smile much, and you took for granted, because it never seemed to have been any different, the frequent knocking at the back door and the young men standing there, mumbling or thrusting defiantly their requests for a drink of water and a sandwich if you could spare it. They were riding the freights, and you never knew where they had come from, or where they might end up, if anywhere. The Drought and Depression were like evil deities which had been there always. You understood and did not understand.

6   Yet the outside world had its continuing marvels. The poplar bluffs and the small river were filled and surrounded with a zillion different grasses, stones, and weed flowers. The meadowlarks sang undaunted from the twanging telephone wires along the gravel highway. Once we found an old flat-bottomed scow, and launched her, poling along the shallow brown waters, mending her with wodges of hastily chewed Spearmint, grounding her among the tangles of yellow marsh marigolds that grew succulently along the banks of the shrunken river, while the sun made our skins smell dusty-warm.

7   My best friend lived in an apartment above some stores on Main Street (its real name was Mountain Avenue, goodness knows why), an elegant apartment with royal-blue velvet curtains. The back roof, scarcely sloping at all, was corrugated tin, of a furnace-like warmth on a July afternoon, and we would sit there drinking lemonade and looking across the back lane at the Fire Hall. Sometimes our vigil would be rewarded. Oh joy! Somebody's house burning down! We had an almost-perfect callousness in some ways. Then the wooden tower's bronze bell would clonk and toll like a thousand speeded funerals in a time of plague, and

in a few minutes the team of giant black horses would cannon forth, pulling the fire wagon like some scarlet chariot of the Goths, while the firemen clung with one hand, adjusting their helmets as they went.

8   The oddities of the place were endless. An elderly lady used to serve, as her afternoon tea offering to other ladies, soda biscuits spread with peanut butter and topped with a whole marshmallow. Some considered this slightly eccentric, when compared with chopped egg sandwiches, and admittedly talked about her behind her back, but no one ever refused these delicacies or indicated to her that they thought she had slipped a cog. Another lady dyed her hair a bright and cherry orange, by strangers often mistaken at twenty paces for a feather hat. My own beloved stepmother wore a silver fox neckpiece, a whole pelt, *with the embalmed (?) head still on.* My Ontario Irish grandfather said, "sparrow grass," a more interesting term than asparagus. The town dump was known as "the nuisance grounds," phrase fraught with weird connotations, as though the effluvia of our lives was beneath contempt but at the same time was subtly threatening to the determined and sometimes hysterical propriety of our ways.

9   Some oddities were, as idiom had it, "funny ha ha"; others were "funny peculiar." Some were not so very funny at all. An old man lived, deranged, in a shack in the valley. Perhaps he wasn't even all that old, but to us he seemed a wild Methuselah figure, shambling among the underbrush and the tall couchgrass, muttering indecipherable curses or blessings, a prophet who had forgotten his prophecies. Everyone in town knew him, but no one knew him. He lived among us as though only occasionally and momentarily visible. The kids called him Andy Gump, and feared him. Some sought to prove their bravery by tormenting him. They were the medieval bear baiters, and he the lumbering bewildered bear, half blind, only rarely turning to snarl. Everything is to be found in a town like mine. Belsen, writ small but with the same ink.

10   All of us cast stones in one shape or another. In grade school, among the vulnerable and violet girls we were, the feared and despised were those few older girls from what was charmingly termed "the wrong side of the tracks." Tough in talk and tougher in muscle, they were said to be whores already. And may have been, that being about the only profession readily available to them.

11   The dead lived in that place, too. Not only the grandparents who

had, in local parlance, "passed on" and who gloomed, bearded or bonneted, from the sepia photographs in old albums, but also the uncles, forever eighteen or nineteen, whose names were carved on the granite family stones in the cemetery, but whose bones lay in France. My own young mother lay in that graveyard, beside other dead of our kin, and when I was ten, my father, too, only forty, left the living town for the dead dwelling on the hill.

12 When I was eighteen, I couldn't wait to get out of that town, away from the prairies. I did not know then that I would carry the land and town all my life within my skull, that they would form the mainspring and source of the writing I was to do, wherever and however far away I might live.

13 This was my territory in the time of my youth, and in a sense my life since then has been an attempt to look at it, to come to terms with it. Stultifying to the mind it certainly could be, and sometimes was, but not to the imagination. It was many things, but it was never dull.

14 The same, I now see, could be said for Canada in general. Why on earth did generations of Canadians pretend to believe this country dull? We knew perfectly well it wasn't. Yet for so long we did not proclaim what we knew. If our upsurge of so-called nationalism seems odd or irrelevant to outsiders, and even to some of our own people (*what's all the fuss about?*), they might try to understand that for many years we valued ourselves insufficiently, living as we did under the huge shadows of those two dominating figures, Uncle Sam and Britannia. We have only just begun to value ourselves, our land, our abilities. We have only just begun to recognize our legends and to give shape to our myths.

15 There are, God knows, enough aspects to deplore about this country. When I see the killing of our lakes and rivers with industrial wastes, I feel rage and despair. When I see our industries and natural resources increasingly taken over by America, I feel an overwhelming discouragement, especially as I cannot simply say "damn Yankees." It should never be forgotten that it is we ourselves who have sold such a large amount of our birthright for a mess of plastic Progress. When I saw the War Measures Act being invoked in 1970, I lost forever the vestigial remains of the naïve wish-belief that repression could not happen here, or would not. And yet, of course, I had known all along in the deepest and often hidden caves of the heart that anything can happen anywhere,

for the seeds of both man's freedom and his captivity are found everywhere, even in the microcosm of a prairie town. But in raging against our injustices, our stupidities, I do so *as family,* as I did, and still do in writing, about those aspects of my town which I hated and which are always in some ways aspects of myself.

16   The land still draws me more than other lands. I have lived in Africa and in England, but splendid as both can be, they do not have the power to move me in the same way as, for example, that part of southern Ontario where I spent four months last summer in a cedar cabin beside a river. "Scratch a Canadian, and you find a phony pioneer," I used to say to myself in warning. But all the same it is true, I think, that we are not yet totally alienated from physical earth, and let us only pray we do not become so. I once thought that my lifelong fear and mistrust of cities made me a kind of old-fashioned freak; now I see it differently.

17   The cabin has a long window across its front western wall, and sitting at the oak table there in the mornings, I used to look out at the river and at the tall trees beyond, green-gold in the early light. The river was bronze; the sun caught it strangely, reflecting upon its surface the near-shore sand ripples underneath. Suddenly, the crescenting of a fish, gone before the eye could clearly give image to it. The old man next door said these leaping fish were carp. Himself, he preferred muskie, for he was a real fisherman and the muskie gave him a fight. The wind most often blew from the south, and the river flowed toward the south, so when the water was wind-riffled, and the current was strong, the river seemed to be flowing both ways. I liked this, and interpreted it as an omen, a natural symbol.

18   A few years ago, when I was back in Winnipeg, I gave a talk at my old college. It was open to the public, and afterward a very old man came up to me and asked me if my maiden name had been Wemyss. I said yes, thinking he might have known my father or my grandfather. But no. "When I was a young lad," he said, "I once worked for your great-grandfather, Robert Wemyss, when he had the sheep ranch at Raeburn." I think that was a moment when I realized all over again something of great importance to me. My long-ago families came from Scotland and Ireland, but in a sense that no longer mattered so much. My true roots were here.

19   I am not very patriotic, in the usual meaning of that word. I cannot

say "My country right or wrong" in any political, social or literary context. But one thing is inalterable, for better or worse, for life.

20   This is where my world began. A world which includes the ancestors—both my own and other people's ancestors who become mine. A world which formed me, and continues to do so, even while I found it in some of its aspects, and continue to do so. A world which gave me my own lifework to do, because it was here that I learned the sight of my own particular eyes.

On Going Home

Joan Didion

1   I am home for my daughter's first birthday. By "home" I do not mean the house in Los Angeles where my husband and I and the baby live, but the place where my family is, in the Central Valley of California. It is a vital although troublesome distinction. My husband likes my family but is uneasy in their house, because once there I fall into their ways, which are difficult, oblique, deliberately inarticulate, not my husband's ways. We live in dusty houses ("D-U-S-T," he once wrote with his finger on surfaces all over the house, but no one noticed it) filled with mementos quite without value to him (what could the Canton dessert plates mean to him? how could he have known about the assay scales, why should he care if he did know?), and we appear to talk exclusively about people we know who have been committed to mental hospitals, about people we know who have been booked on drunk-driving charges, and about property, particularly about property, land, price per acre and C-2 zoning and assessments and freeway access. My brother does not understand my husband's inability to perceive the advantage in the rather common real-estate transaction known as "sale-leaseback," and my husband in turn does not understand why so many of the people he hears about in my father's house have recently been committed to mental hospitals or booked on drunk-driving charges. Nor does he understand that when we talk about sale-leasebacks and right-of-way condemnations we are talking in code about the things we like best, the yellow fields and the cottonwoods and the rivers rising and falling and the mountain roads closing when the heavy snow comes in. We miss each other's points, have another drink and regard the fire. My brother refers to my husband, in his presence, as "Joan's husband." Marriage is the classic betrayal.

2   Or perhaps it is not any more. Sometimes I think that those of us who are now in our thirties were born into the last generation to carry the burden of "home," to find in family life the source of all tension

and drama. I had by all objective accounts a "normal" and a "happy" family situation, and yet I was almost thirty years old before I could talk to my family on the telephone without crying after I had hung up. We did not fight. Nothing was wrong. And yet some nameless anxiety colored the emotional charges between me and the place that I came from. The question of whether or not you could go home again was a very real part of the sentimental and largely literary baggage with which we left home in the fifties; I suspect that it is irrelevant to the children born of the fragmentation after World War II. A few weeks ago in a San Francisco bar I saw a pretty young girl on crystal take off her clothes and dance for the cash prize in an "amateur-topless" contest. There was no particular sense of moment about this, none of the effect of romantic degradation, of "dark journey," for which my generation strived so assiduously. What sense could that girl possibly make of, say, *Long Day's Journey into Night?* Who is beside the point?

3   That I am trapped in this particular irrelevancy is never more apparent to me than when I am home. Paralyzed by the neurotic lassitude engendered by meeting one's past at every turn, around every corner, inside every cupboard, I go aimlessly from room to room. I decide to meet it head-on and clean out a drawer, and I spread the contents on the bed. A bathing suit I wore the summer I was seventeen. A letter of rejection from *The Nation,* an aerial photograph of the site for a shopping center my father did not build in 1954. Three teacups hand-painted with cabbage roses and signed "E. M.," my grandmother's initials. There is no final solution for letters of rejection from *The Nation* and teacups hand-painted in 1900. Nor is there any answer to snapshots of one's grandfather as a young man on skis, surveying around Donner Pass in the year 1910. I smooth out the snapshot and look into his face, and do and do not see my own. I close the drawer, and have another cup of coffee with my mother. We get along very well, veterans of a guerrilla war we never understood.

4   Days pass. I see no one. I come to dread my husband's evening call, not only because he is full of news of what by now seems to me our remote life in Los Angeles, people he has seen, letters which require attention, but because he asks what I have been doing, suggests uneasily that I get out, drive to San Francisco or Berkeley. Instead I drive across the river to a family graveyard. It has been vandalized since my last visit and the monuments are broken, overturned in the dry grass. Be-

cause I once saw a rattlesnake in the grass I stay in the car and listen
to a country-and-Western station. Later I drive with my father to a ranch
he has in the foothills. The man who runs his cattle on it asks us to the
roundup, a week from Sunday, and although I know that I will be in
Los Angeles I say, in the oblique way my family talks, that I will come.
Once home I mention the broken monuments in the graveyard. My
mother shrugs.

5   I go to visit my great-aunts. A few of them think now that I am
my cousin, or their daughter who died young. We recall an anecdote
about a relative last seen in 1948, and they ask if I still like living in
New York City. I have lived in Los Angeles for three years, but I say
that I do. The baby is offered a horehound drop, and I am slipped a
dollar bill "to buy a treat." Questions trail off, answers are abandoned,
the baby plays with the dust motes in a shaft of afternoon sun.

6   It is time for the baby's birthday party: a white cake, strawberry-
marshmallow ice cream, a bottle of champagne saved from another
party. In the evening, after she has gone to sleep, I kneel beside the
crib and touch her face, where it is pressed against the slats, with mine.
She is an open and trusting child, unprepared for and unaccustomed to
the ambushes of family life, and perhaps it is just as well that I can
offer her little of that life. I would like to give her more. I would like
to promise her that she will grow up with a sense of her cousins and
of rivers and of her great-grandmother's teacups, would like to pledge
her a picnic on a river with fried chicken and her hair uncombed, would
like to give her *home* for her birthday, but we live differently now and
I can promise her nothing like that. I give her a xylophone and a sundress
from Madeira, and promise to tell her a funny story.

The Libido for the Ugly

H. L. Mencken

1   On a Winter day some years ago, coming out of Pittsburgh on one of the expresses of the Pennsylvania Railroad, I rolled eastward for an hour through the coal and steel towns of Westmoreland county. It was familiar ground; boy and man, I had been through it often before. But somehow I had never quite sensed its appalling desolation. Here was the very heart of industrial America, the center of its most lucrative and characteristic activity, the boast and pride of the richest and grandest nation ever seen on earth—and here was a scene so dreadfully hideous, so intolerably bleak and forlorn that it reduced the whole aspiration of man to a macabre and depressing joke. Here was wealth beyond computation, almost beyond imagination—and here were human habitations so abominable that they would have disgraced a race of alley cats.

2   I am not speaking of mere filth. One expects steel towns to be dirty. What I allude to is the unbroken and agonizing ugliness, the sheer revolting monstrousness, of every house in sight. From East Liberty to Greensburg, a distance of twenty-five miles, there was not one in sight from the train that did not insult and lacerate the eye. Some were so bad, and they were among the most pretentious—churches, stores, warehouses, and the like—that they were downright startling; one blinked before them as one blinks before a man with his face shot away. A few linger in memory, horrible even there: a crazy little church just west of Jeannette, set like a dormer-window on the side of a bare, leprous hill; the headquarters of the Veterans of Foreign Wars at another forlorn town, a steel stadium like a huge rat-trap somewhere further down the line. But most of all I recall the general effect—of hideousness without a break. There was not a single decent house within eye-range from the Pittsburgh suburbs to the Greensburg yards. There was not one that was not misshapen, and there was not one that was not shabby.

3   The country itself is not uncomely, despite the grime of the endless mills. It is, in form, a narrow river valley, with deep gullies running

up into the hills. It is thickly settled, but not noticeably overcrowded. There is still plenty of room for building, even in the larger towns, and there are very few solid blocks. Nearly every house, big and little, has space on all four sides. Obviously, if there were architects of any professional sense or dignity in the region, they would have perfected a chalet to hug the hillsides—a chalet with a high-pitched roof, to throw off the heavy Winter snows, but still essentially a low and clinging building, wider than it was tall. But what have they done? They have taken as their model a brick set on end. This they have converted into a thing of dingy clapboards, with a narrow, low-pitched roof. And the whole they have set upon thin, preposterous brick piers. By the hundreds and thousands these abominable houses cover the bare hillsides, like gravestones in some gigantic and decaying cemetery. On their deep sides they are three, four and even five stories high; on their low sides they bury themselves swinishly in the mud. Not a fifth of them are perpendicular. They lean this way and that, hanging on to their bases precariously. And one and all they are streaked in grime, with dead and eczematous patches of paint peeping through the streaks.

4   Now and then there is a house of brick. But what brick! When it is new it is the color of a fried egg. When it has taken on the patina of the mills it is the color of an egg long past all hope or caring. Was it necessary to adopt that shocking color? No more than it was necessary to set all of the houses on end. Red brick, even in a steel town, ages with some dignity. Let it become downright black, and it is still sightly, especially if its trimmings are of white stone, with soot in the depths and the high spots washed by the rain. But in Westmoreland they prefer that uremic yellow, and so they have the most loathsome towns and villages ever seen by mortal eye.

5   I award this championship only after laborious research and incessant prayer. I have seen, I believe, all of the most unlovely towns of the world; they are all to be found in the United States. I have seen the mill towns of decomposing New England and the desert towns of Utah, Arizona and Texas. I am familiar with the back streets of Newark, Brooklyn and Chicago, and have made scientific explorations to Camden, N.J. and Newport News, Va. Safe in a Pullman, I have whirled through the gloomy, God-forsaken villages of Iowa and Kansas, and the malarious tide-water hamlets of Georgia. I have been to Bridgeport, Conn., and to Los Angeles. But nowhere on this earth, at home or

abroad, have I seen anything to compare to the villages that huddle along the line of the Pennsylvania from the Pittsburgh yards to Greensburg. They are incomparable in color, and they are incomparable in design. It is as if some titanic and aberrant genius, uncompromisingly inimical to man, had devoted all the ingenuity of Hell to the making of them. They show grotesqueries of ugliness that, in retrospect, become almost diabolical. One cannot imagine mere human beings concocting such dreadful things, and one can scarcely imagine human beings bearing life in them.

6   Are they so frightful because the valley is full of foreigners— dull, insensate brutes, with no love of beauty in them? Then why didn't these foreigners set up similar abominations in the countries that they came from? You will, in fact, find nothing of the sort in Europe—save perhaps in the more putrid parts of England. There is scarcely an ugly village on the whole Continent. The peasants, however poor, somehow manage to make themselves graceful and charming habitations, even in Spain. But in the American village and small town the pull is always toward ugliness, and in that Westmoreland valley it has been yielded to with an eagerness bordering upon passion. It is incredible that mere ignorance should have achieved such masterpieces of horror.

7   On certain levels of the American race, indeed, there seems to be a positive libido for the ugly, as on other and less Christian levels there is a libido for the beautiful. It is impossible to put down the wallpaper that defaces the average American home of the lower middle class to mere inadvertence, or to the obscene humor of the manufacturers. Such ghastly designs, it must be obvious, give a genuine delight to a certain type of mind. They meet, in some unfathomable way, its obscure and unintelligible demands. They caress it as "The Palms" caresses it, or the art of the movie, or jazz. The taste for them is as enigmatical and yet as common as the taste for dogmatic theology and the poetry of Edgar A. Guest.

8   Thus I suspect (though confessedly without knowing) that the vast majority of the honest folk of Westmoreland county, and especially the 100% Americans among them, actually admire the houses they live in, and are proud of them. For the same money they could get vastly better ones, but they prefer what they have got. Certainly there was no pressure upon the Veterans of Foreign Wars to choose the dreadful edifice that bears their banner, for there are plenty of vacant buildings along the

track-side, and some of them are appreciably better. They might, indeed, have built a better one of their own. But they chose that clapboarded horror with their eyes open, and having chosen it, they let it mellow into its present shocking depravity. They like it as it is: beside it, the Parthenon would no doubt offend them. In precisely the same way the authors of the rat-trap stadium that I have mentioned made a deliberate choice. After painfully designing and erecting it, they made it perfect in their own sight by putting a completely impossible pent-house, painted a staring yellow, on top of it. The effect is that of a fat woman with a black eye. It is that of a Presbyterian grinning. But they like it.

9   Here is something that the psychologists have so far neglected: the love of ugliness for its own sake, the lust to make the world intolerable. Its habitat is the United States. Out of the melting pot emerges a race which hates beauty as it hates truth. The etiology of this madness deserves a great deal more study than it has got. There must be causes behind it; it arises and flourishes in obedience to biological laws, and not as a mere act of God. What, precisely, are the terms of those laws? And why do they run stronger in America than elsewhere? Let some honest *Privat Dozent* in pathological sociology apply himself to the problem.

Once More to the Lake

E. B. White

August 1941

1   One summer, along about 1904, my father rented a camp on a lake in Maine and took us all there for the month of August. We all got ringworm from some kittens and had to rub Pond's Extract on our arms and legs night and morning, and my father rolled over in a canoe with all his clothes on; but outside of that the vacation was a success and from then on none of us ever thought there was any place in the world like that lake in Maine. We returned summer after summer— always on August 1 for one month. I have since become a salt-water man, but sometimes in summer there are days when the restlessness of the tides and the fearful cold of the sea water and the incessant wind that blows across the afternoon and into the evening make me wish for the placidity of a lake in the woods. A few weeks ago this feeling got so strong I bought myself a couple of bass hooks and a spinner and returned to the lake where we used to go, for a week's fishing and to revisit old haunts.

2   I took along my son, who had never had any fresh water up his nose and who had seen lily pads only from train windows. On the journey over to the lake I began to wonder what it would be like. I wondered how time would have marred this unique, this holy spot— the coves and streams, the hills that the sun set behind, the camps and the paths behind the camps. I was sure that the tarred road would have found it out, and I wondered in what other ways it would be desolated. It is strange how much you can remember about places like that once you allow your mind to return into the grooves that lead back. You remember one thing, and that suddenly reminds you of another thing. I guess I remembered clearest of all the early mornings, when the lake was cool and motionless, remembered how the bedroom smelled of the lumber it was made of and of the wet woods whose scent entered through the screen. The partitions in the camp were thin and did not extend

clear to the top of the rooms, and as I was always the first up I would dress softly so as not to wake the others, and sneak out into the sweet outdoors and start out in the canoe, keeping close along the shore in the long shadows of the pines. I remembered being very careful never to rub my paddle against the gunwale for fear of disturbing the stillness of the cathedral.

3   The lake had never been what you would call a wild lake. There were cottages sprinkled around the shores, and it was in farming country although the shores of the lake were quite heavily wooded. Some of the cottages were owned by nearby farmers, and you would live at the shore and eat your meals at the farmhouse. That's what our family did. But although it wasn't wild, it was a fairly large and undisturbed lake and there were places in it that, to a child at least, seemed infinitely remote and primeval.

4   I was right about the tar: it led to within half a mile of the shore. But when I got back there, with my boy, and we settled into a camp near a farmhouse and into the kind of summertime I had known, I could tell that it was going to be pretty much the same as it had been before— I knew it, lying in bed the first morning smelling the bedroom and hearing the boy sneak quietly out and go off along the shore in a boat. I began to sustain the illusion that he was I, and therefore, by simple transposition, that I was my father. This sensation persisted, kept cropping up all the time we were there. It was not an entirely new feeling, but in this setting it grew much stronger. I seemed to be living a dual existence. I would be in the middle of some simple act, I would be picking up a bait box or laying down a table fork, or I would be saying something and suddenly it would be not I but my father who was saying the words or making the gesture. It gave me a creepy sensation.

5   We went fishing the first morning. I felt the same damp moss covering the worms in the bait can, and saw the dragonfly alight on the tip of my rod as it hovered a few inches from the surface of the water. It was the arrival of this fly that convinced me beyond any doubt that everything was as it always had been, that the years were a mirage and that there had been no years. The small waves were the same, chucking the rowboat under the chin as we fished at anchor, and the boat was the same boat, the same color green and the ribs broken in the same places, and under the floorboards the same fresh water leavings and débris—the dead hellgrammite, the wisps of moss, the rusty discarded

fishhook, the dried blood from yesterday's catch. We stared silently at the tips of our rods, at the dragonflies that came and went. I lowered the tip of mine into the water, tentatively, pensively dislodging the fly, which darted two feet away, poised, darted two feet back, and came to rest again a little farther up the rod. There had been no years between the ducking of this dragonfly and the other one—the one that was part of memory. I looked at the boy, who was silently watching his fly, and it was my hands that held his rod, my eyes watching. I felt dizzy and didn't know which rod I was at the end of.

6   We caught two bass, hauling them in briskly as though they were mackerel, pulling them over the side of the boat in a businesslike manner without any landing net, and stunning them with a blow on the back of the head. When we got back for a swim before lunch, the lake was exactly where we had left it, the same number of inches from the dock, and there was only the merest suggestion of a breeze. This seemed an utterly enchanted sea, this lake you could leave to its own devices for a few hours and come back to, and find that it had not stirred, this constant and trustworthy body of water. In the shallows, the dark, water-soaked sticks and twigs, smooth and old, were undulating in clusters on the bottom against the clean ribbed sand, and the track of the mussel was plain. A school of minnows swam by, each minnow with its small individual shadow, doubling the attendance, so clear and sharp in the sunlight. Some of the other campers were in swimming, along the shore, one of them with a cake of soap, and the water felt thin and clear and unsubstantial. Over the years there had been this person with the cake of soap, this cultist, and here he was. There had been no years.

7   Up to the farmhouse to dinner through the teeming dusty field, the road under our sneakers was only a two-track road. The middle track was missing, the one with the marks of the hooves and the splotches of dried, flaky manure. There had always been three tracks to choose from in choosing which track to walk in; now the choice was narrowed down to two. For a moment I missed terribly the middle alternative. But the way led past the tennis court, and something about the way it lay there in the sun reassured me; the tape had loosened along the backline, the alleys were green with plantains and other weeds, and the net (installed in June and removed in September) sagged in the dry noon, and the whole place steamed with midday heat and hunger and emptiness. There was a choice of pie for dessert, and one was blueberry

and one was apple, and the waitresses were the same country girls, there having been no passage of time, only the illusion of it as in a dropped curtain—the waitresses were still fifteen; their hair had been washed, that was the only difference—they had been to the movies and seen the pretty girls with the clean hair.

8   Summertime, oh, summertime, pattern of life indelible with fade-proof lake, the wood unshatterable, the pasture with the sweetfern and the juniper forever and ever, summer without end; this was the background, and the life along the shore was the design, the cottages with their innocent and tranquil design, their tiny docks with the flagpole and the American flag floating against the white clouds in the blue sky, the little paths over the roots of the trees leading from camp to camp and the paths leading back to the outhouses and the can of lime for sprinkling, and at the souvenir counters at the store the miniature birch-bark canoes and the postcards that showed things looking a little better than they looked. This was the American family at play, escaping the city heat, wondering whether the newcomers in the camp at the head of the cove were "common" or "nice," wondering whether it was true that the people who drove up for Sunday dinner at the farmhouse were turned away because there wasn't enough chicken.

9   It seemed to me, as I kept remembering all this, that those times and those summers had been infinitely precious and worth saving. There had been jollity and peace and goodness. The arriving (at the beginning of August) had been so big a business in itself, at the railway station the farm wagon drawn up, the first smell of the pine-laden air, the first glimpse of the smiling farmer, and the great importance of the trunks and your father's enormous authority in such matters, and the feel of the wagon under you for the long ten-mile haul, and at the top of the last long hill catching the first view of the lake after eleven months of not seeing this cherished body of water. The shouts and cries of the other campers when they saw you, and the trunks to be unpacked, to give up their rich burden. (Arriving was less exciting nowadays, when you sneaked up in your car and parked it under a tree near the camp and took out the bags and in five minutes it was all over, no fuss, no loud wonderful fuss about trunks.)

10   Peace and goodness and jollity. The only thing that was wrong now, really, was the sound of the place, an unfamiliar nervous sound of the outboard motors. This was the note that jarred, the one thing that

would sometimes break the illusion and set the years moving. In those other summertimes all motors were inboard; and when they were at a little distance, the noise they made was a sedative, an ingredient of summer sleep. They were one-cylinder and two-cylinder engines, and some were make-and-break and some were jump-spark, but they all made a sleepy sound across the lake. The one-lungers throbbed and fluttered, and the twin-cylinder ones purred and purred, and that was a quiet sound, too. But now the campers all had outboards. In the daytime, in the hot mornings, these motors made a petulant, irritable sound; at night in the still evening when the afterglow lit the water, they whined about one's ears like mosquitoes. My boy loved our rented outboard, and his great desire was to achieve single-handed mastery over it, and authority, and he soon learned the trick of choking it a little (but not too much), and the adjustment of the needle valve. Watching him I would remember the things you could do with the old one-cylinder engine with the heavy flywheel, how you could have it eating out of your hand if you got really close to it spiritually. Motorboats in those days didn't have clutches, and you would make a landing by shutting off the motor at the proper time and coasting in with a dead rudder. But there was a way of reversing them, if you learned the trick, by cutting the switch and putting it on again exactly on the final dying revolution of the flywheel, so that it would kick back against compression and begin reversing. Approaching a dock in a strong following breeze, it was difficult to slow up sufficiently by the ordinary coasting method, and if a boy felt he had complete mastery over his motor, he was tempted to keep it running beyond its time and then reverse it a few feet from the dock. It took a cool nerve, because if you threw the switch a twentieth of a second too soon you would catch the flywheel when it still had speed enough to go up past center, and the boat would leap ahead, charging bull-fashion at the dock.

11   We had a good week at the camp. The bass were biting well and the sun shone endlessly, day after day. We would be tired at night and lie down in the accumulated heat of the little bedrooms after the long hot day and the breeze would stir almost imperceptibly outside and the smell of the swamp drift in through the rusty screens. Sleep would come easily and in the morning the red squirrel would be on the roof, tapping out his gay routine. I kept remembering everything, lying in bed in the mornings—the small steamboat that had a long rounded stern like the

lip of a Ubangi, and how quietly she ran on the moonlight sails, when the older boys played their mandolins and the girls sang and we ate doughnuts dipped in sugar, and how sweet the music was on the water in the shining night, and what it had felt like to think about girls then. After breakfast we would go up to the store and the things were in the same place—the minnows in a bottle, the plugs and spinners disarranged and pawed over by the youngsters from the boys' camp, the Fig Newtons and the Beeman's gum. Outside, the road was tarred and cars stood in front of the store. Inside, all was just as it had always been, except there was more Coca-Cola and not so much Moxie and root beer and birch beer and sarsaparilla. We would walk out with the bottle of pop apiece and sometimes the pop would backfire up our noses and hurt. We explored the streams, quietly, where the turtles slid off the sunny logs and dug their way into the soft bottom; and we lay on the town wharf and fed worms to the tame bass. Everywhere we went I had trouble making out which was I, the one walking at my side, the one walking in my pants.

12   One afternoon while we were at that lake a thunderstorm came up. It was like the revival of an old melodrama that I had seen long ago with childish awe. The second-act climax of the drama of the electrical disturbance over a lake in America had not changed in any important respect. This was the big scene, still the big scene. The whole thing was so familiar, the first feeling of oppression and heat and a general air around camp of not wanting to go very far away. In mi-dafternoon (it was all the same) a curious darkening of the sky, and a lull in everything that had made life tick; and then the way the boats suddenly swung the other way at their moorings with the coming of a breeze out of the new quarter, and the premonitory rumble. Then the kettle drum, then the snare, then the bass drum and cymbals, then crackling light against the dark, and the gods grinning and licking their chops in the hills. Afterward the calm, the rain steadily rustling in the calm lake, the return of light and hope and spirits, and the campers running out in joy and relief to go swimming in the rain, their bright cries perpetuating the deathless joke about how they were getting simply drenched, and the children screaming with delight at the new sensation of bathing in the rain, and the joke about getting drenched linking the generations in a strong indestructible chain. And the comedian who waded in carrying an umbrella.

13   When the others went swimming my son said he was going in, too. He pulled his dripping trunks from the line where they had hung all through the shower and wrung them out. Languidly, and with no thought of going in, I watched him, his hard little body, skinny and bare, saw him wince slightly as he pulled up around his vitals the small, soggy, icy garment. As he buckled the swollen belt, suddenly my groin felt the chill of death.

Main Street

Mordecai Richler

1   Two streets below our own came the Main. Rich in delights, but also squalid, filthy, and hollering with stores whose wares, whether furniture or fruit, were ugly or damaged. The signs still say FANTASTIC DISCOUNTS or FORCED TO SELL PRICES HERE, but the bargains so bitterly sought after are illusory—and perhaps they always were.

2   The Main, with something for all our appetites, was dedicated to pinching pennies from the poor, but it was there to entertain, educate and comfort us too. Across the street from the synagogue you could see THE PICTURE THEY CLAIMED COULD NEVER BE MADE. A little further down the street there was the Workman's Circle and, if you liked, a strip show. Peaches, Margo, Lili St. Cyr. Around the corner there was the ritual baths, the *shvitz* or *mikva,* where my grandfather and his cronies went before the High Holidays, emerging boiling red from the highest reaches of the steam rooms to happily flog each other with brushes fashioned of pine tree branches. Where supremely orthodox women went once a month to purify themselves.

3   It was to the Main, once a year before the High Holidays, that I was taken for a new suit (the itch of the cheap tweed was excruciating) and shoes (with a built-in squeak). We also shopped for fruit on the Main, meat and fish, and here the important thing was to watch the man at the scales. On the Main, too, was the Chinese laundry—"Have you ever seen such hard workers?"—the Italian hat-blocker—"Tony's a good goy, you know. Against Mussolini from the very first."—and strolling French Canadian priests—"Some of them speak Hebrew now." "Well, if you ask me, it's none of their business. Enough's enough, you know." Kids like myself were dragged along on shopping expeditions to carry parcels. Old men gave us snuff, at the delicatessens we were allowed salami butts, card players pushed candies on us for luck,

and everywhere we were poked and pinched by the mothers. Absolutely the best that could be said of us was, "He eats well, knock wood," and later, as we went off to school, "He's a rank-one boy."

4   After the shopping, once our errands had been done, we returned to the Main once more, either for part-time jobs or to study with our *melamud*. Jobs going on the Main included spotting pins in a bowling alley, collecting butcher bills and, best of all, working at a newsstand, where you could devour the *Police Gazette* free and pick up a little extra short-changing strangers during the rush hour. Work was supposed to be good for our character development and the fact that we were paid was incidental. To qualify for a job we were supposed to be "bright, ambitious, and willing to learn." An ad I once saw in a shoe store window read:

> PART-TIME BOY WANTED FOR EXPANDING BUSINESS. EXPERIENCE
> ABSOLUTELY NECESSARY, BUT NOT ESSENTIAL

5   Our jobs and lessons finished, we would wander the street in small groups smoking Turret cigarettes and telling jokes.

6   "Hey, *shmo-hawk,* what's the difference between a mail box and an elephant's ass?"

7   "I dunno."

8   "Well, I wouldn't send *you* to mail my letters."

9   As the French Canadian factory girls passed arm-in-arm we would call out, "I've got the time, if you've got the place."

10   *Shabus* it was back to the Main again and the original Young Israel synagogue. While our grandfathers and fathers prayed and gossiped and speculated about the war in Europe in the musty room below, we played chin the bar in the upstairs attic and told jokes that began, "Confucius say. . . ." or, "Once there was an Englishman, an Irishman, and a Hebe. . . ."

11   We would return to the Main once more when we wanted a fight with the pea-soups. Winter, as I recall it, was best for this type of sport. We could throw snowballs packed with ice or frozen horse buns, and with darkness falling early, it was easier to elude pursuers. Soon, however, we developed a technique of battle that served us well even in the spring. Three of us would hide under an outside staircase while the fourth member of our group, a kid named Eddy, would idle provocatively on the sidewalk. Eddy was a good head-and-a-half shorter than

the rest of us. (For this, it was rumoured, his mother was to blame. She wouldn't let Eddy have his tonsils removed and that's why he was such a runt. It was not that Eddy's mother feared surgery, but Eddy sang in the choir of a rich synagogue, bringing in some thirty dollars a month, and if his tonsils were removed it was feared that his voice would go too.) Anyway, Eddy would stand out there alone and when the first solitary pea-soup passed he would kick him in the shins. "Your mother fucks," he'd say.

12   The pea-soup, looking down on little Eddy, would naturally knock him one on the head. Then, and only then, would we emerge from under the staircase.

13   "Hey, that's my kid brother you just slugged."

14   And before the bewildered pea-soup could protest, we were scrambling all over him.

15   These and other fights, however, sprang more out of boredom than from racial hatred, not that there were no racial problems on the Main.

16   If the Main was a poor man's street, it was also a dividing line. Below, the French Canadians. Above, some distance above, the dreaded WASPS. On the Main itself there were some Italians, Yugoslavs and Ukrainians, but they did not count as true Gentiles. Even the French Canadians, who were our enemies, were not entirely unloved. Like us, they were poor and coarse with large families and spoke English badly.

17   Looking back, it's easy to see that the real trouble was there was no dialogue between us and the French Canadians, each elbowing the other, striving for WASP acceptance. We fought the French Canadians stereotype for stereotype. If many of them believed that the St. Urbain Street Jews were secretly rich, manipulating the black market, then my typical French Canadian was a moronic gum-chewer. He wore his greasy black hair parted down the middle and also affected an eyebrow moustache. His zoot trousers were belted just under the breastbone and ended in a peg hugging his ankles. He was the dolt who held up your uncle endlessly at the liquor commission while he tried unsuccessfully to add three figures or, if he was employed at the customs office, never knew which form to give you. Furthermore, he only held his liquor commission or customs or any other government job because he was the second cousin of a backwoods notary who had delivered the village

vote to the *Union Nationale* for a generation. Other French Canadians were speed cops, and if any of these ever stopped you on the highway you made sure to hand him a folded two dollar bill with your licence.

18   Wartime shortages, the admirable Protestant spirit of making-do, benefited both Jews and French Canadians. Jews with clean fingernails were allowed to teach within the Protestant School system and French Canadians off the Atwater League and provincial sandlots broke into the International Baseball League. Jean-Pierre Roy won twenty-five games for the Montreal Royals one year and a young man named Stan Breard enjoyed a season as a stylish but no-hit shortstop. Come to think of it, the only French Canadians I heard of were athletes. Of course there was Maurice Richard, the superb hockey player, but there was also Dave Castiloux, a cunning welterweight, and, above all, the wrestler-hero, Yvon Robert, who week after week gave the blond Anglo-Saxon wrestlers what for at the Forum.

19   Aside from boyhood street fights and what I read on the sports pages, all I knew of French Canadians was that they were clearly hilarious. Our Scots schoolmaster would always raise a laugh in class by reading us the atrocious Uncle Tom-like dialect verse of William Henry Drummond: *Little Baptiste & Co.*

> On wan dark night on Lac St. Pierre,
> De win' she blow, blow, blow,
> An' de crew of de wood scow "Julie Plante"
> Got scar't and' run below—
> Bimeby she blow some more,
> An' de scow bus' up on Lac St. Pierre
> Wan arpent from de shore.

20   Actually, it was only the WASPS who were truly hated and feared. "Among them," I heard it said, "with those porridge faces, who can tell what they're thinking?" It was, we felt, their country, and given sufficient liquor who knew when they would make trouble?

21   We were a rude, aggressive bunch round the Main. Cocky too. But bring down the most insignificant, pinched WASP fire insurance inspector and even the most arrogant merchant on the street would dip into the drawer for a ten spot or a bottle and bow and say, "Sir."

22   After school we used to race down to the Main to play snooker

at the Rachel or the Mount Royal. Other days, when we chose to avoid school altogether, we would take the No. 55 streetcar as far as St. Catherine Street, where there was a variety of amusements offered. We could play the pinball machines and watch archaic strip-tease movies for a nickel at the Silver Gameland. At the Midway or the Crystal Palace we could see a double feature and a girlie show for as little as thirty-five cents. The Main, at this juncture, was thick with drifters, panhandlers and whores. Available on both sides of the street were "Tourist Rooms by Day and Night," and everywhere there was the smell of french fried potatoes cooking in stale oil. Tough, unshaven men in checked shirts stood in knots outside the taverns and cheap cafés. There was the promise of violence.

23   As I recall it, we were always being warned about the Main. Our grandparents and parents had come there by steerage from Rumania or by cattleboat from Poland by way of Liverpool. No sooner had they unpacked their bundles and cardboard suitcases than they were planning a better, brighter life for us, the Canadian-born children. The Main, good enough for them, was not to be for us, and that they told us again and again was what the struggle was for. The Main was for *bummers,* drinkers, and (heaven forbid) failures.

24   During the years leading up to the war, the ideal of the ghetto, no different from any other in America, was the doctor. This, mistakenly, was taken to be the very apogee of learning and refinement. In those days there also began the familiar and agonizing process of alienation between immigrant parents and Canadian-born children. Our older brothers and cousins, off to university, came home to realize that our parents spoke with embarrassing accents. Even the younger boys, like myself, were going to "their" schools. According to them, the priests had made a tremendous contribution to the exploration and development of this country. Some were heroes. But our parents had other memories, different ideas, about the priesthood. At school we were taught about the glory of the Crusades and at home we were instructed in the bloodier side of the story. Though we wished Lord Tweedsmuir, the Governor-General, a long life each Saturday morning in the synagogue, there were those among us who knew him as John Buchan. From the very beginning there was their history, and ours. Our heroes, and theirs.

25   Our parents used to apply a special standard to all men and events.

"Is it good for the Jews?" By this test they interpreted the policies of Mackenzie King and the Stanley Cup play-offs and earthquakes in Japan. To take one example—if the Montreal *Canadiens* won the Stanley Cup it would infuriate the WASPS in Toronto, and as long as the English and French were going at each other they left us alone: *ergo,* it was good for the Jews if the *Canadiens* won the Stanley Cup.

26   We were convinced that we gained from dissension between Canada's two cultures, the English and the French, and we looked neither to England nor France for guidance. We turned to the United States. The real America.

27   America was Roosevelt, the Yeshiva College, Max Baer, Mickey Katz records, Danny Kaye, a Jew in the Supreme Court, the *Jewish Daily Forward,* Dubinsky, Mrs. Nussbaum of Allen's Alley, and Gregory Peck looking so cute in *Gentleman's Agreement.* Why, in the United States a Jew even wrote speeches for the president. Returning cousins swore they had heard a cop speak Yiddish in Brooklyn. There were the Catskill hotels, Jewish soap operas on the radio and, above all earthly pleasure grounds, Florida. Miami. No manufacturer had quite made it in Montreal until he was able to spend a month each winter in Miami.

28   We were governed by Ottawa, we were also British subjects, but our true capital was certainly New York. Success was (and still is) acceptance by the United States. For a boxer this meant a main bout at Madison Square Garden, for a writer or an artist, praise from New York critics, for a businessman, a Miami tan and, today, for comics, an appearance on the Ed Sullivan Show or for actors, not an important part at the Stratford Festival, but Broadway, or the lead in a Hollywood TV series (Lorne Green in *Bonanza*). The outside world, "their" Canada, only concerned us insofar as it affected our living conditions. All the same, we liked to impress the *goyim*. A knock on the knuckles from time to time wouldn't hurt them. So, while we secretly believed that the baseball field or the prize-fighting ring was no place for a Jewish boy, we took enormous pleasure in the accomplishments of, say, Kermit Kitman, the Montreal Royals outfielder, and Maxie Berger, the welterweight.

29   Streets such as ours and Outremont, where the emergent middle-class and the rich lived, comprised an almost self-contained world.

Outside of business there was a minimal contact with the Gentiles. This was hardly petulant clannishness or naive fear. In the years leading up to the war neo-fascist groups were extremely active in Canada. In the United States there was Father Coughlin, Lindberg, and others. We had Adrian Arcand. The upshot was almost the same. So I can recall seeing swastikas and *"A bas les Juifs"* painted on the Laurentian highway. There were suburbs and hotels in the mountains and country clubs where we were not wanted, beaches with signs that read GENTILES ONLY, quotas at the universities, and occasional racial altercations on Park Avenue. The democracy we were being invited to defend was flawed and hostile to us. Without question it was better for us in Canada than in Europe, but this was still their country, not ours.

30   I was only a boy during the war. I can remember signs in cigar stores that warned us THE WALLS HAVE EARS and THE ENEMY IS EVERY-WHERE. I can also recall my parents, uncles and aunts, cracking peanuts on a Friday night and waiting for those two unequalled friends of the Jews, Roosevelt and Walter Winchell, to come off it and get into the war. We admired the British, they were gutsy, but we had more confidence in the United States Marines. Educated by Hollywood, we could see the likes of John Wayne, Gable, and Robert Taylor making minced meat out of the Panzers, while Noel Coward, Laurence Olivier, and others, seen in a spate of British war films, looked all too humanly vulnerable to us. Briefly, then, Pearl Harbour was a day of jubilation, but the war itself made for some confusions. In another country, relatives recalled by my grandparents were being murdered. But on the street in our air cadet uniforms, we F.F.H.S. boys were more interested in seeking out the fabulously wicked V-girls ("They go the limit with guys in uniform, see.") we had read about in the *Herald*. True, we made some sacrifices. American comic books were banned for the duration due, I think, to a shortage of U.S. funds. So we had to put up a quarter on the black market for copies of the *Batman* and *Tip-Top Comics*. But at the same newsstand we bought a page on which four pigs had been printed. When we folded the paper together, as directed, the four pigs' behinds made up Hitler's hateful face. Outside Cooperman's Superior Provisions, where if you were a regular customer you could get sugar without ration coupons, we would chant "Black-market Cooperman! Black-

market Cooperman!" until the old man came out, wielding his broom, and sent us flying down the street.

31   The war in Europe brought about considerable changes within the Jewish community in Montreal. To begin with, there was the coming of the refugees. These men, interned in England as enemy aliens and sent to Canada where they were eventually released, were to make a profound impact on us. I think we had conjured up a picture of the refugees as penurious *hassidim* with packs on their backs. We were eager to be helpful, our gestures were large, but in return we expected more than a little gratitude. As it turned out, the refugees, mostly German and Austrian Jews, were far more sophisticated and better educated than we were. They had not, like our immigrant grandparents, come from *shtetls* in Galicia or Russia. Neither did they despise Europe. On the contrary, they found our culture thin, the city provincial, and the Jews narrow. This bewildered and stung us. But what cut deepest, I suppose, was that the refugees spoke English better than many of us did and, among themselves, had the effrontery to talk in the abhorred German language. Many of them also made it clear that Canada was no more than a frozen place to stop over unitil a U.S. visa was forthcoming. So for a while we real Canadians were hostile.

32   For our grandparents who remembered those left behind in Rumania and Poland the war was a time of unspeakable grief. Parents watched their sons grow up too quickly and stood by helplessly as the boys went off to the fighting one by one. They didn't have to go, either, for until the last days of the war Canadians could only be drafted for service within Canada. A boy had to volunteer before he could be sent overseas.

33   For those of my age the war was something else. I cannot remember it as a black time, and I think it must be so for most boys of my generation. The truth is that for many of us to look back on the war is to recall the first time our fathers earned a good living. Even as the bombs fell and the ships went down, always elsewhere, our country was bursting out of a depression into a period of hitherto unknown prosperity. For my generation the war was hearing of death and sacrifice but seeing with our own eyes the departure from cold-water flats to apartments in Outremont, duplexes and split-levels in the suburbs. It was when we read of the uprising in the Warsaw ghetto and saw, in

Montreal, the changeover from poky little *shuls* to big synagogue-cum-parochial schools with stained glass windows and mosaics outside. During the war some of us lost brothers and cousins but in Canada we had never had it so good, and we began the run from rented summer shacks with outhouses in Shawbridge to Colonial-style summer houses of our own and speedboats on the lake in Ste Agathe.

The Death of the Moth

Virginia Woolf

1   Moths that fly by day are not properly to be called moths; they do not excite that pleasant sense of dark autumn nights and ivy-blossom which the commonest yellow-underwing asleep in the shadow of the curtain never fails to rouse in us. They are hybrid creatures, neither gay like butterflies nor sombre like their own species. Nevertheless the present specimen, with his narrow hay-coloured wings, fringed with a tassel of the same colour, seemed to be content with life. It was a pleasant morning, mid-September, mild, benignant, yet with a keener breath than that of the summer months. The plough was already scoring the field opposite the window, and where the share had been, the earth was pressed flat and gleamed with moisture. Such vigour came rolling in from the fields and the down beyond that it was difficult to keep the eyes strictly turned upon the book. The rooks too were keeping one of their annual festivities; soaring round the tree tops until it looked as if a vast net with thousands of black knots in it had been cast up into the air; which, after a few moments sank slowly down upon the trees until every twig seemed to have a knot at the end of it. Then, suddenly, the net would be thrown into the air again in a wider circle this time, with the utmost clamour and vociferation, as though to be thrown into the air and settle slowly down upon the tree tops were a tremendously exciting experience.

2   The same energy which inspired the rooks, the ploughmen, the horses, and even, it seemed, the lean bare-backed downs, sent the moth fluttering from side to side of his square of the window-pane. One could not help watching him. One was, indeed, conscious of a queer feeling of pity for him. The possibilities of pleasure seemed that morning so enormous and so various that to have only a moth's part in life, and a day moth's at that, appeared a hard fate, and his zest in enjoying his meagre opportunities to the full, pathetic. He flew vigorously to one corner of his compartment, and, after waiting there a second, flew across

to the other. What remained for him but to fly to a third corner and then to a fourth? That was all he could do, in spite of the size of the downs, the width of the sky, the far-off smoke of houses, and the romantic voice, now and then, of a steamer out at sea. What he could do he did. Watching him, it seemed as if a fibre, very thin but pure, of the enormous energy of the world had been thrust into his frail and diminutive body. As often as he crossed the pane, I could fancy that a thread of vital light became visible. He was little or nothing but life.

3   Yet, because he was so small, and so simple a form of the energy that was rolling in at the open window and driving its way through so many narrow and intricate corridors in my own brain and in those of other human beings, there was something marvellous as well as pathetic about him. It was as if someone had taken a tiny bead of pure life and decking it as lightly as possible with down and feathers, had set it dancing and zig-zagging to show us the true nature of life. Thus displayed one could not get over the strangeness of it. One is apt to forget all about life, seeing it humped and bossed and garnished and cumbered so that it has to move with the greatest circumspection and dignity. Again, the thought of all that life might have been had he been born in any other shape caused one to view his simple activities with a kind of pity.

4   After a time, tired by his dancing apparently, he settled on the window ledge in the sun, and, the queer spectacle being at an end, I forgot about him. Then, looking up, my eye was caught by him. He was trying to resume his dancing, but seemed either so stiff or so awkward that he could only flutter to the bottom of the windowpane; and when he tried to fly across it he failed. Being intent on other matters I watched these futile attempts for a time without thinking, unconsciously waiting for him to resume his flight, as one waits for a machine, that has stopped momentarily, to start again without considering the reason of its failure. After perhaps a seventh attempt he slipped from the wooden ledge and fell, fluttering his wings, on to his back on the window sill. The helplessness of his attitude roused me. It flashed upon me that he was in difficulties; he could no longer raise himself; his legs struggled vainly. But, as I stretched out a pencil, meaning to help him to right himself, it came over me that the failure and awkwardness were the approach of death. I laid the pencil down again.

5   The legs agitated themselves once more. I looked as if for the

enemy against which he struggled. I looked out of doors. What had happened there? Presumably it was midday, and work in the fields had stopped. Stillness and quiet had replaced the previous animation. The birds had taken themselves off to feed in the brooks. The horses stood still. Yet the power was there all the same, massed outside indifferent, impersonal, not attending to anything in particular. Somehow it was opposed to the little hay-coloured moth. It was useless to try to do anything. One could only watch the extraordinary efforts made by those tiny legs against an oncoming doom which could, had it chosen, have submerged an entire city, not merely a city, but masses of human beings; nothing, I knew, had any chance against death. Nevertheless after a pause of exhaustion the legs fluttered again. It was superb this last protest, and so frantic that he succeeded at last in righting himself. One's sympathies, of course, were all on the side of life. Also, when there was nobody to care or to know, this gigantic effort on the part of an insignificant little moth, against a power of such magnitude, to retain what no one else valued or desired to keep, moved one strangely. Again, somehow, one saw life, a pure bead. I lifted the pencil again, useless though I knew it to be. But even as I did so, the unmistakable tokens of death showed themselves. The body relaxed, and instantly grew stiff. The struggle was over. The insignificant little creature now knew death. As I looked at the dead moth, this minute wayside triumph of so great a force over so mean an antagonist filled me with wonder. Just as life had been strange a few minutes before, so death was now as strange. The moth having righted himself now lay most decently and uncomplainingly composed. O yes, he seemed to say, death is stronger than I am.

Anatomy of a Martian

Isaac Asimov

[Almost all we know about Mars today was not known at the time this article was written, in 1964.]

1   Conditions are so different on Mars and—to our earth-centered feelings—so inferior from those on earth that scientists are confident no intelligent life exists there. If life on Mars exists at all (the probability of which is small, but not zero) it probably resembles only the simplest and most primitive terrestrial plant life.

2   Still, even granted that the likelihood of complex life is virtually nonexistent, we can still play games and let our fancy roam. Let us suppose that we are told flatly: "There is intelligent life on Mars, roughly man-shaped in form." What reasonable picture can we draw on the basis of what we now know of Mars—bearing always in mind that the conclusions we reach are not to be taken seriously, but only as an exercise in fantasy?

3   In the first place, Mars is a small world with a gravitational force only two-fifths of the earth. If the Martian is a boned creature, those bones can be considerably slenderer than ours and still support a similar mass of material (an inevitable mechanical consequence of decreased weight). Therefore, even if the torso itself were of human bulk, the legs and arms of the Martian would seem grotesquely thin to us.

4   Objects fall more slowly in a weak gravitational field and thus the Martians could afford to have slower reflexes. Therefore, they would seem rather slow and sleepy to us (and they might be longer-lived because of their less intense fight with gravitation). Since things are less top-heavy in a low-gravity world, the Martian would probably be taller than earth people. The Martian backbone need not be so rigid as ours and might have two or three elbowlike joints, making stooping from his (possible) eight-foot height more convenient.

5   The Martian surface has been revealed by the Mars-probe, Mariner

IV, to be heavily pockmarked with craters, but the irregularities they introduce are probably not marked to a creature on the surface. Between and within the craters, much of the surface is probably sandy desert. Yellow clouds obscuring the surface are occasionally detected and, in the 1920s, the astronomer E. M. Antoniadi interpreted these as dust storms. To travel over shifting-sands, the Martian foot (like that of the earthly camel) would have to be flat and broad. That type of foot, plus the weak gravity, would keep him from sinking into the sand.

6   As a guess, the feet might be essentially triangular, with three toes set at 120° separation, with webbing between. (No earthly species has any such arrangement, but it is not an impossible one. Extinct flying reptiles, such as the pterodactyl, possessed wings formed out of webbing extending from a *single* line of bones.) The hands would have the same tripod development, each consisting of three long fingers, equally spaced. If the slender finger bones were numerous, the Martian finger would be the equivalent of a short tentacle. Each might end in a blunt swelling (like that of the earthly lizard called the gecko), where a rich network of nerve endings, as in human fingertips, would make it an excellent organ for touching.

7   The Martian day and night are about as long as our own, but Mars is half again as far from the sun as we are, and it lacks oceans and a thick atmosphere to serve as heat reservoirs. The Martian surface temperature therefore varies from an occasional 90° Fahrenheit, at the equatorial noon, down to a couple of hundred degrees below zero, by the end of the frigid night. The Martian would require an insulating coating. Such insulation might be possible with a double skin; the outer one, tough, horny, and water impervious, like that of an earthly reptile; the inner one, soft, pliable, and richly set with blood vessels, like that of an earthly man. Between the two skins would be an air space which the Martian could inflate or deflate.

8   At night the air space would be full and the Martian would appear balloonlike. The trapped air would serve as an insulator, protecting the warmth of the body proper. In the warm daytime, the Martian would deflate, making it easier for his body to lose heat. During deflation, the outer skin would come together in neat, vertical accordion pleats.

9   The Martian atmosphere, according to Mariner IV data, is extremely thin, perhaps a hundredth the density of our own and consisting almost entirely of carbon dioxide. Thus, the Martian will not breathe

and will not have a nose, though he will have a strongly muscled slit—in his neck, perhaps—through which he can pump up or deflate the air space.

10   What oxygen he requires for building his tissue structure must be obtained from the food he eats. It will take energy to obtain that oxygen, and the energy supply for this and other purposes may come directly from the sun. We can picture each Martian equipped with a capelike extension of tissue attached, perhaps to the backbone. Ordinarily, this would be folded close to the body and so would be inconspicuous.

11   During the day, however, the Martian may spend some hours in sunlight (clouds are infrequent in the thin, dry Martian air) with his cape fully expanded, and resembling a pair of thin, membranous wings reaching several feet to either side. Its rich supply of blood vessels will be exposed to the ultraviolet rays of the sun, and these will be absorbed through the thin, translucent skin. The energy so gained can then be used during the night to enable the necessary chemical reactions to proceed in his body.

12   Although the sun is at a great distance from Mars, the Martian atmosphere is too thin to absorb much of its ultraviolet, so that the Martian will receive more of these rays than we do. His eyes will be adapted to this, and his chief pair, centered in his face, will be small and slitlike to prevent too much radiation from entering. We can guess at two eyes in front, as in the human being, since two are necessary for stereoscopic vision—a very handy thing to have for estimating distance.

13   It is very likely that the Martian will also be adapted to underground existence, for conditions are much more equable underground. One might expect therefore that the Martian would also have two large eyes set on either side of his head, for seeing by feeble illumination. Their function would be chiefly to detect light, not to estimate distance, so they can be set at opposite sides of the head, like those of an earthly dolphin (also an intelligent creature) and stereoscopic vision in feeble light can be sacrificed. These eyes might even be sensitive to the infrared so that Martians can see each other by the heat they radiate. These dim-vision eyes would be enormous enough to make the Martian face wider than it is long. In daytime, of course, they would be tightly closed behind tough-skinned lids and would appear as rounded bulges.

14   The thin atmosphere carries sound poorly, and if the Martian is

to take advantage of the sense of hearing, he will have to have large, flaring, trumpetlike ears, rather like those of a jackrabbit, but capable of independent motion, flaring open and furling shut (during sandstorms, for instance).

15   Exposed portions of the body, such as the arms, legs, ears, and even portions of the face which are not protected by the outer skin and the airtrap within, could be feathered for warmth in the night.

16   The food of the Martian would consist chiefly of simple plant life, which would be tough and hardy and which might incorporate silicon compounds in its structure so that it would be gritty indeed. The earthly horse has teeth with elaborate grinding surfaces to handle coarse, gritty grass, but the Martian would have to carry this to a further extreme. The Martian mouth, therefore, might contain siliceous plates behind a rounded opening which could expand and contract like a diaphragm of a camera. Those plates would work almost like a ball mill, grinding up the tough plants.

17   Water is the great need. The entire water supply on Mars is equal only to that contained in Lake Erie, according to an estimate cited by astronomer Robert S. Richardson. Consequently, the Martian would hoard the water he consumes, never eliminating it as perspiration or wastes, for instance. Wastes would appear in absolutely dry form and would be delivered perhaps in the consistency, even something of the chemical makeup, of earthly bricks.

18   The Martian blood would not be used to carry oxygen, and would contain no oxygen-absorbing compound, a type of substance which in earthly creatures is almost invariably strongly colored. Martian blood, therefore, would be colorless. Thus the Martian skin, adapted to ultraviolet and absorbing it as an energy source, would not have to contain pigment to ward it off. The Martian therefore would be creamy in color.

19   The extensible light-absorbing cape, particularly designed for ultraviolet absorption, might reflect longwave visible light as useless. This reflected light could be yellowish in color. This would cause our Martian to seem to be (when he was busily absorbing energy from solar radiation) a dazzling white creature with golden wings and occasional feathers.

20   So ends our speculation—in a vision of Martian forms not so far removed from the earthman's fantasies of the look of angels.

All Aboa-r-rd!

Dorothy Livesay

1   The difference between childhood and adulthood is so simple that we forget to think about it. It lies in the fact that a child does not have to make decisions. His world is not one of action, but of sensations. It is as if he were being hush-a-byed in a cradle "on the treetop." And if the cradle were whisked away from beneath him he'd still believe he could be cushioned on air, for "When the wind blows the cradle will rock!" Or, there is the possibility, if he is less than three years old, that he would be put aboard a train with his parents but without any idea as to whether this is a stationary new home or an automobile on rails. He has no responsibility except to be there, rejoicing in the cries of "All aboa-r-rd!"; in the feeling of being shunted backward, then forward; the jolt, the chug of wheels; and "Mommy, we're moving!" Now his breath is released as the city's bones are cast behind and through the racing window his eyes devour the grassy plain.

2   Or so it was in my day. Is that why, as adults, we so love trains? Suddenly, we are safe. That sense of security is bliss. As a child at home in the west end of Winnipeg, I remember my early "train thoughts": waking to the deep sound of an engine's moose call; lying in the half light, the green blind being drawn. Passers-by on the wooden sidewalk cast strange shadows on the ceiling above my head and I imagine fairy princesses, carriages, men on horseback, gnomes. Then outside again there's the *clop clop* of the milkman's horse, the clatter of the huge silvery can of milk from which he will measure pints and quarts and pour them into our jugs on the kitchen table. He may leave butter also, in striped pats, all to go into the ice box beside the block of ice hewed from the river, smelling of sawdust. In hot summer we dream of ice and snow. The trains shunt, the black engine lets forth its call. Soon it will be autumn, dark evening, when the train's necklace of lights winks its messages across the prairie.

3   We took the train every summer to go to a cottage in Keewatin (northern Ontario). That was a dull, boring, daytime journey, no air conditioning, the sun sticky yellow on the green plush seats. The real excitement would be to travel overnight on the CPR, west to Regina for camping at Fort Qu'Appelle. The conductor would be out on a wooden platform, the neat grey-clad Negro porters grinning under their red caps, chaffing the children. How tense we felt when the steam began puffing furiously under the wheels, the conductor waved a signal to the engineer leaning out of his black window, and the magic words echoed from car to car: "ALL ABOA-R-RD!" You had to kiss your grannie quickly and be lifted by the porter in a flying movement up the iron steps past the corridor of "staterooms" into the sleeping car.

4   Dinner in the dining car was a deeply satisfying adventure: just getting there, pushing doors through car after car. The head steward kept you waiting a moment until he led you to a table for four, a snowy tablecloth with white table napkins folded like wigwams presiding over the population—those knives, forks, three kinds of spoons, the jug of ice water, silver sugar-and-cream bowls, balls of butter on ice, and that most fascinating basket containing crisp round rolls and soda biscuits. You did not have to feel hungry. You knew there would be good things coming. Five courses! The waiter would shake out the napkin by your plate and tie it round your neck with a flourish. There! Tuck. To begin with: celery sticks and olives. Soup was served from a silver tureen. Then the Winnipeg goldeye, mashed potatoes, carrots, cabbage, turnips, or beets. For dessert you might have to choose between blueberry pie and orange water-ice sherbet (not the strange starch pudding called sherbet today) or, perhaps, strawberry ice cream and pound cake. Father always asked for seed cake, but rarely got it—for which I was thankful. How could anyone like eating that? Perhaps the divine moment of delight was when the waiter had left the bill for a parent to sign. For each person he brought round silver bowls of warm water. "Do we drink it?" "Oh dear no! In these you dip your fingers, delicately, and dry them on your napkin." Delicious ritual, and perhaps the train slowed down at that point. The evening sun shone over the golden prairie fields.

5   There followed childhood sleep—"rocked on the cradle" of the wheels! And sometimes with all the shunting and grunting one could be thrown out of the berth. Then back into the warm womb, utter silence as the train waited in some country siding—waited and waited for the

oncoming monster burdened with freight cars. Finally the shunting began again, until we took flight along the rails. In that dark behind the green curtain the child feels completely protected, with no will, no needs, ready to be rocked to sleep by the *thumpety thump* over the rails and the ever-so-often tilting from side to side. That foetal feeling! In adults, it becomes sexual arousal. From my far off ten-year-old childhood I remember listening on the stairs when our latest maid was telling my mother about her experience in an upper berth. "Never travel that way!" It seems as she lay there in the dark, a man's hand crept up from below and began "feeling" her leg. Quick as a flash she seized her straw hat from the net hammock where such things were put at night. From the hat she pulled out her hat pin and stabbed the offending hand. It worked! And though at that age I was completely innocent, the incident must have plunged deeper into my unconscious, imprinting a sense of mystery and fear into sleeping on a train.

6   Years later, travelling at night with my young family to Penticton, we encountered the rockiest roadbed in Canada—the Kettle Valley line (vanished now). A married friend of mine was aboard in the next double berth. In the morning, hanging on in the swaying washroom, I asked her if she had been able to sleep "with all that shunting?" "Shunting!" she retorted. "*He* shunted down from his upper to my lower. What a time to make love! But that's the way men are—unpredictable."

7   So nowadays fun on the train is no longer to be looked forward to. The mysteries of train travel for child or adult have vanished. And forgotten also is the lifestyle of those men who carried us across the continent. What of the engineers faced with an avalanche of snow? The conductors, trainmen, and porters called in to shovel in emergencies? The cooks running out of supplies on some ice-bound siding? The passengers playing cards endlessly to while away the interminable waits, digging for a bottle hidden in their carpet bags (those one-handled bulging cloth or leather bags that men carried). Nowadays there are a lot of retired conductors and engineers on the CP and CN who travel free and for pleasure, whose stories are juicy enough to make a novel. But no one has written it. The feuds that went on between the private CPR enterprise railwaymen (and all their cousins, families, friends) and the public CN personnel represented the real Canadian game in those days. Not hockey held your obsessed attention, but the latest Canadian National derailment. My mother's family, ardent Conservatives and

upholders of the status quo, had a further stake in the CPR because my Uncle Phil was a baggage clerk at the Winnipeg station. Whatever disaster hit the CN, they cheered. The CPR disasters went unsung.

8   So today, if you listen to those old railwaymen in the lounge car or at the table, you'll note how drastically times have changed. "I think it's time now for unification," I heard the other day. "All the logistics point to amalgamation of the CN and CP, but the government does nothing." "Oh *them* fellows?" exclaims an eighty-five-year-old ex-conductor. "Them politicians take off in orbit and then they can't see where they've gone." So, although they were stimulated by the game, the uncertainties, the night shifts, the absences from home often as not, in their middle age they have a sense of having been cheated by that travelling life. They lost touch with their children. "You can live or die alone. The offspring don't care." Or: "The wife and the kids all ganged up against me—then they left me." "Were you so poor a husband?" "I don't think so. I was boss on the job but she was boss at home . . . but I was away a lot. Many's the time I had to work nights. I didn't see too much of the kids." He was sitting opposite me, a worn-out deeply lined face, a gesture of defeat. "Who wants me now?" Railroading had been his life but it had also destroyed him. So he travelled continuously, compulsively: seeking, seeking. For today "the times is different."

9   That old fellow reminds me of a children's story that fascinated me when young. It was called "All Change Here." Instead of obeying the command to get off the train, the children grew bigger and bigger while their mother and nanny grew smaller and smaller. Changed indeed! And now the aging conductor and my aging self are shrinking down. It seems to be the children who are making decisions, managing our affairs, running the computers—and those computerized, sleek, and silent trains.

Chapter Three

Process

The Spider and the Wasp

Alexander Petrunkevitch

1   To hold its own in the struggle for existence, every species of animal must have a regular source of food, and if it happens to live on other animals, its survival may be very delicately balanced. The hunter cannot exist without the hunted; if the latter should perish from the earth, the former would, too. When the hunted also prey on some of the hunters, the matter may become complicated.

2   This is nowhere better illustrated than in the insect world. Think of the complexity of a situation such as the following: There is a certain wasp, *Pimpla inquisitor,* whose larvae feed on several years in succession. In a Paris museum is a tropical specimen which is said to have been living in captivity for 25 years.

3   A fertilized female tarantula lays from 200 to 400 eggs at a time; thus it is possible for a single tarantula to produce several thousand young. She takes no care of them beyond weaving a cocoon of silk to enclose the eggs. After they hatch, the young walk away, find convenient places in which to dig their burrows and spend the rest of their lives in solitude. Tarantulas feed mostly on insects and millipedes. Once their appetite is appeased, they digest the food for several days before eating again. Their sight is poor, being limited to sensing a change in the intensity of light and to the perception of moving objects. They apparently have little or no sense of hearing, for a hungry tarantula will pay no attention to a loudly chirping cricket placed in its cage unless the insect happens to touch one of its legs.

4   But all spiders, and especially hairy ones, have an extremely delicate sense of touch. Laboratory experiments prove that tarantulas can distinguish three types of touch: pressure against the body wall, stroking of the body hair, and riffling of certain very fine hairs on the legs called trichobothria. Pressure against the body, by a finger or the end of a pencil, causes the tarantula to move off slowly for a short distance. The touch excites no defensive response unless the approach

is from above, where the spider can see the motion, in which case it rises on its hind legs, lifts its front legs, opens its fangs and holds this threatening posture as long as the object continues to move. When the motion stops, the spider drops back to the ground, remains quiet for a few seconds, and then moves slowly away.

5   The entire body of a tarantula, especially its legs, is thickly clothed with hair. Some of it is short and woolly, some long and stiff. Touching this body hair produces one of two distinct reactions. When the spider is hungry, it responds with an immediate and swift attack. At the touch of a cricket's antennae the tarantula seizes the insect so swiftly that a motion picture taken at the rate of 64 frames per second shows only the result not the process of capture. But when the spider is not hungry, the stimulation of its hair merely causes it to shake the touched limb. An insect can walk under its hairy belly unharmed.

6   The trichobothria, very fine hairs growing from disklike membranes of the legs, were once thought to be the spider's hearing organs, but we now know that they have nothing to do with sound. They are sensitive only to air movement. A light breeze makes them vibrate slowly without disturbing the common hair. When one blows gently on the trichobothria, the tarantula reacts with a quick jerk of its four front legs. If the front and hind legs are stimulated at the same time, the spider makes a sudden jump. This reaction is quite independent of the state of its appetite.

7   These three tactile responses—to pressure on the body wall, to moving of the common hair, and to flexing of the trichobothria—are so different from one another that there is no possibility of confusing them. They serve the tarantula adequately for most of its needs and enable it to avoid most annoyances and dangers. But they fail the spider completely when it meets its deadly enemy, the digger wasp *Pepsis*.

8   These solitary wasps are beautiful and formidable creatures. Most species are either a deep shiny blue all over, or deep blue with rusty wings. The largest have a wing span of about four inches. They live on nectar. When excited, they give off a pungent odor—a warning that they are ready to attack. The sting is much worse than that of a bee or common wasp, and the pain and swelling last longer. In the adult stage the wasp lives only a few months. The female produces but a few eggs, one at a time at intervals of two or three days. For each egg the mother must provide one adult tarantula, alive but paralyzed. The tarantula

must be of the correct species to nourish the larva. The mother wasp attaches the egg to the paralyzed spider's abdomen. Upon hatching from the egg, the larva is many hundreds of times smaller than its living but helpless victim. It eats no other food and drinks no water. By the time it has finished its single gargantuan meal and becomes ready for wasp-hood, nothing remains of the tarantula but its indigestible chitinous skeleton.

9   The mother wasp goes tarantula-hunting when the egg in her ovary is almost ready to be laid. Flying low over the ground late on a sunny afternoon, the wasp looks for its victim or for the mouth of a tarantula burrow, a round hole edged by a bit of silk. The sex of the spider makes no difference, but the mother is highly discriminating as to species. Each species of *Pepsis* requires a certain species of tarantula, and the wasp will not attack the wrong species. In a cage with a tarantula which is not its normal prey the wasp avoids the spider, and is usually killed by it in the night.

10   Yet when a wasp finds the correct species, it is the other way about. To identify the species the wasp apparently must explore the spider with her antennae. The tarantula shows an amazing tolerance to this exploration. The wasp crawls under it and walks over it without evoking any hostile response. The molestation is so great and so persistent that the tarantula often rises on all eight legs, as if it were on stilts. It may stand this way for several minutes. Meanwhile the wasp, having satisfied itself that the victim is of the right species, moves off a few inches to dig the spider's grave. Working vigorously with legs and jaws, it excavates a hole 8 to 10 inches deep with a diameter slightly larger than the spider's girth. Now and again the wasp pops out of the hole to make sure that the spider is still there.

11   When the grave is finished, the wasp returns to the tarantula to complete her ghastly enterprise. First she feels it all over once more with her antennae. Then her behavior becomes more aggressive. She bends her abdomen, protruding her sting, and searches for the soft membrane at the point where the spider's leg joins its body—the only spot where she can penetrate the horny skeleton. From time to time, as the exasperated spider slowly shifts ground, the wasp turns on her back and slides along with the aid of her wings, trying to get under the tarantula for a shot at the vital spot. During all this maneuvering, which can last for several minutes, the tarantula makes no move to save itself.

Finally the wasp corners it against some obstruction and grasps one of its legs in her powerful jaws. Now at last the harassed spider tries a desperate but vain defense. The two contestants roll over and over on the ground. It is a terrifying sight and the outcome is always the same. The wasp finally manages to thrust her sting into the soft spot and holds it there for a few seconds while she pumps in the poison. Almost immediately the tarantula falls paralyzed on its back. Its legs stop twitching; its heart stops beating. Yet it is not dead, as is shown by the fact that if taken from the wasp it can be restored to some sensitivity by being kept in a moist chamber for several months.

12   After paralyzing the tarantula, the wasp cleans herself by dragging her body along the ground and rubbing her feet, sucks the drop of blood oozing from the wound in the spider's abdomen, then grabs a leg of the flabby, helpless animal in her jaws and drags it down to the bottom of the grave. She stays there for many minutes, sometimes for several hours, and what she does all that time in the dark we do not know. Eventually she lays her egg and attaches it to the side of the spider's abdomen with a sticky secretion. Then she emerges, fills the grave with soil carried bit by bit in her jaws, and finally tramples the ground all around to hide any trace of the grave from prowlers. Then she flies away, leaving her descendant safely started in life.

13   In all this the behavior of the wasp evidently is qualitatively different from that of the spider. The wasp acts like an intelligent animal. This is not to say that instinct plays no part or that she reasons as man does. But her actions are to the point; they are not automatic and can be modified to fit the situation. We do not know for certain how she identifies the tarantula—probably it is by some olfactory or chemo-tactile sense—but she does it purposefully and does not blindly tackle a wrong species.

14   On the other hand, the tarantula's behavior shows only confusion. Evidently the wasp's pawing gives it no pleasure, for it tries to move away. That the wasp is not simulating sexual stimulation is certain, because male and female tarantulas react in the same way to its advances. That the spider is not anesthetized by some odorless secretion is easily shown by blowing lightly at the tarantula and making it jump suddenly. What, then, makes the tarantula behave as stupidly as it does?

15   No clear, simple answer is available. Possibly the stimulation by the wasp's antennae is masked by a heavier pressure on the spider's

body, so that it reacts as when prodded by a pencil. But the explanation may be much more complex. Initiative in attack is not in the nature of tarantulas; most species fight only when cornered so that escape is impossible. Their inherited patterns of behavior apparently prompt them to avoid problems rather than attack them. For example, spiders always weave their webs in three dimensions, and when a spider finds that there is insufficient space to attach certain threads in the third dimension, it leaves the place and seeks another, instead of finishing the web in a single plane. This urge to escape seems to arise under all circumstances, in all phases of life, and to take the place of reasoning. For a spider to change the pattern of its web is as impossible as for an inexperienced man to build a bridge across a chasm obstructing his way.

16   In a way the instinctive urge to escape is not only easier but more efficient than reasoning. The tarantula does exactly what is most efficient in all cases except in an encounter with a ruthless and determined attacker dependent for the existence of her own species on killing as many tarantulas as she can lay eggs. Perhaps in this case the spider follows its usual pattern of trying to escape, instead of seizing and killing the wasp, because it is not aware of its danger. In any case, the survival of the tarantula species as a whole is protected by the fact that the spider is much more fertile than the wasp.

The Grey Beginnings

Rachel Carson

And the earth was without form, and void; and darkness was upon the face of the deep.

Genesis

1   Beginnings are apt to be shadowy, and so it is with the beginnings of that great mother of life the sea. Many people have debated how and when the earth got its ocean, and it is not surprising that their explanations do not always agree. For the plain and inescapable truth is that no one was there to see, and in the absence of eyewitness accounts there is bound to be a certain amount of disagreement. So if I tell here the story of how the young planet Earth acquired an ocean, it must be a story pieced together from many sources and containing whole chapters the details of which we can only imagine. The story is founded on the testimony of the earth's most ancient rocks, which were young when the earth was young; on other evidence written on the face of the earth's satellite, the moon; and on hints contained in the history of the sun and the whole universe of star-filled space. For although no man was there to witness this cosmic birth, the stars and the moon and the rocks were there, and, indeed, had much to do with the fact that there is an ocean.

2   The events of which I write must have occurred somewhat more than 2 billion years ago. As nearly as science can tell that is the approximate age of the earth, and the ocean must be very nearly as old. It is possible now to discover the age of the rocks that compose the crust of the earth by measuring the rate of decay of the radioactive materials they contain. The oldest rocks found anywhere on earth—in Manitoba—are about 2.3 billion years old. Allowing 100 million years or so for the cooling of the earth's materials to form a rocky crust, we arrive at the supposition that the tempestuous and violent events connected with our planet's birth occurred nearly $2\frac{1}{2}$ billion years ago.

But this is only a minimum estimate, for rocks indicating an even greater age may be found at any time.

3   The new earth, freshly torn from its parent sun, was a ball of whirling gases, intensely hot, rushing through the black spaces of the universe on a path and at a speed controlled by immense forces. Gradually the ball of flaming gases cooled. The gases began to liquefy, and Earth became a molten mass. The materials of this mass eventually became sorted out in a definite pattern: the heaviest in the center, the less heavy surrounding them, and the least heavy forming the outer rim. This is the pattern which persists today—a central sphere of molten iron, very nearly as hot as it was 2 billion years ago, an intermediate sphere of semiplastic basalt, and a hard outer shell, relatively quite thin and composed of solid basalt and granite.

4   The outer shell of the young earth must have been a good many millions of years changing from the liquid to the solid state, and it is believed that, before this change was completed, an event of the greatest importance took place—the formation of the moon. The next time you stand on a beach at night, watching the moon's bright path across the water, and conscious of the moon-drawn tides, remember that the moon itself may have been born of a great tidal wave of earthly substance, torn off into space. And remember that if the moon was formed in this fashion, the event may have had much to do with shaping the ocean basins and the continents as we know them.

5   There were tides in the new earth, long before there was an ocean. In response to the pull of the sun the molten liquids of the earth's whole surface rose in tides that rolled unhindered around the globe and only gradually slackened and diminished as the earthly shell cooled, congealed, and hardened. Those who believe that the moon is a child of earth say that during an early stage of the earth's development something happened that caused this rolling, viscid tide to gather speed and momentum and to rise to unimaginable heights. Apparently the force that created these greatest tides the earth has ever known was the force of resonance, for at this time the period of the solar tides had come to approach, then equal, the period of the free oscillation of the liquid earth. And so every sun tide was given increased momentum by the push of the earth's oscillation, and each of the twice-daily tides was larger than the one before it. Physicists have calculated that, after 500 years of such monstrous, steadily increasing tides, those on the side

toward the sun became too high for stability, and a great wave was torn away and hurled into space. But immediately, of course, the newly created satellite became subject to physical laws that sent it spinning in an orbit of its own about the earth. This is what we call the moon.

6   There are reasons for believing that this event took place after the earth's crust had become slightly hardened, instead of during its partly liquid state. There is to this day a great scar on the surface of the globe. This scar or depression holds the Pacific Ocean. According to some geophysicists, the floor of the Pacific is composed of basalt, the substance of the earth's middle layer, while all other oceans are floored with a thin layer of granite, which makes up most of the earth's outer layer. We immediately wonder what became of the Pacific's granite covering and the most convenient assumption is that it was torn away when the moon was formed. There is supporting evidence. The mean density of the moon is much less than that of the earth (3.3 compared with 5.5), suggesting that the moon took away none of the earth's heavy iron core, but that it is composed only of the granite and some of the basalt of the outer layers.

7   The birth of the moon probably helped shape other regions of the world ocean besides the Pacific. When part of the crust was torn away, strains must have been set up in the remaining granite envelope. Perhaps the granite mass cracked open on the side opposite the moon scar. Perhaps, as the earth spun on its axis and rushed on its orbit through space, the cracks widened and the masses of granite began to drift apart, moving over a tarry, slowly hardening layer of basalt. Gradually the outer portions of the basalt layer became solid and the wandering continents came to rest, frozen into place with oceans between them. In spite of theories to the contrary, the weight of geologic evidence seems to be that the locations of the major ocean basins and the major continental land masses are today much the same as they have been since a very early period of the earth's history.

8   But this is to anticipate the story, for when the moon was born there was no ocean. The gradually cooling earth was enveloped in heavy layers of cloud, which contained much of the water of the new planet. For a long time its surface was so hot that no moisture could fall without immediately being reconverted to steam. This dense, perpetually renewed cloud covering must have been thick enough that no rays of sunlight could penetrate it. And so the rough outlines of the continents

and the empty ocean basins were sculptured out of the surface of the earth in darkness, in a Stygian world of heated rock and swirling clouds and gloom.

9   As soon as the earth's crust cooled enough, the rains began to fall. Never have there been such rains since that time. They fell continuously, day and night, days passing into months, into years, into centuries. They poured into the waiting ocean basins, or, falling upon the continental masses, drained away to become sea.

10   That primeval ocean, growing in bulk as the rains slowly filled its basins, must have been only faintly salt. But the falling rains were the symbol of the dissolution of the continents. From the moment the rains began to fall, the lands began to be worn away and carried to the sea. It is an endless, inexorable process that has never stopped—the dissolving of the rocks, the leaching out of their contained minerals, the carrying of the rock fragments and dissolved minerals to the ocean. And over the eons of time, the sea has grown ever more bitter with the salt of the continents.

11   In what manner the sea produced the mysterious and wonderful stuff called protoplasm we cannot say. In its warm, dimly lit waters the unknown conditions of temperature and pressure and saltiness must have been the critical ones for the creation of life from nonlife. At any rate they produced the result that neither the alchemists with their crucibles nor modern scientists in their laboratories have been able to achieve.

12   Before the first living cell was created, there may have been many trials and failures. It seems probable that, within the warm saltiness of the primeval sea, certain organic substances were fashioned from carbon dioxide, sulphur, nitrogen, phosphorus, potassium, and calcium. Perhaps these were transition steps from which the complex molecules of protoplasm arose—molecules that somehow acquired the ability to reproduce themselves and begin the endless stream of life. But at present no one is wise enough to be sure.

13   Those first living things may have been simple microorganisms rather like some of the bacteria we know today—mysterious borderline forms that were not quite plants, not quite animals, barely over the intangible line that separates the non-living from the living. It is doubtful that this first life possessed the substance chlorophyll, with which plants in sunlight transform lifeless chemicals into the living stuff of their

tissues. Little sunshine could enter their dim world, penetrating the cloud banks from which fell the endless rains. Probably the sea's first children lived on the organic substances then present in the ocean waters, or, like the iron and sulphur bacteria that exist today, lived directly on inorganic food.

14   All the while the cloud cover was thinning, the darkness of the nights alternated with palely illumined days, and finally the sun for the first time shone through upon the sea. By this time some of the living things that floated in the sea must have developed the magic of chlorophyll. Now they were able to take the carbon dioxide of the air and the water of the sea and of these elements, in sunlight, build the organic substances they needed. So the first true plants came into being.

15   Another group of organisms, lacking the chlorophyll but needing organic food, found they could make a way of life for themselves by devouring the plants. So the first animals arose, and from that day to this, every animal in the world has followed the habit it learned in the ancient seas and depends, directly or through complex food chains, on the plants for food and life.

16   As the years passed, and the centuries, and the millions of years, the stream of life grew more and more complex. From simple, one-celled creatures, others that were aggregations of specialized cells arose, and then creatures with organs for feeding, digesting, breathing, reproducing. Sponges grew on the rocky bottom of the sea's edge and coral animals built their habitations in warm, clear waters. Jellyfish swam and drifted in the sea. Worms evolved, and starfish, and hard-shelled creatures with many-jointed legs, the arthropods. The plants, too, progressed, from the microscopic algae to branched and curiously fruiting seaweeds that swayed with the tides and were plucked from the coastal rocks by the surf and cast adrift.

17   During all this time the continents had no life. There was little to induce living things to come ashore, forsaking their all-providing, all-embracing mother sea. The lands must have been bleak and hostile beyond the power of words to describe. Imagine a whole continent of naked rock, across which no covering mantle of green had been drawn— a continent without soil, for there were no land plants to aid in its formation and bind it to the rocks with their roots. Imagine a land of stone, a silent land, except for the sound of the rains and winds that

swept across it. For there was no living voice, and no living thing moved over the surface of the rocks.

18   Meanwhile, the gradual cooling of the planet, which had first given the earth its hard granite crust, was progressing into its deeper layers; and as the interior slowly cooled and contracted, it drew away from the outer shell. This shell, accommodating itself to the shrinking sphere within it, fell into folds and wrinkles—the earth's first mountain ranges.

19   Geologists tell us that there must have been at least two periods of mountain building (often called "revolutions") in that dim period, so long ago that the rocks have no record of it, so long ago that the mountains themselves have long since been worn away. Then there came a third great period of upheaval and readjustment of the earth's crust, about a billion years ago, but of all its majestic mountains the only reminders today are the Laurentian hills of eastern Canada, and a great shield of granite over the flat country around Hudson Bay.

20   The epochs of mountain building only served to speed up the processes of erosion by which the continents were worn down and their crumbling rock and contained minerals returned to the sea. The uplifted masses of the mountains were prey to the bitter cold of the upper atmosphere and under the attacks of frost and snow and ice the rocks cracked and crumbled away. The rains beat with greater violence upon the slopes of the hills and carried away the substance of the mountains in torrential streams. There was still no plant covering to modify and resist the power of the rains.

21   And in the sea, life continued to evolve. The earliest forms have left no fossils by which we can identify them. Probably they were soft-bodied, with no hard parts that could be preserved. Then, too, the rock layers formed in those early days have since been so altered by enormous heat and pressure, under the foldings of the earth's crust, that any fossils they might have contained would have been destroyed.

22   For the past 500 million years, however, the rocks have preserved the fossil record. By the dawn of the Cambrian period, when the history of living things was first inscribed on rock pages, life in the sea had progressed so far that all the main groups of back boneless or invertebrate animals had been developed. But there were no animals with backbones, no insects or spiders, and still no plant or animal had been evolved that

was capable of venturing on to the forbidding land. So for more than three-fourths of geologic time the continents were desolate and uninhabited, while the sea prepared the life that was later to invade them and make them habitable. Meanwhile, with violent tremblings of the earth and with the fire and smoke of roaring volcanoes, mountains rose and wore away, glaciers moved to and fro over the earth, and the sea crept over the continents and again receded.

23   It was not until Silurian time, some 350 million years ago, that the first pioneer of land life crept out on the shore. It was an arthropod, one of the great tribe that later produced crabs and lobsters and insects. It must have been something like a modern scorpion, but, unlike some of its descendants, it never wholly severed the ties that united it to the sea. It lived a strange life, half-terrestrial, half-aquatic, something like that of the ghost crabs that speed along the beaches today, now and then dashing into the surf to moisten their gills.

24   Fish, tapered of body and stream-molded by the press of running waters, were evolving in Silurian rivers. In times of drought, in the drying pools and lagoons, the shortage of oxygen forced them to develop swim bladders for the storage of air. One form that possessed an air-breathing lung was able to survive the dry period by burying itself in mud, leaving a passage to the surface through which it breathed.

25   It is very doubtful that the animals alone would have succeeded in colonizing the land, for only the plants had the power to bring about the first amelioration of its harsh conditions. They helped make soil of the crumbling rocks, they held back the soil from the rains that would have swept it away, and little by little they softened and subdued the bare rock, the lifeless desert. We know very little about the first land plants, but they must have been closely related to some of the larger seaweeds that had learned to live in the coastal shallows, developing strengthened stems and grasping, rootlike holdfasts to resist the drag and pull of the waves. Perhaps it was in some coastal lowlands, periodically drained and flooded, that some such plants found it possible to survive, though separated from the sea. This also seems to have taken place in the Silurian period.

26   The mountains that had been thrown up by the Laurentian revolution gradually wore away, and as the sediments were washed from their summits and deposited on the lowlands, great areas of the continents sank under the load. The seas crept out of their basins and spread

over the lands. Life fared well and was exceedingly abundant in those shallow, sunlit seas. But with the later retreat of the ocean water into the deeper basins, many creatures must have been left stranded in shallow, landlocked bays. Some of these animals found means to survive on land. The lakes, the shores of the rivers, and the coastal swamps of those days were the testing grounds in which plants and animals either became adapted to the new conditions or perished.

27   As the lands rose and the seas receded, a strange fishlike creature emerged on the land, and over the thousands of years its fins became legs, and instead of gills it developed lungs. In the Devonian sandstone this first amphibian left its footprint.

28   On land and sea the stream of life poured on. New forms evolved; some old ones declined and disappeared. On land the mosses and the ferns and the seed plants developed. The reptiles for a time dominated the earth, gigantic, grotesque, and terrifying. Birds learned to live and move in the ocean of air. The first small mammals lurked inconspicuously in hidden crannies of the earth as though in fear of the reptiles.

29   When they went ashore the animals that took up a land life carried with them part of the sea in their bodies, a heritage which they passed on to their children and which even today links each land animal with its origin in the ancient sea. Fish, amphibian, and reptile, warm-blooded bird and mammal—each of us carries in our veins a salty stream in which the elements sodium, potassium, and calcium are combined in almost the same proportions as in sea water. This is our inheritance from the day untold millions of years ago, when a remote ancestor, having progressed from the one-celled to the many-celled stage, first developed a circulatory system in which the fluid was merely the water of the sea. In the same way, our lime-hardened skeletons are a heritage from the calcium-rich ocean of Cambrian time. Even the protoplasm that streams within each cell of our bodies has the chemical structure impressed upon all living matter when the first simple creatures were brought forth in the ancient sea. And as life itself began in the sea, so each of us begins his individual life in a miniature ocean within his mother's womb, and in the stages of his embryonic development repeats the steps by which his race evolved, from gill-breathing inhabitants of a water world to creatures able to live on land.

30   Some of the land animals later returned to the ocean. After perhaps 50 million years of land life, a number of reptiles entered the sea about

170 million years ago, in the Triassic period. They were huge and formidable creatures. Some had oarlike limbs by which they rowed through the water; some were web-footed, with long, serpentine necks. These grotesque monsters disappeared millions of years ago, but we remember them when we come upon a large sea turtle swimming many miles at sea, its barnacle-encrusted shell eloquent of its marine life. Much later, perhaps no more than 50 million years ago, some of the mammals, too, abandoned a land life for the ocean. Their descendants are the sea lions, seals, sea elephants, and whales of today.

31   Among the land mammals there was a race of creatures that took to an arboreal existence. Their hands underwent remarkable development, becoming skilled in manipulating and examining objects, and along with this skill came a superior brain power that compensated for what these comparatively small mammals lacked in strength. At last, perhaps somewhere in the vast interior of Asia, they descended from the trees and became again terrestrial. The past million years have seen their transformation into beings with the body and brain of man.

32   Eventually man, too, found his way back to the sea. Standing on its shores, he must have looked out upon it with wonder and curiosity, compounded with an unconscious recognition of his lineage. He could not physically re-enter the ocean as the seals and whales had done. But over the centuries, with all the skill and ingenuity and reasoning powers of his mind, he has sought to explore and investigate even its most remote parts, so that he might re-enter it mentally and imaginatively.

33   He built boats to venture out on its surface. Later he found ways to descend to the shallow parts of its floor, carrying with him the air that, as a land mammal long unaccustomed to aquatic life, he needed to breathe. Moving in fascination over the deep sea he could not enter, he found ways to probe its depths, he let down nets to capture its life, he invented mechanical eyes and ears that could re-create for his senses a world long lost, but a world that, in the deepest part of his subconscious mind, he had never wholly forgotten.

34   And yet he has returned to his mother sea only on her own terms. He cannot control or change the ocean as, in his brief tenancy of earth, he has subdued and plundered the continents. In the artificial world of his cities and towns, he often forgets the true nature of his planet and the long vistas of its history, in which the existence of the race of men has occupied a mere moment of time. The sense of all these things

comes to him most clearly in the course of a long ocean voyage, when he watches day after day the receding rim of the horizon, ridged and furrowed by waves; when at night he becomes aware of the earth's rotation as the stars pass overhead; or when, alone in this world of water and sky, he feels the loneliness of his earth in space. And then, as never on land, he knows the truth that his world is a water world, a planet dominated by its covering mantle of ocean, in which the continents are but transient intrusions of land above the surface of the all-encircling sea.

In the Toils of the Law

Edward Hoagland

1   Lately people seem to want to pigeonhole themselves ("I'm 'into' this," "I'm 'into' that"), and the anciently universal experiences like getting married or having a child, like voting or jury duty, acquire a kind of poignancy. We hardly believe that our vote will count, we wonder whether the world will wind up uninhabitable for the child, but still we do vote with a rueful fervor and look at new babies with undimmed tenderness, because who knows what will become of these old humane responsibilities? Sadism, homosexuality and other inversions that represent despair for the race of man may be the wave of the future, the wise way to survive.

2   Jury duty. Here one sits listening to evidence: thumbs up for a witness or thumbs down. It's unexpectedly moving; everybody tries so hard to be fair. For their two weeks of service people really try to be better than themselves. In Manhattan eighteen hundred are called each week from the voters' rolls, a third of whom show up and qualify. Later this third is divided into three groups of two hundred, one for the State Supreme Court of New York County, one for the Criminal Court, and one for the Civil Court. At Civil Court, 111 Centre Street, right across from the Tombs, there are jury rooms on the third and eleventh floors, and every Monday a new pool goes to one or the other. The building is relatively modern, the chairs upholstered as in an airport lounge, and the two hundred people sit facing forward like a school of fish until the roll is called. It's like waiting six or seven hours a day for an unscheduled flight to leave. They read and watch the clock, go to the drinking fountain, strike up a conversation, dictate business letters into the pay telephones. When I served, one man in a booth was shouting, "I'll knock your teeth down your throat! I don't want to hear, I don't want to know!"

3   Women are exempt from jury duty if they wish to be because of their sensibilities, their menstrual delicacy, and the care that they must

98

give their babies, so usually not many serve. Instead there are lots of retired men and institutional employees from banks, the Post Office or the Transit Authority whose bosses won't miss them, as well as people at loose ends who welcome the change. But some look extremely busy, rushing back to the office when given a chance or sitting at the tables at the front of the room, trying to keep up with their work. They'll write payroll checks, glancing to see if you notice how important they are, or pore over statistical charts or contact sheets with a magnifying glass, if they are in public relations or advertising. Once in a while a clerk emerges to rotate a lottery box and draw the names of jurors, who go into one of the challenge rooms—six jurors, six alternates—to be interviewed by the plaintiff's and defendant's lawyers. Unless the damages asked are large, in civil cases the jury has six members, only five of whom must agree on a decision, and since no one is going to be sentenced to jail, the evidence for a decision need merely seem preponderant, not "beyond a reasonable doubt."

4　　The legal fiction is maintained that the man or woman you see as defendant is actually going to have to pay, but the defense attorneys are generally insurance lawyers from a regular battery which each big company keeps at the courthouse to handle these matters, or from the legal corps of the City of New York, Con Edison, Hertz Rent A Car, or whoever. If so, they act interchangeably and you may see a different face in court than you saw in the challenge room, and still another during the judge's charge. During my stint most cases I heard about went back four or five years, and the knottiest problem for either side was producing witnesses who were still willing to testify. In negligence cases, so many of which involve automobiles, there are several reasons why the insurers haven't settled earlier. They've waited for the plaintiff to lose hope or greed, and to see what cards each contestant will finally hold in his hands when the five years have passed. More significantly, it's a financial matter. The straight-arrow companies that do right by a sufferer and promptly pay him off lose the use as capital of that three thousand dollars or so meanwhile—multiplied perhaps eighty thousand times, for all the similar cases they have.

5　　Selecting a jury is the last little battle of nerves between the two sides. By now the opposing attorneys know who will testify and have obtained pretrial depositions; this completes the hand each of them holds. Generally they think they know what will happen, so to save time and costs they settle the case either before the hearing starts or out of the jury's earshot during the hearing with the judge's help. Seeing a good sober jury waiting to hear them attempt to justify a bad case greases the wheels.

6   In the challenge room, though, the momentum of confrontation goes on. With a crowded court calendar, the judge in these civil cases is not present, as a rule. It's a small room, and there's an opportunity for the lawyers to be folksy or emotional in ways not permitted them later on. For example, in asking the jurors repeatedly if they will "be able to convert pain and suffering into dollars and cents" the plaintiff's attorney is preparing the ground for his more closely supervised presentation in court. By asking them if they own any stock in an insurance company he can get across the intelligence, which is otherwise *verboten,* that not the humble "defendant" but some corporation is going to have to pay the tab. His opponent will object if he tells too many jokes and wins too many friends, but both seek not so much a sympathetic jury as a jury that is free of nuts and grudge-holders, a jury dependably ready to give everybody "his day in court"—a phrase one hears over and over. The questioning we were subjected to was so polite as to be almost apologetic, however, because of the danger of unwittingly offending any of the jurors who remained. Having to size up a series of strangers, on the basis of some monosyllabic answers and each fellow's face, profession and address, was hard work for these lawyers. Everybody was on his best behavior, the jurors too, because the procedure so much resembled a job interview, and no one wanted to be considered less than fair-minded, unfit to participate in the case; there was a vague sense of shame about being excused.

7   The six alternates sat listening. The lawyers could look at them and draw any conclusions they wished, but they could neither question them until a sitting juror had been challenged, nor know in advance which one of the alternates would be substituted first. Each person was asked about his work, about any honest bias or special knowledge he might have concerning cases of the same kind, or any lawsuits he himself might have been involved in at one time. Some questions were probably partly designed to educate us in the disciplines of objectivity, lest we think it was all too easy, and one or two lawyers actually made an effort to educate us in the majesty of the law, since, as they said, the judges sometimes are "dingbats" and don't. We were told there should be no

opprobrium attached to being excused, that we must not simply assume a perfect impartiality in ourselves but should help them to examine us. Jailhouse advocates, or Spartan types who might secretly believe that the injured party should swallow his misfortune and grin and bear a stroke of bad luck, were to be avoided, of course, along with the mingy, the flippant, the grieved and the wronged, as well as men who might want to redistribute the wealth of the world by finding for the plaintiff, or who might not limit their deliberations to the facts of the case, accepting the judge's interpretation of the law as law. We were told that our common sense and experience of life was what was wanted to sift out the likelihood of the testimony we heard.

8   Most dismissals were caused just by a lawyer's hunch—or figuring the percentages as baseball managers do. After the first day's waiting in the airport lounge, there wasn't anybody who didn't want to get on a case; even listening as an alternate in the challenge room was a relief. I dressed in a suit and tie and shined my shoes. I'd been afraid that when I said I was a novelist no lawyer would have me, on the theory that novelists favor the underdog. On the contrary, I was accepted every time; apparently a novelist was considered ideal, having no allegiances at all, no expertise, no professional link to the workaday world. I stutter and had supposed that this too might disqualify me [but] these lawyers did not think it so. What they seemed to want was simply a balanced group, because when a jury gets down to arguing there's no telling where its leadership will arise. The rich man from Sutton Place whom the plaintiff's lawyer almost dismissed, fearing he'd favor the powers that be, may turn out to be a fighting liberal whose idea of what constitutes proper damages is much higher than what the machinist who sits next to him has in mind. In one case I heard about, a woman was clonked by a Christmas tree in a department store and the juror whose salary was lowest suggested an award of fifty dollars, and the man who earned the most, fifty thousand dollars (they rounded it off to fifteen hundred dollars). These were the kind of cases Sancho Panza did so well on when he was governor of Isle Barataria, and as I was questioned about my prejudices, and solemnly looking into each lawyer's eyes, shook my head—murmuring, No, I had no prejudices—all the time my true unreliable quirkiness filled my head. All I could do was resolve to try to be fair.

9   By the third day, we'd struck up shipboard friendships. There

was a babbling camaraderie in the jury pool, and for lunch we plunged into that old, eclipsed, ethnic New York near City Hall—Chinese roast ducks hanging in the butcher's windows on Mulberry Street next door to an Italian store selling religious candles. We ate at Cucina Luna and Giambone's. Eating at Ping Ching's, we saw whole pigs, blanched white, delivered at the door. We watched an Oriental funeral with Madame Nhu the director waving the limousines on. The deceased's picture, heaped with flowers, was in the lead car, and all his beautiful daughters wept with faces disordered and long black hair streaming down. One of the Italian bands which plays on feast days was mourning over a single refrain—two trumpets, a clarinet, a mellophone and a drum.

10   As an alternate I sat in on the arguments for a rent-a-car crash case, with four lawyers, each of whom liked to hear himself talk, representing the different parties. The theme was that we were New Yorkers and therefore streetwise and no fools. The senior fellow seemed to think that all his years of trying these penny-ante negligence affairs had made him very good indeed, whereas my impression was that the reason he was still trying them was because he was rather bad. The same afternoon I got on a jury to hear the case of a cleaning woman, sixty-four, who had slipped on the floor of a Harlem ballroom in 1967 and broken her ankle. She claimed the floor was overwaxed. She'd obviously been passed from hand to hand within the firm that had taken her case and had wound up with an attractive young man who was here cutting his teeth. What I liked about her was her abusive manner, which expected no justice and made no distinction at all between her own lawyer and that of the ballroom owner, though she was confused by the fact that the judge was black. He was from the Supreme Court, assigned to help cut through this backlog, had a clerk with an Afro, and was exceedingly brisk and effective.

11   The porter who had waxed the floor testified—a man of good will, long since at another job. The ballroom owner had operated the hall for more than thirty years, and his face was fastidious, Jewish, sensitive, sad, like that of a concertgoer who is not unduly pleased with his life. He testified, and it was not *his* fault. Nevertheless the lady had hurt her ankle and been out of pocket and out of work. It was a wedding reception, and she'd just stepped forward, saying, "Here comes the bride!"

12   The proceedings were interrupted while motions were heard in another case, and we sat alone in a jury room, trading reading material, obeying the injunction not to discuss the case, until after several hours we were called back and thanked by the judge. "They also serve who stand and wait." He said that our presence next door as a deliberative body, passive though we were, had pressured a settlement. It was for seven hundred and fifty dollars, a low figure to me (the court attendant told me that there had been a legal flaw in the plaintiff's case), but some of the other jurors thought she'd deserved no money; they were trying to be fair to the ballroom man. Almost always that's what the disputes boiled down to: one juror trying to be fair to one person, another to another.

13   On Friday of my first week I got on a jury to hear the plight of a woman who had been standing at the front of a bus and had been thrown forward and injured when she stooped to pick up some change that had spilled from her purse. The bus company's lawyer was a ruddy, jovial sort. "Anybody here have a bone to pick with our New York City buses?" We laughed and said, no, we were capable of sending her away without any award if she couldn't prove negligence. Nevertheless, he settled with her attorney immediately after we left the challenge room. (These attorneys did not necessarily run to type. There was a Transit Authority man who shouted like William Kunstler; five times the judge had an officer make him sit down, and once threatened to have the chap bound to his chair.)

14   I was an alternate for another car crash. With cases in progress all over the building, the jury pool had thinned out, so that no sooner were we dropped back into it than our names were called again. Even one noteworthy white-haired fellow who was wearing a red velvet jump suit, a dragon-colored coat and a dangling gold talisman had some experiences to talk about. I was tabbed for a panel that was to hear from a soft-looking, tired, blond widow of fifty-seven who, while walking home at night five years before from the shop where she worked, had tripped into an excavation only six inches deep but ten feet long and three feet wide. She claimed that the twists and bumps of this had kept her in pain and out of work for five months. She seemed natural and truthful on the witness stand, yet her testimony was so brief and flat that one needed to bear in mind how much time had passed. As we'd first filed into the courtroom she had watched us with the ironic

gravity that a person inevitably would feel who has waited five years for a hearing and now sees the cast of characters who will decide her case. This was a woeful low point of her life, but the memory of how badly she'd felt was stale.

15   The four attorneys on the case were straightforward youngsters getting their training here. The woman's was properly aggressive; Con Edison's asked humorously if we had ever quarreled with Con Edison over a bill; the city's, who was an idealist with shoulder-length hair, asked with another laugh if we disliked New York; and the realty company's, whether we fought with our landlords. Of course, fair-minded folk that we were, we told them no. They pointed out that just as the code of the law provides that a lone woman, fifty-seven, earning a hundred dollars a week, must receive the same consideration in court as a great city, so must the city be granted an equal measure of justice as that lone woman was.

16   Our panel included a bank guard, a lady loan officer, a young black Sing Sing guard, a pale, slim middle-aged executive from Coca-Cola, a hale fellow who sold package tours for an airline and looked like the Great Gildersleeve, and me. If her attorney had successfully eliminated Spartans from the jury, we'd surely award her something; the question was how much. I wondered about the five months. No bones broken—let's say, being rather generous, maybe two months of rest. But couldn't the remainder be one of those dead-still intermissions that each of us must stop and take once or twice in a life, not from any single blow but from the accumulating knocks and scabby disappointments that pile up, the harshness of winning a living, and the rest of it—for which the government in its blundering wisdom already makes some provision through unemployment insurance?

17   But there were no arguments. The judge had allowed the woman to testify about her injuries on the condition that her physician appear. When, the next day, he didn't, a mistrial was declared.

Behind the Formaldehyde Curtain

Jessica Mitford

1   The drama begins to unfold with the arrival of the corpse at the mortuary.

2   Alas, poor Yorick! How surprised he would be to see how his counterpart of today is whisked off to a funeral parlor and is in short order sprayed, sliced, pierced, pickled, trussed, trimmed, creamed, waxed, painted, rouged and neatly dressed—transformed from a common corpse into a Beautiful Memory Picture. This process is known in the trade as embalming and restorative art, and is so universally employed in the United States and Canada that the funeral director does it routinely, without consulting corpse or kin. He regards as eccentric those few who are hardy enough to suggest that it might be dispensed with. Yet no law requires embalming, no religious doctrine commends it, nor is it dictated by considerations of health, sanitation, or even of personal daintiness. In no part of the world but in Northern America is it widely used. The purpose of embalming is to make the corpse presentable for viewing in a suitably costly container; and here too the funeral director routinely, without first consulting the family, prepares the body for public display.

3   Is all this legal? The processes to which a dead body may be subjected are after all to some extent circumscribed by law. In most states, for instance, the signature of next of kin must be obtained before an autopsy may be performed, before the deceased may be cremated, before the body may be turned over to a medical school for research purposes; or such provision must be made in the decedent's will. In the case of embalming, no such permission is required nor is it ever sought. A textbook, *The Principles and Practices of Embalming,* comments on this: "There is some question regarding the legality of much that is done within the preparation room." The author points out that it would be most unusual for a responsible member of a bereaved family to instruct the mortician, in so many words, to *"embalm"* the body of a deceased

relative. The very term "embalming" is so seldom used that the mortician must rely upon custom in the matter. The author concludes that unless the family specifies otherwise, the act of entrusting the body to the care of a funeral establishment carries with it an implied permission to go ahead and embalm.

4   Embalming is indeed a most extraordinary procedure, and one must wonder at the docility of Americans who each year pay hundreds of millions of dollars for its perpetuation, blissfully ignorant of what it is all about, what is done, how it is done. Not one in ten thousand has any idea of what actually takes place. Books on the subject are extremely hard to come by. They are not to be found in most libraries or bookshops.

5   In an era when huge television audiences watch surgical operations in the comfort of their living rooms, when, thanks to the animated cartoon, the geography of the digestive system has become familiar territory even to the nursery school set, in a land where the satisfaction of curiosity about almost all matters is a national pastime, the secrecy surrounding embalming can, surely, hardly be attributed to the inherent gruesomeness of the subject. Custom in this regard has within this century suffered a complete reversal. In the early days of American embalming, when it was performed in the home of the deceased, it was almost mandatory for some relative to stay by the embalmer's side and witness the procedure. Today, family members who might wish to be in attendance would certainly be dissuaded by the funeral director. All others, except apprentices, are excluded by law from the preparation room.

6   A close look at what does actually take place may explain in large measure the undertaker's intractable reticence concerning a procedure that has become his major *raison d'être*. It is possible he fears that public information about embalming might lead patrons to wonder if they really want this service? If the funeral men are loath to discuss the subject outside the trade, the reader may, understandably, be equally loath to go on reading at this point. For those who have the stomach for it, let us part the formaldehyde curtain. . . .

7   The body is first laid out in the undertaker's morgue—or rather, Mr. Jones is reposing in the preparation room—to be readied to bid the world farewell.

8   The preparation room in any of the better funeral establishments

has the tiled and sterile look of a surgery, and indeed the embalmer-restorative artist who does his chores there is beginning to adopt the term "dermasurgeon" (appropriately corrupted by some mortician-writers as "demi-surgeon") to describe his calling. His equipment, consisting of scalpels, scissors, augers, forceps, clamps, needles, pumps, tubes, bowls and basins, is crudely imitative of the surgeon's, as is his technique, acquired in a nine- or twelve-month post-high-school course in an embalming school. He is supplied by an advanced chemical industry with a bewildering array of fluids, sprays, pastes, oils, powders, creams, to fix or soften tissue, shrink or distend it as needed, dry it here, restore the moisture there. There are cosmetics, waxes and paints to fill and cover features, even plaster of Paris to replace entire limbs. There are ingenious aids to prop and stabilize the cadaver: a Vari-Pose Head Rest, the Edwards Arm and Hand Positioner, the Repose Block (to support the shoulders during the embalming), and the Throop Foot Positioner, which resembles an old-fashioned stocks.

9   Mr. John H. Eckels, president of the Eckels College of Mortuary Science, thus describes the first part of the embalming procedure: "In the hands of a skilled practitioner, this work may be done in a comparatively short time and without mutilating the body other than by slight incision—so slight that it scarcely would cause serious inconvenience if made upon a living person. It is necessary to remove the blood, and doing this not only helps in the disinfecting, but removes the principal cause of disfigurements due to discoloration."

10   Another textbook discusses the all-important time element: "The earlier this is done, the better, for every hour that elapses between death and embalming will add to the problems and complications encountered. . . ." Just how soon should one get going on the embalming? The author tells us, "On the basis of such scanty information made available to this profession through its rudimentary and haphazard system of technical research, we must conclude that the best results are to be obtained if the subject is embalmed before life is completely extinct—that is, before cellular death has occurred. In the average case, this would mean within an hour after somatic death." For those who feel that there is something a little rudimentary, not to say haphazard, about this advice, a comforting thought is offered by another writer. Speaking of fears entertained in early days of premature burial, he points out,

"One of the effects of embalming by chemical injection, however, has been to dispel fears of live burial." How true; once the blood is removed, chances of live burial are indeed remote.

11   To return to Mr. Jones, the blood is drained out through the veins and replaced by embalming fluid pumped in through the arteries. As noted in *The Principles and Practices of Embalming,* "every operator has a favorite injection and drainage point—a fact which becomes a handicap only if he fails or refuses to forsake his favorites when conditions demand it." Typical favorites are the carotid artery, femoral artery, jugular vein, subclavian vein. There are various choices of embalming fluid. If Flextone is used, it will produce a "mild, flexible rigidity. The skin retains a velvety softness, the tissues are rubbery and pliable. Ideal for women and children." It may be blended with B. and G. Products Company's Lyf-Lyk tint, which is guaranteed to reproduce "nature's own skin texture . . . the velvety appearance of living tissue." Suntone comes in three separate tints: Suntan; Special Cosmetic Tint, a pink shade "especially indicated for female subjects"; and Regular Cosmetic Tint, moderately pink.

12   About three to six gallons of a dyed and perfumed solution of formaldehyde, glycerin, borax, phenol, alcohol and water is soon circulating through Mr. Jones, whose mouth has been sewn together with a "needle directed upward between the upper lip and gum and brought out through the left nostril," with the corners raised slightly "for a more pleasant expression." If he should be bucktoothed, his teeth are cleaned with Bon Ami and coated with colorless nail polish. His eyes, meanwhile, are closed with flesh-tinted eye caps and eye cement.

13   The next step is to have at Mr. Jones with a thing called a trocar. This is a long, hollow needle attached to a tube. It is jabbed into the abdomen, poked around the entrails and chest cavity, the contents of which are pumped out and replaced with "cavity fluid." This done, and the hole in the abdomen sewn up, Mr. Jones's face is heavily creamed (to protect the skin from burns which may be caused by leakage of the chemicals), and he is covered with a sheet and left unmolested for a while. But not for long—there is more, much more, in store for him. He has been embalmed, but not yet restored, and the best time to start the restorative work is eight to ten hours after embalming, when the tissues have become firm and dry.

14   The object of all this attention to the corpse, it must be remem-

bered, is to make it presentable for viewing in an attitude of healthy repose. "Our customs require the presentation of our dead in the semblance of normality . . . unmarred by the ravages of illness, disease or multilation," says Mr. J. Sheridan Mayer in his *Restorative Art*. This is rather a large order since few people die in the full bloom of health, unravaged by illness and unmarked by some disfigurement. The funeral industry is equal to the challenge: "In some cases the gruesome appearance of a mutilated or disease-ridden subject may be quite discouraging. The task of restoration may seem impossible and shake the confidence of the embalmer. This is the time for intestinal fortitude and determination. Once the formative work is begun and affected tissues are cleaned or removed, all doubts of success vanish. It is surprising and gratifying to discover the results which may be obtained."

15   The embalmer, having allowed an appropriate interval to elapse, returns to the attack, but now he brings into play the skill and equipment of sculptor and cosmetician. Is a hand missing? Casting one in plaster of Paris is a simple matter. "For replacement purposes, only a cast of the back of the hand is necessary; this is within the ability of the average operator and is quite adequate." If a lip or two, a nose or an ear should be missing, the embalmer has at hand a variety of restorative waxes with which to model replacements. Pores and skin texture are simulated by stippling with a little brush, and over this cosmetics are laid on. Head off? Decapitation cases are rather routinely handled. Ragged edges are trimmed, and head joined to torso with a series of splints, wires and sutures. It is a good idea to have a little something at the neck— a scarf or a high collar—when time for viewing comes. Swollen mouth? Cut out tissue as needed from inside the lips. If too much is removed, the surface contour can easily be restored by padding with cotton. Swollen necks and cheeks are reduced by removing tissue through vertical incisions made down each side of the neck. "When the deceased is casketed, the pillow will hide the suture incisions . . . as an extra precaution against leakage, the suture may be painted with liquid sealer."

16   The opposite condition is more likely to present itself—that of emaciation. His hypodermic syringe now loaded with massage cream, the embalmer seeks out and fills the hollowed and sunken areas by injection. In this procedure the backs of the hands and fingers and the under-chin area should not be neglected.

17   Positioning the lips is a problem that recurrently challenges the

ingenuity of the embalmer. Closed too tightly, they tend to give a stern, even disapproving expression. Ideally, embalmers feel, the lips should give the impression of being ever so slightly parted, the upper lip protruding slightly for a more youthful appearance. This takes some engineering, however, as the lips tend to drift apart. Lip drift can sometimes be remedied by pushing one or two straight pins through the inner margin of the lower lip and then inserting them between tne two front upper teeth. If Mr. Jones happens to have no teeth, the pins can just as easily be anchored in his Armstrong Face Former and Denture Replacer. Another method to maintain lip closure is to dislocate the lower jaw, which is then held in its new position by a wire run through holes which have been drilled through the upper and lower jaws at the midline. As the French are fond of saying, *il faut souffrir pour être belle*.

18   If Mr. Jones has died of jaundice, the embalming fluid will very likely turn him green. Does this deter the embalmer? Not if he has intestinal fortitude. Masking pastes and cosmetics are heavily laid on, burial garments and casket interiors are color-correlated with particular care, and Jones is displayed beneath rose-colored lights. Friends will say "How *well* he looks." Death by carbon monoxide, on the other hand, can be rather a good thing from the embalmer's viewpoint: "One advantage is the fact that this type of discoloration is an exaggerated form of a natural pink coloration." This is nice because the healthy glow is already present and needs but little attention.

19   The patching and filling completed, Mr. Jones is now shaved, washed and dressed. Cream-based cosmetic, available in pink, flesh, suntan, brunette and blond, is applied to his hands and face, his hair is shampooed and combed (and, in the case of Mrs. Jones, set), his hands manicured. For the horny-handed son of toil special care must be taken; cream should be applied to remove ingrained grime, and the nails cleaned. "If he were not in the habit of having them manicured in life, trimming and shaping is advised for better appearance—never questioned by kin."

20   Jones is now ready for casketing (this is the present participle of the verb "to casket"). In this operation his right shoulder should be depressed slightly "to turn the body a bit to the right and soften the appearance of lying flat on the back." Positioning the hands is a matter of importance, and special rubber positioning blocks may be used. The

hands should be cupped slightly for a more lifelike, relaxed appearance. Proper placement of the body requires a delicate sense of balance. It should lie as high as possible in the casket, yet not so high that the lid, when lowered, will hit the nose. On the other hand, we are cautioned, placing the body too low "creates the impression that the body is in a box."

21   Jones is next wheeled into the appointed slumber room where a few last touches may be added—his favorite pipe placed in his hand or, if he was a great reader, a book propped into position. (In the case of little Master Jones a Teddy bear may be clutched.) Here he will hold open house for a few days, visiting hours 10 A.M. to 9 P.M.

22   All now being in readiness, the funeral director calls a staff conference to make sure that each assistant knows his precise duties. Mr. Wilber Kriege writes: "This makes your staff feel that they are a part of the team, with a definite assignment that must be properly carried out if the whole plan is to succeed. You never heard of a football coach who failed to talk to his entire team before they go on the field. They have drilled on the plays they are to execute for hours and days, and yet the successful coach knows the importance of making even the bench-warming third-string substitute feel that he is important if the game is to be won." The winning of *this* game is predicated upon glass-smooth handling of the logistics. The funeral director has notified the pallbearers whose names were furnished by the family, has arranged for the presence of clergyman, organist, and soloist, has provided transportation for everybody, has organized and listed the flowers sent by friends. In *Psychology of Funeral Service* Mr. Edward A. Martin points out: "He may not always do as much as the family thinks he is doing, but it is his helpful guidance that they appreciate in knowing they are proceeding as they should. . . . The important thing is how well his services can be used to make the family believe they are giving unlimited expression to their own sentiment."

23   The religious service may be held in a church or in the chapel of the funeral home; the funeral director vastly prefers the latter arrangement, for not only is it more convenient for him but it affords him the opportunity to show off his beautiful facilities to the gathered mourners. After the clergyman has had his say, the mourners queue up to file past the casket for a last look at the deceased. The family is *never* asked whether they want an open-casket ceremony; in the absence of their

instruction to the contrary, this is taken for granted. Consequently well over 90 per cent of all American funerals feature the open casket—a custom unknown in other parts of the world. Foreigners are astonished by it. An English woman living in San Francisco described her reaction in a letter to the writer:

> I myself have attended only one funeral here—that of an elderly fellow worker of mine. After the service I could not understand why everyone was walking towards the coffin (sorry, I mean casket), but thought I had better follow the crowd. It shook me rigid to get there and find the casket open and poor old Oscar lying there in his brown tweed suit, wearing a suntan makeup and just the wrong shade of lipstick. If I had not been extremely fond of the old boy, I have a horrible feeling that I might have giggled. Then and there I decided that I could never face another American funeral—even dead.

24   The casket (which has been resting throughout the service on a Classic Beauty Ultra Metal Casket Bier) is now transferred by a hydraulically operated device called Porto-Lift to a balloon-tired, Glide Easy casket carriage which will wheel it to yet another conveyance, the Cadillac Funeral Coach. This may be lavender, cream, light green— anything but black. Interiors, of course, are color-correlated, "for the man who cannot stop short of perfection."

25   At graveside, the casket is lowered into the earth. This office, once the prerogative of friends of the deceased, is now performed by a patented mechanical lowering device. A "Lifetime Green" artificial grass mat is at the ready to conceal the sere earth, and overhead, to conceal the sky, is a portable Steril Chapel Tent ("resists the intense heat and humidity of of summer and the terrific storms of winter . . . available in Silver Grey, Rose or Evergreen"). Now is the time for the ritual scattering of earth over the coffin, as the solemn words "earth to earth, ashes to ashes, dust to dust" are pronounced by the officiating cleric. This can today be accomplished "with a mere flick of the wrist with the Gordon Leak-Proof Earth Dispenser. No grasping of a handful of dirt, no soiled fingers. Simple, dignified, beautiful, reverent! The modern way!" The Gordon Earth Dispenser (at $5) is of nickel-plated brass construction. It is not only "attractive to the eye and long wearing"; it is also "one of the 'tools' for building better public

relations" if presented as "an appropriate non-commercial gift" to the clergyman. It is shaped something like a saltshaker.

26   Untouched by human hand, the coffin and the earth are now united.

27   It is in the function of directing the participants through this maze of gadgetry that the funeral director has assigned to himself his relatively new role of "grief therapist." He has relieved the family of every detail, he has revamped the corpse to look like a living doll, he has arranged for it to nap for a few days in a slumber room, he has put on a well-oiled performance in which the concept of *death* has played no part whatsoever—unless it was inconsiderately mentioned by the clergyman who conducted the religious service. He has done everything in his power to make the funeral a real pleasure for everybody concerned. He and his team have given their all to score an upset victory over death.

The Maker's Eye: Revising Your Own Manuscripts

Donald M. Murray

1   When students complete a first draft, they consider the job of writing done—and their teachers too often agree. When professional writers complete a first draft, they usually feel that they are at the start of the writing process. When a draft is completed, the job of writing can begin.

2   That difference in attitude is the difference between amateur and professional, inexperience and experience, journeyman and craftsman. Peter F. Drucker, the prolific business writer, calls his first draft "the zero draft"—after that he can start counting. Most writers share the feeling that the first draft, and all of those which follow, are opportunities to discover what they have to say and how best they can say it.

3   To produce a progression of drafts, each of which says more and says it more clearly, the writer has to develop a special kind of reading skill. In school we are taught to decode what appears on the page as finished writing. Writers, however, face a different category of possibility and responsibility when they read their own drafts. To them the words on the page are never finished. Each can be changed and rearranged, can set off a chain reaction of confusion or clarified meaning. This is a different kind of reading which is possibly more difficult and certainly more exciting.

4   Writers must learn to be their own best enemy. They must accept the criticism of others and be suspicious of it; they must accept the praise of others and be even more suspicious of it. Writers cannot depend on others. They must detach themselves from their own pages so that they can apply both their caring and their craft to their own work.

5   Such detachment is not easy. Science fiction writer Ray Bradbury supposedly puts each manuscript away for a year to the day and then rereads it as a stranger. Not many writers have the discipline or the

time to do this. We must read when our judgment may be at its worst, when we are close to the euphoric moment of creation.

6   Then the writer, counsels novelist Nancy Hale, "should be critical of everything that seems to him most delightful in his style. He should excise what he most admires, because he wouldn't thus admire it if he weren't . . . in a sense protecting it from criticism." John Ciardi, the poet, adds, "The last act of the writing must be to become one's own reader. It is, I suppose, a schizophrenic process, to begin passionately and to end critically, to begin hot and to end cold; and, more important, to be passion-hot and critic-cold at the same time."

7   Most people think that the principal problem is that writers are too proud of what they have written. Actually, a greater problem for most professional writers is one shared by the majority of students. They are overly critical, think everything is dreadful, tear up page after page, never complete a draft, see the task as hopeless.

8   The writer must learn to read critically but constructively, to cut what is bad, to reveal what is good. Eleanor Estes, the children's book author, explains: "The writer must survey his work critically, cooly, as though he were a stranger to it. He must be willing to prune, expertly and hard-heartedly. At the end of each revision, a manuscript may look . . . worked over, torn apart, pinned together, added to, deleted from, words changed and words changed back. Yet the book must maintain its original freshness and spontaneity."

9   Most readers underestimate the amount of rewriting it usually takes to produce spontaneous reading. This is a great disadvantage to the student writer, who sees only a finished product and never watches the craftsman who takes the necessary step back, studies the work carefully, returns to the task, steps back, returns, steps back, again and again. Anthony Burgess, one of the most prolific writers in the English-speaking world, admits, "I might revise a page twenty times." Ronald Dahl, the popular children's writer, states, "By the time I'm nearing the end of a story, the first part will have been reread and altered and corrected at least 150 times. . . . Good writing is essentially rewriting. I am positive of this."

10   Rewriting isn't virtuous. It isn't something that ought to be done. It is simply something that most writers find they have to do to discover what they have to say and how to say it. It is a condition of the writer's life.

11   There are, however, a few writers who do little formal rewriting, primarily because they have the capacity and experience to create and review a large number of invisible drafts in their minds before they approach the page. And some writers slowly produce finished pages, performing all the tasks of revision simultaneously, page by page, rather than draft by draft. But it is still possible to see the sequence followed by most writers most of the time in rereading their own work.

12   Most writers scan their drafts first, reading as quickly as possible to catch the larger problems of subject and form, then move in closer and closer as they read and write, reread and rewrite.

13   The first thing writers look for in their drafts is *information*. They know that a good piece of writing is built from specific, accurate, and interesting information. The writer must have an abundance of information from which to construct a readable piece of writing.

14   Next writers look for *meaning* in the information. The specifics must build to a pattern of significance. Each piece of specific information must carry the reader toward meaning.

15   Writers reading their own drafts are aware of *audience*. They put themselves in the reader's situation and make sure that they deliver information which a reader wants to know or needs to know in a manner which is easily digested. Writers try to be sure that they anticipate and answer the questions a critical reader will ask when reading the piece of writing.

16   Writers make sure that the *form* is appropriate to the subject and the audience. Form, or genre, is the vehicle which carries meaning to the reader, but form cannot be selected until the writer has adequate information to discover its significance and an audience which needs or wants that meaning.

17   Once writers are sure the form is appropriate, they must then look at the *structure,* the order of what they have written. Good writing is built on a solid framework of logic, argument, narrative, or motivation which runs through the entire piece of writing and holds it together. This is the time when many writers find it most effective to outline as a way of visualizing the hidden spine by which the piece of writing is supported.

18   The element on which writers may spend a majority of their time is *development*. Each section of a piece of writing must be adequately developed. It must give readers enough information so that they are

satisfied. How much information is enough? That's as difficult as asking how much garlic belongs in a salad. It must be done to taste, but most beginning writers underdevelop, underestimating the reader's hunger for information.

19   As writers solve development problems, they often have to consider questions of *dimension*. There must be a pleasing and effective proportion among all the parts of the piece of writing. There is a continual process of subtracting and adding to keep the piece of writing in balance.

20   Finally, writers have to listen to their own voices. *Voice* is the force which drives a piece of writing forward. It is an expression of the writer's authority and concern. It is what is between the words on the page, what glues the piece of writing together. A good piece of writing is always marked by a consistent, individual voice.

21   As writers read and reread, write and rewrite, they move closer and closer to the page until they are doing line-by-line editing. Writers read their own pages with infinite care. Each sentence, each line, each clause, each phrase, each word, each mark of punctuation, each section of white space between the type has to contribute to the clarification of meaning.

22   Slowly the writer moves from word to word, looking through language to see the subject. As a word is changed, cut, or added, as a construction is rearranged, all the words used before that moment and all those that follow that moment must be considered and reconsidered.

23   Writers often read aloud at this stage of the editing process, muttering or whispering to themselves, calling on the ear's experience with language. Does this sound right—or that? Writers edit, shifting back and forth from eye to page to ear to page. I find I must do this careful editing in short runs, no more than fifteen or twenty minutes at a stretch, or I become too kind with myself. I begin to see what I hope is on the page, not what actually is on the page.

24   This sounds tedious if you haven't done it, but actually it is fun. Making something right is immensely satisfying, for writers begin to learn what they are writing about by writing. Language leads them to meaning, and there is the joy of discovery, of understanding, of making meaning clear as the writer employs the technical skills of language.

25   Words have double meanings, even triple and quadruple meanings. Each word has its own potential for connotation and denotation.

And when writers rub one word against the other, they are often rewarded with a sudden insight, an unexpected clarification.

26   The maker's eye moves back and forth from word to phrase to
sentence to paragraph to sentence to phrase to word. The maker's eye
sees the need for variety and balance, for a firmer structure, for a more
appropriate form. It peers into the interior of the paragraph, looking for
coherence, unity, and emphasis, which make meaning clear.

27   I learned something about this process when my first bifocals were
prescribed. I had ordered a larger section of the reading portion of the
glass because of my work, but even so, I could not contain my eyes
within this new limit of vision. And I still find myself taking off my
glasses and bending my nose towards the page, for my eyes unconsciously flick back and forth across the page, back to another page,
forward to still another, as I try to see each evolving line in relation to
every other line.

28   When does this process end? Most writers agree with the great
Russian writer Tolstoy, who said, "I scarcely ever reread my published
writings, if by chance I come across a page, it always strikes me: all
this must be rewritten; this is how I should have written it."

29   The maker's eye is never satisfied, for each word has the potential
to ignite new meaning. This article has been twice written all the way
through the writing process, and it was published four years ago. Now
it is to be republished in a book. The editors made a few small suggestions, and then I read it with my maker's eye. Now it has been re-
edited, re-revised, re-read, re-re-edited, for each piece of writing to the
writer is full of potential and alternatives.

30   A piece of writing is never finished. It is delivered to a deadline,
torn out of the typewriter on demand, sent off with a sense of accomplishment and shame and pride and frustration. If only there were a
couple more days, time for just another run at it, perhaps then. . . .

Desperation Writing

Peter Elbow

1   I know I am not alone in my recurring twinges of panic that I won't be able to write something when I need to, I won't be able to produce coherent speech or thought. And that lingering doubt is a great hindrance to writing. It's a constant fog or static that clouds the mind. I never got out of its clutches till I discovered that it was possible to write something—not something great or pleasing but at least something usable, workable—when my mind is out of commission. The trick is that you have to do all your cooking out on the table: your mind is incapable of doing any inside. It means using symbols and pieces of paper not as a crutch but as a wheel chair.

2   The first thing is to admit your condition: because of some mood or event or whatever, your mind is incapable of anything that could be called thought. It can put out a babbling kind of speech utterance, it can put a simple feeling, perception, or sort-of-thought into understandable (though terrible) words. But it is incapable of considering anything in relation to anything else. The moment you try to hold that thought or feeling up against some other to see the relationship, you simply lose the picture—you get nothing but buzzing lines or waving colors.

3   So admit this. Avoid anything more than one feeling, perception, or thought. Simply write as much as possible. Try simply to steer your mind in the direction or general vicinity of the thing you are trying to write about and start writing and keep writing.

4   Just write and keep writing. (Probably best to write on only one side of the paper in case you should want to cut parts out with scissors—but you probably won't.) Just write and keep writing. It will probably come in waves. After a flurry, stop and take a brief rest. But don't stop too long. Don't think about what you are writing or what you have written or else you will overload the circuit again. Keep writing as though you are drugged or drunk. Keep doing this till you feel you have a lot of material that might be useful; or, if necessary, till you

119

can't stand it any more—even if you doubt that there's anything useful there.

5   Then take a pad of little pieces of paper—or perhaps 3 × 5 cards—and simply start at the beginning of what you were writing, and as you read over what you wrote, every time you come to any thought, feeling, perception, or image that could be gathered up into one sentence or one assertion, do so and write it by itself on a little sheet of paper. In short, you are trying to turn, say, ten or twenty pages of wandering mush into twenty or thirty hard little crab apples. Sometimes there won't be many on a page. But if it seems to you that there are none on a page, you are making a serious error—the same serious error that put you in this comatose state to start with. You are mistaking lousy, stupid, second-rate, wrong, childish, foolish, worthless ideas for no ideas at all. Your job is not to pick out *good* ideas but to pick out ideas. As long as you were conscious, your words will be full of things that could be called feelings, utterances, ideas—things that can be squeezed into one simple sentence. This is your job. Don't ask for too much.

6   After you have done this, take those little slips or cards, read through them a number of times—not struggling with them, simply wandering and mulling through them; perhaps shifting them around and looking through them in various sequences. In a sense these are cards you are playing solitaire with, and the rules of this particular game permit shuffling the unused pile.

7   The goal of this procedure with the cards is to get them to distribute themselves in two or three or ten or fifteen different piles on your desk. You can get them to do this almost by themselves if you simply keep reading through them in different orders; certain cards will begin to feel like they go with other cards. I emphasize this passive, thoughtless mode because I want to talk about desperation writing in its pure state. In practice, almost invariably at some point in the procedure, your sanity begins to return. It is often at this point. You actually are moved to have thoughts or—and the difference between active and passive is crucial here—to *exert* thought; to hold two cards together and *build* or *assert* a relationship. It is a matter of bringing energy to bear.

8   So you may start to be able to do something active with these cards, and begin actually to think. But if not, just allow the cards to find their own piles with each other by feel, by drift, by intuition, by mindlessness.

9   You have now engaged in the two main activities that will permit you to get something cooked out on the table rather than in your brain: writing out into messy words, summing up into single assertions, and even sensing relationships between assertions. You can simply continue to deploy these two activities.

10   If, for example, after that first round of writing, assertion-making, and pile-making, your piles feel as though they are useful and satisfactory for what you are writing—paragraphs or sections or trains of thought—then you can carry on from there. See if you can gather each pile up into a single assertion. When you can, then put the subsidiary assertions of that pile into their best order to fit with that single unifying one. If you *can't* get the pile into one assertion, then take the pile as the basis for doing some more writing out into words. In the course of this writing, you may produce for yourself the single unifying assertion you were looking for; or you may have to go through the cycle of turning the writing into assertions and piles and so forth. Perhaps more than once. The pile may turn out to want to be two or more piles itself; or it may want to become part of a pile you already have. This is natural. This kind of meshing into one configuration, then coming apart, then coming together and meshing into a different configuration—this is growing and cooking. It makes a terrible mess, but if you can't do it in your head, you have to put up with a cluttered desk and a lot of confusion.

11   If, on the other hand, all that writing *didn't* have useful material in it, it means that your writing wasn't loose, drifting, quirky, jerky, associative enough. This time try especially to let things simply remind you of things that are seemingly crazy or unrelated. Follow these odd associations. Make as many metaphors as you can—be as nutty as possible—and explore the metaphors themselves—open them out. You may have all your energy tied up in some area of your experience that you are leaving out. Don't refrain from writing about whatever else is on your mind: how you feel at the moment, what you are losing your mind over, randomness that intrudes itself on your consciousness, the pattern on the wallpaper, what those people you see out the window have on their minds—though keep coming back to the whateveritis you are supposed to be writing about. Treat it, in short, like ten-minute writing exercises. Your best perceptions and thoughts are always going to be tied up in whatever is really occupying you, and that is also where

your energy is. You may end up writing a love poem—or a hate poem—in one of those little piles while the other piles will finally turn into a lab report on data processing or whatever you have to write about. But you couldn't, in your present state of having your head shot off, have written that report without also writing the poem. And the report will have some of the juice of the poem in it and vice versa.

How to Write a Rotten Poem with Almost No Effort

Richard Howey

1   So you want to write a poem. You've had a rotten day or an astounding thought or a car accident or a squalid love affair and you want to record it for all time. You want to organize those emotions that are pounding through your veins. You have something to communicate via a poem but you don't know where to start.

2   This, of course, is the problem with poetry. Most people find it difficult to write a poem so they don't even try. What's worse, they don't bother reading any poems either. Poetry has become an almost totally foreign art form to many of us. As a result, serious poets either starve or work as account executives.[1] There is no middle ground. Good poets and poems are lost forever simply because there is no market for them, no people who write their own verse and seek out further inspiration from other bards.

3   Fortunately, there is a solution for this problem, as there are for all imponderables. The answer is to make it easy for everyone to write at least one poem in his life. Once a person has written a poem, of whatever quality, he will feel comradeship with fellow poets and, hopefully, read their works. Ideally, there would evolve a veritable society of poet-citizens, which would elevate the quality of life worldwide. Not only that, good poets could make a living for a change.

4   So, to begin. Have your paper ready. You must first understand that the poem you write here will not be brilliant. It won't even be mediocre. But it will be better than 50% of all song lyrics and at least equal to one of Rod McKuen's best efforts. You will be instructed how to write a four-line poem but the basic structure can be repeated at will to create works of epic length.

[1]Upper-level positions in advertising agencies.

5   The first line of your poem should start and end with these words: "In the———of my mind." The middle word of this line is optional. Any word will do. It would be best not to use a word that has been overdone, such as "windmills" or "gardens" or "playground." Just think of as many nouns as you can and see what fits best. The rule of thumb is to pick a noun that seems totally out of context, such as "filing cabinet" or "radiator" or "parking lot." Just remember, the more unusual the noun, the more profound the image.

6   The second line should use two or more of the human senses[2] in a conflicting manner, as per the famous, "listen to the warm." This is a sure way to conjure up "poetic" feeling and atmosphere. Since there are five different senses, the possibilities are endless. A couple that come to mind are "see the noise" and "touch the sound." If more complexity is desired other senses can be added, as in "taste the color of my hearing," or "I cuddled your sight in the aroma of the night." Rhyming, of course, is optional.

7   The third line should be just a simple statement. This is used to break up the insightful images that have been presented in the first two lines. This line should be as prosaic as possible to give a "down-to-earth" mood to the poem. An example would be "she gave me juice and toast that morning," or perhaps "I left for work next day on the 8:30 bus." The content of this line may or may not relate to what has gone before.

8   The last line of your poem should deal with the future in some way. This gives the poem a forward thrust that is always helpful. A possibility might be, "tomorrow will be a better day," or "I'll find someone sometime," or "maybe we'll meet again in July." This future-oriented ending lends an aura of hope and yet need not be grossly optimistic.

9   By following the above structure, anyone can write a poem. For example, if I select one each of my sample lines, I come up with:

> In the parking lot of my mind,
>
>> I cuddled your sight in the aroma of the night.
>
> I left for work next day on the 8:30 bus.
>
>> Maybe we'll meet again in July.

---

[2]The five senses are taste, touch, smell, hearing, and sight.

10   Now that poem (like yours, when your're finished) is rotten. But at least it's a poem and you've written it, which is an accomplishment that relatively few people can claim.

11   Now that you're a poet, feel free to read poetry by some of your more accomplished brothers and sisters in verse. Chances are, you'll find their offerings stimulating and refreshing. You might even try writing some more of your own poems, now that you've broken the ice. Observe others' emotions and experience your own—that's what poetry is all about.

12   Incidentally, if you find it impossible to sell the poem you write to Bobby Goldsboro or John Denver, burn it. It will look terrible as the first page of your anthology when it's published.

Chapter Four

Definition

The Holocaust

Bruno Bettelheim

1   To begin with, it was not the hapless victims of the Nazis who named their incomprehensible and totally unmasterable fate the "holocaust." It was the Americans who applied this artificial and highly technical term to the Nazi extermination of the European Jews. But while the event when named as mass murder most foul evokes the most immediate, most powerful revulsion, when it is designated by a rare technical term, we must first in our minds translate it back into emotionally meaningful language. Using technical or specially created terms instead of words from our common vocabulary is one of the best-known and most widely used distancing devices, separating the intellectual from the emotional experience. Talking about "the holocaust" permits us to manage it intellectually where the raw facts, when given their ordinary names, would overwhelm us emotionally—because it was catastrophe beyond comprehension, beyond the limits of our imagination, unless we force ourselves against our desire to extend it to encompass these terrible events.

2   This linguistic circumlocution began while it all was only in the planning stage. Even the Nazis—usually given to grossness in language and action—shied away from facing openly what they were up to and called this vile mass murder "the final solution of the Jewish problem." After all, solving a problem can be made to appear like an honorable enterprise, as long as we are not forced to recognize that the solution we are about to embark on consists of the completely unprovoked, vicious murder of millions of helpless men, women, and children. The Nuremberg judges of these Nazi criminals followed their example of circumlocution by coining a neologism out of one Greek and one Latin root: genocide. These artificially created technical terms fail to connect with our strongest feelings. The horror of murder is part of our most common human heritage. From earliest infancy on, it arouses violent abhorrence in us. Therefore in whatever form it appears we should give

such an act its true designation and not hide it behind polite, erudite terms created out of classical words.

3   To call this vile mass murder "the holocaust" is not to give it a special name emphasizing its uniqueness which would permit, over time, the word becoming invested with feelings germane to the event it refers to. The correct definition of "holocaust" is "burnt offering." As such, it is part of the language of the psalmist, a meaningful word to all who have some acquaintance with the Bible, full of the richest emotional connotations. By using the term "holocaust," entirely false associations are established through conscious and unconscious connotations between the most vicious of mass murders and ancient rituals of a deeply religious nature.

4   Using a word with such strong unconscious religious connotations when speaking of the murder of millions of Jews robs the victims of this abominable mass murder of the only thing left to them: their uniqueness. Calling the most callous, most brutal, most horrid, most heinous mass murder a burnt offering is a sacrilege, a profanation of God and man.

5   Martyrdom is part of our religious heritage. A martyr, burned at the stake, is a burnt offering to his god. And it is true that after the Jews were asphyxiated, the victims' corpses were burned. But I believe we fool ourselves if we think we are honoring the victims of systematic murder by using this term, which has the highest moral connotations. By doing so, we connect for our own psychological reasons what happened in the extermination camps with historical events we deeply regret, but also greatly admire. We do so because this makes it easier for us to cope; only in doing so we cope with our distorted image of what happened, not with the events the way they did happen.

6   By calling the victims of the Nazis "martyrs," we falsify their fate. The true meaning of "martyr" is: "one who voluntarily undergoes the penalty of death for refusing to renounce his faith" (*Oxford English Dictionary*). The Nazis made sure that nobody could mistakenly think that their victims were murdered for their religious beliefs. Renouncing their faith would have saved none of them. Those who had converted to Christianity were gassed, as were those who were atheists, and those who were deeply religious Jews. They did not die for any conviction, and certainly not out of choice.

7   Millions of Jews were systematically slaughtered, as were untold other "undesirables," not for any convictions of theirs, but only because

they stood in the way of the realization of an illusion. They neither died for their convictions, nor were they slaughtered because of their convictions, but only in consequence of the Nazis' delusional belief about what was required to protect the purity of their assumed superior racial endowment, and what they thought necessary to guarantee them the living space they believed they needed and were entitled to. Thus while these millions were slaughtered for an idea, they did not die for one.

8   Millions—men, women, and children—were processed after they had been utterly brutalized, their humanity destroyed, their clothes torn from their bodies. Naked, they were sorted into those who were destined to be murdered immediately, and those others who had a short-term usefulness as slave labor. But after a brief interval they, too, were to be herded into the same gas chambers into which the others were immediately piled, there to be asphyxiated so that, in their last moments, they could not prevent themselves from fighting each other in vain for a last breath of air.

9   To call these most wretched victims of a murderous delusion, of destructive drives run rampant, martyrs or a burnt offering is a distortion invented for our comfort, small as it may be. It pretends that this most vicious of mass murders had some deeper meaning; that in some fashion the victims either offered themselves or at least became sacrifices to a higher cause. It robs them of the last recognition which could be theirs, denies them the last dignity we could accord them: to face and accept what their death was all about, not embellishing it for the small psychological relief this may give us.

10   We could feel so much better if the victims had acted out of choice. For our emotional relief, therefore, we dwell on the tiny minority who did exercise some choice: the resistance fighters of the Warsaw ghetto, for example, and others like them. We are ready to overlook the fact that these people fought back only at a time when everything was lost, when the overwhelming majority of those who had been forced into the ghettos had already been exterminated without resisting. Certainly those few who finally fought for their survival and their convictions, risking and losing their lives in doing so, deserve our admiration; their deeds give us a moral lift. But the more we dwell on these few, the more unfair are we to the memory of the millions who were slaughtered—who gave in, did not fight back—because we deny them the only thing which up to the very end remained uniquely their own: their fate.

Beauty

Susan Sontag

1   For the Greeks, beauty was a virtue: a kind of excellence. Persons then were assumed to be what we now have to call—lamely, enviously—*whole* persons. If it did occur to the Greeks to distinguish between a person's "inside" and "outside," they still expected that inner beauty would be matched by beauty of the other kind. The well-born young Athenians who gathered around Socrates found it quite paradoxical that their hero was so intelligent, so brave, so honorable, so seductive—and so ugly. One of Socrates' main pedagogical acts was to be ugly—and teach those innocent, no doubt splendid-looking disciples of his how full of paradoxes life really was.

2   They may have resisted Socrates' lesson. We do not. Several thousand years later, we are more wary of the enchantments of beauty. We not only split off—with the greatest facility—the "inside" (character, intellect) from the "outside" (looks); but we are actually surprised when someone who is beautiful is also intelligent, talented, good.

3   It was principally the influence of Christianity that deprived beauty of the central place it had in classical ideals of human excellence. By limiting excellence (*virtus* in Latin) to *moral* virtue only, Christianity set beauty adrift—as an alienated, arbitrary, superficial enchantment. And beauty has continued to lose prestige. For close to two centuries it has become a convention to attribute beauty to only one of the two sexes: the sex which, however Fair, is always Second. Associating beauty with women has put beauty even further on the defensive, morally.

4   A beautiful woman, we say in English. But a handsome man. "Handsome" is the masculine equivalent of—and refusal of—a compliment which has accumulated certain demeaning overtones, by being reserved for women only. That one can call a man "beautiful" in French and in Italian suggests that Catholic countries—unlike those countries shaped by the Protestant version of Christianity—still retain some ves-

tiges of the pagan admiration for beauty. But the difference, if one exists, is of degree only. In every modern country that is Christian or post-Christian, women *are* the beautiful sex—to the detriment of the notion of beauty as well as of women.

5   To be called beautiful is thought to name something essential to women's character and concerns. (In contrast to men—whose essence is to be strong, or effective, or competent.) It does not take someone in the throes of advanced feminist awareness to perceive that the way women are taught to be involved with beauty encourages narcissism, reinforces dependence and immaturity. Everybody (women and men) knows that. For it is "everybody," a whole society, that has identified being feminine with caring about how one *looks*. (In contrast to being masculine—which is identified with caring about what one *is* and *does* and only secondarily, if at all, about how one looks.) Given these stereotypes, it is no wonder that beauty enjoys, at best, a rather mixed reputation.

6   It is not, of course, the desire to be beautiful that is wrong but the obligation to be—or to try. What is accepted by most women as a flattering idealization of their sex is a way of making women feel inferior to what they actually are—or normally grow to be. For the ideal of beauty is administered as a form of self-oppression. Women are taught to see their bodies in *parts,* and to evaluate each part separately. Breasts, feet, hips, waistline, neck, eyes, nose, complexion, hair, and so on— each in turn is submitted to an anxious, fretful, often despairing scrutiny. Even if some pass muster, some will always be found wanting. Nothing less than perfection will do.

7   In men, good looks is a whole, something taken in at a glance. It does not need to be confirmed by giving measurements of different regions of the body, nobody encourages a man to dissect his appearance, feature by feature. As for perfection, that is considered trivial—almost unmanly. Indeed, in the ideally good-looking man a small imperfection or blemish is considered positively desirable. According to one movie critic (a woman) who is a declared Robert Redford fan, it is having that cluster of skin-colored moles on one cheek that saves Redford from being merely a "pretty face." Think of the depreciation of women—as well as of beauty—that is implied in that judgment.

8   "The privileges of beauty are immense," said Cocteau. To be sure, beauty is a form of power. And deservedly so. What is lamentable

is that it is the only form of power that most women are encouraged to seek. This power is always conceived in relation to men; it is not the power to do but the power to attract. It is a power that negates itself. For this power is not one that can be chosen freely—at least, not by women—or renounced without social censure.

9   To preen, for a woman, can never be just a pleasure. It is also a duty. It is her work. If a woman does real work—and even if she has clambered up to a leading position in politics, law, medicine, business, or whatever—she is always under pressure to confess that she still works at being attractive. But in so far as she is keeping up as one of the Fair Sex, she brings under suspicion her very capacity to be objective, professional, authoritative, thoughtful. Damned if they do—women are. And damned if they don't.

10   One could hardly ask for more important evidence of the dangers of considering persons as split between what is "inside" and what is "outside" than that interminable half-comic half-tragic tale, the oppression of women. How easy it is to start off by defining women as caretakers of their surfaces, and then to disparage them (or find them adorable) for being "superficial." It is a crude trap, and it has worked for too long. But to get out of the trap requires that women get some critical distance from that excellence and privilege which is beauty, enough distance to see how much beauty itself has been abridged in order to prop up the mythology of the "feminine." There should be a way of saving beauty *from* women—and *for* them.

Roughing It in the Bush: My Plans for Moose Hunting in the Canadian Wilderness

Stephen Leacock

1   The season is now opening when all those who have a manly streak in them like to get out into the bush and 'rough it' for a week or two of hunting or fishing. For myself, I never feel that the autumn has been well spent unless I can get out after the moose. And, when I go, I like to go right into the bush and 'rough it'—get clear away from civilization, out in the open, and take fatigue and hardship just as it comes.

2   So this year I am making all my plans to get away for a couple of weeks of moose-hunting along with my brother George and my friend Tom Gass. We generally go together because we are all of us men who like the rough stuff, and are tough enough to stand the hardship of living in the open. The place we go to is right in the heart of the primitive Canadian forest, among big timber, broken with lakes as still as glass, just the very ground for moose.

3   We have a kind of lodge up there. It's just a rough place that we put up, the three of us, the year before last—built out of tamarack logs faced with a broad axe. The flies, while we were building it, were something awful. Two of the men that we sent in there to build it were so badly bitten that we had to bring them out a hundred miles to a hospital. None of us saw the place while we were building it—we were all busy at the time—but the teamsters who took in our stuff said it was the worst season for the black flies that they ever remembered.

4   Still we hung to it, in spite of the flies, and stuck at it till we got it built. It is, as I say, only a plain place, but good enough to rough it in. We have one big room with a stone fireplace, and bedrooms round the sides, with a wide veranda, properly screened, all along the front. The veranda has a row of upright tamaracks for its posts, and doesn't

look altogether bad. In the back part we have quarters where our man sleeps. We had an ice-house knocked up while they were building, and water laid on in pipes from a stream. So that, on the whole, the place has a kind of rough comfort about it—good enough, anyway, for fellows hunting moose all day.

5   The place, nowadays, is not hard to get at. The Government has just built a colonization highway, quite all right for motors, that happens to go within a hundred yards of our lodge.

6   We can get the railway for a hundred miles, and then the highway for forty, and the last hundred yards we can walk. But this season we are going to cut out the railway and go the whole way from the city in George's car, with our kit with us.

7   George has one of those great big cars with a roof and thick glass sides. Personally, none of the three of us would have preferred to ride in a luxurious darned thing like that. Tom says that, as far as he is concerned, he'd much sooner go into the bush over a rough trail in a buckboard; and, for my own part, a team of oxen would be more the kind of thing I'd wish.

8   However, the car is there, so we might as well use the thing, especially as the provincial Government has built the fool highway right into the wilderness. By taking the big car also we can not only carry all the hunting outfit that we need, but we can also, if we like, shove in a couple of small trunks with a few clothes. This may be necessary, as it seems that somebody has gone and slapped a great big frame hotel right there in the wilderness, not half a mile from the place we go to. The hotel we find a regular nuisance. It gave us the advantage of electric light for our lodge (a thing none of us cares about), but it means more fuss about clothes. Clothes, of course, don't really matter when a fellow is roughing it in the bush, but Tom says that we might find it necessary to go over to the hotel in the evenings to borrow coal-oil or a side of bacon or any rough stuff that we need; and they do such a lot of dressing up at these fool hotels now, that if we do go over for bacon or anything in the evening we might just as well slip on our evening clothes, as we could chuck them off the minute we get back. George thinks it might not be a bad idea—just as a way of saving all our energy for getting after the moose—to dine each evening at the hotel itself. He knew some men who did that last year, and they told him that the time saved for

moose-hunting in that way is extraordinary. George's idea is that we could come in each night with our moose—such-and-such a number as the case might be—either bringing them with us or burying them where they die, change our things, slide over to the hotel and get dinner, and then beat it back into the bush by moonlight and fetch in the moose. It seems they have a regular two-dollar table d'hôte dinner at the hotel— just rough stuff of course, but after all, as we all admit, we don't propose to go out into the wilds to pamper ourselves with high feeding; a plain hotel meal in a home-like style at two dollars a plate is better than cooking up a lot of rich stuff over a camp-fire.

9   If we *do* dine at the hotel we could take our choice each evening between going back into the bush by moonlight to fetch in the dead moose from the different caches where we had hidden them, or sticking round the hotel itself for a while. It seems that there is dancing there. Nowadays such a lot of women and girls get the open-air craze for the life in the bush that these big wilderness hotels are crowded with them. There is something about living in the open that attracts modern women, and they like to get right away from everybody and everything; and, of course, hotels of this type in the open are nowadays always well closed in with screens so that there are no flies or anything of that sort.

10   So it seems that there is dancing at the hotel every evening, nothing on a large scale or pretentious, just an ordinary hardwood floor—they may wax it a little for all I know—and some sort of plain, rough Italian orchestra that they fetch up from the city. Not that any of us care for dancing. It's a thing that, personally, we wouldn't bother with. But it happens that there are a couple of young girls that Tom knows that are going to be staying at the hotel, and, of course, naturally he wants to give them a good time. They are only eighteen and twenty (sisters), and that's really younger than we care for, but with young girls like that—practically kids—any man wants to give them a good time. So Tom says, and I think quite rightly, that as the kids are going to be there we may as well put in an appearance at the hotel and see that they are having a good time. Their mother is going to be with them too, and of course we want to give her a good time as well; in fact, I think I will lend her my moose rifle and let her go out and shoot moose. One thing we are all agreed upon in the arrangement of our hunting trip is in not taking along anything to drink. Drinking spoils a trip of

that sort. We all remember how in the old days we'd go out into a camp in the bush (I mean before there used to be any highway or any hotel), and carry in rye whisky in demi-johns (two dollars a gallon it was), and sit around the camp-fire drinking it in the evenings.

11   But there's nothing in it. We all agree that, the law being what it is, it is better to stick to it. It makes a fellow feel better. So we shall carry nothing in. I don't say that one might not have a flask of something in one's pocket in the car; but only as a precaution against accident or cold. And when we get to our lodge we all feel that we are a darned sight better without it. If we *should* need anything—though it isn't likely—there are still three cases of old Scotch whisky kicking around the lodge somewhere: I think they are kicking around in a little cement cellar with a locked door that we had made so as to use it for butter or anything of that sort. Anyway, there are three, possibly four, or maybe five, cases of Scotch there, and, if we should for any reason want it, there it is. But we are hardly likely to touch it—unless we hit a cold snap, or a wet spell; then we might; or if we strike hot, dry weather. Tom says he thinks there are a couple of cases of champagne still in the cellar—some stuff that one of us must have shot in there just before Prohibition came in. But we'll hardly use it. When a man is out moose-hunting from dawn to dusk he hasn't much use for champagne—not till he gets home, anyway. The only thing that Tom says the champagne might come in useful for would be if we cared to ask the two kids over to some sort of dinner; it would be just a rough kind of camp dinner (we could hardly ask their mother to it), but we think we could manage it. The man we keep there used to be a butler in England, or something of the sort, and he could manage some kind of rough meal where the champagne might fit in.

12   There's only one trouble about our plans for our fall camp that bothers us just a little. The moose are getting damn scarce about that place. There used, so they say, to be any quantity of them. There's an old settler up there that our man buys all our cream from, who says that he remembers when the moose were so thick that they would come up and drink whisky out of his dipper. But somehow they seem to have quit the place. Last year we sent our man out again and again looking for them, and he never saw any. Three years ago a boy that works at the hotel said he saw a moose in the cow pasture back of the hotel, and there were the tracks of a moose seen last year at the place not ten miles

from the hotel where it had come to drink. But, apart from these two exceptions, the moose-hunting has been poor.

13   Still, what does it matter? What we want is the *life,* the rough life, just as I have described it. If any moose comes to our lodge, we'll shoot him, or tell the butler to. But if not—well, we've got along without for ten years. I don't suppose we shall worry.

The Discovery and Assumption of Old Age

Simone de Beauvoir

1   Die early or grow old: there is no other alternative. And yet, as Goethe said, "Age takes hold of us by surprise." For himself each man is the sole, unique subject, and we are often astonished when the common fate becomes our own—when we are struck by sickness, a shattered relationship, or bereavement. I remember my own stupefaction when I was seriously ill for the first time in my life and I said to myself, "This woman they are carrying on a stretcher is me." Nevertheless, we accept fortuitous accidents readily enough, making them part of our history, because they affect us as unique beings: but old age is the general fate, and when it seizes upon our own personal life we are dumbfounded. "Why, what has happened?" writes Aragon. "It is life that has happened; and I am old." The fact that the passage of universal time should have brought about a private, personal metamorphosis is something that takes us completely aback. When I was only forty I still could not believe it when I stood there in front of the looking-glass and said to myself, "I am forty." Children and adolescents are of some particular age. The mass of prohibitions and duties to which they are subjected and the behaviour of others towards them do not allow them to forget it. When we are grown up we hardly think about our age any more: we feel that the notion does not apply to us; for it is one which assumes that we look back towards the past and draw a line under the total, whereas in fact we are reaching out towards the future, gliding on imperceptibly from day to day, from year to year. Old age is particularly difficult to assume because we have always regarded it as something alien, a foreign species: "Can I have become a different being while I still remain myself?"

2   "False dilemma," people have said to me. "So long as you feel young, you are young." This shows a complete misunderstanding of the complex truth of old age: for the outsider it is a dialectic relationship

between my being as he defines it objectively and the awareness of myself that I acquire by means of him. Within me it is the Other—that is to say the person I am for the outsider—who is old: and that Other is myself. In most cases, for the rest of the world our being is as many-sided as the rest of the world itself. Any observation made about us may be challenged on the basis of some differing opinion. But in this particular instance no challenge is permissible: the words "a sixty-year-old" interpret the same fact for everybody. They correspond to biological phenomena that may be detected by examination. Yet our private, inward experience does not tell us the number of our years; no fresh perception comes into being to show us the decline of age. This is one of the characteristics that distinguish growing old from disease. Illness warns us of its presence and the organism defends itself, sometimes in a way that is more harmful than the initial stimulus: the existence of the disease is more evident to the subject who undergoes it than to those around him, who often do not appreciate its importance. Old age is more apparent to others than to the subject himself: it is a new state of biological equilibrium, and if the aging individual adapts himself to it smoothly he does not notice the change. Habit and compensatory attitudes mean that psychomotor shortcomings can be alleviated for a long while.

3   Even if the body does send us signals, they are ambiguous. There is a temptation to confuse some curable disease with irreversible old age. Trotsky lived only for working and fighting, and he dreaded growing old: he was filled with anxiety when he remembered Turgenev's remark, one that Lenin often quoted—"Do you know the worst of all vices? It is being over fifty-five." And in 1933, when he was exactly fifty-five himself, he wrote a letter to his wife, complaining of tiredness, lack of sleep, a failing memory; it seemed to him that his strength was going, and it worried him. "Can this be age that has come for good, or is it no more than a temporary, though sudden, decline that I shall recover from? We shall see." Sadly he called the past to mind: "I have a painful longing for your old photograph, the picture that shows us both when we were so young." He did get better and he took up all his activities again.

4   The reverse applies: the discomforts caused by age may sometimes be scarcely noticed or mentioned. They are taken for superficial and curable disorders. One must already be fully aware of one's age before

it can be detected in one's body. And even then, the body does not always help us to a full inward realization of our condition. We know that this rheumatism, for example, or that arthritis, are caused by old age; yet we fail to see that they represent a new status. We remain what we were, with the rheumatism as something additional. . . .

5   All in all, there is truth in the idea of Galen, who placed old age half-way between illness and health. What is so disconcerting about old age is that normally it is an abnormal condition. As Canghilem says, "It is normal, that is to say it is in accordance with the biological laws of aging, that the progressive diminution of the margins of safety should bring about a lowering of the threshold of resistance to attack from the environment. What is normal for an old man would be reckoned deficient in the same person in his middle years." When elderly people say that they are ill—even when they are not—they are emphasizing this anomaly: they are adopting the point of view of a man who is still young, and who would be worried by being rather deaf and dim-sighted, by feeling poorly from time to time and by tiring easily. When they say that they are satisfied with their health and when they will not look after themselves, then they are settling down into old age—they realize what is the matter. Their attitude depends upon how they choose to regard age in general. They know that elderly people are looked upon as an inferior species. So many of them take any allusion to their age as an insult: they want to regard themselves as young come what may, and they would rather think of themselves as unwell than old. Others find it convenient to speak of themselves as elderly, even before the time has really come—age provides alibis; it allows them to lower their standards; and it is less tiring to let oneself go than to fight.

What Is Poverty?

Jo Goodwin Parker

1   You ask me what is poverty? Listen to me. Here I am, dirty, smelly, and with no "proper" underwear on and with the stench of my rotting teeth near you. I will tell you. Listen to me. Listen without pity. I cannot use your pity. Listen with understanding. Put yourself in my dirty, worn out, ill-fitting shoes, and hear me.

2   Poverty is getting up every morning from a dirt- and illness-stained mattress. The sheets have long since been used for diapers. Poverty is living in a smell that never leaves. This is a smell of urine, sour milk, and spoiling food sometimes joined with the strong smell of long-cooked onions. Onions are cheap. If you have smelled this smell, you did not know how it came. It is the smell of the outdoor privy. It is the smell of young children who cannot walk the long dark way in the night. It is the smell of the mattresses where years of "accidents" have happened. It is the smell of the milk which has gone sour because the refrigerator long has not worked, and it costs money to get it fixed. It is the smell of rotting garbage. I could bury it, but where is the shovel? Shovels cost money.

3   Poverty is being tired. I have always been tired. They told me at the hospital when the last baby came that I had chronic anemia caused from poor diet, a bad case of worms, and that I needed a corrective operation. I listened politely—the poor are always polite. The poor always listen. They don't say that there is no money for iron pills, or better food, or worm medicine. The idea of an operation is frightening and costs so much that, if I had dared, I would have laughed. Who takes care of my children? Recovery from an operation takes a long time. I have three children. When I left them with "Granny" the last time I had a job, I came home to find the baby covered with fly specks, and a diaper that had not been changed since I left. When the dried diaper came off, bits of my baby's flesh came with it. My other child was playing with a sharp bit of broken glass, and my oldest was playing

alone at the edge of a lake. I made twenty-two dollars a week, and a good nursery school costs twenty dollars a week for three children. I quit my job.

4   Poverty is dirt. You can say in your clean clothes coming from your clean house, "Anybody can be clean." Let me explain about house-keeping with no money. For breakfast I give my children grits with no oleo or cornbread without eggs and oleo. This does not use up many dishes. What dishes there are, I wash in cold water and with no soap. Even the cheapest soap has to be saved for the baby's diapers. Look at my hands, so cracked and red. Once I saved for two months to buy a jar of Vaseline for my hands and the baby's diaper rash. When I had saved enough, I went to buy it and the price had gone up two cents. The baby and I suffered on. I have to decide every day if I can bear to put my cracked sore hands into the cold water and strong soap. But you ask, why not hot water? Fuel costs money. If you have a wood fire it costs money. If you burn electricity, it costs money. Hot water is a luxury. I do not have luxuries. I know you will be surprised when I tell you how young I am. I look so much older. My back has been bent over the wash tubs every day for so long, I cannot remember when I ever did anything else. Every night I wash every stitch my school age child has on and just hope her clothes will be dry by morning.

5   Poverty is staying up all night on cold nights to watch the fire knowing one spark on the newspaper covering the walls means your sleeping child dies in flames. In summer poverty is watching gnats and flies devour your baby's tears when he cries. The screens are torn and you pay so little rent you know they will never be fixed. Poverty means insects in your food, in your nose, in your eyes, and crawling over you when you sleep. Poverty is hoping it never rains because diapers won't dry when it rains and soon you are using newspapers. Poverty is seeing your children forever with runny noses. Paper handkerchiefs cost money and all your rags you need for other things. Even more costly are antihistamines. Poverty is cooking without food and cleaning without soap.

6   Poverty is asking for help. Have you ever had to ask for help, knowing your children will suffer unless you get it? Think about asking for a loan from a relative, if this is the only way you can imagine asking for help. I will tell you how it feels. You find out where the office is

that you are supposed to visit. You circle that block four or five times. Thinking of your children, you go in. Everyone is very busy. Finally, someone comes out and you tell her that you need help. That never is the person you need to see. You go see another person, and after spilling the whole shame of your poverty all over the desk between you, you find that this isn't the right office after all—you must repeat the whole process, and it never is any easier at the next place.

7   You have asked for help, and after all it has a cost. You are again told to wait. You are told why, but you don't really hear because of the red cloud of shame and the rising cloud of despair.

8   Poverty is remembering. It is remembering quitting school in junior high because "nice" children had been so cruel about my clothes and my smell. The attendance officer came. My mother told him I was pregnant. I wasn't, but she thought that I could get a job and help out. I had jobs off and on, but never long enough to learn anything. Mostly I remember being married. I was so young then. I am still young. For a time, we had all the things you have. There was a little house in another town, with hot water and everything. Then my husband lost his job. There was unemployment insurance for a while and what few jobs I could get. Soon, all our nice things were repossessed and we moved back here. I was pregnant then. This house didn't look so bad when we first moved in. Every week it gets worse. Nothing is ever fixed. We now had no money. There were a few odd jobs for my husband, but everything went for food then, as it does now. I don't know how we lived through three years and three babies, but we did. I'll tell you something, after the last baby I destroyed my marriage. It had been a good one, but could you keep on bringing children in this dirt? Did you ever think how much it costs for any kind of birth control? I knew my husband was leaving the day he left, but there were no good-bys between us. I hope he has been able to climb out of this mess somewhere. He never could hope with us to drag him down.

9   That's when I asked for help. When I got it, you know how much it was? It was, and is, seventy-eight dollars a month for the four of us; that is all I ever can get. Now you know why there is no soap, no needles and thread, no hot water, no aspirin, no worm medicine, no hand cream, no shampoo. None of these things forever and ever and ever. So that you can see clearly, I pay twenty dollars a month rent,

and most of the rest goes for food. For grits and cornmeal, and rice and milk and beans. I try my best to use only the minimum electricity. If I use more, there is that much less for food.

10   Poverty is looking into a black future. Your children won't play with my boys. They will turn to other boys who steal to get what they want. I can already see them behind the bars of their prison instead of behind the bars of my poverty. Or they will turn to the freedom of alcohol or drugs, and find themselves enslaved. And my daughter? At best, there is for her a life like mine.

11   But you say to me, there are schools. Yes, there are schools. My children have no extra books, no magazines, no extra pencils, or crayons, or paper and most important of all, they do not have health. They have worms, they have infections, they have pink-eye all summer. They do not sleep well on the floor, or with me in my one bed. They do not suffer from hunger, my seventy-eight dollars keeps us alive, but they do suffer from malnutrition. Oh yes, I do remember what I was taught about health in school. It doesn't do much good. In some places there is a surplus commodities program. Not here. The country said it cost too much. There is a school lunch program. But I have two children who will already be damaged by the time they get to school.

12   But, you say to me, there are health clinics. Yes, there are health clinics and they are in the towns. I live out here eight miles from town. I can walk that far (even if it is sixteen miles both ways), but can my little children? My neighbor will take me when he goes; but he expects to get paid, *one way or another*. I bet you know my neighbor. He is that large man who spends his time at the gas station, the barbershop, and the corner store complaining about the government spending money on the immoral mothers of illegitimate children.

13   Poverty is an acid that drips on pride until all pride is worn away. Poverty is a chisel that chips on honor until honor is worn away. Some of you say that you would do *something* in my situation, and maybe you would, for the first week or the first month, but for year after year after year?

14   Even the poor can dream. A dream of a time when there is money. Money for the right kinds of food, for worm medicine, for iron pills, for toothbrushes, for hand cream, for a hammer and nails and a bit of screening, for a shovel, for a bit of paint, for some sheeting, for needles and thread. Money to pay *in money* for a trip to town. And, oh, money

for hot water and money for soap. A dream of when asking for help does not eat away the last bit of pride. When the office you visit is as nice as the offices of other governmental agencies, when there are enough workers to help you quickly, when workers do not quit in defeat and despair. When you have to tell your story to only one person, and that person can send you for other help and you don't have to prove your poverty over and over and over again.

15   I have come out of my despair to tell you this. Remember I did not come from another place or another time. Others like me are all around you. Look at us with an angry heart, anger that will help you help me. Anger that will let you tell of me. The poor are always silent. Can you be silent too?

Pornoviolence

Tom Wolfe

1   *"Keeps His Mom-in-law in Chains,* meet *Kills Son and Feeds Corpse to Pigs."*

2   "Pleased to meet you."

3   *"Teenager Twists Off Corpse's Head . . . to Get Gold Teeth,* meet *Strangles Girl Friend, Then Chops Her to Pieces."*

4   "How you doing?"

5   *"Nurse's Aide Sees Fingers Chopped Off in Meat Grinder,* meet *I Left My Babies in the Deep Freeze."*

6   "It's a pleasure."

7   It's a pleasure! No doubt about that! In all these years of journalism I have covered more conventions than I care to remember. Podiatrists, theosophists, Professional Budget Finance dentists, oyster farmers, mathematicians, truckers, dry cleaners, stamp collectors, Esperantists, nudists, and newspaper editors—I have seen them all, together, in vast assemblies, sloughing through the wall-to-wall of a thousand hotel lobbies (the nudists excepted) in their shimmering gray-metal suits and pajama-stripe shirts with white Plasti-Coat name cards on their chests, and I have sat through their speeches and seminars (the nudists included) and attentively endured ear baths such as you wouldn't believe. And yet none has ever been quite like the convention of the stringers for *The National Enquirer.*

8   *The Enquirer* is a weekly newspaper that is probably known by sight to millions more than know it by name. No one who ever came face-to-face with *The Enquirer* on a newsstand in its wildest days is likely to have forgotten the sight: a tabloid with great inky shocks of type all over the front page saying something on the order of *Gouges Out Wife's Eyes to Make Her Ugly, Dad Hurls Hot Grease in Daughter's Face, Wife Commits Suicide after 2 Years of Poisoning Fails to Kill Husband . . .*

9   The stories themselves were supplied largely by stringers, i.e.,

correspondents, from all over the country, the world, for that matter, mostly copy editors and reporters on local newspapers. Every so often they would come upon a story, usually via the police beat, that was so grotesque the local sheet would discard it or run it in a highly glossed form rather than offend or perplex its readers. The stringers would preserve them for *The Enquirer,* which always rewarded them well and respectfully.

10   One year *The Enquirer* convened and feted them at a hotel in Manhattan. This convention was a success in every way. The only awkward moment was at the outset when the stringers all pulled in. None of them knew each other. Their hosts got around the problem by introducing them by the stories they had supplied. The introductions went like this:

11   "Harry, I want you to meet Frank here. Frank did that story, you remember that story, *Midget Murderer Throws Girl Off Cliff after She Refuses to Dance with Him.*"

12   "Pleased to meet you. That was some story."

13   "And Harry did the one about *I Spent Three Days Trapped at Bottom of Forty-Foot-Deep Mine Shaft and Was Saved by a Swarm of Flies.*"

14   "Likewise, I'm sure."

15   And *Midget Murderer Throws Girl Off Cliff* shakes hands with *I Spent Three Days Trapped at Bottom of Forty-Foot-Deep Mine Shaft,* and *Buries Her Baby Alive* shakes hands with *Boy, Twelve, Strangles Two-Year-Old Girl,* and *Kills Son and Feeds Corpse to Pigs* shakes hands with *He Strangles Old Woman and Smears Corpse with Syrup, Ketchup, and Oatmeal* . . . and . . .

16   . . . There was a great deal of esprit about the whole thing. These men were, in fact, the avant-garde of a new genre that since then has become institutionalized throughout the nation without anyone knowing its proper name. I speak of the new pornography, the pornography of violence.

17   Pornography comes from the Greek word *"porne,"* meaning harlot, and pornography is literally the depiction of the acts of harlots. In the new pornography, the theme is not sex. The new pornography depicts practitioners acting out another, murkier drive: people staving teeth in, ripping guts open, blowing brains out, and getting even with all those bastards . . .

18   The success of *The Enquirer* prompted many imitators to enter the field, *Midnight, The Star Chronicle, The National Insider, Inside News, The National Close-up, The National Tattler, The National Examiner*. A truly competitive free press evolved, and soon a reader could go to the newspaper of his choice for *Kill the Retarded! (Won't You Join My Movement?)* and *Unfaithful Wife? Burn Her Bed!, Harem Master's Mistress Chops Him with Machete, Babe Bites Off Boy's Tongue,* and *Cuts Buddy's Face to Pieces for Stealing His Business and Fiancée.*

19   And yet the last time I surveyed the Violence press, I noticed a curious thing. These pioneering journals seem to have pulled back. They seem to be regressing to what is by now the Redi-Mix staple of literate Americans, mere sex. *Ecstasy and Me (by Hedy Lamarr),* says *The National Enquirer. I Run a Sex Art Gallery,* says *The National Insider.* What has happened, I think, is something that has happened to avant-gardes in many fields, from William Morris and the Craftsmen to the Bauhaus group. Namely, their discoveries have been preempted by the Establishment and so thoroughly dissolved into the mainstream they no longer look original.

20   Robert Harrison, the former publisher of *Confidential,* and later publisher of the aforementioned *Inside News,* was perhaps the first person to see it coming. I was interviewing Harrison early in January 1964 for a story in *Esquire* about six weeks after the assassination of President Kennedy, and we were in a cab in the West Fifties in Manhattan, at a stoplight, by a newsstand, and Harrison suddenly pointed at the newsstand and said, "Look at that. They're doing the same thing *The Enquirer* does."

21   There on the stand was a row of slick-paper, magazine-size publications, known in the trade as one-shots, with titles like *Four Days That Shook the World, Death of a President, An American Tragedy,* or just *John Fitzgerald Kennedy (1921–1963).* "You want to know why people buy those things?" said Harrison. "People buy those things to see a man get his head blown off."

22   And, of course, he was right. Only now the publishers were in many cases the pillars of the American press. Invariably, these "special coverages" of the assassination bore introductions piously commemorating the fallen President, exhorting the American people to strength and unity in a time of crisis, urging greater vigilance and safeguards

for the new President, and even raising the nice metaphysical question of collective guilt in "an age of violence."

23   In the years since then, of course, there has been an incessant replay, with every recoverable clinical detail, of those less than five seconds in which a man got his head blown off. And throughout this deluge of words, pictures, and film frames, I have been intrigued with one thing: The point of view, the vantage point, is almost never that of the victim, riding in the Presidential Lincoln Continental. What you get is . . . the view from Oswald's rifle. You can step right up here and look point-blank right through the very hairline cross in Lee Harvey Oswald's Optics Ordnance in weaponry four-power Japanese telescope sight and watch, frame by frame by frame by frame, as that man there's head comes apart. Just a little History there before your very eyes.

24   The television networks have schooled us in the view from Oswald's rifle and made it seem a normal pastime. The TV viewpoint is nearly always that of the man who is going to strike. The last time I watched *Gunsmoke*, which was not known as a very violent Western in TV terms, the action went like this: The Wellington agents and the stagecoach driver pull guns on the badlands gang leader's daughter and Kitty, the heart-of-gold saloonkeeper, and kidnap them. Then the badlands gang shoots two Wellington agents. Then they tie up five more and talk about shooting them. Then they desist because they might not be able to get a hotel room in the next town if the word got around. Then one badlands gang gunslinger attempts to rape Kitty while the gang leader's younger daughter looks on. Then Kitty resists, so he slugs her one in the jaw. Then the gang leader slugs him. Then the gang leader slugs Kitty. Then Kitty throws hot stew in a gang member's face and hits him over the back of the head with a revolver. Then he knocks her down with a rock. Then the gang sticks up a bank. Here comes the marshal, Matt Dillon. He shoots a gang member and breaks it up. Then the gang leader shoots the guy who was guarding his daughter and the woman. Then the marshal shoots the gang leader. The final exploding bullet signals The End.

25   It is not the accumulated slayings and bone crushings that make this pornoviolence, however. What makes it pornoviolence is that in almost every case the camera angle, therefore the viewer, is with the gun, the fist, the rock. The pornography of violence has no point of view in the old sense that novels do. You do not live the action through

the hero's eyes. You live with the aggressor, whoever he may be. One moment you are the hero. The next you are the villain. No matter whose side you may be on consciously, you are in fact with the muscle, and it is you who disintegrate all comers, villains, lawmen, women, anybody. On the rare occasions in which the gun is emptied into the camera—i.e., into your face—the effect is so startling that the pornography of violence all but loses its fantasy charm. There are not nearly so many masochists as sadists among those little devils whispering into one's ears.

26   In fact, sex—"sadomasochism"—is only a part of the pornography of violence. Violence is much more wrapped up, simply, with status. Violence is the simple, ultimate solution for problems of status competition, just as gambling is the simple, ultimate solution for economic competition. The old pornography was the fantasy of easy sexual delights in a world where sex was kept unavailable. The new pornography is the fantasy of easy triumph in a world where status competition has become so complicated and frustrating.

27   Already the old pornography is losing its kick because of overexposure. In the late thirties, Nathanael West published his last and best-regarded novel, *The Day of the Locust,* and it was a terrible flop commercially, and his publisher said if he ever published another book about Hollywood it would "have to be *My Thirty-nine Ways of Making Love by Hedy Lamarr."* He thought he was saying something that was funny because it was beyond the realm of possibility. Less than thirty years later, however, Hedy Lamarr's *Ecstasy and Me* was published. Whether she mentions thirty-nine ways, I'm not sure, but she gets off to a flying start: "The men in my life have ranged from a classic case history of impotence, to a whip-brandishing sadist who enjoyed sex only after he tied my arms behind me with the sash of his robe. There was another man who took his pleasure with a girl in my own bed, while he thought I was asleep in it."

28   Yet she was too late. The book very nearly sank without a trace. The sin itself is wearing out. Pornography cannot exist without certified taboo to violate. And today Lust, like the rest of the Seven Deadly Sins—Pride, Sloth, Envy, Greed, Anger, and Gluttony—is becoming a rather minor vice. The Seven Deadly Sins, after all, are only sins against the self. Theologically, the idea of Lust—well, the idea is that if you seduce some poor girl from Akron, it is not a sin because you

are ruining her, but because you are wasting your time and your energies and damaging your own spirit. This goes back to the old work ethic, when the idea was to keep every able-bodied man's shoulder to the wheel. In an age of riches for all, the ethic becomes more nearly: Let him do anything he pleases, as long as he doesn't get in my way. And if he does get in my way, or even if he doesn't . . . well . . . we have *new* fantasies for that. *Put hair on the walls.*

29   "Hair on the walls" is the invisible subtitle of Truman Capote's book *In Cold Blood.* The book is neither a who-done-it nor a will-they-be-caught, since the answers to both questions are known from the outset. It does ask why-did-they-do-it, but the answer is soon as clear as it is going to be. Instead, the book's suspense is based largely on a totally new idea in detective stories: the promise of gory details, and the withholding of them until the end. Early in the game one of the two murderers, Dick, starts promising to put "plenty of hair on them-those walls" with a shotgun. So read on, gentle readers, and on and on; you are led up to the moment before the crime on page 60—yet the specifics, what happened, the gory details, are kept out of sight, in grisly dangle, until page 244.

30   But Dick and Perry, Capote's killers, are only a couple of Low Rent bums. With James Bond the new pornography reached a dead center, the bureaucratic middle class. The appeal of Bond has been explained as the appeal of the lone man who can solve enormously complicated, even world problems through his own bravery and initiative. But Bond is not a lone man at all, of course. He is not the Lone Ranger. He is much easier to identify than that. He is a salaried functionary in a bureaucracy. He is a sport, but a believable one; not a millionaire, but a bureaucrat on an expense account. He is not even a high-level bureaucrat. He is an operative. This point is carefully and repeatedly made by having his superiors dress him down for violations of standard operating procedure. Bond, like the Lone Ranger, solves problems with guns and fists. When it is over, however, the Lone Ranger leaves a silver bullet. Bond, like the rest of us, fills out a report in triplicate.

31   Marshall McLuhan says we are in a period in which it will become harder and harder to stimulate lust through words and pictures—i.e., the old pornography. In the latest round of pornographic movies the producers have found it necessary to introduce violence, bondage, tor-

ture, and aggressive physical destruction to an extraordinary degree. The same sort of bloody escalation may very well happen in the pure pornography of violence. Even such able craftsmen as Truman Capote, Ian Fleming, NBC, and CBS may not suffice. Fortunately, there are historical models to rescue us from this frustration. In the latter days of the Roman Empire, the Emperor Commodus became jealous of the celebrity of the great gladiators. He took to the arena himself, with his sword, and began dispatching suitably screened cripples and hobbled fighters. Audience participation became so popular that soon various *illuminati* of the Commodus set, various boys and girls of the year, were out there, suited up, gaily cutting a sequence of dwarfs and feebles down to short ribs. Ah, swinging generations, what new delights await?

Slang Origins

Woody Allen

1   How many of you have ever wondered where certain slang expressions come from? Like "She's the cat's pajamas," or to "take it on the lam." Neither have I. And yet for those who are interested in this sort of thing I have provided a brief guide to a few of the more interesting origins.

2   Unfortunately, time did not permit consulting any of the established works on the subject, and I was forced to either obtain the information from friends or fill in certain gaps by using my own common sense.

3   Take, for instance, the expression "to eat humble pie." During the reign of Louis the Fat, the culinary arts flourished in France to a degree unequaled anywhere. So obese was the French monarch that he had to be lowered onto the throne with a winch and packed into the seat itself with a large spatula. A typical dinner (according to DeRochet) consisted of a thin crêpe appetizer, some parsley, an ox, and custard. Food became the court obsession, and no other subject could be discussed under penalty of death. Members of a decadent aristocracy consumed incredible meals and even dressed as foods. DeRochet tells us that M. Monsant showed up at the coronation as a wiener, and Étienne Tisserant received papal dispensation to wed his favorite codfish. Desserts grew more and more elaborate and pies grew larger until the minister of justice suffocated trying to eat a seven-foot "Jumbo Pie." *Jumbo* pie soon became *jumble* pie and "to eat a jumble pie" referred to any kind of humiliating act. When the Spanish seamen heard the word *jumble,* they pronounced it "humble," although many preferred to say nothing and simply grin.

4   Now, while "humble pie" goes back to the French, "take it on the lam" is English in origin. Years ago, in England, "lamming" was a game played with dice and a large tube of ointment. Each player in turn threw dice and then skipped around the room until he hemorrhaged.

If a person threw a seven or under he would say the word "quintz" and proceed to twirl in a frenzy. If he threw over seven, he was forced to give every player a portion of his feathers and was given a good "lamming." Three "lammings" and a player was "kwirled" or declared a moral bankrupt. Gradually any game with feathers was called "lamming" and feathers became "lams." To "take it on the lam" meant to put on feathers and later, to escape, although the transition is unclear.

5   Incidentally, if two players disagreed on rules, we might say they "got into a beef." This term goes back to the Renaissance when a man would court a woman by stroking the side of her head with a slab of meat. If she pulled away, it meant she was spoken for. If, however, she assisted by clamping the meat to her face and pushing it all over her head, it meant she would marry him. The meat was kept by the bride's parents and worn as a hat on special occasions. If, however, the husband took another lover, the wife could dissolve the marriage by running with the meat to the town square and yelling, "With thine own beef, I do reject thee. Aroo! Aroo!" If a couple "took to the beef" or "had a beef" it meant they were quarreling.

6   Another marital custom gives us that eloquent and colorful expression of disdain, "to look down one's nose." In Persia it was considered a mark of great beauty for a woman to have a long nose. In fact, the longer the nose, the more desirable the female, up to a certain point. Then it became funny. When a man proposed to a beautiful woman he awaited her decision on bended knee as she "looked down her nose at him." If her nostrils twitched, he was accepted, but if she sharpened her nose with pumice and began pecking him on the neck and shoulders, it meant she loved another.

7   Now, we all know when someone is very dressed up, we say he looks "spiffy." The term owes its origin to Sir Oswald Spiffy, perhaps the most renowned fop of Victorian England. Heir to treacle millions, Spiffy squandered his money on clothes. It was said that at one time he owned enough handkerchiefs for all the men, women and children in Asia to blow their noses for seven years without stopping. Spiffy's sartorial innovations were legend, and he was the first man ever to wear gloves on his head. Because of extra-sensitive skin, Spiffy's underwear had to be made of the finest Nova Scotia salmon, carefully sliced by one particular tailor. His libertine attitudes involved him in several notorious scandals, and he eventually sued the government over the right to wear earmuffs while fondling a dwarf. In the end Spiffy died

a broken man in Chichester, his total wardrobe reduced to kneepads and a sombrero.

8   Looking "spiffy," then, is quite a compliment, and one who does is liable to be dressed "to beat the band," a turn-of-the-century expression that originated from the custom of attacking with clubs any symphony orchestra whose conductor smiled during Berlioz. "Beating the band" soon became a popular evening out, and people dressed up in their finest clothes, carrying with them sticks and rocks. The practice was finally abandoned, during a performance of the *Symphonie fantastique* in New York when the entire string section suddenly stopped playing and exchanged gunfire with the first ten rows. Police ended the melee but not before a relative of J. P. Morgan's was wounded in the soft palate. After that, for a while at least, nobody dressed "to beat the band."

9   If you think some of the above derivations questionable, you might throw up your hands and say, "Fiddlesticks." This marvelous expression originated in Austria many years ago. Whenever a man in the banking profession announced his marriage to a circus pinhead, it was the custom for friends to present him with a bellows and a three-year supply of wax fruit. Legend has it that when Leo Rothschild made known his betrothal, a box of cello bows was delivered to him by mistake. When it was opened and found not to contain the traditional gift, he exclaimed, "What are these? Where are my bellows and fruit? Eh? All I rate is fiddlesticks!" The term "fiddlesticks" became a joke overnight in the taverns amongst the lower classes, who hated Leo Rothschild for never removing the comb from his hair after combing it. Eventually "fiddlesticks" meant any foolishness.

10   Well, I hope you've enjoyed some of these slang origins and that they stimulate you to investigate some of your own. And in case you were wondering about the term used to open this study, "the cat's pajamas," it goes back to an old burlesque routine of Chase and Rowe's, the two nutsy German professors. Dressed in oversized tails, Bill Rowe stole some poor victim's pajamas. Dave Chase, who got great mileage out of his "hard of hearing" specialty, would ask him:

11   *Chase:* Ach, Herr Professor. Vot is dot bulge under your pocket?

12   *Rowe:* Dot? Dot's de chap's pajamas.

13   *Chase:* The cat's pajamas? Ut mein Gott?

14   Audiences were convulsed by this sort of repartee and only a premature death of the team by strangulation kept them from stardom.

Chapter Five

Division and Classification

Thinking as a Hobby

William Golding

1   While I was still a boy, I came to the conclusion that there were three grades of thinking; and since I was later to claim thinking as my hobby, I came to an even stranger conclusion—namely, that I myself could not think at all.

2   I must have been an unsatisfactory child for grownups to deal with. I remember how incomprehensible they appeared to me at first, but not, of course, how I appeared to them. It was the headmaster of my grammar school who first brought the subject of thinking before me—though neither in the way, nor with the result he intended. He had some statuettes in his study. They stood on a high cupboard behind his desk. One was a lady wearing nothing but a bath towel. She seemed frozen in an eternal panic lest the bath towel slip down any farther; and since she had no arms, she was in an unfortunate position to pull the towel up again. Next to her, crouched the statuette of a leopard, ready to spring down at the top drawer of a filing cabinet labeled A-AH. My innocence interpreted this as the victim's last, despairing cry. Beyond the leopard was a naked, muscular gentleman, who sat, looking down, with his chin on his fist and his elbow on his knee. He seemed utterly miserable.

3   Some time later, I learned about these statuettes. The headmaster had placed them where they would face delinquent children, because they symbolized to him the whole of life. The naked lady was the Venus of Milo. She was Love. She was not worried about the towel. She was just busy being beautiful. The leopard was Nature, and he was being natural. The naked, muscular gentleman was not miserable. He was Rodin's Thinker, an image of pure thought. It is easy to buy small plaster models of what you think life is like.

4   I had better explain that I was a frequent visitor to the headmaster's study, because of the latest thing I had done or left undone. As we now say, I was not integrated. I was, if anything, disintegrated; and I was

puzzled. Grownups never made sense. Whenever I found myself in a penal position before the headmaster's desk, with the statuettes glimmering whitely above him, I would sink my head, clasp my hands behind my back and writhe one shoe over the other.

5   The headmaster would look opaquely at me through flashing spectacles.

6   "What are we going to do with you?"

7   Well, what *were* they going to do with me? I would writhe my shoe some more and stare down at the worn rug.

8   "Look up, boy! Can't you look up?"

9   Then I would look up at the cupboard, where the naked lady was frozen in her panic and the muscular gentleman contemplated the hindquarters of the leopard in endless gloom. I had nothing to say to the headmaster. His spectacles caught the light so that you could see nothing human behind them. There was no possibility of communication.

10   "Don't you ever think at all?"

11   No, I didn't think, wasn't thinking, couldn't think—I was simply waiting in anguish for the interview to stop.

12   "Then you'd better learn—hadn't you?"

13   On one occasion the headmaster leaped to his feet, reached up and plonked Rodin's masterpiece on the desk before me.

14   "That's what a man looks like when he's really thinking."

15   I surveyed the gentleman without interest or comprehension.

16   "Go back to your class."

17   Clearly there was something missing in me. Nature had endowed the rest of the human race with a sixth sense and left me out. This must be so, I mused, on my way back to the class, since whether I had broken a window, or failed to remember Boyle's Law, or been late for school, my teachers produced me one, adult answer: "Why can't you think?"

18   As I saw the case, I had broken the window because I had tried to hit Jack Arney with a cricket ball and missed him; I could not remember Boyle's Law because I had never bothered to learn it; and I was late for school because I preferred looking over the bridge into the river. In fact, I was wicked. Were my teachers, perhaps, so good that they could not understand the depths of my depravity? Were they clear, untormented people who could direct their every action by this mysterious business of thinking? The whole thing was incomprehensible.

In my earlier years, I found even the statuette of the Thinker confusing. I did not believe any of my teachers were naked, ever. Like someone born deaf, but bitterly determined to find out about sound, I watched my teachers to find out about thought.

19   There was Mr. Houghton. He was always telling me to think. With a modest satisfaction, he would tell me that he had thought a bit himself. Then why did he spend so much time drinking? Or was there more sense in drinking than there appeared to be? But if not, and if drinking were in fact ruinous to health—and Mr. Houghton was ruined, there was no doubt about that—why was he always talking about the clean life and the virtues of fresh air? He would spread his arms wide with the action of a man who habitually spent his time striding along mountain ridges.

20   "Open air does me good, boys—I know it!"

21   Sometimes, exalted by his own oratory, he would leap from his desk and hustle us outside into a hideous wind.

22   "Now, boys! Deep breaths! Feel it right down inside you—huge draughts of God's good air!"

23   He would stand before us, rejoicing in his perfect health, an open-air man. He would put his hands on his waist and take a tremendous breath. You could hear the wind, trapped in the cavern of his chest and struggling with all the unnatural impediments. His body would reel with shock and his ruined face go white at the unaccustomed visitation. He would stagger back to his desk and collapse there, useless for the rest of the morning.

24   Mr. Houghton was given to high-minded monologues about the good life, sexless and full of duty. Yet in the middle of one of these monologues, if a girl passed the window, tapping along on her neat little feet, he would interrupt his discourse, his neck would turn of itself and he would watch her out of sight. In this instance, he seemed to me ruled not by thought but by an invisible and irresistible spring in his nape.

25   His neck was an object of great interest to me. Normally it bulged a bit over his collar. But Mr. Houghton had fought in the First World War alongside both Americans and French, and had come—by who knows what illogic?—to a settled detestation of both countries. If either happened to be prominent in current affairs, no argument could make Mr. Houghton think well of it. He would bang the desk, his neck would

bulge still further and go red. "You can say what you like," he would cry, "but I've thought about this—and I know what I think!"

26   Mr. Houghton thought with his neck.

27   There was Miss Parsons. She assured us that her dearest wish was our welfare, but I knew even then, with the mysterious clairvoyance of childhood, that what she wanted most was the husband she never got. There was Mr. Hands—and so on.

28   I have dealt at length with my teachers because this was my introduction to the nature of what is commonly called thought. Through them I discovered that thought is often full of unconscious prejudice, ignorance and hypocrisy. It will lecture on disinterested purity while its neck is being remorselessly twisted toward a skirt. Technically, it is about as proficient as most businessmen's golf, as honest as most politicians' intentions, or—to come near my own preoccupation—as coherent as most books that get written. It is what I came to call grade-three thinking, though more properly, it is feeling, rather than thought.

29   True, often there is a kind of innocence in prejudices, but in those days I viewed grade-three thinking with an intolerant contempt and an incautious mockery. I delighted to confront a pious lady who hated the Germans with the proposition that we should love our enemies. She taught me a great truth in dealing with grade-three thinkers; because of her, I no longer dismiss lightly a mental process which for nine-tenths of the population is the nearest they will ever get to thought. They have immense solidarity. We had better respect them, for we are outnumbered and surrounded. A crowd of grade-three thinkers, all shouting the same thing, all warming their hands at the fire of their own prejudices, will not thank you for pointing out the contradictions in their beliefs. Man is a gregarious animal, and enjoys agreement as cows will graze all the same way on the side of a hill.

30   Grade-two thinking is the detection of contradictions. I reached grade two when I trapped the poor, pious lady. Grade-two thinkers do not stampede easily, though often they fall into the other fault and lag behind. Grade-two thinking is a withdrawal, with eyes and ears open. It became my hobby and brought satisfaction and loneliness in either hand. For grade-two thinking destroys without having the power to create. It set me watching the crowds cheering His Majesty and King and asking myself what all the fuss was about, without giving me anything positive to put in the place of that heady patriotism. But there

were compensations. To hear people justify their habit of hunting foxes and tearing them to pieces by claiming that the foxes liked it. To hear our Prime Minister talk about the great benefit we conferred on India by jailing people like Pandit Nehru and Gandhi. To hear American politicians talk about peace in one sentence and refuse to join the League of Nations in the next. Yes, there were moments of delight.

31   But I was growing toward adolescence and had to admit that Mr. Houghton was not the only one with an irresistible spring in his neck. I, too, felt the compulsive hand of nature and began to find that pointing out contradiction could be costly as well as fun. There was Ruth, for example, a serious and attractive girl. I was an atheist at the time. Grade-two thinking is a menace to religion and knocks down sects like skittles. I put myself in a position to be converted by her with an hypocrisy worthy of grade three. She was a Methodist—or at least, her parents were, and Ruth had to follow suit. But, alas, instead of relying on the Holy Spirit to convert me, Ruth was foolish enough to open her pretty mouth in argument. She claimed that the Bible (King James Version) was literally inspired. I countered by saying that the Catholics believed in the literal inspiration of Saint Jerome's *Vulgate,* and the two books were different. Argument flagged.

32   At last she remarked that there were an awful lot of Methodists, and they couldn't be wrong, could they—not all those millions? That was too easy, said I restively (for the nearer you were to Ruth, the nicer she was to be near to) since there were more Roman Catholics than Methodists anyway; and they couldn't be wrong, could they—not all those hundreds of millions? An awful flicker of doubt appeared in her eyes. I slid my arm around her waist and murmured breathlessly that if we were counting heads, the Buddhists were the boys for my money. But Ruth had *really* wanted to do me good, because I was so nice. She fled. The combination of my arm and those countless Buddhists was too much for her.

33   That night her father visited my father and left, red-cheeked and indignant. I was given the third degree to find out what had happened. It was lucky we were both of us only fourteen. I lost Ruth and gained an undeserved reputation as a potential libertine.

34   So grade-two thinking could be dangerous. It was in this knowledge, at the age of fifteen, that I remember making a comment from the heights of grade two, on the limitations of grade three. One evening

I found myself alone in the school hall, preparing it for a party. The door of the headmaster's study was open. I went in. The headmaster had ceased to thump Rodin's Thinker down on the desk as an example to the young. Perhaps he had not found any more candidates, but the statuettes were still there, glimmering and gathering dust on top of the cupboard. I stood on a chair and rearranged them. I stood Venus in her bath towel on the filing cabinet, so that now the top drawer caught its breath in a gasp of sexy excitement. "A-ah!" The portentous Thinker I placed on the edge of the cupboard so that he looked down at the bath towel and waited for it to slip.

35   Grade-two thinking, though it filled life with fun and excitement, did not make for content. To find out the deficiencies of our elders bolsters the young ego but does not make for personal security. I found that grade two was not only the power to point out contradictions. It took the swimmer some distance from the shore and left him there, out of his depth. I decided that Pontius Pilate was a typical grade-two thinker. "What is truth?" he said, a very common grade-two thought, but one that is used always as the end of an argument instead of the beginning. There is still a higher grade of thought which says, "What is truth?" and sets out to find it.

36   But these grade-one thinkers were few and far between. They did not visit my grammar school in the flesh though they were there in books. I aspired to them, partly because I was ambitious and partly because I now saw my hobby as an unsatisfactory thing if it went no further. If you set out to climb a mountain, however high you climb, you have failed if you cannot reach the top.

37   I *did* meet an undeniably grade-one thinker in my first year at Oxford. I was looking over a small bridge in Magdalen Deer Park, and a tiny mustached and hatted figure came and stood by my side. He was a German who had just fled from the Nazis to Oxford as a temporary refuge. His name was Einstein.

38   But Professor Einstein knew no English at that time and I knew only two words of German. I beamed at him, trying wordlessly to convey by my bearing all the affection and respect that the English felt for him. It is possible—and I have to make the admission—that I felt here were two grade-one thinkers standing side by side; yet I doubt if my face conveyed more than a formless awe. I would have given my Greek and Latin and French and a good slice of my English for enough

German to communicate. But we were divided; he was as inscrutable as my headmaster. For perhaps five minutes we stood together on the bridge, undeniable grade-one thinker and breathless aspirant. With true greatness, Professor Einstein realized that my contact was better than none. He pointed to a trout wavering in midstream.

39   He spoke: *"Fisch."*

40   My brain reeled. Here I was, mingling with the great, and yet helpless as the veriest grade-three thinker. Desperately I sought for some sign by which I might convey that I, too, revered pure reason. I nodded vehemently. In a brilliant flash I used up half of my German vocabulary.

41   *"Fisch. Ja Ja."*

42   For perhaps another five minutes we stood side by side. Then Professor Einstein, his whole figure still conveying good will and amiability, drifted away out of sight.

43   I, too, would be a grade-one thinker. I was irreverent at the best of times. Political and religious systems, social customs, loyalties and traditions, they all came tumbling down like so many rotten apples off a tree. This was a fine hobby and a sensible substitute for cricket, since you could play it all the year round. I came up in the end with what must always remain the justification for grade-one thinking, its sign, seal and charter. I devised a coherent system for living. It was a moral system, which was wholly logical. Of course, as I readily admitted, conversion of the world to my way of thinking might be difficult, since my system did away with a number of trifles, such as big business, centralized government, armies, marriage. . . .

44   It was Ruth all over again. I had some very good friends who stood by me, and still do. But my acquaintances vanished, taking the girls with them. Young women seemed oddly contented with the world as it was. They valued the meaningless ceremony with a ring. Young men, while willing to concede the chaining sordidness of marriage, were hesitant about abandoning the organizations which they hoped would give them a career. A young man on the first rung of the Royal Navy, while perfectly agreeable to doing away with big business and marriage, got as rednecked as Mr. Houghton when I proposed a world without any battleships in it.

45   Had the game gone too far? Was it a game any longer? In those prewar days, I stood to lose a great deal, for the sake of a hobby.

46   Now you are expecting me to describe how I saw the folly of my ways and came back to the warm nest, where prejudices are so often called loyalties, where pointless actions are hallowed into custom by repetition, where we are content to say we think when all we do is feel.

47   But you would be wrong. I dropped my hobby and turned professional.

48   If I were to go back to the headmaster's study and find the dusty statuettes still there, I would arrange them differently. I would dust Venus and put her aside, for I have come to love her and know her for the fair thing she is. But I would put the Thinker, sunk in his desperate thought, where there were shadows before him—and at his back, I would put the leopard, crouched and ready to spring.

Territorial Behavior

Desmond Morris

1   A territory is a defended space. In the broadest sense, there are three kinds of human territory: tribal, family and personal.

2   It is rare for people to be driven to physical fighting in defense of these "owned" spaces, but fight they will, if pushed to the limit. The invading army encroaching on national territory, the gang moving into a rival district, the trespasser climbing into an orchard, the burglar breaking into a house, the bully pushing to the front of a queue, the driver trying to steal a parking space, all of these intruders are liable to be met with resistance varying from the vigorous to the savagely violent. Even if the law is on the side of the intruder, the urge to protect a territory may be so strong that otherwise peaceful citizens abandon all their usual controls and inhibitions. Attempts to evict families from their homes, no matter how socially valid the reasons, can lead to siege conditions reminiscent of the defence of a medieval fortress.

3   The fact that these upheavals are so rare is a measure of the success of Territorial Signals as a system of dispute prevention. It is sometimes cynically stated that "all property is theft," but in reality it is the opposite. Property, as owned space which is *displayed* as owned space, is a special kind of sharing system which reduces fighting much more than it causes it. Man is a co-operative species, but he is also competitive, and his struggle for dominance has to be structured in some way if chaos is to be avoided. The establishment of territorial rights is one such structure. It limits dominance geographically. I am dominant in my territory and you are dominant in yours. In other words, dominance is shared out spatially, and we all have some. Even if I am weak and unintelligent and you can dominate me when we meet on neutral ground, I can still enjoy a thoroughly dominant role as soon as I retreat to my private base. Be it ever so humble, there is no place like a home territory.

4   Of course, I can still be intimidated by a particularly dominant individual who enters my home base, but his encroachment will be

169

dangerous for him and he will think twice about it, because he will know that here my urge to resist will be dramatically magnified and my usual subservience banished. Insulted at the heart of my own territory, I may easily explode into battle—either symbolic or real—with a result that may be damaging to both of us.

5   In order for this to work, each territory has to be plainly advertised as such. Just as a dog cocks its leg to deposit its personal scent on the trees in its locality, so the human animal cocks its leg symbolically all over his home base. But because we are predominantly visual animals we employ mostly visual signals, and it is worth asking how we do this at the three levels: tribal, family and personal.

6   First: the Tribal Territory. We evolved as tribal animals, living in comparatively small groups, probably of less than a hundred, and we existed like that for millions of years. It is our basic social unit, a group in which everyone knows everyone else. Essentially, the tribal territory consisted of a home base surrounded by extended hunting grounds. Any neighbouring tribe intruding on our social space would be repelled and driven away. As these early tribes swelled into agricultural super-tribes, and eventually into industrial nations, their territorial defence systems became increasingly elaborate. The tiny, ancient home base of the hunting tribe became the great capital city, the primitive war-paint became the flags, emblems, uniforms and regalia of the specialized military, and the war-chants became national anthems, marching songs and bugle calls. Territorial boundary-lines hardened into fixed borders, often conspicuously patrolled and punctuated with defensive structures—forts and lookout posts, checkpoints and great walls, and, today, customs barriers.

7   Today each nation flies its own flag, a symbolic embodiment of its territorial status. But patriotism is not enough. The ancient tribal hunter lurking inside each citizen finds himself unsatisfied by membership of such a vast conglomeration of individuals, most of whom are totally unknown to him personally. He does his best to feel that he shares a common territorial defence with them all, but the scale of the operation has become inhuman. It is hard to feel a sense of belonging with a tribe of fifty million or more. His answer is to form sub-groups, nearer to his ancient pattern, smaller and more personally known to him—the local club, the teenage gang, the union, the specialist society, the sports association, the political party, the college fraternity, the

social clique, the protest group, and the rest. Rare indeed is the individual who does not belong to at least one of these splinter groups, and take from it a sense of tribal allegiance and brotherhood. Typical of all these groups is the development of Territorial Signals—badges, costumes, headquarters, banners, slogans, and all the other displays of group identity. This is where the action is, in terms of tribal territorialism, and only when a major war breaks out does the emphasis shift upwards to the higher group level of the nation.

8   Each of these modern pseudo-tribes sets up its own special kind of home base. In extreme cases non-members are totally excluded, in others they are allowed in as visitors with limited rights and under a control system of special rules. In many ways they are like miniature nations, with their own flags and emblems and their own border guards. The exclusive club has its own "customs barrier": the doorman who checks your "passport" (your membership card) and prevents strangers from passing in unchallenged. There is a government: the club committee; and often special displays of the tribal elders: the photographs or portraits of previous officials on the walls. At the heart of the specialized territories there is a powerful feeling of security and importance, a sense of shared defence against the outside world. Much of the club chatter, both serious and joking, directs itself against the rottenness of everything outside the club boundaries—in that "other world" beyond the protected portals.

9   In social organizations which embody a strong class system, such as military units and large business concerns, there are many territorial rules, often unspoken, which interfere with the official hierarchy. High-status individuals, such as officers or managers, could in theory enter any of the regions occupied by the lower levels in the peck order, but they limit this power in a striking way. An officer seldom enters a sergeant's mess or a barrack room unless it is for a formal inspection. He respects those regions as alien territories even though he has the power to go there by virtue of his dominant role. And in businesses, part of the appeal of unions, over and above their obvious functions, is that with their officials, headquarters and meetings they add a sense of territorial power for the staff workers. It is almost as if each military organization and business concern consists of two warring tribes: the officers versus the other ranks, and the management versus the workers. Each has its special home base within the system, and the territorial

defence pattern thrusts itself into what, on the surface, is a pure social hierarchy. Negotiations between managements and unions are tribal battles fought out over the neutral ground of a boardroom table, and are as much concerned with territorial display as they are with resolving problems of wages and conditions. Indeed, if one side gives in too quickly and accepts the other's demands, the victors feel strangely cheated and deeply suspicious that it may be a trick. What they are missing is the protracted sequence of ritual and counter-ritual that keeps alive their group territorial identity.

10   Likewise, many of the hostile displays of sports fans and teenage gangs are primarily concerned with displaying their group image to rival fan-clubs and gangs. Except in rare cases, they do not attack one another's headquarters, drive out the occupants, and reduce them to a submissive, subordinate condition. It is enough to have scuffles on the borderlands between the two rival territories. This is particularly clear at football matches, where the fan-club headquarters becomes temporarily shifted from the club-house to a section of the stands, and where minor fighting breaks out at the unofficial boundary line between the massed groups of rival supporters. Newspaper reports play up the few accidents and injuries which do occur on such occasions, but when these are studied in relation to the total numbers of displaying fans involved it is clear that the serious incidents represent only a tiny fraction of the overall group behaviour. For every actual punch or kick there are a thousand war-cries, war-dances, chants and gestures.

11   Second: the Family Territory. Essentially, the family is a breeding unit and the family territory is a breeding ground. At the centre of this space, there is the nest—the bedroom—where, tucked up in bed, we feel at our most territorially secure. In a typical house the bedroom is upstairs, where a safe nest should be. This puts it farther away from the entrance hall, the area where contact is made, intermittently, with the outside world. The less private reception rooms, where intruders are allowed access, are the next line of defence. Beyond them, outside the walls of the building, there is often a symbolic remnant of the ancient feeding grounds—a garden. Its symbolism often extends to the plants and animals it contains, which cease to be nutritional and become merely decorative—flowers and pets. But like a true territorial space it has a conspicuously displayed boundary-line, the garden fence, wall,

or railings. Often no more than a token barrier, this is the outer territorial demarcation, separating the private world of the family from the public world beyond. To cross it puts any visitor or intruder at an immediate disadvantage. As he crosses the threshold, his dominance wanes, slightly but unmistakably. He is entering an area where he senses that he must ask permission to do simple things that he would consider a right elsewhere. Without lifting a finger, the territorial owners exert their dominance. This is done by all the hundreds of small ownership "markers" they have deposited on their family territory: the ornaments, the "possessed" objects positioned in the rooms and on the walls; the furnishings, the furniture, the colours, the patterns, all owner-chosen and all making this *particular* home base unique to them.

12   It is one of the tragedies of modern architecture that there has been a standardization of these vital territorial living-units. One of the most important aspects of a home is that it should be similar to other homes only in a general way, and that in detail it should have many differences, making it a *particular* home. Unfortunately, it is cheaper to build a row of houses, or a block of flats, so that all the family living-units are identical, but the territorial urge rebels against this trend and house-owners struggle as best they can to make their mark on their mass-produced properties. They do this with garden-design, with front-door colours, with curtain patterns, with wallpaper and all the other decorative elements that together create a unique and different family environment. Only when they have completed this nest-building do they feel truly "at home" and secure.

13   When they venture forth as a family unit they repeat the process in a minor way. On a day-trip to the seaside, they load the car with personal belongings and it becomes their temporary, portable territory. Arriving at the beach they stake out a small territorial claim, marking it with rugs, towels, baskets and other belongings to which they can return from their seaboard wanderings. Even if they all leave it at once to bathe, it retains a characteristic territorial quality and other family groups arriving will recognize this by setting up their own "home" bases at a respectful distance. Only when the whole beach has filled up with these marked spaces will newcomers start to position themselves in such a way that the inter-base distance becomes reduced. Forced to pitch between several existing beach territories they will feel a momentary

sensation of intrusion, and the established "owners" will feel a similar sensation of invasion, even though they are not being directly inconvenienced.

14   The same territorial scene is being played out in parks and fields and on riverbanks, wherever family groups gather in their clustered units. But if rivalry for spaces creates mild feelings of hostility, it is true to say that, without the territorial system of sharing and space-limited dominance, there would be chaotic disorder.

15   Third: the Personal Space. If a man enters a waiting-room and sits at one end of a long row of empty chairs, it is possible to predict where the next man to enter will seat himself. He will not sit next to the first man, nor will he sit at the far end, right away from him. He will choose a position about halfway between these two points. The next man to enter will take the largest gap left, and sit roughly in the middle of that, and so on, until eventually the latest newcomer will be forced to select a seat that places him right next to one of the already seated men. Similar patterns can be observed in cinemas, public urinals, aeroplanes, trains and buses. This is a reflection of the fact that we all carry with us, everywhere we go, a portable territory called a Personal Space. If people move inside this space, we feel threatened. If they keep too far outside it, we feel rejected. The result is a subtle series of spatial adjustments, usually operating quite unconsciously and producing ideal compromises as far as this is possible. If a situation becomes too crowded, then we adjust our reactions accordingly and allow our personal space to shrink. Jammed into an elevator, a rush-hour compartment, or a packed room, we give up altogether and allow body-to-body contact, but when we relinquish our Personal Space in this way, we adopt certain special techniques. In essence, what we do is to convert these other bodies into "nonpersons." We studiously ignore them, and they us. We try not to face them if we can possibly avoid it. We wipe all expressiveness from our faces, letting them go blank. We may look up at the ceiling or down at the floor, and we reduce body movements to a minimum. Packed together like sardines in a tin, we stand dumbly still, sending out as few social signals as possible.

16   Even if the crowding is less severe, we still tend to cut down our social interactions in the presence of large numbers. Careful observations of children in play groups revealed that if they are high density groupings there is less social interaction between the individual children,

even though there is theoretically more opportunity for such contacts. At the same time, the high-density groups show a higher frequency of aggressive and destructive behaviour patterns in their play. Personal Space—"elbow room"—is a vital commodity for the human animal, and one that cannot be ignored without risking serious trouble.

17   Of course, we all enjoy the excitement of being in a crowd, and this reaction cannot be ignored. But there are crowds and crowds. It is pleasant enough to be in a "spectator crowd," but not so appealing to find yourself in the middle of a rush-hour crush. The difference between the two is that the spectator crowd is all facing in the same direction and concentrating on a distant point of interest. Attending a theatre, there are twinges of rising hostility towards the stranger who sits down immediately in front of you or the one who squeezes into the seat next to you. The shared armrest can become a polite, but distinct, territorial boundary-dispute region. However, as soon as the show begins, these invasions of Personal Space are forgotten and the attention is focused beyond the small space where the crowding is taking place. Now, each member of the audience feels himself spatially related, not to his cramped neighbours, but to the actor on the stage, and this distance is, if anything, too great. In the rush-hour crowd, by contrast, each member of the pushing throng is competing with his neighbours all the time. There is no escape to a spatial relation with a distant actor, only the pushing, shoving bodies all around.

18   Those of us who have to spend a great deal of time in crowded conditions become gradually better able to adjust, but no one can ever become completely immune to invasions of Personal Space. This is because they remain forever associated with either powerful hostile or equally powerful loving feelings. All through our childhood we will have been held to be loved and held to be hurt, and anyone who invades our Personal Space when we are adults is, in effect, threatening to extend his behaviour into one of these two highly charged areas of human interaction. Even if his motives are clearly neither hostile nor sexual, we still find it hard to suppress our reactions to his close approach. Unfortunately, different countries have different ideas about exactly how close is close. It is easy enough to test your own "space reaction": when you are talking to someone in the street or in any open space, reach out with your arm and see where the nearest point on his body comes. If you hail from western Europe, you will find that he is

at roughly fingertip distance from you. In other words, as you reach out, your fingertips will just about make contact with his shoulder. If you come from eastern Europe you will find you are standing at "wrist distance." If you come from the Mediterranean region you will find that you are much closer to your companion, at little more than "elbow distance."

19   Trouble begins when a member of one of these cultures meets and talks to one from another. Say a British diplomat meets an Italian or an Arab diplomat at an embassy function. They start talking in a friendly way, but soon the fingertips man begins to feel uneasy. Without knowing quite why, he starts to back away gently from his companion. The companion edges forward again. Each tries in this way to set up a Personal Space relationship that suits his own background. But it is impossible to do. Every time the Mediterranean diplomat advances to a distance that feels comfortable for him, the British diplomat feels threatened. Every time the Briton moves back, the other feels rejected. Attempts to adjust this situation often lead to a talking pair shifting slowly across a room, and many an embassy reception is dotted with western-European fingertip-distance men pinned against the walls by eager elbow-distance men. Until such differences are fully understood, and allowances made, these minor differences in "body territories" will continue to act as an alienation factor which may interfere in a subtle way with diplomatic harmony and other forms of international trans-action.

20   If there are distance problems when engaged in conversation, then there are clearly going to be even bigger difficulties where people must work privately in a shared space. Close proximity of others, pressing against the invisible boundaries of our personal body-territory, makes it difficult to concentrate on non-social matters. Flatmates, students sharing a study, sailors in the cramped quarters of a ship, and office staff in crowded workplaces, all have to face this problem. They solve it by "cocooning." They use a variety of devices to shut themselves off from the others present. The best possible cocoon, of course, is a small private room—a den, a private office, a study or a studio—which phys-ically obscures the presence of other nearby territory-owners. This is the ideal situation for non-social work, but the space-sharers cannot enjoy this luxury. Their cocooning must be symbolic. They may, in certain cases, be able to erect small physical barriers, such as screens

and partitions, which give substance to their invisible Personal Space boundaries, but when this cannot be done, other means must be sought. One of these is the "favoured object." Each space-sharer develops a preference, repeatedly expressed until it becomes a fixed pattern, for a particular chair, or table, or alcove. Others come to respect this, and friction is reduced. This system is often formally arranged (this is my desk, that is yours), but even where it is not, favoured places soon develop. Professor Smith has a favourite chair in the library. It is not formally his, but he always uses it and others avoid it. Seats around a mess-room table, or a boardroom table, become almost personal property for specific individuals. Even in the home, father has his favourite chair for reading the newspaper or watching television. Another device is the blinkers-posture. Just as a horse that over-reacts to other horses and the distractions of the noisy race-course is given a pair of blinkers to shield its eyes, so people studying privately in a public place put on pseudo-blinkers in the form of shielding hands. Resting their elbows on the table, they sit with their hands screening their eyes from the scene on either side.

21   A third method of reinforcing the body-territory is to use personal markers. Books, papers and other personal belongings are scattered around the favoured site to render it more privately owned in the eyes of companions. Spreading out one's belongings is a well-known trick in public-transport situations, where a traveller tries to give the impression that seats next to him are taken. In many contexts carefully arranged personal markers can act as an effective territorial display, even in the absence of the territory owner. Experiments in a library revealed that placing a pile of magazines on the table in one seating position successfully reserved that place for an average of 77 minutes. If a sports-jacket was added, draped over the chair, then the "reservation effect" lasted for over two hours.

22   In these ways, we strengthen the defences of our Personal Spaces, keeping out intruders with the minimum of open hostility. As with all territorial behaviour, the object is to defend space with signals rather than with fists and at all three levels—the tribal, the family and the personal—it is a remarkably efficient system of space-sharing. It does not always seem so, because newspapers and newscasts inevitably magnify the exceptions and dwell on those cases where the signals have failed and wars have broken out, gangs have fought, neighbouring

families have feuded, or colleagues have clashed, but for every territorial signal that has failed, there are millions of others that have not. They do not rate a mention in the news, but they nevertheless constitute a dominant feature of human society—the society of a remarkably territorial animal.

The Sound of Music: Enough Already

Fran Lebowitz

1   First off, I want to say that as far as I am concerned, in instances where I have not personally and deliberately sought it out, the only difference between music and Muzak is the spelling. Pablo Casals practicing across the hall with the door open—being trapped in an elevator, the ceiling of which is broadcasting "Parsley, Sage, Rosemary, and Thyme"—it's all the same to me. Harsh words? Perhaps. But then again these are not gentle times we live in. And they are being made no more gentle by this incessant melody that was once real life.

2   There was a time when music knew its place. No longer. Possibly this is not music's fault. It may be that music fell in with a bad crowd and lost its sense of common decency. I am willing to consider this. I am willing even to try and help. I would like to do my bit to set music straight in order that it might shape up and leave the mainstream of society. The first thing that music must understand is that there are two kinds of music—good music and bad music. Good music is music that I want to hear. Bad music is music that I don't want to hear.

3   So that music might more clearly see the error of its ways I offer the following. If you are music and you recognize yourself on this list, you are bad music.

1. MUSIC IN OTHER PEOPLE'S CLOCK RADIOS

4   There are times when I find myself spending the night in the home of another. Frequently the other is in a more reasonable line of work than I and must arise at a specific hour. Ofttimes the other, unbeknownst to me, manipulates an appliance in such a way that I am awakened by Stevie Wonder. On such occasions I announce that if I wished to be awakened by Stevie Wonder I would sleep with Stevie Wonder. I do

not, however, wish to be awakened by Stevie Wonder and that is why God invented alarm clocks. Sometimes the other realizes that I am right. Sometimes the other does not. And that is why God invented *many* others.

2. MUSIC RESIDING IN THE HOLD BUTTONS OF OTHER PEOPLE'S BUSINESS TELEPHONES

5   I do not under any circumstances enjoy hold buttons. But I am a woman of reason. I can accept reality. I can face the facts. What I cannot face is the music. Just as there are two kinds of music—good and bad—so there are two kinds of hold buttons—good and bad. Good hold buttons are hold buttons that hold one silently. Bad hold buttons are hold buttons that hold one musically. When I hold I want to hold silently. That is the way it was meant to be, for that is what God was talking about when he said, "Forever hold your peace." He would have added, "and quiet," but he thought you were smarter.

3. MUSIC IN THE STREETS

6   The past few years have seen a steady increase in the number of people playing music in the streets. The past few years have also seen a steady increase in the number of malignant diseases. Are these two facts related? One wonders. But even if they are not—and, as I have pointed out, one cannot be sure—music in the streets has definitely taken its toll. For it is at the very least disorienting. When one is walking down Fifth Avenue, one does not expect to hear a string quartet playing a Strauss waltz. What one expects to hear while walking down Fifth Avenue is traffic. When one does indeed hear a string quartet playing a Strauss waltz while one is walking down Fifth Avenue, one is apt to become confused and imagine that one is not walking down Fifth Avenue at all but rather that one has somehow wound up in Old Vienna. Should one imagine that one is in Old Vienna one is likely to become quite upset when one realizes that in Old Vienna there is no sale at Charles Jourdan. And that is why when I walk down Fifth Avenue I want to hear traffic.

4. MUSIC IN THE MOVIES

7   I'm not talking about musicals. Musicals are movies that warn you by saying, "Lots of music here. Take it or leave it." I'm talking about regular movies that extend no such courtesy but allow unsuspecting people to come to see them and then assault them with a barrage of unasked-for tunes. There are two major offenders in this category: black movies and movies set in the fifties. Both types of movies are afflicted with the same misconception. They don't know that movies are supposed to be movies. They think that movies are supposed to be records with pictures. They have failed to understand that if God had wanted records to have pictures, he would not have invented television.

5. MUSIC IN PUBLIC PLACES SUCH AS RESTAURANTS, SUPERMARKETS, HOTEL LOBBIES, AIRPORTS, ETC.

8   When I am in any of the above-mentioned places I am not there to hear music. I am there for whatever reason is appropriate to the respective place. I am no more interested in hearing "Mack the Knife" while waiting for the shuttle to Boston than someone sitting ringside at the Sands Hotel is interested in being forced to choose between sixteen varieties of cottage cheese. If God had meant for everything to happen at once, he would not have invented desk calendars.

EPILOGUE

9   Some people talk to themselves. Some people sing to themselves. Is one group better than the other? Did not God create all people equal? Yes, God created all people equal. Only to some he gave the ability to make up their own words.

Presidential Character and How To Foresee It

James David Barber

1 When a citizen votes for a Presidential candidate he makes, in effect, a prediction. He chooses from among the contenders the one he thinks (or feels, or guesses) would be the best President. He operates in a situation of immense uncertainty. If he has a long voting history, he can recall time and time again when he guessed wrong. He listens to the commentators, the politicians, and his friends, then adds it all up in some rough way to produce his prediction and his vote. Earlier in the game, his anticipations have been taken into account, either directly in the polls and primaries or indirectly in the minds of politicians who want to nominate someone he will like. But he must choose in the midst of a cloud of confusion, a rain of phony advertising, a storm of sermons, a hail of complex issues, a fog of charisma and boredom, and a thunder of accusation and defense. In the face of this chaos, a great many citizens fall back on the past, vote their old allegiances, and let it go at that. Nevertheless, the citizen's vote says that on balance he expects Mr. X would outshine Mr. Y in the Presidency. . . .

2 The burden of this book is that the crucial differences can be anticipated by an understanding of a potential President's character, his world view, and his style. This kind of prediction is not easy; well-informed observers often have guessed wrong as they watched a man step toward the White House. One thinks of Woodrow Wilson, the scholar who would bring reason to politics; of Herbert Hoover, the Great Engineer who would organize chaos into progress; of Franklin D. Roosevelt, that champion of the balanced budget; of Harry Truman, whom the office would surely overwhelm; of Dwight D. Eisenhower, militant crusader; of John F. Kennedy, who would lead beyond moralisms to achievements; of Lyndon B. Johnson, the Southern conservative; and of Richard M. Nixon, conciliator. Spotting the errors is

easy. Predicting with even approximate accuracy is going to require some sharp tools and close attention in their use. But the experiment is worth it because the question is critical and because it lends itself to correction by evidence.

3   My argument comes in layers.

4   First, a President's personality is an important shaper of his Presidential behavior on nontrivial matters.

5   Second, Presidential personality is patterned. His character, world view, and style fit together in a dynamic package understandable in psychological terms.

6   Third, a President's personality interacts with the power situation he faces and the national "climate of expectations" dominant at the time he serves. The tuning, the resonance—or lack of it—between these external factors and his personality sets in motion the dynamic of his Presidency.

7   Fourth, the best way to predict a President's character, world view, and style is to see how they were put together in the first place. That happened in his early life, culminating in his first independent political success.

8   But the core of the argument (which organizes the structure of the book) is that Presidential character—the basic stance a man takes toward his Presidential experience—comes in four varieties. The most important thing to know about a President or candidate is where he fits among these types, defined according to (a) how active he is and (b) whether or not he gives the impression he enjoys his political life.

9   Let me spell out these concepts briefly before getting down to cases. . . .

FOUR TYPES OF PRESIDENTIAL CHARACTER

10   The five concepts—character, world view, style, power situation, and climate of expectations—run through the accounts of Presidents in the chapters to follow, which cluster the Presidents since Theodore Roosevelt into four types. This is the fundamental scheme of the study. It offers a way to move past the complexities to the main contrasts and comparisons.

11   The first baseline in defining Presidential types is *activity-passivity*. How much energy does the man invest in his Presidency? Lyndon

Johnson went at his day like a human cyclone, coming to rest long after the sun went down. Calvin Coolidge often slept eleven hours a night and still needed a nap in the middle of the day. In between the Presidents array themselves on the high or low side of the activity line.

12   The second baseline is *positive-negative affect* toward one's activity—that is, how he feels about what he does. Relatively speaking, does he seem to experience his political life as happy or sad, enjoyable or discouraging, positive or negative in its main effect. The feeling I am after here is not grim satisfaction in a job well done, not some philosophical conclusion. The idea is this: is he someone who, on the surfaces we can see, gives forth the feeling that he has *fun* in political life? Franklin Roosevelt's Secretary of War, Henry L. Stimson wrote that the Roosevelts "not only understood the *use* of power, they knew the *enjoyment* of power, too. . . . Whether a man is burdened by power or enjoys power; whether he is trapped by responsibility or made free by it; whether he is moved by other people and outer forces or moves them—that is the essence of leadership."

13   The positive-negative baseline then, is a general symptom of the fit between the man and his experience, a kind of register of *felt* satisfaction.

14   Why might we expect these two simple dimensions to outline the main character types? Because they stand for two central features of anyone's orientation toward life. In nearly every study of personality, some form of the active-passive contrast is critical; the general tendency to act or be acted upon is evident in such concepts as dominance-submission, extraversion-introversion, aggression-timidity, attack-defense, fight-flight, engagement-withdrawal, approach-avoidance. In everyday life we sense quickly the general energy output of the people we deal with. Similarly we catch on fairly quickly to the affect dimension—whether the person seems to be optimistic or pessimistic, hopeful or skeptical, happy or sad. The two baselines are clear and they are also independent of one another: all of us know people who are very active but seem discouraged, others who are quite passive but seem happy, and so forth. The activity baseline refers to what one does, the affect baseline to how one feels about what he does.

15   Both are crude clues to character. They are leads into four basic character patterns long familiar in psychological research. In summary form, these are the main configurations:

16   **Active-positive:**   There is a congruence, a consistency, between much activity and the enjoyment of it, indicating relatively high self-esteem and relative success in relating to the environment. The man shows an orientation toward productiveness as a value and an ability to use his styles flexibly, adaptively, suiting the dance to the music. He sees himself as developing over time toward relatively well defined personal goals—growing toward his image of himself as he might yet be. There is an emphasis on rational mastery, on using the brain to move the feet. This may get him into trouble; he may fail to take account of the irrational in politics. Not everyone he deals with sees things his way and he may find it hard to understand why.

17   **Active-negative:**   The contradiction here is between relatively intense effort and relatively low emotional reward for that effort. The activity has a compulsive quality, as if the man were trying to make up for something or to escape from anxiety into hard work. He seems ambitious, striving upward, power-seeking. His stance toward the environment is aggressive and he has a persistent problem in managing his aggressive feelings. His self-image is vague and discontinuous. Life is a hard struggle to achieve and hold power, hampered by the condemnations of a perfectionistic conscience. Active-negative types pour energy into the political system, but it is an energy distorted from within.

18   **Passive-positive:**   This is the receptive, compliant, other-directed character whose life is a search for affection as a reward for being agreeable and cooperative rather than personally assertive. The contradiction is between low self-esteem (on grounds of being unlovable, unattractive) and a superficial optimism. A hopeful attitude helps dispel doubt and elicits encouragement from others. Passive-positive types help soften the harsh edges of politics. But their dependence and the fragility of their hopes and enjoyments make disappointment in politics likely.

19   **Passive-negative:**   The factors are consistent—but how are we to account for the man's *political* role-taking? Why is someone who does little in politics and enjoys it less there at all? The answer lies in the passive-negative's character-rooted orientation toward doing dutiful service; this compensates for low self-esteem based on a sense of use-

lessness. Passive-negative types are in politics because they think they ought to be. They may be well adapted to certain nonpolitical roles, but they lack the experience and flexibility to perform effectively as political leaders. Their tendency is to withdraw, to escape from the conflict and uncertainty of politics by emphasizing vague principles (especially prohibitions) and procedural arrangements. They become guardians of the right and proper way, above the sordid politicking of lesser men.

20   Active-positive Presidents want most to achieve results. Active-negatives aim to get and keep power. Passive-positives are after love. Passive-negatives emphasize their civic virtue. The relation of activity to enjoyment in a President thus tends to outline a cluster of characteristics, to set apart the adapted from the compulsive, compliant, and withdrawn types.

21   The first four Presidents of the United States, conveniently, ran through this gamut of character types. (Remember, we are talking about tendencies, broad directions; no individual man exactly fits a category.) George Washington—clearly the most important President in the pantheon—established the fundamental legitimacy of an American government at a time when this was a matter in considerable question. Washington's dignity, judiciousness, his aloof air of reserve and dedication to duty fit the passive-negative or withdrawing type best. Washington did not seek innovation, he sought stability. He longed to retire to Mount Vernon, but fortunately was persuaded to stay on through a second term, in which, by rising above the political conflict between Hamilton and Jefferson and inspiring confidence in his own integrity, he gave the nation time to develop the organized means for peaceful change.

22   John Adams followed, a dour New England Puritan, much given to work and worry, an impatient and irascible man—an active-negative President, a compulsive type. Adams was far more partisan than Washington; the survival of the system through his Presidency demonstrated that the nation could tolerate, for a time, domination by one of its nascent political parties. As President, an angry Adams brought the United States to the brink of war with France, and presided over the new nation's first experiment in political repression: the Alien and Sedition Acts, forbidding, among other things, unlawful combinations "with intent to oppose any measure or measures of the government of

the United States," or "any false, scandalous, and malicious writing or writings against the United States, or the President of the United States, with intent to defame . . . or to bring them or either of them, into contempt or disrepute."

23   Then came Jefferson. He too had his troubles and failures—in the design of national defense, for example. As for his Presidential character (only one element in success or failure), Jefferson was clearly active-positive. A child of the Enlightenment, he applied his reason to organizing connections with Congress aimed at strengthening the more popular forces. A man of catholic interests and delightful humor, Jefferson combined a clear and open vision of what the country could be with a profound political sense, expressed in his famous phrase, "Every difference of opinion is not a difference of principle."

24   The fourth President was James Madison, "Little Jemmy," the constitutional philosopher thrown into the White House at a time of great international turmoil. Madison comes closest to the passive-positive, or compliant, type; he suffered from irresolution, tried to compromise his way out, and gave in too readily to the "warhawks" urging combat with Britain. The nation drifted into war, and Madison wound up ineptly commanding his collection of amateur generals in the streets of Washington. General Jackson's victory at New Orleans saved the Madison administration's historical reputation; but he left the Presidency with the United States close to bankruptcy and secession.

25   These four Presidents—like all Presidents—were persons trying to cope with the roles they had won by using the equipment they had built over a lifetime. The President is not some shapeless organism in a flood of novelties, but a man with a memory in a system with a history. Like all of us, he draws on his past to shape his future. The pathetic hope that the White House will turn a Caligula into a Marcus Aurelius is as naive as the fear that ultimate power inevitably corrupts. The problem is to understand—and to state understandably—what in the personal past foreshadows the Presidential future.

Three Kinds of Symbols

Erich Fromm

1   One of the current definitions of a symbol is that it is "something that stands for something else." The definition is too general to be useful, unless we can be more specific with regard to the crucial question concerning the nature of the connection between symbol and that which it symbolizes. . . .

2   We can differentiate between three kinds of symbols: the *conventional,* the *accidental,* and the *universal* symbol.

3   The *conventional* symbol is the best known of the three, since we employ it in everyday language. If we see the word "table" or hear the sound "table," the letters *t-a-b-l-e* stand for something else. They stand for the thing "table" that we see, touch, and use. What is the connection between the *word* "table" and the *thing* "table"? Is there any inherent relationship between them? Obviously not. The *thing* table has nothing to do with the *sound* table, and the only reason the word symbolizes the thing is the convention of calling this particular thing by a name. We learn this connection as children by the repeated experience of hearing the word in reference to the thing until a lasting association is formed so that we don't have to think to find the right word.

4   There are some words, however, in which the association is not only conventional. When we say "phooey," for instance, we make with our lips a movement of dispelling the air quickly. By this quick expulsion of air we imitate and thus express our intention to expel something, to get it out of our system. In this case, as in some others, the symbol has an inherent connection with the feeling it symbolizes. But even if we assume that originally many or even all words had their origins in some such inherent connection between symbol and the symbolized, most words no longer have this meaning for us when we learn a language.

5   Words are not the only illustration for conventional symbols, although they are the most frequent and best-known ones. Pictures also can be conventional symbols. A flag, for instance, may stand for a specific country, and yet there is no intrinsic connection between the specific colors and the country for which they stand. They have been accepted as denoting that particular country, and we translate the visual impression of the flag into the concept of that country, again on conventional grounds. Some pictorial symbols are not entirely conventional; for example, the cross. The cross can be merely a conventional symbol of the Christian Church and in that respect no different from a flag. But the specific content of the cross referring to Jesus' death or, beyond that, to the interpenetration of the material and spiritual planes, puts the connection between the symbol and what it symbolizes beyond the level of mere conventional symbols.

6   The opposite to the conventional symbol is the *accidental* symbol, although they have one thing in common: there is no intrinsic relationship between the symbol and that which it symbolizes. Let us assume that someone has had a saddening experience in a certain city; when he hears the name of that city, he will easily connect the name with a mood of sadness, just as he would connect it with a mood of joy had his experience been a happy one. Quite obviously there is nothing in the nature of the city that is either sad or joyful. It is the individual experience connected with the city that makes it a symbol of a mood. The same reaction could occur in connection with a house, a street, a certain dress, certain scenery, or anything once connected with a specific mood. . . . The connection between the symbol and the experience symbolized is entirely accidental.

7   In contrast to the conventional symbol, the accidental symbol cannot be shared by anyone else except as we relate the events connected with the symbol. For this reason accidental symbols are rarely used in myths, fairy tales, or works of art written in symbolic language because they are not communicable unless the writer adds a lengthy comment to each symbol he uses. In dreams, however, accidental symbols are frequent, and Freud by his method of free association devised a method for understanding their meaning.

8   The *universal* symbol is one in which there is an intrinsic relationship between the symbol and that which it represents. Take, for

instance, the symbol of fire. We are fascinated by certain qualities of fire in a fireplace. First of all, by its aliveness. It changes continuously, it moves all the time, and yet there is constancy in it. It remains the same without being the same. It gives the impression of power, of energy, of grace and lightness. It is as if it were dancing, and had an inexhaustible source of energy. When we use fire as a symbol, we describe the *inner experience* characterized by the same elements which we notice in the sensory experience of fire—the mood of energy, lightness, movement, grace, gaiety, sometimes one, sometimes another of these elements being predominant in the feeling.

9   Similar in some ways and different in others is the symbol of water—of the ocean or of the stream. Here, too, we find the blending of change and constant movement and yet of permanence. We also feel the quality of aliveness, continuity, and energy. But there is a difference; where fire is adventurous, quick, exciting, water is quiet, slow, and steady. Fire has an element of surprise; water an element of predictability. Water symbolizes the mood of aliveness, too, but one which is "heavier," "slower," and more comforting than exciting. . . .

10   The universal symbol is the only one in which the relationship between the symbol and that which is symbolized is not coincidental but intrinsic. It is rooted in the experience of the affinity between an emotion or thought, on the one hand, and a sensory experience, on the other. It can be called universal because it is shared by all men, in contrast not only to the accidental symbol, which is by its very nature entirely personal, but also to the conventional symbol, which is restricted to a group of people sharing the same convention. The universal symbol is rooted in the properties of our body, our senses, and our mind, which are common to all men and, therefore, not restricted to individuals or to specific groups. Indeed, *the language of the universal symbol is the one common tongue developed by the human race,* a language which it forgot before it succeeded in developing a universal conventional language.

11   There is no need to speak of a racial inheritance in order to explain the universal character of symbols. Every human being sharing the essential features of bodily and mental equipment with the rest of mankind is capable of speaking and understanding the symbolic language that is based upon these common properties. Just as we do not need to

learn to cry when we are sad or to get red in the face when we are angry, and just as these reactions are not restricted to any particular race or group of people, symbolic language does not have to be learned and is not restricted to any segment of the human race. Evidence for this is to be found in the fact that symbolic language as it is employed in myths and dreams is found in all cultures, in the so-called primitive as well as such developed cultures as those of Egypt and Greece. Furthermore, the symbols used in these various cultures are strikingly similar since they all go back to the basic sensory as well as emotional experiences shared by men of all cultures. Dreams of people living in the United States, India, or China today, as well as those which are reported to us from Greece, Palestine, or Egypt 3000 years ago, are essentially the same in content and structure.

12   The foregoing statement needs qualification, however. Some symbols differ in meaning according to the difference in their realistic significance in various cultures. For instance, the function and consequently the meaning of the sun is different in northern countries and in tropical countries. In norther countries, where water is plentiful, all growth depends on sufficient sunshine. The sun is the warm, life-giving, protecting, loving power. In the Near East, where the heat of the sun is much more powerful, the sun is a dangerous and even threatening power from which man must protect himself, while water is felt to be the source of all life and the main condition for growth. We may speak of *dialects of universal symbolic language*, which are determined by those differences in natural conditions which cause certain symbols to have a different meaning in different regions of the earth.

13   Different from these "symbol dialects" is the fact that many symbols have more than one meaning in accordance with various kinds of experiences which can be connected with one and the same natural phenomenon. Let us take the symbol of fire again. If we watch fire in the fireplace, which is a source of pleasure and comfort, it is expressive of a mood of aliveness, warmth, and pleasure. But if we see a building or forest on fire, it conveys to us an experience of threat and terror, of the powerlessness of man against the elements of nature. Fire, then, can be the symbolic representation of inner aliveness and happiness as well as of fear, powerlessness, or of one's own destructive tendencies. The same holds true of the symbol of water. Water can be a most

destructive force when it is whipped up by a storm or when a swollen river floods its banks. Therefore, it can be the symbolic expression of horror and chaos as well as of comfort and peace.

14   Another illustration of the same principle is a symbol of a valley. The valley enclosed between mountains can arouse in us the feeling of security and comfort, of protection against all dangers from the outside. But the protecting mountains can also mean isolating walls which do not permit us to get out of the valley and thus the valley can become a symbol of imprisonment.

15   The particular meaning of the symbol in any given place can only be determined from the whole context in which the symbol appears, and in terms of the predominant experiences of the person using the symbol. . . .

Reflections on Horror Movies

Robert Brustein

1   Although horror movies have recently been enjoying a vogue, they have always been perennial supporting features among Grade B and C fare. The popularity of the form is no doubt partly explained by its ability to engage the spectator's feelings without making any serious demand on his mind. In addition, however, horror movies covertly embody certain underground assumptions about science which reflect popular opinions.

2   The horror movies I am mainly concerned with I have divided into three major categories: Mad Doctor, Atomic Beast and Interplanetary Monster. They do not exhaust all the types but they each contain two essential characters, the Scientist and the Monster, towards whom the attitudes of the movies are in a revealing state of change.

3   The Mad Doctor series is by far the most long lived of the three. It suffered a temporary decline in the Forties when Frankenstein, Dracula, and the Wolfman (along with their countless offspring) were first loaned out as straight men to Abbott and Costello, and then set out to graze in the parched pastures of the cheap all-night movie houses, but it has recently demonstrated its durability in a group of English remakes and a Teen-age Monster craze. These films find their roots in certain European folk myths. Dracula was inspired by an ancient Balkan superstition about vampires, the Werewolf is a Middle European folk myth recorded, among other places, in the Breton *lais* of Marie de France, and even Frankenstein, though out of Mary Shelley by the Gothic tradition, has a medieval prototype in the Golem, a monster the Jews fashioned from clay and earth to free them from oppression. The spirit of these films is still medieval, combining a vulgar religiosity with folk superstitions. Superstition now, however, has been crudely transferred from magic and alchemy to creative science, itself a form of magic to the untutored mind. The devil of the Vampire and Werewolf myths, who turned human beings into baser animals, today has become

a scientist, and the metamorphosis is given a technical name—it is a "regression" into an earlier state of evolution. The alchemist and devil-conjuring scholar, Dr. Faustus, gives way to Dr. Frankenstein, the research physician, while the magic circle, the tetragrammaton, and the full moon are replaced by test tubes, complicated electrical apparatus, and Bunsen burners.

4   Frankenstein, like Faustus, defies God by exploring areas where humans are not meant to trespass. In Mary Shelley's book (it is subtitled *A Modern Prometheus*), Frankenstein is a latter-day Faustus, a super-human creature whose aspiration embodies the expansiveness of his age. In the movies, however, Frankenstein loses his heroic quality and becomes a lunatic monomaniac, so obsessed with the value of his work that he no longer cares whether his discovery proves a boon or a curse to mankind. When the mad doctor, his eyes wild and inflamed, bends over his intricate equipment, pouring in a little of this and a little of that, the spectator is confronted with an immoral being whose mental superiority is only a measure of his madness. Like the popular image of the theoretical scientist engaged in basic research ("Basic research," says Charles Wilson, "is science's attempt to prove the grass is green"), he succeeds only in creating something badly which nature has already made well. The Frankenstein monster is a parody of man. Ghastly in appearance, clumsy in movement, criminal in behavior, imbecilic of mind, it is superior only in physical strength and resistance to destruction. The scientist has fashioned it in the face of divine disapproval (the heavens disgorge at its birth)—not to mention the disapproval of friends and frightened townspeople—and it can lead only to trouble.

5   For Dr. Frankenstein, however, the monster symbolizes the triumph of his intellect over the blind morality of his enemies and it confirms him in the ultimate soundness of his thought ("They thought I was mad, but this proves who is the superior being"). When it becomes clear that his countrymen are unimpressed by his achievement and regard him as a menace to society, the monster becomes the agent of his revenge. As it ravages the countryside and terrorizes the inhabitants, it embodies and expresses the scientist's own lust and violence. It is an extension of his own mad soul, come to life not in a weak and ineffectual body but in a body of formidable physical power. (In a movie like *Dr. Jekyll and Mr. Hyde,* the identity of monster and doctor is even clearer; Mr. Hyde, the monster, is the aggressive and libidinous element in the

benevolent Dr. Jekyll's personality.) The rampage of the monster is the rampage of mad, unrestrained science which inevitably turns on the scientist, destroying him too. As the lava bubbles over the sinking head of the monster, the crude moral of the film frees itself from the horror and is asserted. Experimental science (and by extension knowledge itself) is superfluous, dangerous, and unlawful, for in exploring the unknown, it leads man to usurp God's creative power. Each of these films is a victory for obscurantism, flattering the spectator into believing that his intellectual inferiority is a sign that he is loved by God.

6   The Teen-age Monster films, a very recent phenomenon, amend the assumptions of these horror movies in a startling manner. Their titles—*I Was a Teenage Werewolf, I Was a Teenage Frankenstein, Blood of Dracula,* and *Teenage Monster*—(some wit awaits one called *I Had a Teenage Monkey on My Back*)—suggest a Hollywood prank, but they are deadly serious, mixing the conventions of early horror movies with the ingredients of adolescent culture. The doctor, significantly enough, is no longer a fringe character whose madness can be inferred from the rings around his eyes and his wild hair but a respected member of society, a high-school chemistry teacher (*Blood of Dracula*) or a psychoanalyst (*Teenage Werewolf*) or a visiting lecturer from Britain (*Teenage Frankenstein*). Although he gives the appearance of benevolence—he pretends to help teen-agers with their problems—behind this facade he hides evil experimental designs. The monster, on the other hand, takes on a more fully developed personality. He is a victim who begins inauspiciously as an average, though emotionally troubled, adolescent and ends, through the influence of the doctor, as a voracious animal. The monster as teen-ager becomes the central character in the film and the teen-age audience is expected to identify and sympathize with him.

7   In *I Was a Teenage Werewolf,* the hero is characterized as brilliant but erratic in his studies and something of a delinquent. At the suggestion of his principal, he agrees to accept therapy from an analyst helping maladjusted students. The analyst gets the boy under his control and, after injecting him with a secret drug, turns him into a werewolf. Against his will he murders a number of his contemporaries. When the doctor refuses to free him from this curse, he kills him and is himself killed by the police. In death, his features relax into the harmless countenance of an adolescent.

8   The crimes of the adolescent are invariably committed against other youths (the doctor has it in for teen-agers) and are always connected with those staples of juvenile culture, sex and violence. The advertising displays show the male monsters, dressed in leather jackets and blue jeans, bending ambiguously over the diaphanously draped body of a luscious young girl while the female teen-age vampire of *Blood of Dracula,* her nails long and her fangs dripping, is herself half-dressed and lying on top of a struggling male (whether to rape or murder him is not clear). The identification of sex and violence is further underlined by the promotion blurbs: "In her eyes DESIRE! in her veins—the blood of a MONSTER!" (*Blood of Dracula*); "A Teenage Titan on a Lustful Binge that Paralyzed a Town with Fear" (*Teenage Monster*). It is probable that these crimes are performed less reluctantly than is suggested and that the adolescent spectator is more thrilled than appalled by this "lustful binge" which captures the attention of the adult community. The acquisition of power and prestige through delinquent sexual and aggressive activity is a familiar juvenile fantasy (the same distributors exploit it more openly in films like *Reform School Girl* and *Drag-Strip Girl*), one which we can see frequently acted out by delinquents in our city schools. In the Teen-age Monster films, however, the hero is absolved of his aggressive and libidinous impulses. Although he both feels and acts on them, he can attribute the responsibility to the mad scientist who controls his behavior. What these films seem to be saying, in their underground manner, is that behind the harmless face of the high-school chemistry teacher and the intellectual countenance of the psychoanalyst lies the warped authority responsible for teen-age violence. The adolescent feels victimized by society—turned into a monster by society— and if he behaves in a delinquent manner, society and not he is to blame. Thus, we can see one direction in which the hostility for experimental research, explicit in the Mad Doctor films, can go—it can be transmuted into hatred of adult authority itself.

9   Or it can go underground, as in the Atomic Beast movies. The Mad Doctor movies, in exploiting the supernatural, usually locate their action in Europe (often a remote Bavarian village) where wild fens, spectral castles, and ominous graveyards provide the proper eerie background. The Atomic Beast movies depend for their effect on the contemporary and familiar and there is a corresponding change in locale. The monster (or "thing" as it is more often called) appears now in a

busy American city—usually Los Angeles to save the producer money—where average men walk about in business suits. The thing terrorizes not only the hero, the heroine, and a few anonymous (and expendable) characters in Tyrolean costumes, but the entire world. Furthermore, it has lost all resemblance to anything human. It appears as a giant ant (*Them!*), a prehistoric animal (*Beast from Twenty Thousand Fathoms*), an outsized grasshopper (*Beginning of the End*) or a monstrous spider (*Tarantula*). Although these films, in their deference to science fiction, seem to smile more benignly on scientific endeavor, they are unconsciously closer to the anti-theoretical biases of the Mad Doctor series than would first appear.

10   All these films are similarly plotted, so the plot of *Beginning of the End* will serve as an example of the whole genre. The scene opens on a pair of adolescents necking in their car off a desert road. Their attention is caught by a weird clicking sound, the boy looks up in horror, the girl screams, the music stings and the scene fades. In the next scene, we learn that the car has been completely demolished and its occupants have disappeared. The police, totally baffled, are conducting fruitless investigations when word comes that a small town nearby has been destroyed in the same mysterious way. Enter the young scientist hero. Examining the wreckage of the town, he discovers a strange fluid which when analyzed proves to have been manufactured by a giant grasshopper. The police ridicule his conclusions and are instantly attacked by a fleet of these grasshoppers, each fifteen feet high, which wipe out the entire local force and a few state troopers. Interrupting a perfunctory romance with the heroine, the scientist flies to Washington to alert the nation. He describes the potential danger to a group of bored politicians and yawning big brass, but they remain skeptical until word comes that the things have reached Chicago and are crushing buildings and eating the occupants. The scientist is then put in charge of the army and air force. Although the military men want to evacuate the city and drop an atomic bomb on it, the scientist devises a safer method of destroying the creatures and proceeds to do so through exemplary physical courage and superior knowledge of their behavior. The movie ends on a note of foreboding: have the things been completely exterminated?

11   Externally, there seem to be very significant changes indeed, especially in the character of the scientist. No longer fang-toothed, long-haired, and subject to delirious ravings (Bela Lugosi, John Carradine,

Basil Rathbone), the doctor is now a highly admired member of society, muscular, handsome, and heroic (John Agar). He is invariably wiser, more reasonable, and more humane than the bone-headed bureaucrats and trigger-happy brass that compose the members of his "team," and he even has sexual appeal, a quality which Hollywood's eggheads have never enjoyed before. The scientist-hero, however, is not a very convincing intellectual. Although he may use technical, polysyllabic language when discussing his findings, he always yields gracefully to the admonition to "tell us in our own words, Doc" and proves that he can speak as simply as you or I; in the crisis, in fact, he is almost monosyllabic. When the chips are down, he loses his glasses (a symbol of his intellectualism) and begins to look like everyone else. The hero's intellect is part of his costume and makeup, easily shed when heroic action is demanded. That he is always called upon not only to outwit the thing but to wrestle with it as well (in order to save the heroine) indicates that he is in constant danger of tripping over the thin boundary between specialist and average Joe.

12   The fact remains that there is a new separation between the scientist and the monster. Rather than being an extension of the doctor's evil will, the monster functions completely on its own, creating havoc through its predatory nature. We learn through charts, biological film, and the scientist's patient explanations that ants and grasshoppers are not the harmless little beasties they appear but actually voracious insects who need only the excuse of size to prey upon humanity. The doctor, rather than allying himself with the monster in its rampage against our cities, is in strong opposition to it, and reverses the pattern of the Mad Doctor films by destroying it.

13   And yet, if the individual scientist is absolved of all responsibility for the "thing," science somehow is not. These films suggest an uneasiness about science which, though subtle and unpremeditated, reflects unconscious American attitudes. These attitudes are sharpened when we examine the genesis of the thing for, though it seems to rise out of nowhere, it is invariably caused by a scientific blunder. The giant ants of *Them!*, for example, result from a nuclear explosion which caused a mutation in the species; another fission test has awakened, in *Beast from Twenty Thousand Fathoms*, a dinosaur encrusted in polar icecaps; the spider of *Tarantula* grows in size after having been injected with

radioactive isotopes, and escapes during a fight in the lab between two scientists; the grasshoppers of *Beginning of the End* enlarge after crawling into some radioactive dust carelessly left about by a researcher. We are left with a puzzling substatement: science destroys the thing but scientific experimentation has created it.

14   I think we can explain this equivocal attitude when we acknowledge that the thing "which is too horrible to name," which owes its birth to an atomic or nuclear explosion, which begins in a desert or frozen waste and moves from there to cities, and which promises ultimately to destroy the world, is probably a crude symbol for the bomb itself. The scientists we see represented in these films are unlike the Mad Doctors in another more fundamental respect: they are never engaged in basic research. The scientist uses his knowledge in a purely defensive manner, like a specialist working on rocket interception or a physician trying to cure a disease. The isolated theoretician who tinkers curiously in his lab (and who invented the atomic bomb) is never shown, only the practical working scientist who labors to undo the harm. The thing's destructive rampage against cities, like the rampage of the Frankenstein monster, is the result of too much cleverness, and the consequences for all the world are only too apparent.

15   These consequences are driven home more powerfully in movies like *The Incredible Shrinking Man* and *The Amazing Colossal Man* where the audience gets the opportunity to identify closely with the victims of science's reckless experimentation. The hero of the first movie is an average man who, through contact with fallout while on his honeymoon, begins to shrink away to nothing. As he proceeds to grow smaller, he finds himself in much the same dilemma as the other heroes of the *Atomic Beast* series: he must do battle with (now) gigantic insects in order to survive. Scientists can do nothing to save him—after a while they can't even find him—so as he dwindles into an atomic particle he finally turns to God for whom "there is no zero." The inevitable sequel, *The Amazing Colossal Man,* reverses the dilemma. The hero grows to enormous size through the premature explosion of a plutonium bomb. Size carries with it the luxury of power but the hero cannot enjoy his new stature. He feels like a freak and his body is proceeding to outgrow his brain and heart. Although the scientists labor to help him and even succeed in reducing an elephant to the size of a cat, it is too late; the

hero has gone mad, demolished Las Vegas and fallen over Boulder
Dam. The victimization of man by theoretical science has become, in
these two movies, less of a suggestion and more of a fact.

16   In the Interplanetary Monster movies, Hollywood handles the
public's ambivalence towards science in a more obvious way, by split-
ting the scientist in two. Most of these movies feature both a practical
scientist who wishes to destroy the invader and a theoretical scientist
who wants to communicate with it. In *The Thing,* for example, we find
billeted among a group of more altruistic average-Joe colleagues with
crew cuts an academic long-haired scientist of the Dr. Frankenstein
type. When the evil thing (a highly evolved vegetable which, by mul-
tiplying itself, threatens to take over the world) descends in a flying
saucer, this scientist tries to perpetuate its life in order "to find out what
it knows." He is violently opposed in this by the others who take the
occasion to tell him that such amoral investigation produced the atomic
bomb. But he cannot be reasoned with and almost wrecks the entire
party. After both he and the thing are destroyed, the others congratulate
themselves on remaining safe, though in the dark. In *Forbidden Planet*
(a sophisticated thriller inspired in part by Shakespeare's *Tempest*), the
good and evil elements in science are represented, as in *Dr. Jekyll and
Mr. Hyde,* by the split personality of the scientist. He is urbane and
benevolent (Walter Pidgeon plays the role) and is trying to realize an
ideal community on the far-off planet he has discovered. Although he
has invented a robot (Ariel) who cheerfully performs man's baser tasks,
we learn that he is also responsible, though unwittingly, for a terrible
invisible force (Caliban) overwhelming in its destructiveness. While he
sleeps, the aggressive forces in his libido activate a dynamo he has been
tinkering with which gives them enormous power to kill those the doctor
unconsciously resents. Thus, Freudian psychology is evoked to endow
the scientist with guilt. At the end, he accepts his guilt and sacrifices
his life in order to combat the being he has created.

17   The Interplanetary Monster series sometimes reverses the central
situation of most horror films. We often find the monster controlling
the scientist and forcing him to do its evil will. In *It Conquered the
World* (the first film to capitalize on Sputnik and Explorer), the projection of a space satellite proves to be a mistake, for it results in the
invasion of America by a monster from Venus. The monster takes
control of the scientist who, embittered by the indifference of the masses

towards his ideas, mistakenly thinks the monster will free men from stupidity. This muddled egghead finally discovers the true intentions of the monster and destroys it, dying himself in the process. In *The Brain from Planet Arous,* a hideous brain inhabits the mind of a nuclear physicist with the intention of controlling the universe. As the physical incarnation of the monster, the scientist is at the mercy of its will until he can free himself of its influence. The monster's intellect, like the intellect of the Mad Doctor, is invariably superior, signified graphically by its large head and small body (in the last film named it is nothing but Brain). Like the Mad Doctor, its superior intelligence is always accompanied by moral depravity and an unconscionable lust for power. If the monster is to be destroyed at all, this will not be done by matching wits with it but by finding some chink in its armor. The chink quite often is a physical imperfection: in *War of the Worlds,* the invading Martians are stopped, at the height of their victory, by their vulnerability to the disease germs of earth. Before this Achilles heel is discovered, however, the scientist is controlled to do evil, and with the monster and the doctor in collaboration again, even in this qualified sense, the wheel has come full circle.

18   The terror of most of these films, then, stems from the matching of knowledge with power, always a source of fear for Americans— when Nietzsche's Superman enters comic book culture he loses his intellectual and spiritual qualities and becomes a muscle man. The muscle man, even with X-ray vision, poses no threat to the will, but muscle in collaboration with mind is generally thought to have a profound effect on individual destinies. The tendency to attribute everything that happens in the heavens, from flying saucers to Florida's cold wave, to science and the bomb ("Why don't they stop," said an old lady on the bus behind me the other day, "they don't know what they're doing") accounts for the extreme ways in which the scientist is regarded in our culture: either as a protective savior or as a destructive blunderer. It is little wonder that America exalts the physician (and the football player) and ignores the physicist. These issues, the issues of the great debate over scientific education and basic research, assert themselves crudely through the unwieldy monster and the Mad Doctor. The films suggest that the academic scientist, in exploring new areas, has laid the human race open to devastation either by human or interplanetary enemies— the doctor's madness, then, is merely a suitable way of expressing a

conviction that the scientist's idle curiosity has shaken itself loose from prudence or principle. There is obviously a sensitive moral problem involved here, one which needs more articulate treatment than the covert and superstitious way it is handled in horror movies. That the problem is touched there at all is evidence of how profoundly it has stirred the American psyche.

Notes on Punctuation

Lewis Thomas

1   There are no precise rules about punctuation (Fowler lays out some general advice (as best he can under the complex circumstances of English prose (he points out, for example, that we possess only four stops (the comma, the semicolon, the colon and the period (the question mark and exclamation point are not, strictly speaking, stops; they are indicators of tone (oddly enough, the Greeks employed the semicolon for their question mark (it produces a strange sensation to read a Greek sentence which is a straightforward question: Why weepest thou; (instead of Why weepest thou? (and, of course, there are parentheses (which are surely a kind of punctuation making this whole matter much more complicated by having to count up the left-handed parentheses in order to be sure of closing with the right number (but if the parentheses were left out, with nothing to work with but the stops, we would have considerably more flexibility in the deploying of layers of meaning than if we tried to separate all the clauses by physical barriers (and in the latter case, while we might have more precision and exactitude for our meaning, we would lose the essential flavor of language, which is its wonderful ambiguity)))))))))))))).

2   The commas are the most useful and usable of all the stops. It is highly important to put them in place as you go along. If you try to come back after doing a paragraph and stick them in the various spots that tempt you you will discover that they tend to swarm like minnows into all sorts of crevices whose existence you hadn't realized and before you know it the whole long sentence becomes immobilized and lashed up squirming in commas. Better to use them sparingly, and with affection, precisely when the need for each one arises, nicely, by itself.

3   I have grown fond of semicolons in recent years. The semicolon tells you that there is still some question about the preceding full sentence; something needs to be added; it reminds you sometimes of the Greek usage. It is almost always a greater pleasure to come across a

semicolon than a period. The period tells you that that is that; if you didn't get all the meaning you wanted or expected, anyway you got all the writer intended to parcel out and now you have to move along. But with a semicolon there you get a pleasant little feeling of expectancy; there is more to come; read on; it will get clearer.

4   Colons are a lot less attractive, for several reasons: firstly, they give you the feeling of being rather ordered around, or at least having your nose pointed in a direction you might not be inclined to take if left to yourself, and, secondly, you suspect you're in for one of those sentences that will be labeling the points to be made: firstly, secondly and so forth, with the implication that you haven't sense enough to keep track of a sequence of notions without having them numbered. Also, many writers use this system loosely and incompletely, starting out with number one and number two as though counting off on their fingers but then going on and on without the succession of labels you've been led to expect, leaving you floundering about searching for the ninethly or seventeenthly that ought to be there but isn't.

5   Exclamation points are the most irritating of all. Look! they say, look at what I just said! How amazing is my thought! It is like being forced to watch someone else's small child jumping up and down crazily in the center of the living room shouting to attract attention. If a sentence really has something of importance to say, something quite remarkable, it doesn't need a mark to point it out. And if it is really, after all, a banal sentence needing more zing, the exclamation point simply emphasizes its banality!

6   Quotation marks should be used honestly and sparingly, when there is a genuine quotation at hand, and it is necessary to be very rigorous about the words enclosed by the marks. If something is to be quoted, the *exact* words must be used. If part of it must be left out because of space limitations, it is good manners to insert three dots to indicate the omission, but it is unethical to do this if it means connecting two thoughts which the original author did not intend to have tied together. Above all, quotation marks should not be used for ideas that you'd like to disown, things in the air so to speak. Nor should they be put in place around clichés; if you want to use a cliché you must take full responsibility for it yourself and not try to job it off on anon., or on society. The most objectionable misuse of quotation marks, but one which illustrates the dangers of misuse in ordinary prose, is seen in

advertising, especially in advertisements for small restaurants, for example "just around the corner," or "a good place to eat." No single, identifiable, citable person ever really said, for the record, "just around the corner," much less "a good place to eat," least likely of all for restaurants of the type that use this type of prose.

7   The dash is a handy device, informal and essentially playful, telling you that you're about to take off on a different tack but still in some way connected with the present course—only you have to remember that the dash is there, and either put a second dash at the end of the notion to let the reader know that he's back on course, or else end the sentence, as here, with a period.

8   The greatest danger in punctuation is for poetry. Here it is necessary to be as economical and parsimonious with commas and periods as with the words themselves, and any marks that seem to carry their own subtle meanings, like dashes and little rows of periods, even semicolons and question marks, should be left out altogether rather than inserted to clog up the thing with ambiguity. A single exclamation point in a poem, no matter what else the poem has to say, is enough to destroy the whole work.

9   The things I like best in T. S. Eliot's poetry, especially in the *Four Quartets,* are the semicolons. You cannot hear them, but they are there, laying out the connections between the images and the ideas. Sometimes you get a glimpse of a semicolon coming, a few lines farther on, and it is like climbing a steep path through woods and seeing a wooden bench just at a bend in the road ahead, a place where you can expect to sit for a moment, catching your breath.

10   Commas can't do this sort of thing; they can only tell you how the different parts of a complicated thought are to be fitted together, but you can't sit, not even take a breath, just because of a comma,

Chapter Six

Comparison and Contrast

Grant and Lee: A Study in Contrasts

Bruce Catton

1   When Ulysses S. Grant and Robert E. Lee met in the parlor of a modest house at Appomattox Court House, Virginia, on April 9, 1865, to work out the terms for the surrender of Lee's Army of Northern Virginia, a great chapter in American life came to a close, and a great new chapter began.

2   These men were bringing the Civil War to its virtual finish. To be sure, other armies had yet to surrender, and for a few days the fugitive Confederate government would struggle desperately and vainly, trying to find some way to go on living now that its chief support was gone. But in effect it was all over when Grant and Lee signed the papers. And the little room where they wrote out the terms was the scene of one of the poignant, dramatic contrasts in American history.

3   They were two strong men, these oddly different generals, and they represented the strengths of two conflicting currents that, through them, had come into final collision.

4   Back of Robert E. Lee was the notion that the old aristocratic concept might somehow survive and be dominant in American life.

5   Lee was tidewater Virginia, and in his background were family, culture, and tradition . . . the age of chivalry transplanted to a New World which was making its own legends and its own myths. He embodied a way of life that had come down through the age of knighthood and the English country squire. America was a land that was beginning all over again, dedicated to nothing much more complicated than the rather hazy belief that all men had equal rights, and should have an equal chance in the world. In such a land Lee stood for the feeling that it was somehow of advantage to human society to have a pronounced inequality in the social structure. There should be a leisure class, backed by ownership of land; in turn, society itself should be keyed to the land as the chief source of wealth and influence. It would bring forth (according to this ideal) a class of men with a strong sense

of obligation to the community; men who lived not to gain advantage for themselves, but to meet the solemn obligations which had been laid on them by the very fact that they were privileged. From them the country would get its leadership; to them it could look for the higher values—of thought, of conduct, of personal deportment—to give it strength and virtue.

6   Lee embodied the noblest elements of this aristocratic ideal. Through him, the landed nobility justified itself. For four years, the Southern states had fought a desperate war to uphold the ideals for which Lee stood. In the end, it almost seemed as if the Confederacy fought for Lee; as if he himself was the Confederacy . . . the best thing that the way of life for which the Confederacy stood could ever have to offer. He had passed into legend before Appomattox. Thousands of tired, underfed, poorly clothed Confederate soldiers, long-since past the simple enthusiasm of the early days of the struggle, somehow considered Lee the symbol of everything for which they had been willing to die. But they could not quite put this feeling into words. If the Lost Cause, sanctified by so much heroism and so many deaths, had a living justification, its justification was General Lee.

7   Grant, the son of a tanner on the Western frontier, was everything Lee was not. He had come up the hard way, and embodied nothing in particular except the eternal toughness and sinewy fiber of the men who grew up beyond the mountains. He was one of a body of men who owed reverence and obeisance to no one, who were self-reliant to a fault, who cared hardly anything for the past but who had a sharp eye for the future.

8   These frontier men were the precise opposites of the tidewater aristocrats. Back of them, in the great surge that had taken people over the Alleghenies and into the opening Western country, there was a deep, implicit dissatisfaction with a past that had settled into grooves. They stood for democracy, not from any reasoned conclusion about the proper ordering of human society, but simply because they had grown up in the middle of democracy and knew how it worked. Their society might have privileges, but they would be privileges each man had won for himself. Forms and patterns meant nothing. No man was born to anything, except perhaps to a chance to show how far he could rise. Life was competition.

9   Yet along with this feeling had come a deep sense of belonging to a national community. The Westerner who developed a farm, opened a shop or set up in business as a trader, could hope to prosper only as his own community prospered—and his community ran from the Atlantic to the Pacific and from Canada down to Mexico. If the land was settled, with towns and highways and accessible markets, he could better himself. He saw his fate in terms of the nation's own destiny. As its horizons expanded, so did his. He had, in other words, an acute dollars-and-cents stake in the continued growth and development of his country.

10   And that, perhaps, is where the contrast between Grant and Lee becomes most striking. The Virginia aristocrat, inevitably, saw himself in relation to his own region. He lived in a static society which could endure almost anything except change. Instinctively, his first loyalty would go to the locality in which that society existed. He would fight to the limit of endurance to defend it, because in defending it he was defending everything that gave his own life its deepest meaning.

11   The Westerner, on the other hand, would fight with an equal tenacity for the broader concept of society. He fought so because everything he lived by was tied to growth, expansion, and a constantly widening horizon. What he lived by would survive or fall with the nation itself. He could not possibly stand by unmoved in the face of an attempt to destroy the Union. He would combat it with everything he had, because he could only see it as an effort to cut the ground out from under his feet.

12   So Grant and Lee were in complete contrast, representing two diametrically opposed elements in American life. Grant was the modern man emerging; beyond him, ready to come on the stage, was the great age of steel and machinery, of crowded cities and a restless, burgeoning vitality. Lee might have ridden down from the old age of chivalry, lance in hand, silken banner fluttering over his head. Each man was the perfect champion of his cause, drawing both his strengths and his weaknesses from the people he led.

13   Yet it was not all contrast, after all. Different as they were—in background, in personality, in underlying aspiration—these two great soldiers had much in common. Under everything else, they were marvelous fighters. Furthermore, their fighting qualities were really very much alike.

14   Each man had, to begin with, the great virtue of utter tenacity and fidelity. Grant fought his way down the Mississippi Valley in spite of acute personal discouragement and profound military handicaps. Lee hung on in the trenches at Petersburg after hope itself had died. In each man there was an indomitable quality . . . the born fighter's refusal to give up as long as he can still remain on his feet and lift his two fists.

15   Daring and resourcefulness they had, too; the ability to think faster and move faster than the enemy. These were the qualities which gave Lee the dazzling campaigns of Second Manassas and Chancellorsville and won Vicksburg for Grant.

16   Lastly, and perhaps greatest of all, there was the ability, at the end, to turn quickly from war to peace once the fighting was over. Out of the way these two men behaved at Appomattox came the possibility of a peace of reconciliation. It was a possibility not wholly realized, in the years to come, but which did, in the end, help the two sections to become one nation again . . . after a war whose bitterness might have seemed to make such a reunion wholly impossible. No part of either man's life became him more than the part he played in their brief meeting in the McLean house at Appomattox. Their behavior there put all succeeding generations of Americans in their debt. Two great Americans, Grant and Lee—very different, yet under everything very much alike. Their encounter at Appomattox was one of the great moments of American history.

The Black and White Truth About Basketball: A Skin-deep Theory of Style

Jeff Greenfield

1   The dominance of black athletes over professional basketball is beyond dispute. Two thirds of the players are black, and the number would be greater were it not for the continuing practice of picking white bench warmers for the sake of balance. The Most Valuable Player award of the National Basketball Association has gone to blacks for sixteen of the last twenty years, and in the newer American Basketball Association, blacks have won it all but once in the league's eight years. In the 1974–75 season, four of the top five All-Stars and seven of the top ten were black. The N.B.A. was the first pro sports league of any stature to hire a black coach (Bill Russell of the Celtics) and the first black general manager (Wayne Embry of the Bucks). What discrimination remains—lack of opportunity for lucrative benefits such as speaking engagements and product endorsements—has more to do with society than with basketball.

2   This dominance reflects a natural inheritance; basketball is a pastime of the urban poor. The current generation of black athletes are heirs to a tradition half a century old: in a neighborhood without the money for bats, gloves, hockey sticks, tennis rackets, or shoulder pads, basketball is accessible. "Once it was the game of the Irish and Italian Catholics in Rockaway and the Jews on Fordham Road in the Bronx," writes David Wolf in his brilliant book, *Foul!* "It was recreation, status, and a way out." But now the ethnic names are changed; instead of Red Holzmans, Red Auerbachs, and McGuire brothers, there are Earl Monroes and Connie Hawkins and Nate Archibalds. And professional basketball is a sport with a national television contract and million-dollar salaries.

3   But the mark on basketball of today's players can be measured by more than money or visibility. It is a question of style. For there is a clear difference between "black" and "white" styles of play that is as clear as the difference between 155th Street at Eighth Avenue and Crystal City, Missouri. Most simply (remembering we are talking about culture, not chromosomes), "black" basketball is the use of superb athletic skill to adapt to the limits of space imposed by the game. "White" ball is the pulverization of that space by sheer intensity.

4   It takes a conscious effort to realize how constricted the space is on a basketball court. Place a regulation court (ninety-four by fifty feet) on a football field, and it will reach from the back of the end zone to the twenty-one-yard line; its width will cover less than a third of the field. On a baseball diamond, a basketball court will reach from home plate to just beyond first base. Compared to its principal indoor rival, ice hockey, basketball covers about one fourth the playing area. And during the normal flow of the game, most of the action takes place on about the third of the court nearest the basket. It is in this dollhouse space that ten men, each of them half a foot taller than the average man, come together to battle each other.

5   There is, thus, no room; basketball is a struggle for the edge: the half step with which to cut around the defender for a lay-up, the half second of freedom with which to release a jump shot, the instant a head turns allowing a pass to a teammate breaking for the basket. It is an arena for the subtlest of skills: the head fake, the shoulder fake, the shift of body weight to the right and the sudden cut to the left. Deception is crucial to success; and to young men who have learned early and painfully that life is a battle for survival, basketball is one of the few games in which the weapon of deception is a legitimate rule and not the source of trouble.

6   If there is, then, the need to compete in a crowd, to battle for the edge, then the surest strategy is to develop the *unexpected;* to develop a shot that is simply and fundamentally different from the usual methods of putting the ball in the basket. Drive to the hoop, but go under it and come up the other side; hold the ball at waist level and shoot from there instead of bringing the ball up to eye level; leap into the air and fall away from the basket instead of toward it. All these tactics take maximum advantage of the crowding on a court; they also stamp uniqueness on young men who may feel it nowhere else.

7   "For many young men in the slums," David Wolf writes, "the school yard is the only place they can feel true pride in what they do, where they can move free of inhibitions and where they can, by being spectacular, rise for the moment against the drabness and anonymity of their lives. Thus, when a player develops extraordinary 'school yard' moves and shots . . .[they] become his measure as a man."

8   So the moves that begin as tactics for scoring soon become calling cards. You don't just lay the ball in for an uncontested basket; you take the ball in both hands, leap as high as you can, and slam the ball through the hoop. When you jump in the air, fake a shot, bring the ball back to your body, and throw up a shot, all without coming back down, you have proven your worth in uncontestable fashion.

9   This liquid grace is an integral part of "black" ball, almost exclusively the province of the playground player. Some white stars like Richie Guerin, Bob Cousy, and Billy Cunningham have it: the body control, the moves to the basket, the free-ranging mobility. They also have the surface ease that is integral to the "black" style; an incorporation of the ethic of mean streets—to "make it" is not just to have wealth, but to have it without strain. Whatever the muscles and organs are doing, the face of the "black" star almost never shows it. Bob McAdoo of the Buffalo Braves can drive to the basket with two men on him, pull up, turn around, and hit a basket without the least flicker of emotion. The Knicks' Walt Frazier, flamboyant in dress, cars, and companions, displays nothing but a quickly raised fist after scoring a particularly important basket. (Interestingly, the black coaches in the N.B.A. exhibit far less emotion on the bench than their white counterparts; Washington's K. C. Jones and Seattle's Bill Russell are statuelike compared with Tommy Heinsohn, Jack Ramsay, or Dick Motta.)

10   If there is a single trait that characterizes "black" ball it is leaping agility. Bob Cousy, ex-Celtic great and former pro coach, says that "when coaches get together, one is sure to say, 'I've got the one black kid in the country who can't jump.' When coaches see a white boy who can jump or who moves with extraordinary quickness, they say, 'He should have been born black, he's that good.'"

11   Don Nelson of the Celtics recalls that in 1970, Dave Cowens, then a relatively unknown Florida State graduate, prepared for his rookie season by playing in the Rucker League, an outdoor Harlem competition that pits pros against playground stars and college kids. So ferocious

was Cowens' leaping power, Nelson says, that "when the summer was over, every one wanted to know who the white son of a bitch was who could jump so high." That's another way to overcome a crowd around the basket—just go over it.

12   Speed, mobility, quickness, acceleration, "the moves"—all of these are catchphrases that surround the "black" playground style of play. So does the most racially tinged of attributes, "rhythm." Yet rhythm is what the black stars themselves talk about; feeling the flow of the game, finding the tempo of the dribble, the step, the shot. It is an instinctive quality, one that has led to difficulty between systematic coaches and free-form players. "Cats from the street have their own rhythm when they play," said college dropout Bill Spivey, onetime New York high-school star. "It's not a matter of somebody setting you up and you shooting. You *feel* the shot. When a coach holds you back, you lose the feel and it isn't fun anymore."

13   Connie Hawkins, the legendary Brooklyn playground star, said of Laker coach Bill Sharman's methodical style of teaching, "He's systematic to the point where it begins to be a little too much. It's such an action-reaction type of game that when you have to do everything the same way, I think you lose something."

14   There is another kind of basketball that has grown up in America. It is not played on asphalt playgrounds with a crowd of kids competing for the court; it is played on macadam driveways by one boy with a ball and a backboard nailed over the garage; it is played in Midwestern gyms and on Southern dirt courts. It is a mechanical, precise development of skills (when Don Nelson was an Iowa farm boy, his incentive to make his shots was that an errant rebound would land in the middle of chicken droppings), without frills, without flow, but with effectiveness. It is "white" basketball: jagged, sweaty, stumbling, intense. A "black" player overcomes an obstacle with finesse and body control; a "white" player reacts by outrunning or outpowering the obstacle.

15   By this definition, the Boston Celtics and the Chicago Bulls are classically "white" teams. The Celtics almost never use a player with dazzling moves; that would probably make Red Auerbach swallow his cigar. Instead, the Celtics wear you down with execution, with constant running, with the same play run again and again. The rebound triggers the fast break, with everyone racing downcourt; the ball goes to John Havlicek, who pulls up and takes the jump shot, or who fakes the shot

and passes off to the man following, the "trailer," who has the momentum to go inside for a relatively easy shot.

16   The Bulls wear you down with punishing intensity, hustling, and defensive tactics which are either aggressive or illegal, depending on what side you're on. The Bulls—particularly Jerry Sloan and Norm Van Lier (one white, one black for the quota-minded)—seem to reject the concept of an out-of-bounds line. They are as likely to be found under the press table or wrapped around the ushers as on the court.

17   Perhaps the most classically "white" position is that of the quick forward, one without great moves to the basket, without highly developed shots, without the height and mobility for rebounding effectiveness. What does he do? He runs. He runs from the opening jump to the last horn. He runs up and down the court, from base line to base line, back and forth under the basket, looking for the opening, for the pass, for the chance to take a quick step and the high-percentage shot. To watch Boston's Don Nelson, a player without speed or moves, is to wonder what this thirty-five-year-old is doing in the N.B.A.—until you see him swing free and throw up a shot that, without demanding any apparent skill, somehow goes in the basket more frequently than the shots of any of his teammates. And to watch his teammate John Havlicek, also thirty-five, is to see "white" ball at its best.

18   Havlicek stands in dramatic contrast to Julius Erving of the New York Nets. Erving has the capacity to make legends come true; leaping from the foul line and slam-dunking the ball on his way down; going up for a lay-up, pulling the ball to his body and throwing under and up the other side of the rim, defying gravity and probability with moves and jumps. Havlicek looks like the living embodiment of his small-town Ohio background. He brings the ball downcourt, weaving left, then right, looking for the path. He swings the ball to a teammate, cuts behind a pick, takes the pass and releases the shot in a flicker of time. It looks plain, unvarnished. But there are not half a dozen players in the league who can see such possibilities for a free shot, then get that shot off as quickly and efficiently as Havlicek.

19   To Jim McMillian of Buffalo, a black with "white" attributes, himself a quick forward, "it's a matter of environment. Julius Erving grew up in a different environment from Havlicek—John came from a very small town in Ohio. There everything was done the easy way, the shortest distance between two points. It's nothing fancy, very few times

will he go one-on-one; he hits the lay-up, hits the jump shot, makes the free throw, and after the game you look and you say, 'How did he hurt us that much?'"

20   "White" ball, then, is the basketball of patience and method. "Black" ball is the basketball of electric self-expression. One player has all the time in the world to perfect his skills, the other a need to prove himself. These are slippery categories, because a poor boy who is black can play "white" and a white boy of middle-class parents can play "black." K. C. Jones and Pete Maravich are athletes who seem to defy these categories. And what makes basketball the most intriguing of sports is how these styles do not necessarily clash; how the punishing intensity of "white" players and the dazzling moves of the "blacks" can fit together, a fusion of cultures that seems more and more difficult in the world beyond the out-of-bounds line.

Football Red and Baseball Green

Murray Ross

1   The 1970 Superbowl, the final game of the professional football season, drew a larger television audience than either the moonwalk or Tiny Tim's wedding. This revelation is one way of indicating just how popular spectator sports are in this country. Americans, or American men anyway, seem to care about the games they watch as much as the Elizabethans cared about their plays, and I suspect for some of the same reasons. There is, in sport, some of the rudimentary drama found in popular theater: familiar plots, type characters, heroic and comic action spiced with new and unpredictable variations. And common to watching both activities is the sense of participation in a shared tradition and in shared fantasies. If it is true that sport exploits these fantasies without significantly transcending them, it seems no less satisfying for all that.

2   It is my guess that sport spectating involves something more than the vicarious pleasures of identifying with athletic prowess. I suspect that each sport contains a fundamental myth which it elaborates for its fans, and that our pleasure in watching such games derives in part from belonging briefly to the mythic world which the game and its players bring to life. I am especially interested in baseball and football because they are so popular and so uniquely *American;* they began here and unlike basketball they have not been widely exported. Thus whatever can be said, mythically, about these games would seem to apply directly and particularly to our own culture.

3   Baseball's myth may be the easier to identify since we have a greater historical perspective on the game. It was an instant success during the Industrialization, and most probably it was a reaction to the squalor, the faster pace and the dreariness of the new conditions. Baseball was old fashioned right from the start; it seems conceived in nostalgia, in the resuscitation of the Jeffersonian dream. It established an artificial rural environment, one removed from the toil of an urban life,

219

which spectators could be admitted to and temporarily breathe in. Baseball is a *pastoral* sport, and I think the game can be best understood as this kind of art. For baseball does what all good pastoral does—it creates an atmosphere in which everything exists in harmony.

4   Consider, for instance, the spatial organization of the game. A kind of controlled openness is created by having everything fan out from home plate, and the crowd sees the game through an arranged perspective that is rarely violated. Visually this means that the game is always seen as a constant, rather calm whole, and that the players and the playing field are viewed in relationship to each other. Each player has a certain position, a special area to tend, and the game often seems to be as much a dialogue between the fielders and the field as it is a contest between the players themselves: will that ball get through the hole? Can that outfielder run under that fly? As a moral genre pastoral asserts the virtue of communion with nature. As a competitive game, baseball asserts that the team which best relates to the playing field (by hitting the ball in the right places) will be the team which wins.

5   I suspect baseball's space has a subliminal function too, for topographically it is a sentimental mirror of older America. Most of the game is played between the pitcher and the hitter in the extreme corner of the playing area. This is the busiest, most sophisticated part of the ball park, where something is always happening, and from which all subsequent action depends. From this urban corner we move to a supporting infield, active but a little less crowded, and from there we come to the vast stretches of the outfield. As is traditional in American lore danger increases with distance, and the outfield action is often the most spectacular in the game. The long throw, the double off the wall, the leaping catch—these plays take place in remote territory, and they belong, like most legendary feats, to the frontier.

6   Having established its landscape, pastoral art operates to eliminate any references to that bigger, more disturbing, more real world it has left behind. All games are to some extent insulated from the outside by having their own rules, but baseball has a circular structure as well which furthers its comfortable feeling of self-sufficiency. By this I mean that every motion of extension is also one of return—a ball hit outside is a *home* run, a full circle. Home—familiar, peaceful, secure—it is the beginning and end of everything. You must go out and you must come back, for only the completed movement is registered.

7   Time is a serious threat to any form of pastoral. The genre poses a timeless world of perpetual spring, and it does its best to silence the ticking of clocks which remind us that in time the green world fades into winter. One's sense of time is directly related to what happens in it, and baseball is so structured as to stretch out and ritualize whatever action it contains. Dramatic moments are few, and they are almost always isolated by the routine texture of normal play. It is certainly a game of climax and drama, but it is perhaps more a game of repeated and predictable action: the foul balls, the walks, the pitcher fussing around on the mound, the lazy fly ball to centerfield. This is, I think, as it should be, for baseball exists as an alternative to a world of too much action, struggle and change. It is a merciful release from a more grinding and insistent tempo, and its time, as William Carlos Williams suggests, makes a virtue out of idleness simply by providing it:

> The crowd at the ball game
> is moved uniformly
> by a spirit of uselessness
> which delights them . . .

8   Within this expanded and idle time the baseball fan is at liberty to become a ceremonial participant and a lover of style. Because the action is normalized, how something is done becomes as important as the action itself. Thus baseball's most delicate and detailed aspects are often, to the spectator, the most interesting. The pitcher's windup, the anticipatory crouch of the infielders, the quick waggle of the bat as it poises for the pitch—these subtle miniature movements are as meaningful as the home runs and the strikeouts. It somehow matters in baseball that all the tiny rituals are observed: the shortstop must kick the dirt and the umpire must brush the plate with his pocket broom. In a sense baseball is largely a continuous series of small gestures, and I think it characteristic that the game's most treasured moment came when Babe Ruth pointed to the place where he subsequently hit a home run.

9   Baseball is a game where the little things mean a lot, and this, together with its clean serenity, its open space, and its ritualized action is enough to place it in a world of yesterday. Baseball evokes for us a past which may never have been ours, but which we believe was, and

certainly that is enough. In the Second World War, supposedly, we fought for "Baseball, Mom and Apple Pie," and considering what baseball means that phrase is a good one. We fought then for the right to believe in a green world of tranquillity and uninterrupted contentment, where the little things would count. But now the possibilities of such a world are more remote, and it seems that while the entertainment of such a dream has an enduring appeal, it is no longer sufficient for our fantasies. I think this may be why baseball is no longer our preeminent national pastime, and why its myth is being replaced by another more appropriate to the new realities (and fantasies) of our time.

10   Football, especially professional football, is the embodiment of a newer myth, one which in many respects is opposed to baseball's. The fundamental difference is that football is not a pastoral game; it is a heroic one. One way of seeing the difference between the two is by the juxtaposition of Babe Ruth and Jim Brown, both legendary players in their separate genres. Ruth, baseball's most powerful hitter, was a hero maternalized (his name), an epic figure destined for a second immortality as a candy bar. His image was impressive but comfortable and altogether human: round, dressed in a baggy uniform, with a schoolboy's cap and a bat which looked tiny next to him. His spindly legs supported a Santa sized torso, and this comic disproportion would increase when he was in motion. He ran delicately, with quick, very short steps, since he felt that stretching your stride slowed you down. This sort of superstition is typical of baseball players, and typical too is the way in which a personal quirk or mannerism mitigates their awesome skill and makes them poignant and vulnerable.

11   There was nothing funny about Jim Brown. His muscular and almost perfect physique was emphasized further by the uniform which armored him. Babe Ruth had a tough face, but boyish and innocent; Brown was an expressionless mask under the helmet. In action he seemed invincible, the embodiment of speed and power in an inflated human shape. One can describe Brown accurately only with superlatives, for as a player he was a kind of Superman, undisguised.

12   Brown and Ruth are caricatures, yet they represent their games. Baseball is part of a comic tradition which insists that its participants be humans, while football, in the heroic mode, asks that its players be more than that. Football converts men into gods, and suggests that magnificence and glory are as desirable as happiness. Football is de-

signed, therefore, to impress its audience rather differently than baseball, as I think comparison will show.

13   As a pastoral game, baseball attempts to close the gap between
the players and the crowd. It creates the illusion, for instance, that with
a lot of hard work, a little luck, and possibly some extra talent, the
average spectator might well be playing; not watching. For most of us
can do a few of the things the ballplayers do: catch a pop-up, field a
ground ball, and maybe get a hit once in a while. Chance is allotted a
good deal of play in the game. There is no guarantee, for instance, that
a good pitch will not be looped over the infield, or that a solidly batted
ball will turn into a double play. In addition to all of this, almost every
fan feels he can make the manager's decision for him, and not entirely
without reason. Baseball's statistics are easily calculated and rather
meaningful; and the game itself, though a subtle one, is relatively lucid
and comprehensible.

14   As a heroic game football is not concerned with a shared community of near-equals. It seeks almost the opposite relationship between
its spectators and players, one which stresses the distance between them.
We are not allowed to identify directly with Jim Brown any more than
we are with Zeus, because to do so would undercut his stature as
something more than human. The players do much of the distancing
themselves by their own excesses of speed, size and strength. When
Bob Brown, the giant all pro tackle says that he could "block King
Kong all day," we look at him and believe. But the game itself con-
tributes to the players' heroic isolation. As George Plimpton has graphically illustrated in *Paper Lion,* it is almost impossible to imagine
yourself in a professional football game without also considering your
imminent humiliation and possible injury. There is scarcely a single
play that the average spectator could hope to perform adequately, and
there is even a difficulty in really understanding what is going on. In
baseball what happens is what meets the eye, but in football each action
is the result of eleven men acting simultaneously against eleven other
men, and clearly this is too much for the eye to totally comprehend.
Football has become a game of staggering complexity, and coaches are
now wired in to several "spotters" during the games so that they too
can find out what is happening.

15   If football is distanced from its fans by its intricacy and its "su-
perhuman" play, it nonetheless remains an intense spectacle. Baseball,

as I have implied, dissolves time and urgency in a green expanse, thereby creating a luxurious and peaceful sense of leisure. As is appropriate to a heroic enterprise, football reverses this procedure and converts space into time. The game is ideally played in an oval stadium, not in a "park," and the difference is the elimination of perspective. This makes football a perfect television game, because even at first hand it offers a flat, perpetually moving foreground (wherever the ball is). The eye in baseball viewing opens up; in football it zeroes in. There is no democratic vista in football, and spectators are not asked to relax, but to concentrate. You are encouraged to watch the drama, not a medley of ubiquitous gestures, and you are constantly reminded that this event is taking place in time. The third element in baseball is the field; in football this element is the clock. Traditionally heroes do reckon with time, and football players are no exceptions. Time in football is wound up inexorably until it reaches the breaking point in the last minutes of a close game. More often than not it is the clock which emerges as the real enemy, and it is the sense of time running out that regularly produces a pitch of tension uncommon in baseball.

16   A further reason for football's intensity, surely, is that the game is played like a war. The idea is to win by going through, around or over the opposing team and the battle lines, quite literally, are drawn on every play. Violence is somewhere at the heart of the game, and the combat quality is reflected in football's army language ("blitz," "trap," "zone," "bomb," "trenches," etc.). Coaches often sound like generals when they discuss their strategy. Woody Hayes of Ohio State, for instance, explains his quarterback option play as if it had been conceived in the pentagon: "You know," he says, "the most effective kind of warfare is siege. You have to attack on broad fronts. And that's all the option is—attacking on a broad front. You know General Sherman ran an option right through the South."

17   Football like war is an arena for action, and like war football leaves little room for personal style. It seems to be a game which projects "character" more than personality, and for the most part football heroes, publicly, are a rather similar lot. They tend to become personifications rather than individuals, and, with certain exceptions, they are easily read emblematically as embodiments of heroic qualities such as "strength," "confidence," "perfection," etc.—cliches really, but forceful enough when represented by the play of a Dick Butkus, a Johnny Unitas or a

Bart Starr. Perhaps this simplification of personality results in part from the heroes' total identification with their mission, to the extent that they become more characterized by their work than by what they intrinsically "are." At any rate football does not make allowances for the idiosyncrasies that baseball actually seems to encourage, and as a result there have been few football players as uniquely crazy or human as, say, Casey Stengel or Dizzy Dean.

18   A further reason for the underdeveloped qualities of football personalities, and one which gets us to the heart of the game's modernity, is that football is very much a game of modern technology. Football's action is largely interaction, and the game's complexity requires that its players mold themselves into a perfectly coordinated unit. Jerry Kramer, the veteran guard and author of *Instant Replay,* writes how Lombardi would work to develop such integration:

> He makes us execute the same plays over and over, a hundred times, two hundred times, until we do every little thing automatically. He works to make the kickoff team perfect, the punt-return team perfect, the field-goal team perfect. He ignores nothing. Technique, technique, technique, over and over and over, until we feel like we're going crazy. But we win.

19   Mike Garratt, the halfback, gives the player's version:

> After a while you train your mind like a computer—put the ideas in, digest it, and the body acts accordingly.

20   As the quotations imply, pro football is insatiably preoccupied with the smoothness and precision of play execution, and most coaches believe that the team which makes the fewest mistakes will be the team that wins. Individual identity thus comes to be associated with the team or unit that one plays for to a much greater extent than in baseball. To use a reductive analogy, it is the difference between *Bonanza* and *Mission Impossible.* Ted Williams is mostly Ted Williams, but Bart Starr is mostly the Green Bay Packers. The latter metaphor is a precise one, since football heroes stand out not because of purely individual acts, but because they epitomize the action and style of the groups they are connected to. Kramer cites the obvious if somewhat self-glorifying

historical precedent: "Perhaps," he writes, "we're living in Camelot."
Ideally a football team should be what Camelot was supposed to have
been, a group of men who function as equal parts of a larger whole,
entirely dependent on each other for their total meaning. . . .

21   Football's collective pattern is only one aspect of the way in which
it seems to echo our contemporary environment. The game, like our
society, can be thought of as a cluster of people living under great
tension in a state of perpetual flux. The potential for sudden disaster or
triumph is as great in football as it is in our own age, and although
there is something ludicrous in equating interceptions with assassinations and long passes with moonshots, there is also something valid and
appealing in the analogies. It seems to me that football does successfully
reflect those salient and common conditions which affect us all, and it
does so with the end of making us feel better about them and our lot.
For one thing, it makes us feel that something can be connected in all
this chaos; out of the accumulated pile of bodies something can emerge—
a runner breaks into the clear or a pass finds its way to a receiver. To
the spectator plays such as these are human and dazzling. They suggest
to the audience what it has hoped for (and been told) all along, that
technology is still a tool and not a master. Fans get living proof of this
every time a long pass is completed; they see at once that it is the result
of careful planning, perfect integration and an effective "pattern," but
they see too that it is human and that what counts as well is man, his
desire, his natural skill and his "grace under pressure." Football me-
taphysically yokes heroic action and technology together by violence
to suggest that they are mutually supportive. It's a doubtful proposition,
but given how we live it has its attractions.

22   Football, like the space program, is a game in the grand manner,
yet it is a rather sober sport and often seems to lack that positive, comic
vision of which baseball's pastoral is a part. It is a winter game, as
those fans who saw the Minnesota Vikings play the Detroit Lions last
Thanksgiving were graphically reminded. The two teams played in a
blinding snowstorm, and except for the small flags in the corners of the
end zones, and a patch of mud wherever the ball was downed, the field
was totally obscured. Even through the magnified television lenses the
players were difficult to identify; you saw only huge shapes come out
of the gloom, thump against each other and fall in a heap. The movement
was repeated endlessly and silently in a muffled stadium, interrupted

once or twice by a shot of a bare-legged girl who fluttered her pom-poms in the cold. The spectacle was by turns pathetic, compelling and absurd; a kind of theater of oblivion. . . .

23   A final note. It is interesting that the heroic and pastoral conventions which underlie our most popular sports are almost classically opposed. The contrasts are familiar: city vs. country, aspiration vs. contentment, activity vs. peace and so on. Judging from the rise of professional football we seem to be slowly relinquishing that unfettered rural vision of ourselves that baseball so beautifully mirrors, and we have come to cast ourselves in a genre more reflective of a nation confronted by constant and unavoidable challenges. Right now, like the Elizabethans, we seem to share both heroic and pastoral yearnings, and we reach out to both. Perhaps these divided needs account in part for the enormous attention we as a nation now give to spectator sports. For sport provides one place, at least, where we can have our football and our baseball too.

Two Views of the Mississippi

Mark Twain

1   Now when I had mastered the language of this water, and had come to know every trifling feature that bordered the great river as familiarly as I knew the letters of the alphabet, I had made a valuable acquisition. But I had lost something, too. I had lost something which could never be restored to me while I lived. All the grace, the beauty, the poetry, had gone out of the majestic river! I still keep in mind a certain wonderful sunset which I witnessed when steamboating was new to me. A broad expanse of the river was turned to blood; in the middle distance the red hue brightened into gold, through which a solitary log came floating black and conspicuous; in one place a long, slanting mark lay sparkling upon the water; in another the surface was broken by boiling, tumbling rings, that were as many-tinted as an opal; where the ruddy flush was faintest, was a smooth spot that was covered with graceful circles and radiating lines, ever so delicately traced; the shore on our left was densely wooded, and the somber shadow that fell from this forest was broken in one place by a long, ruffled trail that shone like silver; and high above the forest wall a clean-stemmed dead tree waved a single leafy bough that glowed like a flame in the unobstructed splendor that was flowing from the sun. There were graceful curves, reflected images, woody heights, soft distances; and over the whole scene, far and near, the dissolving lights drifted steadily, enriching it every passing moment with new marvels of coloring.

2   I stood like one bewitched. I drank it in, in a speechless rapture. The world was new to me, and I had never seen anything like this at home. But as I have said, a day came when I began to cease from noting the glories and the charms which the moon and the sun and the twilight wrought upon the river's face; another day came when I ceased altogether to note them. Then, if that sunset scene had been repeated, I should have looked upon it without rapture, and should have commented upon it, inwardly, after this fashion: "This sun means that we

are going to have wind to-morrow; that floating log means that the river
is rising, small thanks to it; that slanting mark on the water refers to a
bluff reef which is going to kill somebody's steamboat one of these
nights, if it keeps on stretching out like that; those tumbling 'boils'
show a dissolving bar and a changing channel there; the lines and circles
in the slick water over yonder are a warning that that troublesome place
is shoaling up dangerously; that silver streak in the shadow of the forest
is the 'break' from a new snag, and he has located himself in the very
best place he could have found to fish for steamboats; that tall dead
tree, with a single living branch, is not going to last long, and then
how is a body ever going to get through this blind place at night without the friendly old landmark?"

3   No, the romance and beauty were all gone from the river. All the
value any feature of it had for me now was the amount of usefulness
it could furnish toward compassing the safe piloting of a steamboat.
Since those days, I have pitied doctors from my heart. What does the
lovely flush in a beauty's cheek mean to a doctor but a "break" that
ripples above some deadly disease? Are not all her visible charms sown
thick with what are to him the signs and symbols of hidden decay?
Does he ever see her beauty at all, or doesn't he simply view her
professionally, and comment upon her unwholesome condition all to
himself? And doesn't he sometimes wonder whether he has gained most
or lost most by learning his trade?

Venezuela for Visitors

John Updike

1   All Venezuela, except for the negligible middle class, is divided between the Indians (*los indios*) and the rich (*los ricos*.) The Indians are mostly to be found in the south, amid the muddy tributaries of the Orinoco and the god-haunted *tepuys* (mesas) that rear their fearsome mile-high crowns above the surrounding jungle, whereas the rich tend to congregate in the north, along the sunny littoral, in the burgeoning metropolis of Caracas, and on the semi-circular shores of Lake Maracaibo, from which their sumptuous black wealth is drawn. The negligible middle class occupies a strip of arid savanna in the center of the nation and a few shunned enclaves on the suburban slopes of Monte Avila.

2   The Indians, who range in color from mocha to Dentyne, are generally under five feet tall. Their hair style runs to pageboys and severe bangs, with some tonsures in deference to lice. Neither sex is quite naked: the males wear around their waists a thong to which their foreskins are tied, pulling their penises taut upright; the females, once out of infancy, suffer such adornments as three pale sticks symmetrically thrust into their lower faces. The gazes of both sexes are melting, brown, alert, canny. The visitor, standing among them with his Nikon FE and L. L. Bean fannypack, is shy at first, but warms to their inquisitive touches, which patter and rub across his person with a soft, sandy insistence unlike both the fumblings of children and the caresses one Caucasian adult will give another. There is an infectious, wordless ecstasy in their touches, and a blank eagerness with yet some parameters of tact and irony. *These are human presences,* the visitor comes to realize.

3   The rich, who range in color from porcelain to mocha, are generally under six feet tall. Their hair style runs to chignons and blow-dried trims. Either sex is elegantly clad: the males favor dark suits of medium weight (nights in Caracas can be cool), their close English cut enhanced by a slight Latin flare, and shirts with striped bodies but stark-

white collars and French cuffs held by agates and gold; the females appear in a variety of gowns and mock-military pants suits, Dior and de la Renta originals flown in from Paris and New York. The gazes of both sexes are melting, brown, alert, canny. The visitor, standing among them in his funky Brooks Brothers suit and rumpled blue button-down, is shy at first, but warms to their excellent English, acquired at colleges in London or "the States," and to their impeccable manners, which conceal, as their fine clothes conceal their skins, rippling depths of Spanish and those dark thoughts that the mind phrases to itself in its native language. They tell anecdotes culled from their rich international lives; they offer, as the evening deepens, confidences, feelers, troubles. These, too, are human presences.

4   The Indians live in *shabonos*—roughly circular lean-tos woven beautifully of palm thatch in clearings hacked and burned out of the circumambient rain forest. A *shabono* usually rots and is abandoned within three years. The interiors are smoky, from cooking fires, and eye diseases are common among the Indians. They sleep, rest, and die in hammocks (*cinchorros*) hung as close together as pea pods on a vine. Their technology, involving in its pure state neither iron nor the wheel, is yet highly sophisticated: the chemical intricacies of curare have never been completely plumbed, and with their blowpipes of up to sixteen feet in length the Indians can bring down prey at distances of over thirty meters. They fish without hooks, by employing nets and thrashing the water with poisonous lianas. All this sounds cheerier than it is. It is depressing to stand in the gloom of a *shabono,* the palm thatch overhead infested with giant insects, the Indians drooping in their hammocks, their eyes diseased, their bellies protuberant, their faces and limbs besmirched with the same gray-brown dirt that composes the floor, their possessions a few brown baskets and monkey skins. Their lives are not paradise but full of anxiety—their religion a matter of fear, their statecraft a matter of constant, nagging war. To themselves, they are "the people" (*Yanomami*); to others, they are "the killers" (*Waikás*).

5   The rich dwell in *haciendas*—airy long ranch houses whose roofs are of curved tile and, surprisingly, dried sugar-cane stalks. Some *haciendas* surviving in Caracas date from the sixteenth century, when the great valley was all but empty. The interiors are smoky, from candlelit dinners, and contact lenses are common among the rich. The furniture is solid, black, polished by generations of servants. Large paintings by

Diebenkorn, Stella, Baziotes, and Botero adorn the white plaster walls, along with lurid religious pictures in the colonial Spanish style. The appliances are all modern and paid for; even if the oil in Lake Maracaibo were to give out, vast deposits of heavy crude have been discovered in the state of Bolívar. All this sounds cheerier than it is. The rich wish they were in Paris, London, New York. Many have condominiums in Miami. *Haute couture* and abstract painting may not prove bulwark enough. Constitutional democracy in Venezuela, though the last dictator fled in 1958, is not so assured as may appear. Turbulence and tyranny are traditional. Che Guevara is still idealized among students. To themselves, the rich are good, decent, amusing people; to others, they are *"reaccionarios."*

6   Missionaries, many of them United States citizens, move among the Indians. They claim that since Western civilization, with all its diseases and detritus, must come, it had best come through them. Nevertheless, Marxist anthropologists inveigh against them. Foreign experts, many of them United States citizens, move among the rich. They claim they are just helping out, and that anyway the oil industry was nationalized five years ago. Nevertheless, Marxist anthropologists are not mollified. The feet of the Indians are very broad in front, their toes spread wide for climbing avocado trees. The feet of the rich are very narrow in front, their toes compressed by pointed Italian shoes. The Indians seek relief from tension in the use of *ebene,* or *yopo,* a mind-altering drug distilled from the bark of the *ebene* tree and blown into the user's nose through a hollow cane by a colleague. The rich take cocaine through the nose, and frequent mind-altering discotheques, but more customarily imbibe cognac, *vino blanco,* and Scotch, in association with colleagues.

7   These and other contrasts and comparisons between the Indians and the rich can perhaps be made more meaningful by the following anecdote: A visitor, after some weeks in Venezuela, was invited to fly to the top of a *tepuy* in a helicopter, which crashed. As stated, the *tepuys* are supposed by the Indians to be the forbidden haunts of the gods; and, indeed, they present an exotic, attenuated vegetation and a craggy geology to the rare intruder. The crash was a minor one, breaking neither bones nor bottles (a lavish picnic, including *mucho vino blanco,* had been packed). The bottles were consumed, the exotic vegetation was photographed, and a rescue helicopter arrived. In the Cessna back

to Caracas, the survivors couldn't get enough of discussing the incident and their survival, and the red-haired woman opposite the visitor said, "I *love* the way you pronounce '*tepuy*.'" She imitated him: *tupooey*. "Real zingy," she said. The visitor slowly realized that he was being flirted with, and that therefore *this woman was middle-class*. In Venezuela, only the negligible middle class flirts. The Indians kidnap or are raped; the rich commandeer, or languorously give themselves in imperious surrender.

8   The Indians tend to know only three words of Spanish: "*¿Cómo se llama?*" ("What is your name?"). In Indian belief, to give one's name is to place oneself in the other's power. And the rich, when one is introduced, narrow their eyes and file one's name away in their mysterious depths. Power among them flows along lines of kinship and intimacy. After an imperious surrender, a rich female gazes at her visitor with new interest out of her narrowed, brown, melting, kohl-ringed eyes. He has become someone to be reckoned with, if only as a potential source of financial embarrassment. "Again, what is your name?" she asks.

9   *Los indios* and *los ricos* rarely achieve contact. When they do, *mestizos* result, and the exploitation of natural resources. In such lies the future of Venezuela.

Viewing Vs. Reading

Marie Winn

1   Until the television era a young child's access to symbolic representations of reality was limited. Unable to read, he entered the world of fantasy primarily by way of stories told to him or read to him from a book. But rarely did such "literary" experiences take up a significant proportion of a child's waking time; even when a willing reader or storyteller was available, an hour or so a day was more time than most children spent ensconced in the imagination of others. And when the pre-television child *did* enter those imaginary worlds, he always had a grown-up escort along to interpret, explain, and comfort, if need be. Before he learned to read, it was difficult for the child to enter the fantasy world alone.

2   For this reason the impact of television was undoubtedly greater on preschoolers and pre-readers than on any other group. By means of television, very young children were able to enter and spend sizable portions of their waking time in a secondary world of incorporeal people and intangible things, unaccompanied, in too many cases, by an adult guide or comforter. School-age children fell into a different category. Because they could read, they had other opportunities to leave reality behind. For these children television was merely *another* imaginary world.

3   But since reading, once the school child's major imaginative experience, has now been virtually eclipsed by television, the television experience must be compared with the reading experience to try to discover whether they are, indeed, similar activities fulfilling similar needs in a child's life.

WHAT HAPPENS WHEN YOU READ

4   It is not enough to compare television watching and reading from the viewpoint of quality. Although the quality of the material available in each medium varies enormously, from junky books and shoddy pro-

grams to literary masterpieces and fine, thoughtful television shows, the *nature* of the two experiences is different and that difference significantly affects the impact of the material taken in.

5   Few people besides linguistics students and teachers of reading are aware of the complex mental manipulations involved in the reading process. Shortly after learning to read, a person assimilates the process into his life so completely that the words in books seem to acquire an existence almost equal to the objects or acts they represent. It requires a fresh look at a printed page to recognize that those symbols that we call letters of the alphabet are completely abstract shapes bearing no inherent "meaning" of their own. Look at an "o," for instance, or a "k." The "o" is a curved figure; the "k" is an intersection of three straight lines. Yet it is hard to divorce their familiar figures from their sounds, though there is nothing "o-ish" about an "o" or "k-ish" about a "k." A reader unfamiliar with the Russian alphabet will find it easy to look at the symbol "щ" and see it as an abstract shape; a Russian reader will find it harder to detach that symbol from its sound, *shch*. And even when trying to consider "k" as an abstract symbol, we cannot see it without the feeling of a "k" sound somewhere between the throat and the ears, a silent pronunciation of "k" that occurs the instant we see the letter.

6   That is the beginning of reading: we learn to transform abstract figures into sounds, and groups of symbols into the combined sounds that make up the words of our language. As the mind transforms the abstract symbols into sounds and the sounds into words, it "hears" the words, as it were, and thereby invests them with meanings previously learned in the spoken language. Invariably, as the skill of reading develops, the meaning of each word begins to seem to dwell within those symbols that make up the word. The word "dog," for instance, comes to bear some relationship with the real animal. Indeed, the word "dog" seems to *be* dog in a certain sense, to possess some of the qualities of a dog. But it is only as a result of a swift and complex series of mental activities that the word "dog" is transformed from a series of meaningless squiggles into an idea of something real. This process goes on smoothly and continuously as we read, and yet it becomes no less complex. The brain must carry out all the steps of decoding and investing with meaning each time we read; but it becomes more adept at it as the skill develops, so that we lose the sense of struggling with symbols and meanings that children have when they first learn to read.

7   But not merely does the mind *hear* words in the process of reading; it is important to remember that reading involves images as well. For when the reader sees the word "dog" and understands the idea of "dog," an image representing a dog is conjured up as well. The precise nature of this "reading image" is little understood, nor is there agreement about what relation it bears to visual images taken in directly by the eyes. Nevertheless images necessarily color our reading, else we would perceive no meaning, merely empty words. The great difference between these "reading images" and the images we take in when viewing television is this: we *create* our own images when reading, based upon our own life experiences and reflecting our own individual needs, while we must accept what we receive when watching television images. This aspect of reading, which might be called "creative" in the narrow sense of the word, is present during all reading experiences, regardless of *what* is being read. The reader "creates" his own images as he reads, almost as if he were creating his own, small, inner television program. The result is a nourishing experience for the imagination. As Bruno Bettelheim notes, "Television captures the imagination but does not liberate it. A good book at once stimulates and frees the mind."

8   Television images do not go through a complex symbolic transformation. The mind does not have to decode and manipulate during the television experience. Perhaps this is a reason why the visual images received directly from a television set are strong, stronger, it appears, than the images conjured up mentally while reading. But ultimately they satisfy less. A ten-year-old child reports on the effects of seeing television dramatizations of books he has previously read: "The TV people leave a stronger impression. Once you've seen a character on TV, he'll always look like that in your mind, even if you made a different picture of him in your mind before, when you read the book yourself." And yet, as the same child reports, "the thing about a book is that you have so much freedom. You can make each character look exactly the way you want him to look. You're more in control of things when you read a book than when you see something on TV."

9   It may be that television-bred children's reduced opportunities to indulge in this "inner picture-making" accounts for the curious inability of so many children today to adjust to nonvisual experiences. This is commonly reported by experienced teachers who bridge the gap between the pretelevision and the television eras.

10   "When I read them a story without showing them pictures, the children always complain—'I can't see.' Their attention flags," reports a first-grade teacher. "They'll begin to talk or wander off. I have to really work to develop their visualizing skills. I tell them that there's nothing to see, that the story is coming out of my mouth, and that they can make their own pictures in their 'mind's eye.' They get better at visualizing, with practice. But children never needed to learn how to visualize before television, it seems to me."

VIEWING VS. READING: CONCENTRATION

11   Because reading demands complex mental manipulations, a reader is required to concentrate far more than a television viewer. An audio expert notes that "with the electronic media it is openness [that counts]. Openness permits auditory and visual stimuli more direct access to the brain . . . someone who is taught to concentrate will fail to perceive many patterns of information conveyed by the electronic stimuli."

12   It may be that a predisposition toward concentration, acquired, perhaps, through one's reading experiences, makes one an inadequate television watcher. But it seems far more likely that the reverse situation obtains: that a predisposition toward "openness" (which may be understood to mean the opposite of focal concentration), acquired through years and years of television viewing, has influenced adversely viewers' ability to concentrate, to read, to write clearly—in short, to demonstrate any of the verbal skills a literate society requires.

PACE

13   A comparison between reading and viewing may be made in respect to the pace of each experience, and the relative control a person has over that pace, for the pace may influence the ways one uses the material received in each experience. In addition, the pace of each experience may determine how much it intrudes upon other aspects of one's life.

14   The pace of reading, clearly, depends entirely upon the reader. He may read as slowly or as rapidly as he can or wishes to read. If he does not understand something, he may stop and reread it, or go in

search of elucidation before continuing. The reader can accelerate his pace when the material is easy or less than interesting, and slow down when it is difficult or enthralling. If what he reads is moving, he can put down the book for a few moments and cope with his emotions without fear of losing anything.

15 The pace of the television experience cannot be controlled by the viewer; only its beginning and end are within his control as he clicks the knob on and off. He cannot slow down a delightful program or speed up a dreary one. He cannot "turn back" if a word or phrase is not understood. The program moves inexorably forward, and what is lost or misunderstood remains so.

16 Nor can the television viewer readily transform the material he receives into a form that might suit his particular emotional needs, as he invariably does with material he reads. The images move too quickly. He cannot use his own imagination to invest the people and events portrayed on television with the personal meanings that would help him understand and resolve relationships and conflicts in his own life; he is under the power of the imagination of the show's creators. In the television experience the eyes and ears are overwhelmed with the immediacy of sights and sounds. They flash from the television set just fast enough for the eyes and ears to take them in before moving on quickly to the new pictures and sounds . . . so as *not to lose the thread*.

17 Not to lose the thread . . . it is this need, occasioned by the irreversible direction and relentless velocity of the television experience, that not only limits the workings of the viewer's imagination, but also causes television to intrude into human affairs far more than reading experiences can ever do. If someone enters the room while one is watching television—a friend, a relative, a child, someone, perhaps, one has not seen for some time—one must continue to watch or one will lose the thread. The greetings must wait, for the television program will not. A book, of course, can be set aside, with a pang of regret, perhaps, but with no sense of permanent loss.

18 A grandparent describes a situation that is, by all reports, not uncommon:

19 "Sometimes when I come to visit the girls, I'll walk into their room and they're watching a TV program. Well, I know they love me, but it makes me feel *bad* when I tell them hello, and they say, without

even looking up, 'Wait a minute . . . we have to see the end of this program.' It hurts me to have them care more about that machine and those little pictures than about being glad to see me. I know that they probably can't help it, but still. . . ."

20   Can they help it? Ultimately the power of a television viewer to release himself from his viewing in order to attend to human demands arising in the course of his viewing is not altogether a function of the pace of the program. After all, the viewer might *choose* to operate according to human priorities rather than electronic dictatorship. He might quickly decide "to hell with this program" and simply stop watching when a friend entered the room or a child needed attention.

21   He might . . . but the hypnotic power of television makes it difficult to shift one's attention away, makes one desperate not to lose the thread of the program. . . .

THE BASIC BUILDING BLOCKS

22   There is another difference between reading and television viewing that must affect the response to each experience. This is the relative acquaintance of readers and viewers with the fundamental elements of each medium. While the reader is familiar with the basic building blocks of the reading medium, the television viewer has little acquaintance with those of the television medium.

23   As a person reads, he has his own writing experience to fall back upon. His understanding of what he reads, and his feelings about it, are necessarily affected, and deepened, by his possession of writing as a means of communicating. As a child begins to learn reading, he begins to acquire the rudiments of writing. That these two skills are always acquired together is important and not coincidental. As the child learns to read words, he needs to understand that a word is something he can write himself, though his muscle control may temporarily prevent him from writing it clearly. That he wields such power over the words he is struggling to decipher makes the reading experience a satisfying one right from the start.

24   A young child watching television enters a realm of materials completely beyond his control—and understanding. Though the images that appear on the screen may be reflections of familiar people and

things, they appear as if by magic. The child cannot create similar images, nor even begin to understand how those flickering, electronic shapes and forms come into being. He takes on a far more powerless and ignorant role in front of the television set than in front of a book.

25   There is no doubt that many young children have a confused relationship to the television medium. When a group of preschool children were asked, "How do kids get to be on your TV?" only 22 percent of them showed any real comprehension of the nature of the television images. When asked, "Where do the people and kids and things go when your TV is turned off?" only 20 percent of the three-year-olds showed the smallest glimmer of understanding. Although there was an increase in comprehension among the four-year-olds, the authors of the study note that "even among the older children the vast majority still did not grasp the nature of television pictures."

26   The child's feelings of power and competence are nourished by another feature of the reading experience that does not obtain for television: the nonmechanical, easily accessible, and easily transportable nature of reading matter. The child can always count on a book for pleasure, though the television set may break down at a crucial moment. The child may take a book with him wherever he goes, to his room, to the park, to his friend's house, to school to read under his desk: he can *control* his use of books and reading materials. The television set is stuck in a certain place; it cannot be moved easily. It certainly cannot be casually transported from place to place by a child. The child must not only watch television wherever the set is located, but he must watch certain programs at certain times, and is powerless to change what comes out of the set and when it comes out.

27   In this comparison of reading and television experiences a picture begins to emerge that quite confirms the commonly held notion that reading is somehow "better" than television viewing. Reading involves a complex form of mental activity, trains the mind in concentration skills, develops the powers of imagination and inner visualization; the flexibility of its pace lends itself to a better and deeper comprehension of the material communicated. Reading engrosses, but does not hypnotize or seduce the reader from his human responsibilities. Reading is a two-way process: the reader can also write; television viewing is a one-way street: the viewer cannot create television images. And books are ever available, ever controllable. Television controls.

Conservatives and Liberals

Ralph Waldo Emerson

1   The two parties which divide the state, the party of Conservatism and that of Innovation, are very old, and have disputed the possession of the world ever since it was made. This quarrel is the subject of civil history. The conservative party established the reverend hierarchies and monarchies of the most ancient world. The battle of patrician and plebeian, of parent state and colony, of old usage and accomodation to new facts, of the rich and the poor, reappears in all countries and times. The war rages not only in battle-fields, in national councils, and ecclesiastical synods, but agitates every man's bosom with opposing advantages every hour. On rolls the old world meantime, and now one, now the other gets the day, and still the fight renews itself as if for the first time, under new names and hot personalities.

2   Such an irreconcilable antagonism, of course, must have a correspondent depth of seat in the human constitution. It is the opposition of Past and Future, of Memory and Hope, of the Understanding and the Reason. It is the primal antagonism, the appearance in trifles of the two poles of nature.

3   There is a fragment of old fable which seems somehow to have been dropped from the current mythologies, which may deserve attention, as it appears to relate to this subject.

4   Saturn grew weary of sitting alone, or with none but the great Uranus or Heaven beholding him, and he created an oyster. Then he would act again, but he made nothing more, but went on creating the race of oysters. Then Uranus cried, 'a new work, O Saturn! the old is not good again.'

5   Saturn replied. 'I fear. There is not only the alternative of making and not making, but also of unmaking. Seest thou the great sea, how it ebbs and flows? so is it with me; my power ebbs; and if I put forth my hands, I shall not do, but undo. Therefore I do what I have done; I hold what I have got; and so I resist Night and Chaos.'

6   'O Saturn,' replied Uranus. 'Thou canst not hold thine own, but by making more. Thy oysters are barnacles and cockles, and with the next flowing of the tide, they will be pebbles and sea foam.'

7   'I see,' rejoins Saturn, 'thou art in league with Night, thou art become an evil eye: thou spakest from love; now thy words smite me with hatred. I appeal to Fate, must there not be rest?'—'I appeal to Fate also,' said Uranus, 'must there not be motion?'—But Saturn was silent and went on making oysters for a thousand years.

8   After that, the word of Uranus came into his mind like a ray of the sun, and he made Jupiter; and then he feared again; and nature froze, the things that were made went backward, and to save the world, Jupiter slew his father Saturn.

9   This may stand for the earliest account of a conversation on politics between a Conservative and a Radical, which has come down to us. It is ever thus. It is the counteraction of the centripetal and the centrifugal forces. Innovation is the salient energy; Conservatism the pause on the last movement. 'That which is was made by God,' saith Conservatism. 'He is leaving that, he is entering this other;' rejoins Innovation.

10   There is always a certain meanness in the argument of conservatism, joined with a certain superiority in its fact. It affirms because it holds. Its fingers clutch the fact, and it will not open its eyes to see a better fact. The castle, which conservatism is set to defend, is the actual state of things, good and bad. The project of innovation is the best possible state of things. Of course, conservatism always has the worst of the argument, is always apologizing, pleading a necessity, pleading that to change would be to deteriorate; it must saddle itself with the mountainous load of all the violence and vice of society, must deny the possibility of good, deny ideas, and suspect and stone the prophet; whilst innovation is always in the right, triumphant, attacking, and sure of final success. Conservatism stands on man's incontestable limitations; reform on his indisputable infinitude; conservatism on circumstance; liberalism on power; one goes to make an adroit member of the social frame; the other to postpone all things to the man himself; conservatism is debonnair and social; reform is individual and imperious. We are reformers in spring and summer, in autumn and winter we stand by the old; reformers in the morning, conservers at night. Reform is affirmative, conservatism negative; conservatism goes for comfort, reform for truth. Conservatism is more candid to behold an-

other's worth; reform more disposed to maintain and increase its own. Conservatism makes no poetry, breathes no prayer, has no invention; it is all memory. Reform has no gratitude, no prudence, no husbandry. It makes a great difference to your figure and to your thought, whether your foot is advancing or receding. Conservatism never puts the foot forward; in the hour when it does that, it is not establishment, but reform. Conservatism tends to universal seeming and treachery, believes in a negative fate; believes that men's temper governs them; that for me, it avails not to trust in principles; they will fail me; I must bend a little; it distrusts nature; it thinks there is a general law without a particular application,—law for all that does not include any one. Reform in its antagonism inclines to asinine resistance, to kick with hoofs; it runs to egotism and bloated self-conceit; it runs to a bodiless pretension, to unnatural refining and elevation, which ends in hypocrisy and sensual reaction.

11   And so whilst we do not go beyond general statements, it may be safely affirmed of these two metaphysical antagonists, that each is a good half, but an impossible whole. Each exposes the abuses of the other, but in a true society, in a true man, both must combine. Nature does not give the crown of its approbation, namely, Beauty, to any action or emblem or actor but to one which combines both these elements; not to the rock which resists the waves from age to age, nor to the wave which lashes incessantly the rock, but the superior beauty is with the oak which stands with its hundred arms against the storms of a century and grows every year like a sapling; or the river which ever flowing, yet is found in the same bed from age to age; or, greatest of all, the man who has subsisted for years amid the changes of nature, yet has distanced himself, so that when you remember what he was, and see what he is, you say, what strides! what a disparity is here!

Chapter Seven

Example and Illustration

Kitsch

Gilbert Highet

1   If you have ever passed an hour wandering through an antique shop (not looking for anything exactly, but simply looking), you must have noticed how your taste gradually grows numb, and then—if you stay—becomes perverted. You begin to see unsuspected charm in those hideous pictures of plump girls fondling pigeons, you develop a psychopathic desire for spinning wheels and cobblers' benches, you are apt to pay out good money for a bronze statuette of Otto von Bismarck, with a metal hand inside a metal frock coat and metal pouches under his metallic eyes. As soon as you take the things home, you realize that they are revolting. And yet they have a sort of horrible authority; you don't like them; you know how awful they are; but it is a tremendous effort to drop them in the garbage, where they belong.

2   To walk along a whole street of antique shops—that is an experience which shakes the very soul. Here is a window full of bulbous Chinese deities; here is another littered with Zulu assagais, Indian canoe paddles, and horse pistols which won't fire; the next shopfront is stuffed with gaudy Italian majolica vases, and the next, even worse, with Austrian pottery—tiny ladies and gentlemen sitting on lace cushions and wearing lace ruffles, with every frill, every wrinkle and reticulation translated into porcelain: pink; stiff; but fortunately not unbreakable. The nineteenth century produced an appalling amount of junky art like this, and sometimes I imagine that clandestine underground factories are continuing to pour it out like illicit drugs.

3   There is a name for such stuff in the trade, a word apparently of Russian origin, kitsch:* it means vulgar showoff, and it is applied to anything that took a lot of trouble to make and is quite hideous.

4   It is paradoxical stuff, kitsch. It is obviously bad: so bad that you can scarcely understand how any human being would spend days and

*The Russian verb *keetcheetsya* means 'to be haughty and puffed up.'

weeks making it, and how anybody else would buy it and take it home and keep it and dust it and leave it to her heirs. It is terribly ingenious, and terribly ugly, and utterly useless; and yet it has one of the qualities of good art—which is that, once seen, it is not easily forgotten. Of course it is found in all the arts: think of Milan Cathedral, or the statues in Westminster Abbey, or Liszt's settings of Schubert songs. There is a lot of it in the United States—for instance, the architecture of Miami, Florida, and Forest Lawn Cemetery in Los Angeles. Many of Hollywood's most ambitious historical films are superb kitsch. Most Tin Pan Alley love songs are perfect 100 per cent kitsch.

5   There is kitsch in the world of books also. I collect it. It is horrible, but I enjoy it.

6   The gem of my collection is the work of the Irish novelist Mrs. Amanda McKittrick Ros, whose masterpiece, *Delina Delaney,* was published about 1900. It is a stirringly romantic tale, telling how Delina, a fisherman's daughter from Erin Cottage, was beloved by Lord Gifford, the heir of Columbia Castle, and—after many trials and even imprisonment—married him. The story is dramatic, not to say impossible; but it is almost lost to view under the luxuriant style. Here, for example, is a sentence in which Mrs. Ros explains that her heroine used to earn extra cash by doing needlework.

> She tried hard to assist in keeping herself a stranger to her poor old father's slight income by the use of the finest production of steel, whose blunt edge eyed the reely covering with marked greed, and offered its sharp dart to faultless fabrics of flaxen fineness.

Revolting, but distinctive: what Mr. Polly called 'rockockyo' in manner. For the baroque vein, here is Lord Gifford saying goodby to his sweetheart:

> My darling virgin! my queen! my Delina! I am just in time to hear the toll of a parting bell strike its heavy weight of appalling softness against the weakest fibers of a heart of love, arousing and tickling its dormant action, thrusting the dart of evident separation deeper into its tubes of tenderness, and fanning the flame, already unextinguishable, into volumes of blaze.

Mrs. Ros had a remarkable command of rhetoric, and could coin an unforgettable phrase. She described her hero's black eyes as 'glittering jet revolvers.' When he became ill, she said he fell 'into a state of lofty fever'—doubtless because commoners have high fever, but lords have lofty fever. And her reflections on the moral degeneracy of society have rarely been equaled, in power and penetration:

> Days of humanity, whither hast thou fled? When bows of compulsion, smiles for the deceitful, handshakes for the dogmatic, and welcome for the tool of power live under your objectionable, unambitious beat, not daring to be checked by the tongue of candour because the selfish world refuses to dispense with her rotten policies. The legacy of your fore-fathers, which involved equity, charity, reason, and godliness, is beyond the reach of their frivolous, mushroom offspring—deceit, injustice, mal-ice and unkindness—and is not likely to be codiciled with traits of har-mony so long as these degrading vices of mock ambition fester the human heart.

Perhaps one reason I enjoy this stuff is because it so closely resembles a typical undergraduate translation of one of Cicero's finest perorations: sound and fury, signifying nothing. I regret only that I have never seen Mrs. Ros's poetry. One volume was called *Poems of Puncture* and another *Bayonets of Bastard Sheen:* alas, jewels now almost unprocur-able. But at least I know the opening of her lyric written on first visiting St. Paul's Cathedral:

> Holy Moses, take a look,
> Brain and brawn in every nook!

7   Such genius is indestructible. Soon, soon now, some earnest re-searcher will be writing a Ph.D. thesis on Mrs. Amanda McKittrick Ros, and thus (as she herself might put it) conferring upon her dewy brow the laurels of concrete immortality.

8   Next to Mrs. Ros in my collection of kitsch is the work of the Scottish poet William McGonagall. This genius was born in 1830, but did not find his vocation until 1877. Poor and inadequate poets pullulate in every tongue, but (as the *Times Literary Supplement* observes) McGonagall 'is the only truly memorable bad poet in our language.'

In his command of platitude and his disregard of melody, he was the
true heir of William Wordsworth as a descriptive poet.

9   In one way his talents, or at least his aspirations, exceeded those
of Wordsworth. He was at his best in describing events he had never
witnessed, such as train disasters, shipwrecks, and sanguinary battles,
and in picturing magnificent scenery he had never beheld except with
the eye of the imagination. Here is his unforgettable Arctic landscape:

> Greenland's icy mountains are fascinating and grand,
> And wondrously created by the Almighty's command;
> And the works of the Almighty there's few can understand:
> Who knows but it might be a part of Fairyland?
>
> Because there are churches of ice, and houses glittering like glass,
> And for scenic grandeur there's nothing can it surpass,
> Besides there's monuments and spires, also ruins,
> Which serve for a safe retreat from the wild bruins.
>
> The icy mountains they're higher than a brig's topmast,
> And the stranger in amazement stands aghast
> As he beholds the water flowing off the melted ice
> Adown the mountain sides, that he cries out, Oh! how nice!

10   McGonagall also had a strong dramatic sense. He loved to tell of
agonizing adventures, more drastic perhaps but not less moving than
that related in Wordsworth's 'Vaudracour and Julia.' The happy ending
of one of his 'Gothic' ballads is surely unforgettable:

> So thus ends the story of Hanchen, a heroine brave,
> That tried hard her master's gold to save,
> And for her bravery she got married to the miller's eldest son,
> And Hanchen on her marriage night cried Heaven's will be done.

11   These scanty selections do not do justice to McGonagall's ingenuity as a rhymester. His sound effects show unusual talent. Most poets
would be baffled by the problem of producing rhymes for the proper

names *General Graham* and *Osman Digna,* but McGonagall gets them
into a single stanza, with dazzling effect:

> Ye sons of Great Britain, I think no shame
>
> To write in praise of brave General Graham!
>
> Whose name will be handed down to posterity without any stigma,
>
> Because, at the battle of El-Tab, he defeated Osman Digna.

12   One of McGonagall's most intense personal experiences was his
visit to New York. Financially, it was not a success. In one of his vivid
autobiographical sketches, he says, 'I tried occasionally to get an engagement from theatrical proprietors and music-hall proprietors, but
alas! 'twas all in vain, for they all told me they didn't encourage rivalry.'
However, he was deeply impressed by the architecture of Manhattan.
In eloquent verses he expressed what many others have felt, although
without adequate words to voice their emotion:

> Oh! Mighty City of New York, you are wonderful to behold,
>
> Your buildings are magnificent, the truth be it told;
>
> They were the only thing that seemed to arrest my eye,
>
> Because many of them are thirteen stories high.
>
> And the tops of the houses are all flat,
>
> And in the warm weather the people gather to chat;
>
> Besides on the house-tops they dry their clothes,
>
> And also many people all night on the house-tops repose.

13   Yet McGonagall felt himself a stranger in the United States. And
here again his close kinship with Wordsworth appears. The Poet Laureate, in a powerful sonnet written at Calais, once reproached the English
Channel for delaying his return by one of those too frequent storms in
which (reckless tyrant!) it will indulge itself:

> Why cast ye back upon the Gallic shore,
>
> Ye furious waves! a patriotic Son
>
> Of England?

14   In the same vein McGonagall sings with rapture of his return to his 'ain countree':

> And with regard to New York, and the sights I did see,
> One street in Dundee is more worth to me,
> And, believe me, the morning I sailed from New York,
> For bonnie Dundee—my heart it felt as light as a cork.

15   Indeed, New York is a challenging subject for ambitious poets. Here, from the same shelf, is a delicious poem on the same theme, by Ezra Pound:

> My City, my beloved
> Thou art a maid with no breasts
> Thou art slender as a silver reed.
> Listen to me, attend me!
> And I will breathe into thee a soul,
> And thou shalt live for ever.

16   The essence of this kind of trash is incongruity. The kitsch writer is always sincere. He really means to say something important. He feels he has a lofty spiritual message to bring to an unawakened world, or else he has had a powerful experience which he must communicate to the public. But either his message turns out to be a majestic platitude, or else he chooses the wrong form in which to convey it—or, most delightful of all, there is a fundamental discrepancy between the writer and his subject, as when Ezra Pound, born in Idaho, addresses the largest city in the world as a maid with no breasts, and enjoins it to achieve inspiration and immortality by listening to him. This is like climbing Mount Everest in order to carve a head of Mickey Mouse in the east face.

17   Bad love poetry, bad religious poetry, bad mystical prose, bad novels both autobiographical and historical—one can form a superb collection of kitsch simply by reading with a lively and awakened eye. College songs bristle with it. The works of Father Divine are full of it—all the more delightful because in him it is usually incomprehensible.

One of the Indian mystics, Sri Rama-krishna, charmed connoisseurs by describing the Indian scriptures (in a phrase which almost sets itself to kitsch-music) as

> fried in the butter of knowledge and steeped in the honey of love.

Bad funeral poetry is a rich mine of the stuff. Here, for example, is the opening of a jolly little lament, 'The Funeral' by Stephen Spender, apparently written during his pink period:

> Death is another milestone on their way,
> With laughter on their lips and with winds blowing round them
> They record simply
> How this one excelled all others in making driving belts.

Observe the change from humanism to communism. Spender simply took Browning's 'Grammarian's Funeral,' threw away the humor and the marching rhythm, and substituted wind and the Stakhanovist speed-up. Such also is a delicious couplet from Archibald MacLeish's elegy on the late Harry Crosby:

> He walks with Ernest in the streets in Saragossa
> They are drunk their mouths are hard they say *qué cosa.*

18   From an earlier romantic period, here is a splendid specimen. Coleridge attempted to express the profound truth that men and animals are neighbors in a hard world; but he made the fundamental mistake of putting it into a monologue address to a donkey:

> Poor Ass! Thy master should have learnt to show
> Pity—best taught by fellowship of Woe!
> Innocent foal! thou poor despised forlorn!
> I hail thee brother. . . .

19   Once you get the taste for this kind of thing it is possible to find pleasure in hundreds of experiences which you might otherwise have

thought either anesthetic or tedious: bad translations, abstract painting,
grand opera . . . Dr. Johnson, with his strong sense of humor, had a
fancy for kitsch, and used to repeat a poem in celebration of the marriage
of the Duke of Leeds, composed by 'an inferiour domestick . . . in
such homely rhimes as he could make':

> When the Duke of Leeds shall married be
> To a fine young lady of high quality,
> How happy will that gentlewoman be
> In his Grace of Leed's good company.
>
> She shall have all that's fine and fair,
> And the best of silk and sattin shall wear;
> And ride in a coach to take the air,
> And have a house in St. James's Square.

20   Folk poetry is full of such jewels. Here is the epitaph on an old
gentleman from Vermont who died in a sawmill accident:

> How shocking to the human mind
> The log did him to powder grind.
> God did command his soul away
> His summings we must all obey.

21   Kitsch is well known in drama, although (except for motion pictures) it does not usually last long. One palmary instance was a play
extolling the virtues of the Boy Scout movement, called *Young England*.
It ran for a matter of years during the 1930's, to audiences almost
wholly composed of kitsch-fanciers, who eventually came to know the
text quite as well as the unfortunate actors. I can still remember the
opening of one magnificent episode. Scene: a woodland glade. Enter
the hero, a Scoutmaster, riding a bicycle, and followed by the youthful
members of his troop. They pile bicycles in silence. Then the Scoutmaster raises his finger, and says (accompanied fortissimo by most of
the members of the audience):

> Fresh water must be our first consideration

22   In the decorative arts kitsch flourishes, and is particularly wide-spread in sculpture. One of my favorite pieces of bad art is a statue in Rockefeller Center, New York. It is supposed to represent Atlas, the Titan condemned to carry the sky on his shoulders. That is an ideal of somber, massive tragedy: greatness and suffering combined as in Hercules or Prometheus. But this version displays Atlas as a powerful moron, with a tiny little head, rather like the pan-fried young men who appear in the health magazines. Instead of supporting the heavens, he is lifting a spherical metal balloon: it is transparent, and quite empty; yet he is balancing insecurely on one foot like a furniture mover walking upstairs with a beach ball; and he is scowling like a mad baboon. If he ever gets the thing up, he will drop it; or else heave it onto a Fifth Avenue bus. It is a supremely ridiculous statue, and delights me every time I see it.

23   Perhaps you think this is a depraved taste. But really it is an extension of experience. At one end, Homer. At the other, Amanda McKittrick Ros. At one end, *Hamlet*. At the other, McGonagall, who is best praised in his own inimitable words:

> The poetry is moral and sublime
>
> And in my opinion nothing could be more fine.
>
> True genius there does shine so bright
>
> Like unto the stars of night.

Why Don't We Complain?

William F. Buckley, Jr.

1   It was the very last coach and the only empty seat on the entire train, so there was no turning back. The problem was to breathe. Outside, the temperature was below freezing. Inside the railroad car the temperature must have been about 85 degrees. I took off my overcoat, and a few minutes later my jacket, and noticed that the car was flecked with the white shirts of the passengers. I soon found my hand moving to loosen my tie. From one end of the car to the other, as we rattled through Westchester County, we sweated; but we did not moan.

2   I watched the train conductor appear at the head of the car. "Tickets, all tickets, please!" In a more virile age, I thought, the passengers would seize the conductor and strap him down on a seat over the radiator to share the fate of his patrons. He shuffled down the aisle, picking up tickets, punching commutation cards. *No one addressed a word to him.* He approached my seat, and I drew a deep breath of resolution. "Conductor," I began with a considerable edge to my voice. . . . Instantly the doleful eyes of my seatmate turned tiredly from his newspaper to fix me with a resentful stare: what question could be so important as to justify my sibilant intrusion into his stupor? I was shaken by those eyes. I am incapable of making a discreet fuss, so I mumbled a question about what time we were due in Stamford (I didn't even ask whether it would be before or after dehydration could be expected to set in), got my reply, and went back to my newspaper and to wiping my brow.

3   The conductor had nonchalantly walked down the gauntlet of eighty sweating American freemen, and not one of them had asked him to explain why the passengers in that car had been consigned to suffer. There is nothing to be done when the temperature *outdoors* is 85 degrees, and indoors the air conditioner has broken down; obviously when that happens there is nothing to do, except perhaps curse the day that one was born. But when the temperature outdoors is below freezing, it takes a positive act of will on somebody's part to set the temperature *indoors*

at 85. Somewhere a valve was turned too far, a furnace overstocked, a thermostat maladjusted: something that could easily be remedied by turning off the heat and allowing the great outdoors to come indoors. All this is so obvious. What is not obvious is what has happened to the American people.

4   It isn't just the commuters, whom we have come to visualize as a supine breed who have got on to the trick of suspending their sensory faculties twice a day while they submit to the creeping dissolution of the railroad industry. It isn't just they who have given up trying to rectify irrational vexations. It is the American people everywhere.

5   A few weeks ago at a large movie theatre I turned to my wife and said, "The picture is out of focus." "Be quiet," she answered. I obeyed. But a few minutes later I raised the point again, with mounting impatience. "It will be all right in a minute," she said apprehensively. (She would rather lose her eyesight than be around when I make one of my infrequent scenes.) I waited. It was *just* out of focus—not glaringly out, but out. My vision is 20-20, and I assume that is the vision, adjusted, of most people in the movie house. So, after hectoring my wife throughout the first reel, I finally prevailed upon her to admit that it *was* off, and very annoying. We then settled down, coming to rest on the presumption that: a) someone connected with the management of the theatre must soon notice the blur and make the correction; or b) that someone seated near the rear of the house would make the complaint in behalf of those of us up front; or c) that—any minute now—the entire house would explode into catcalls and foot stamping, calling dramatic attention to the irksome distortion.

6   What happened was nothing. The movie ended, as it had begun *just* out of focus, and as we trooped out, we stretched our faces in a variety of contortions to accustom the eye to the shock of normal focus.

7   I think it is safe to say that everybody suffered on that occasion. And I think it is safe to assume that everyone was expecting someone else to take the initiative in going back to speak to the manager. And it is probably true even that if we had supposed the movie would run right through the blurred image, someone surely would have summoned up the purposive indignation to get up out of his seat and file his complaint.

8   But notice that no one did. And the reason no one did is because we are all increasingly anxious in America to be unobtrusive, we are

reluctant to make our voices heard, hesitant about claiming our rights; we are afraid that our cause is unjust, or that if it is not unjust, that it is ambiguous; or if not even that, that it is too trivial to justify the horrors of a confrontation with Authority; we will sit in an oven or endure a racking headache before undertaking a head-on, I'm-here-to-tell-you complaint. That tendency to passive compliance, to a heedless endurance, is something to keep one's eyes on—in sharp focus.

9   I myself can occasionally summon the courage to complain, but I cannot, as I have intimated, complain softly. My own instinct is so strong to let the thing ride, to forget about it—to expect that someone will take the matter up, when the grievance is collective, in my behalf—that it is only when the provocation is at a very special key, whose vibrations touch simultaneously a complexus of nerves, allergies, and passions, that I catch fire and find the reserves of courage and assertiveness to speak up. When that happens, I get quite carried away. My blood gets hot, my brow wet, I become unbearably and unconscionably sarcastic and bellicose; I am girded for a total showdown.

10   Why should that be? Why could not I (or anyone else) on that railroad coach have said simply to the conductor, "Sir"—I take that back: that sounds sarcastic—"Conductor, would you be good enough to turn down the heat? I am extremely hot. In fact, I tend to get hot every time the temperature reaches 85 degr—" Strike that last sentence. Just end it with the simple statement that you are extremely hot, and let the conductor infer the cause.

11   Every New Year's Eve I resolve to do something about the Milquetoast in me and vow to speak up, calmly, for my rights, and for the betterment of our society, on every appropriate occasion. Entering last New Year's Eve I was fortified in my resolve because that morning at breakfast I had had to ask the waitress three times for a glass of milk. She finally brought it—after I had finished my eggs, which is when I don't want it any more. I did not have the manliness to order her to take the milk back, but settled instead for a cowardly sulk, and ostentatiously refused to drink the milk—though I later paid for it—rather than state plainly to the hostess, as I should have, why I had not drunk it, and would not pay for it.

12   So by the time the New Year ushered out the Old, riding in on my morning's indignation and stimulated by the gastric juices of resolution that flow so faithfully on New Year's Eve, I rendered my vow.

Henceforward I would conquer my shyness, my despicable disposition to supineness. I would speak out like a man against the unnecessary annoyances of our time.

13   Forty-eight hours later, I was standing in line at the ski repair store in Pico Peak, Vermont. All I needed, to get on with my skiing, was the loan, for one minute, of a small screwdriver, to tighten a loose binding. Behind the counter in the workshop were two men. One was industriously engaged in servicing the complicated requirements of a young lady at the head of the line, and obviously he would be tied up for quite a while. The other—"Jiggs," his workmate called him—was a middle-aged man, who sat in a chair puffing a pipe, exchanging small talk with his working partner. My pulse began its telltale acceleration. The minutes ticked on. I stared at the idle shopkeeper, hoping to shame him into action, but he was impervious to my telepathic reproof and continued his small talk with his friend, brazenly insensitive to the nervous demands of six good men who were raring to ski.

14   Suddenly my New Year's Eve resolution struck me. It was now or never. I broke from my place in line and marched to the counter. I was going to control myself. I dug my nails into my palms. My effort was only partially successful.

15   "If you are not too busy," I said icily, "would you mind handing me a screwdriver?"

16   Work stopped and everyone turned his eyes on me, and I experienced that mortification I always feel when I am the center of centripetal shafts of curiosity, resentment, perplexity.

17   But the worst was yet to come. "I am sorry, sir," said Jiggs deferentially, moving the pipe from his mouth. "I am not supposed to move. I have just had a heart attack." That was the signal for a great whirring noise that descended from heaven. We looked, stricken, out the window, and it appeared as though a cyclone had suddenly focused on the snowy courtyard between the shop and the ski lift. Suddenly a gigantic army helicopter materialized, and hovered down to a landing. Two men jumped out of the plane carrying a stretcher, tore into the ski shop, and lifted the shopkeeper onto the stretcher. Jiggs bade his companion goodby, was whisked out the door, into the plane, up to the heavens, down—we learned—to a near-by army hospital. I looked up manfully—into a score of man-eating eyes. I put the experience down as a reversal.

18   As I write this, on an airplane, I have run out of paper and need to reach into my briefcase under my legs for more. I cannot do this until my empty lunch tray is removed from my lap. I arrested the stewardess as she passed empty-handed down the aisle on the way to the kitchen to fetch the lunch trays for the passengers up forward who haven't been served yet. "Would you please take my tray?" "Just a *moment,* sir!" she said, and marched on sternly. Shall I tell her that since she is headed for the kitchen *anyway,* it could not delay the feeding of the other passengers by more than two seconds necessary to stash away my empty tray? Or remind her that not fifteen minutes ago she spoke unctuously into the loudspeaker the words undoubtedly devised by the airline's highly paid public relations counselor: "If there is anything I or Miss French can do for you to make your trip more enjoyable, *please* let us—" I have run out of paper.

19   I think the observable reluctance of the majority of Americans to assert themselves in minor matters is related to our increased sense of helplessness in an age of technology and centralized political and economic power. For generations, Americans who were too hot, or too cold, got up and did something about it. Now we call the plumber, or the electrician, or the furnace man. The habit of looking after our own needs obviously had something to do with the assertiveness that characterized the American family familiar to readers of American literature. With the technification of life goes our direct responsibility for our material environment, and we are conditioned to adopt a position of helplessness not only as regards the broken air conditioner, but as regards the overheated train. It takes an expert to fix the former, but not the latter; yet these distinctions, as we withdraw into helplessness, tend to fade away.

20   Our notorious political apathy is a related phenomenon. Every year, whether the Republican or the Democratic Party is in office, more and more power drains away from the individual to feed vast reservoirs in far-off places; and we have less and less say about the shape of events which shape our future. From this alienation of personal power comes the sense of resignation with which we accept the political dispensations of a powerful government whose hold upon us continues to increase.

21   An editor of a national weekly news magazine told me a few years ago that as few as a dozen letters of protest against an editorial stance of his magazine was enough to convene a plenipotentiary meeting

of the board of editors to review policy. "So few people complain, or make their voices heard," he explained to me, "that we assume a dozen letters represent the inarticulated views of thousands of readers." In the past ten years, he said, the volume of mail has noticeably decreased, even though the circulation of his magazine has risen.

22   When our voices are finally mute, when we have finally suppressed the natural instinct to complain, whether the vexation is trivial or grave, we shall have become automatons, incapable of feeling. When Premier Khrushchev first came to this country late in 1959 he was primed, we are informed, to experience the bitter resentment of the American people against his tyranny, against his persecutions, against the movement which is responsible for the great number of American deaths in Korea, for billions in taxes every year, and for life everlasting on the brink of disaster; but Khrushchev was pleasantly surprised, and reported back to the Russian people that he had been met with overwhelming cordiality (read: apathy), except, to be sure, for "a few fascists who followed me around with their wretched posters, and should be horsewhipped."

23   I may be crazy, but I say there would have been lots more posters in a society where train temperatures in the dead of winter are not allowed to climb to 85 degrees without complaint.

Does America Still Exist?

Richard Rodriguez

1   For the children of immigrant parents the knowledge comes easier. America exists everywhere in the city—on billboards, frankly in the smell of French fries and popcorn. It exists in the pace: traffic lights, the assertions of neon, the mysterious bong-bong-bong through the atriums of department stores. America exists as the voice of the crowd, a menacing sound—the high nasal accent of American English.

2   When I was a boy in Sacramento (California, the fifties), people would ask me, "Where you from?" I was born in this country, but I knew the question meant to decipher my darkness, my looks.

3   My mother once instructed me to say, "I am an American of American descent." By the time I was nine or ten, I wanted to say, but dared not reply, "I am an American."

4   Immigrants come to America and, against hostility or mere loneliness, they recreate a homeland in the parlor, tacking up postcards or calendars of some impossible blue—lake or sea or sky. Children of immigrant parents are supposed to perch on a hyphen between two countries. Relatives assume the achievement as much as anyone. Relatives are, in any case, surprised when the child begins losing old ways. One day at the family picnic the boy wanders away from their spiced food and faceless stories to watch other boys play baseball in the distance.

5   There is sorrow in the American memory, guilty sorrow for having left something behind—Portugal, China, Norway. The American story is the story of immigrant children and of their children—children no longer able to speak to grandparents. The memory of exile becomes inarticulate as it passes from generation to generation, along with wedding rings and pocket watches—like some mute stone in a wad of old lace. Europe. Asia. Eden.

6   But, it needs to be said, if this is a country where one stops being Vietnamese or Italian, this is a country where one begins to be an

American. America exists as a culture and a grin, a faith and a shrug. It is clasped in a handshake, called by a first name.

7   As much as the country is joined in a common culture, however, Americans are reluctant to celebrate the process of assimilation. We pledge allegiance to diversity. America was born Protestant and bred Puritan, and the notion of community we share is derived from a seventeenth-century faith. Presidents and the pages of ninth-grade civics readers yet proclaim the orthodoxy: We are gathered together—but as individuals, with separate pasts, distinct destinies. Our society is as paradoxical as a Puritan congregation: We stand together, alone.

8   Americans have traditionally defined themselves by what they refused to include. As often, however, Americans have struggled, turned in good conscience at last to assert the great Protestant virtue of tolerance. Despite outbreaks of nativist frenzy, America has remained an immigrant country, open and true to itself.

9   Against pious emblems of rural America—soda fountain, Elks hall, Protestant church, and now shopping mall—stands the cold-hearted city, crowded with races and ambitions, curious laughter, much that is odd. Nevertheless, it is the city that has most truly represented America. In the city, however, the millions of singular lives have had no richer notion of wholeness to describe them than the idea of pluralism.

10   *"Where you from?" the American asks the immigrant child. "Mexico," the boy learns to say.*

11   Mexico, the country of my blood ancestors, offers formal contrast to the American achievement. If the United States was formed by Protestant individualism, Mexico was shaped by a medieval Catholic dream of one world. The Spanish journeyed to Mexico to plunder, and they may have gone, in God's name, with an arrogance peculiar to those who intend to convert. But through the conversion, the Indian converted the Spaniard. A new race was born, the *mestizo,* wedding European to Indian. José Vasconcelos, the Mexican philosopher, has celebrated this New World creation, proclaiming it the "cosmic race."

12   Centuries later, in a San Francisco restaurant, a Mexican-American lawyer of my acquaintance says, in English, over *salade niçoise,* that he does not intend to assimilate into gringo society. His claim is echoed by a chorus of others (Italian-Americans, Greeks, Asians) in this era of ethnic pride. The melting pot has been retired, clanking, into the museum of quaint disgrace, alongside Aunt Jemima and the Katz-

enjammer Kids. But resistance to assimilation is characteristically American. It only makes clear how inevitable the process of assimilation actually is.

13   For generations, this has been the pattern. Immigrant parents have sent their children to school (simply, they thought) to acquire the "skills" to survive in the city. The child returned home with a voice his parents barely recognized or understood, couldn't trust, and didn't like.

14   In Eastern cities—Philadelphia, New York, Boston, Baltimore— class after class gathered immigrant children to women (usually women) who stood in front of rooms full of children, changing children. So also for me in the 1950s. Irish-Catholic nuns. California. The old story. The hyphen tipped to the right, away from Mexico and toward a confusing but true American identity.

15   I speak now in the chromium American accent of my grammar school classmates—Billy Reckers, Mike Bradley, Carol Schmidt, Kathy O'Grady. . . . I believe I became like my classmates, became German, Polish, and (like my teachers) Irish. And because assimilation is always reciprocal, my classmates got something of me. (I mean sad eyes; belief in the Indian Virgin; a taste for sugar skulls on the Feast of the Dead.) In the blending, we became what our parents could never have been, and we carried America one revolution further.

16   "Does America still exist?" Americans have been asking the ques- tion for so long that to ask it again only proves our continuous link. But perhaps the question deserves to be asked with urgency—now. Since the black civil rights movement of the 1960s, our tenuous notion of a shared public life has deteriorated notably.

17   The struggle of black men and women did not eradicate racism, but it became the great moment in the life of America's conscience. Water hoses, bulldogs, blood—the images, rendered black, white, rec- tangular, passed into living rooms.

18   It is hard to look at a photograph of a crowd taken, say, in 1890 or in 1930 and not notice the absence of blacks. (It becomes an im- pertinence to wonder if America *still* exists.)

19   In the sixties, other groups of Americans learned to champion their rights by analogy to the black civil rights movement. But the heroic vision faded. Dr. Martin Luther King Jr. had spoken with Pauline eloquence of a nation that would unite Christian and Jew, old and young, rich and poor. Within a decade, the struggles of the 1960s were reduced

to a bureaucratic competition for little more than pieces of a representational pie. The quest for a portion of power became an end in itself. The metaphor for the American city of the 1970s was a committee: one black, one woman, one person under thirty. . . .

20   If the small town had sinned against America by too neatly defining who could be an American, the city's sin was a romantic secession. One noticed the romanticism in the antiwar movement—certain demonstrators who demonstrated a lack of tact or desire to persuade and seemed content to play secular protestants. One noticed the romanticism in the competition among members of "minority groups" to claim the status of Primary Victim. To Americans unconfident of their common identity, minority standing became a way of asserting individuality. Middle-class Americans—men and women clearly not the primary victims of social oppression—brandished their suffering with exuberance.

21   The dream of a single society probably died with *The Ed Sullivan Show*. The reality of America persists. Teenagers pass through big-city high schools banded in racial groups, their collars turned up to a uniform shrug. But then they graduate to jobs at the phone company or in banks, where they end up working alongside people unlike themselves. Typists and tellers walk out together at lunchtime.

22   It is easier for us as Americans to believe the obvious fact of our separateness—easier to imagine the black and white Americas prophesied by the Kerner report (broken glass, street fires)—than to recognize the reality of a city street at lunchtime. Americans are wedded by proximity to a common culture. The panhandler at one corner is related to the pamphleteer at the next who is related to the banker who is kin to the Chinese old man wearing an MIT sweatshirt. In any true national history, Thomas Jefferson begets Martin Luther King Jr. who begets the Gray Panthers. It is because we lack a vision of ourselves entire—the city street is crowded and we are each preoccupied with finding our own way home—that we lack an appropriate hymn.

23   Under my window now passes a little white girl softly rehearsing to herself a Motown obbligato.

I Remember . . .

Joyce Maynard

1   We got our TV set in 1959, when I was 5. So I can barely remember life without television. I have spent 20,000 hours of my life in front of the set. Not all of my contemporaries watched so much, but many did, and what's more, we watched the same programs, heard the same commercials, were exposed to the same end-of-show lessons. So there is, among this generation of television children, a shared history, a tremendous fund of common experience. These massive doses of TV have not affected all of us in an identical way, and it would be risky to draw broad conclusions. But if a sociologist were—rashly—to try to uncover some single most important influence on this generation, which has produced Patty Hearst and Alice Cooper and the Jesus movement and the peace movement; if he were searching for the roots of 1960's psychedelia and 1970's apathy, he would do well to look first at television.

2   My own motives are less ambitious. I know, simply, that a rerun of *I Love Lucy* or *Father Knows Best,* the theme music from *Dr. Kildare* or the sad, whistling refrain from *Lassie* can make me stand, frozen, before the set. It is as if I, and not Timmy Martin, had been stuck in an abandoned mine shaft during a thunderstorm, as if I, and not Lucy Ricardo, had dropped a diamond ring somewhere in the batter of a seven-layer cake. I didn't so much *watch* those shows when I was little; I let them wash over me. Now I study them like a psychiatrist on his own couch, looking hungrily for some clue inside the TV set to explain the person I have become.

3   I was not a dull or energyless child, or neglected by my parents. Our house was full of books and paints, and sometimes I did choose to draw or ride my bike. But the picture of my childhood that comes to mind is one of a dimly lit room in a small New Hampshire town and

a girl listening, leaden-eyed, to some talk-show rendition of "I Left My Heart in San Francisco." It is a picture of myself at age 8, wise to the ways of "Vegas," the timing of standup comics, the marriages of Zsa Zsa Gabor, the advertising slogans of Bufferin and Fab.

4   And what did all this television watching teach me? Well, I rarely swallowed the little pellets of end-of-show morals presented in the television shows I watched (that crime does not pay, that one must always obey one's parents). But I observed something of the way the world works: that life is easier if one fits in with the established conventions; that everything is easier if one has a pretty face.

5   And in the process of acquiring those melancholy truths I picked up an embarrassingly large fund of knowledge that is totally unusable (except, perhaps, ironically, on some television game show). I can hum Perry Mason's theme song or give the name of the actress who played Donna Reed's best friend. I would happily trade that knowledge for the facility with piano or ballet I might have had if I'd spent those television hours practicing music and dance instead. But something else I gained from television should be less lightly dismissed. I guess it is a sense of knowing America, not simply its vulgarities but its strengths as well: the rubber face of Lucille Ball, the lovableness of Americans on *Candid Camera,* an athlete's slow-motion grace in an instant replay on *Monday Night Football.*

6   So many hours of television I watched—hundreds of bank robberies, touch-and-go operations and barroom fights, millions of dollars' worth of refrigerators awarded to thousands of housewives who kissed dozens of game-show moderators—and yet the list of individual programs I remember is very short. One is the Beatles' appearance, the winter I was 10, on *The Ed Sullivan Show.* I remember the on-camera shooting of Lee Oswald, and the face of Jacqueline Kennedy at her husband's funeral. A few particularly marvelous episodes of the old *Dick Van Dyke Show* stand out: Laura Petrie getting her toe stuck in the bathroom faucet; Rob imagining that he's going bald. One or two *I Love Lucy, Andy Griffith* shows, a Miss America contestant who sang a number from "The Sound of Music"—dressed like a nun—and then whipped off her habit to reveal a spangled bathing suit. I remember a special five-part *Dr. Kildare* segment in which a team of doctors had to choose five patients for a lifesaving kidney machine out of eight

candidates. I remember getting up at midnight to watch Neil Armstrong land on the moon—expecting to be awed, but falling asleep instead.

7   My strongest memories are of one series and one character. Not the best, but the one that formed me more than any other, that haunts me still, and left its mark on a good-sized part of a generation: *Leave It to Beaver*. I watched that show every day after school (fresh from my own failures) and studied it, like homework, because the Cleaver family was so steady and normal—and my own was not—and because the boys had so many friends, played basketball, drank sodas, *fit in*. Watching that series and other family situation comedies was almost like taking a course in how to be an American.

8   I loved my father, but I longed secretly for a "Dad" like Ward Cleaver, who puttered in a work shed, building bookcases and oiling hinges, one who spent his Saturday afternoons playing golf or mowing the lawn or dipping his finger into cake batter whipped up by a mother in a frilly apron who spent her time going to PTA meetings and playing bridge with "the girls." Wally Cleaver, the older brother, was one of those boys destined to be captain of every team he plays on. But Beaver had his problems—often he was uncoordinated, gullible, less than perfectly honest, tricked by his older brother's friends, made fun of. He lost library books and haircut money. Once he sent away for a "free" accordion and suddenly found himself wildly in debt. Of course he got caught—he always did. I remember him so clearly, as familiar to me as a brother.

9   Occasionally I go to college campuses. Some student in the audience always mentions Beaver Cleaver, and when the name is spoken, a satisfied murmur can be heard in the crowd. Somebody—a stranger, in his 20s now—wrote to say he watches *Beaver* reruns every morning. He just wanted to share memories of the show with me and recall favorite episodes. We were not readers, after all, this stranger and I. We have no great literary tradition behind us. Our heritage is television. Wally and Beaver Cleaver were our Tom Sawyer and Huck Finn.

10   There's something terribly sad about this need to reminisce, and the lack of real stories, true experiences, to reminisce about. Partly it is that we grew up in the '60s, when life was soft, and partly that we grew up with television, which made life softer. We had Vietnam, of course, and civil-rights battles, and a brief threat of nuclear attack that led neighbors, down the block, to talk of building a fallout shelter. But

I remember the large events, like the Kennedy and King assassinations, the space launches and the war, as I experienced them through television. I watched it all from a goose-down-filled easy chair with a plate of oatmeal cookies on my lap—on television.

11   We grew up to be observers, not participants, to respond to action, not initiate it. And I think finally, it was this lack of real hardship (when we lacked for nothing else) that was our greatest hardship and that led so many among this television generation to seek out some kind of artificial pain. Some of us, for a time at least, gave up matching skirt-and-sweater sets for saffron-colored Hare Krishna robes; some gave up parents and clean-cut fiances for the romance of poverty and the excitement of crime. Rebellion like that is not so much inspired by television violence as it is brought about by television banality: it is a response not to *The Man from U.N.C.L.E.* but to *Father Knows Best.* One hears it said that hatred of an idea is closer to love than to indifference. Large and angry rejections of the bourgeois, the conventional—the Beaver Cleaver life—aren't so surprising, coming from a generation that grew up admiring those things so much.

12   Television smartened us up, expanded our minds, and then proceeded to fill them with the only kinds of knowledge it had to offer: names of Las Vegas nightclubs, brands of detergent, players of bit parts. And knowledge—accurate or not—about life: marriage as we learned about it from Ozzie and Harriet. Justice as practiced by Matt Dillon. Politics as revealed to us on the 6 o'clock news.

13   Anguished, frustrated and enraged by a decade of war in Vietnam as we saw it on the news, we became part of the news ourselves—with peace marches, rallies in the streets. But only briefly; we were easily discouraged, quick to abandon hope for change and to lose interest. That, also, comes from a television-watching childhood, I think: a short attention span, and a limpness, an inertia, acquired from too many hours spent in the easy chair, never getting up except to change the channels.

The Decline of Quality

Barbara Tuchman

1   A question raised by our culture of the last two or three decades is whether quality in product and effort has become a vanishing element of current civilization. The word "quality" has, of course, two meanings: first, the nature or essential characteristic of something, as in "His voice has the quality of command"; second, a condition of excellence implying fine quality as distinct from poor quality. The second, obviously, is my subject.

2   The discussion that follows is not, except for a few samples, based on documentary or other hard evidence according to usual historical method; rather it represents the personal reflections of an observer with half a century's awareness of and occasional participation in public affairs, supported by the study and writing of history. It offers opinion on a pervasive problem and, as opinion, should and, I hope, may be supplemented by factual studies on special areas of the problem, such as education, labor and merchandising.

3   In the hope of possibly reducing the hail of censure which is certain to greet this essay (I am thinking of going to Alaska or possibly Patagonia in the week it is published), let me say that quality, as I understand it, means investment of the best skill and effort possible to produce the finest and most admirable result possible. Its presence or absence in some degree characterizes every man-made object, service, skilled or unskilled labor—laying bricks, painting a picture, ironing shirts, practicing medicine, shoemaking, scholarship, writing a book. You do it well or you do it half-well. Materials are sound and durable or they are sleazy; method is painstaking or whatever is easiest. Quality is achieving or reaching for the highest standard as against being satisfied with the sloppy or fraudulent. It is honesty of purpose as against catering to cheap or sensational sentiment. It does not allow compromise with the second-rate.

4   When Michelangelo started work on the Sistine Chapel ceiling, five friends who were painters came to assist him and advise him in

the techniques of fresco, in which they were practiced and he was not. Finding their work not what he desired, he resolved to accomplish the whole task by himself, locked the doors of the chapel until his friends gave up and went home, and through four painful years on a scaffold carried the work to completion, as Vasari tells us, "with the utmost solicitude, labor and study." That is what makes for quality—and its cost—and what helped to make Michelangelo one of the greatest artists, if not, as some think, the greatest, of all time. Creating quality is self-nourishing. Michelangelo, Vasari goes on to say, "became more and more kindled every day by his fervor in the work and encouraged by his growing proficiency and improvement." Genius and effort go together, or if they do not, the genius will be wasted.

5   Quality, however, can be attained without genius. Art, in any case, is a slippery area for discussion of the problem, because values in the perception of art change radically from one generation to another. Everyone knows how the French Impressionists were scorned when they first exhibited, only in recent decades to reach the peak of repute and honor and what seems to be permanent popularity. Now, in our time, we are confronted by new schools of challenging, not to say puzzling, expression. In some individuals among the moderns, quality is emphatic *because* it is individual: in Louise Nevelson's impressive and innovative work, for example; in the intensity of loneliness in Hopper's mature paintings. With regard to the schools—as distinct from individuals—of Pop Art, Abstract Expressionism, Minimalism, hard-edge, scrawny-edge and whatnot, the two criteria of quality—intensive effort and honesty of purpose—often seem missing. The paintings seem thin, if not empty; one feels nothing behind the surface of the canvas. By contrast, behind the glow and mystery of a Turner, for instance, a whole world of ships and storms and eerie seas and men laboring over mountain passes stretches the imagination far beyond the canvas. It occurs to me to wonder whether museums hang the modern abstracts, and the public crowds to see them, in some vast pretense of seeing something where there is nothing; that in the present state of our culture, many do not know the difference.

6   Here we must confront the contentious question whether quality is something inherent in a given work or something socially induced—as the ultra-feminists say of sex—in the eye and period-consciousness of the beholder. I unhesitatingly opt for the inherent (as I do for sense of gender in the individual). In architecture there is something inherently

right in certain proportions of windows to wall space, or for example in the Double Cube Room at Wilton House in England. One may be an architectural illiterate and still recognize, indeed *feel,* the perfection. Any kind of illiterate will recognize a difference in quality between, let us say, Matisse's exhilarating interiors and hotel art of little waifs with big black eyes, or between Michelangelo's marble Moses or David and that school of sculpture which consists of jigsaw puzzles lying on a museum floor, or, alternatively, the ceramic Snow Whites and Bambis advertised at such fancy prices in The New Yorker.

7   The difference is not only a matter of artistic skill, but of intent. Although the Moses and David are period pieces, they are timeless, universal, noble. They were intended to be—and they are—supreme. The others fall considerably short of that measure because they are designed for lesser reasons: the ceramic princesses and companions for commercial appeal to cheap sentiment, the floor puzzles for appeal to false sentiment—that is, worship of the avant-garde for its own sake as chic.

8   These examples represent the posing of extremes in which quality versus nonquality is unmistakable. If I come closer, however, and suggest that quality is inherent in, let us say, the stark, exquisite fiction of Jean Rhys but not in "Princess Daisy," in New England's white-steepled churches but not in Howard Johnson's orange-roofed eateries, in the film "Ninotchka" but not in "Star Wars," in Fred Astaire but not in Johnny Carson, I shall be pelted with accusations of failure to understand that what was once considered quality has given way under a change of social values to appreciation of new qualities and new values; that the admirers of the ceramic dolls and trash fiction and plastic furniture and television talk and entertainment shows with their idiotic laughter find something in these objects and diversions that means quality to *them*—in short, that quality is subjective. Yes, indeed, just as there are men who believe and loudly insist they are sober and who stumble and weave and pass out five minutes later. The judgment is subjective but the condition is not.

9   Contemporary life undeniably marks many improvements over the past, in freedom and nonconformity and most strikingly in material welfare. Such fine devices as the microchips that govern computer systems, a lifesaving mechanism like the cardiac pacemaker, drip-water techniques that permit arid-zone agriculture and a thousand other de-

velopments that have added to human efficiency and well-being may be cited as evidence of modern quality. Nevertheless, these are technological and seem to me to belong to a different scheme of things from the creative components of civilized life.

10   In two other areas, morals and politics, loss of quality is widely felt, but as I am not sure that the present level in these areas is much lower than at many other periods in history, I shall leave them out of the discussion.

11   In labor and culture, standards are certainly lower. Everyone is conscious of the prevalence of slipshod performance in clerical, manual and bureaucratic work. Much of it is slow, late, inaccurate, inefficient, either from lack of training or lack of caring or both. Secretaries still exist who care and who produce a perfectly typed letter, but more and more letters appear like one I recently received which contained— whether owed to writer or typist—"parred" for "pared," "deline" for "decline," "in tact" for "intact," and the information that removal of portions of an author's text "eschews his political intentions."

12   The writer in this case was certainly ignorant of the meaning of the word "eschews," while it is impossible to say whether the other errors represent ignorance or simple slackness. Either way, though only a sample, no more manifest evidence could be had of what has become prevalent in many fields. Even more striking is recognition that no such letter could have been written from a reasonably literate office 10 or 15 years ago. The decline has been precipitate, perhaps as one result of the student movements of the 1960's, when learning skills [were] renounced in favor of "doing your own thing" or consciousness-raising and other exercises in self-fulfillment. It is good for the self to be fulfilled but better if coping skills are acquired first.

13   In culture the tides of trash rise a little higher by the week: in fast foods and junky clothes and cute greeting cards, in films devoted nowadays either to sadism or teen-agers and consequently either nasty or boring; in the frantic razzle-dazzle of Bloomingdale's and its proliferating imitators; in endless paperbacks of sex and slaughter, Gothics and westerns; in the advertising of sensation-fiction which presents each book as the ultimate in horror, catastrophe, political plot or world crime, each by an unknown author who is never heard from again—fortunately.

14   Examining the evidence, one could apply a system of Q and non-Q for quality, on the model of the famous system of U (for upper-class)

and non-U in language sponsored by Nancy Mitford. Her categories were devised to distinguish social class, which brings us to the dangerous problem of the relationship of quality to class.

15   Quality is undeniably, though not necessarily, related to class, not in its nature but in circumstances. In former times, the princely patron had the resources in wealth and power to commission the finest workmanship, materials and design. Since his motive was generally self-glorification, the result was as beautiful and magnificent as he could command: in crystal and gold and tapestry, in exquisite silks and brocades, in the jeweled and enameled masterpieces of Cellini, the carved staircases of Grinling Gibbons. It is also true that cities and states caused works of equal value to be created not for individual glory but for the good of the whole, as in the Greek temples and theaters, the Colosseum of Rome, the Gothic cathedrals, the public parks of London.

16   The decline that has since set in has a good historical reason: The age of privilege is over and civilization has passed into the age of the masses. The many exceptions that can be made to this statement do not invalidate it. No change takes place wholly or all at once and many components of privilege and of capitalist control remain functioning parts of society and will, I expect, continue as such for some time. Nevertheless, the turn has taken place, with the result that our culture has been taken over by commercialism directed to the mass market and necessarily to mass taste. De Tocqueville stated the problem, already appearing in his time, succinctly when he wrote, "When only the wealthy had watches they were very good ones; few are now made that are worth much but everyone has one in his pocket."

17   In the absence of the princely patron, the public is now the consumer, or if government is the patron, it is answerable to the public. The criterion for the goods and services and arts that society produces is the pleasure and purchasing power of the greatest number, not of the most discerning. Therein lies the history of non-Q. Arts and luxuries may still be directed to the few and most discerning, but when the dominant culture is mass-directed and the rewards in money and celebrity go with it, we have to consider whether popular appeal will become the governing criterion and gradually submerge all but isolated rocks of quality.

18   Will the tides of trash obey Gresham's law to the effect that bad money drives out good? This means, I am told, that as between two

coinages of equal denomination but different intrinsic value in gold or silver content, the one of lesser will drive out the one of higher value. I do not know whether, according to our ever-flexible economists, Gresham's law remains valid, but as regards quality in culture, it has gloomy implications.

19   Quality cannot be put down altogether. As the would-be philosopher said of cheerfulness, it keeps breaking in, and I suspect always will. It appears in the crafts movement that, in a reaction to floods of the tawdry, has been expanding in the last decade, producing fine handwoven fabrics and handmade utensils and ornaments of pottery, glass and wood. There are art and design in these and individual skills that make for Q. We come across Q here and there in every field of endeavor, from a symphony orchestra to a well-run grocery and on the covers of the Audubon bimonthly magazine. For all its appearances we are grateful and by them encouraged, yet we have to recognize that the prevailing tendency is non-Q.

20   This is not confined to the taste of the masses. It reaches into the richer ranks, where purchasing power has outdistanced cultivated judgment. Persons in this difficulty tend to buy purses and scarfs and various garments—even sheets—adorned with the designer's or manufacturer's initials in the illusion that, without risking individual judgment, they are thus acquiring the stamp of Q. In fact, they are merely proclaiming that they lack reliable taste of their own. If I were to adopt the Mitford tone, I would have to say that wearing anything bearing commercial initials is definitely non-Q.

21   Most of the products of non-Q have the economic excuse that they supply needs to pocketbooks that can afford them. An entire level of society has arisen that can now afford to obtain goods, services and entertainment formerly beyond its means. Consequently these are now produced at a price level attractive to the greatest number of consumers and likewise at a cultural level, or level of taste, that presumably the greatest number wants or will respond to. Whether the merchandiser or advertiser is invariably a good judge of what the public wants is open to doubt. Whereas one used naively to believe that, under the infallible test of profit, business knew what it was doing, we have now witnessed the most monumental goof in business history committed by the very king of American enterprise, the auto industry. If Detroit with all its resources errs, can the rest be far behind?

22   A question that puzzles me is why inexpensive things must be ugly; why walking through the aisles in a discount chain store causes acute discomfort in the esthetic nerve cells. I have heard it suggested that raucous colors and hideous decoration are meant to distract the purchaser's eye from shoddy workmanship, but since that only results in a remedy worse than the disease, it cannot be the whole explanation. One had supposed that ugly, oversize packaging obeyed some mysterious law of merchandising, the merchandisers having proved that if the package were neat, discreet and elegant, it would not sell. I wonder if they really know this, based on careful tests, with controls, of consumer response, or whether gratuitous ugliness is not just a presumption of what the public is supposed to like. The automobile companies thought they knew too and they were so wrong that the taxpayer is now bailing them out in survival loans and unemployment insurance to the workers they had to let go.

23   I do not see why the presumption cannot be made the other way: that the consumer would respond to good design rather than bad, and to quality insofar as it can be mass-produced, rather than junk. The answer will doubtless be that when this experiment has been tried the mass of consumers fails to respond. For this failure, I believe, two institutions of our culture are largely to blame: education and advertising.

24   We have some superb schools, public and private, in this country but the dominant tendency, once again, is non-Q. Education for the majority has slipped to a level undemanding of effort, satisfied with the least, lacking respect for its own values, and actually teaching very little. We read in the press that, despite the anxious concern and experiments of educators, college-entrance scores are sinking and the national rate of schoolchildren reading at below-grade levels hovers at 50 percent. The common tendency is to blame television, and while I suppose that the two-minute attention span it fosters, and the passive involvement of the viewer, must negatively affect the learning process, I suspect something more basic is at fault.

25   That something, I believe, lies in new attitudes toward both teaching and learning. Schoolchildren are not taught to work. Homework is frivolous or absent. The idea has grown that learning must be fun; students must study what they like, therefore courses have largely become elective. Work is left to the highly motivated, and failure for the

others does not matter because, owing to certain socially concerned but ill-conceived rules, students in many school systems cannot be flunked. Except by the few who learn because they cannot be stopped, the coping skills society needs are not acquired by the promoted failures, and the gulf between the few and the mass will widen.

26   Further, one becomes aware through occasional glimpses into curriculums, that subject matter makes increasing concessions to junk. Where are the summer reading lists and book reports of former years? A high-school student of my acquaintance in affluent suburbia was recently assigned by his English teacher, no less, to watch television for a week and keep a record on 3-by-5 index cards of what he had seen. This in the literature of Shakespeare to Mark Twain, Jane Austen to J. D. Salinger! How will the young become acquainted with quality if they are not exposed to it?

27   The effect appears at the next level. A professor of classics at a major Eastern university told me recently that, in a discussion with his students of the heroes of Greek legend, he tried to elicit their concept of the hero without success, and resorted to asking if anyone could name a hero. Only one student, a girl, raised her hand, and replied "Dustin Hoffman."

28   I feel sure that Mr. Hoffman, whose real persona is not at stake, will forgive his name being used to illustrate a case of modern know-nothingism. The girl neither knew what a hero was, nor apparently that an actor represents a character without being it. If she could not distinguish between make-believe and real, her school is unlikely to have equipped her to distinguish between quality and vulgarity or fraud, between Q and non-Q. She does not know the difference. Consequently, when the market offers her junk, she and her contemporaries buy it and listen to it and wear it because that is all they know.

29   Advertising augments the condition. From infancy to adulthood, advertising is the air Americans breathe, the information we absorb, almost without knowing it. It floods our minds with pictures of perfection and goals of happiness easy to attain. Face cream will banish age, decaffeinated coffee will banish nerves, floor wax will bring in neighbors for a cheery bridge game or gossip, grandchildren will love you if your disposition improves with the right laxative, storekeepers and pharmacists overflow with sound avuncular advice, the right beer endows you with hearty masculine identity, and almost anything from deodor-

ants to cigarettes, toothpaste, hair shampoo and lately even antacids will bring love affairs, usually on horseback or on a beach. Moreover, all the people engaged in these delights are beautiful. Dare I suggest that this is not the true world? We are feeding on foolery, of which a steady diet, for those who feed on little else, cannot help but leave a certain fuzziness of perceptions.

30   When it comes to standards of labor, the uncomfortable fact must be faced that decline in quality of work is connected with the rise in the security of the worker. No one likes to admit this, because it is depressing and because it does not fit into the sentimental conviction that all's well that is meant well, that good things have only good results. The unhappy fact is that they have mixed results. Work may be a satisfaction to those who can choose their own line of endeavor and who enjoy what they do, but for the majority work is a more or less disagreeable necessity. Therefore, when holding a job no longer depends upon quality of performance but on union rules and bureaucratic protections, the incentive to excellent work is reduced. Like the failing student who cannot be flunked, the inadequate worker cannot be fired, short of some extreme dereliction. If he is laid off or quits for reasons of his own, unemployment insurance provides a temporary substitute for the pay envelope and, in the long run, the various supports of social welfare preclude destitution.

31   No one this side of the lunatic fringe suggests that these rights and protections of labor should be abandoned or weakened because loss of quality has been part of their price. Gain in one aspect of society generally means loss in another, and social gain in the well-being of the masses has been the major development of the last two centuries. We have put a floor under misery in the West and few would wish it removed because its measures have been abused. The privileged abuse their opportunities too, by monopolies, trusts, graft, bribery, tax evasion, pollution—and with far higher returns. At whatever cost, the working class has obtained access to comforts and pleasures, possessions and vacations that have changed immeasurably not only their lives but the whole of our economy and culture. On balance, this is social progress, but let us not suppose it has been unalloyed.

32   Other factors have played a part: The alienating nature of the assembly line and mass production is one, but this has been present since the Industrial Revolution. The great change has come with the

complacency of—on the whole, in America—a comfortable society (previous to present inflation and recession). As in education, the change has been in attitude. The pressures and needs that once drove us have relaxed. Today's watchword is "Why knock yourself out?" The Asians in our midst—Koreans who put a whole family to work in a grocery of neat, washed, fresh produce, and stay open for 24 hours—exemplify the difference.

33   What of prognosis? The new egalitarians would like to make the whole question of quality vanish by adopting a flat philosophy of the equality of everything. No fact or event is of greater or less value than any other; no person or thing is superior or inferior to any other. Any reference to quality is instantly castigated as elitism, which seems to inspire in users of the word the sentiments of Jacobins denouncing aristos to the guillotine.

34   In fact, elitism is the equivalent of quality. Without it, management of everything would be on a par with the United States Postal Service, which, mercifully, is not yet quite the case. Difference in capacity does exist and superiority makes itself felt. It wins the ski race and promotion on the job and admission to the college of its choice. There are A students and D students, and their lives and fortunes will be different. I do not know if egalitarianism applies to horses, but if so how does it account for Seattle Slew and Affirmed sweeping the triple crown; and if all are equal, why do we hold horse races? Given the evidence of daily life, the egalitarian credo must be difficult to maintain and succeeds, I imagine, in deceiving chiefly its advocates.

35   However, because egalitarianism obviously appeals to those least likely to excel—and they are many—its appeal is wide, and not altogether harmless. It sponsors mediocrity, which, as we learned a few years ago on the occasion of President Nixon's nomination of Judge G. Harrold Carswell to the Supreme Court, has an important constituency in this country. The general criticism of Carswell as mediocre prompted from Senator Roman L. Hruska of Nebraska one of the historic remarks of the century. He did not think Carswell should be disqualified on the grounds of an undistinguished judicial career, because, he said, "Even if he were mediocre, there are a lot of mediocre judges and people and lawyers and they are entitled to a little representation, aren't they?"

36   The more I ponder this idea of a seat for mediocrity on the Supreme Court, the more it haunts me. The Hruska Principle is only a logical

extension, after all, of majority rule, and if carried to its logical conclusion must mean that the mediocre shall inherit the earth. (Carswell
was rejected, of course, but for alleged racism, not for mediocrity.)

37   In the 18th century, Montesquieu saw political egalitarianism as
a "dangerous fallacy" that could lead only to incompetence—and, he
added, mob control, by which he meant democracy. We are less afraid
of democracy than he was because we already have it, but growing
incompetence is undoubtedly a feature of contemporary life, although
it is not necessarily an attribute of democracy. There never was greater
incompetence than in the Bourbon monarchy in the last decade before
the French Revolution. It brought the old regime down in ruins, but we
need not take that precedent too closely to heart for, despite present
appearances, I think our society has built itself more safeguards and a
firmer foundation.

38   I cannot believe we shall founder under the rising tide of incompetence and trash. Perhaps that is merely a matter of temperament; it
is difficult to believe in fatality. Although I know we have already
grown accustomed to less beauty, less elegance, less excellence—and
less hypocrisy, too—yet perversely I have confidence in the opposite
of egalitarianism: in the competence and excellence of the best among
us. I meet this often enough, if not quite as often as the reverse, to
believe that the urge for the best is an element of humankind as inherent
as the heartbeat. It does not command society, and it may be crushed
temporarily in a period of heavy non-Q, but it cannot be eliminated. If
incompetence does not kill us first, Q will continue the combat against
numbers. It will not win, but it will provide a refuge for the trash-
beleaguered. It will supply scattered beauty, pride in accomplishment,
the charm of fine things—and it will win horse races. As long as people
exist, some will always strive for the best; some will attain it.

Were Dinosaurs Dumb?

Stephen Jay Gould

1   When Muhammad Ali flunked his army intelligence test, he quipped (with a wit that belied his performance on the exam): "I only said I was the greatest; I never said I was the smartest." In our metaphors and fairy tales, size and power are almost always balanced by a want of intelligence. Cunning is the refuge of the little guy. Think of Br'er Rabbit and Br'er Bear; David smiting Goliath with a slingshot; Jack chopping down the beanstalk. Slow wit is the tragic flaw of a giant.

2   The discovery of dinosaurs in the nineteenth century provided, or so it appeared, a quintessential case for the negative correlation of size and smarts. With their pea brains and giant bodies, dinosaurs became a symbol of lumbering stupidity. Their extinction seemed only to confirm their flawed design.

3   Dinosaurs were not even granted the usual solace of a giant— great physical prowess. God maintained a discreet silence about the brains of behemoth, but he certainly marveled at its strength: "Lo, now, his strength is in his loins, and his force is in the navel of his belly. He moveth his tail like a cedar. . . . His bones are as strong pieces of brass; his bones are like bars of iron [Job 40:16–18]." Dinosaurs, on the other hand, have usually been reconstructed as slow and clumsy. In the standard illustration, *Brontosaurus* wades in a murky pond because he cannot hold up his own weight on land.

4   Popularizations for grade school curricula provide a good illustration of prevailing orthodoxy. I still have my third grade copy (1948 edition) of Bertha Morris Parker's *Animals of Yesterday,* stolen, I am forced to suppose, from P.S. 26, Queens (sorry Mrs. McInerney). In it, boy (teleported back to the Jurassic) meets brontosaur:

> It is huge, and you can tell from the size of its head that it must be stupid. . . . This giant animal moves about very slowly as it eats. No wonder it moves slowly! Its huge feet are very heavy, and its great tail

is not easy to pull around. You are not surprised that the thunder lizard likes to stay in the water so that the water will help it hold up its huge body. . . .Giant dinosaurs were once the lords of the earth. Why did they disappear? You can probably guess part of the answer—their bodies were too large for their brains. If their bodies had been smaller, and their brains larger, they might have lived on.

5   Dinosaurs have been making a strong comeback of late, in this age of "I'm OK, you're OK." Most paleontologists are now willing to view them as energetic, active, and capable animals. The *Brontosaurus* that wallowed in its pond a generation ago is now running on land, while pairs of males have been seen twining their necks about each other in elaborate sexual combat for access to females (much like the neck wrestling of giraffes). Modern anatomical reconstructions indicate strength and agility, and many paleontologists now believe that dinosaurs were warmblooded. . . .

6   The idea of warmblooded dinosaurs has captured the public imagination and received a torrent of press coverage. Yet another vindication of dinosaurian capability has received very little attention, although I regard it as equally significant. I refer to the issue of stupidity and its correlation with size. The revisionist interpretation, which I support in this column, does not enshrine dinosaurs as paragons of intellect, but it does maintain that they were not small brained after all. They had the "right-sized" brains for reptiles of their body size.

7   I don't wish to deny that the flattened, minuscule head of large-bodied *Stegosaurus* houses little brain from our subjective, top-heavy perspective, but I do wish to assert that we should not expect more of the beast. First of all, large animals have relatively smaller brains than related, small animals. The correlation of brain size with body size among kindred animals (all reptiles, all mammals, for example) is remarkably regular. As we move from small to large animals, from mice to elephants or small lizards to Komodo dragons, brain size increases, but not so fast as body size. In other words, bodies grow faster than brains, and large animals have low ratios of brain weight to body weight. In fact, brains grow only about two-thirds as fast as bodies. Since we have no reason to believe that large animals are consistently stupider than their smaller relatives, we must conclude that large animals require

relatively less brain to do as well as smaller animals. If we do not recognize this relationship, we are likely to underestimate the mental power of very large animals, dinosaurs in particular.

8   Second, the relationship between brain and body size is not identical in all groups of vertebrates. All share the same rate of relative decrease in brain size, but small mammals have much larger brains than small reptiles of the same body weight. This discrepancy is maintained at all larger body weights, since brain size increases at the same rate in both groups—two-thirds as fast as body size.

9   Put these two facts together—all large animals have relatively small brains, and reptiles have much smaller brains than mammals at any common body weight—and what should we expect from a normal, large reptile? The answer, of course, is a brain of very modest size. No living reptile even approaches a middle-sized dinosaur in bulk, so we have no modern standard to serve as a model for dinosaurs.

10   Fortunately, our imperfect fossil record has, for once, not severely disappointed us in providing data about fossil brains. Superbly preserved skulls have been found for many species of dinosaurs, and cranial capacities can be measured. (Since brains do not fill craniums in reptiles, some creative, although not unreasonable, manipulation must be applied to estimate brain size from the hole within a skull.) With these data, we have a clear test for the conventional hypothesis of dinosaurian stupidity. We should agree, at the outset, that a reptilian standard is the only proper one—it is surely irrelevant that dinosaurs had smaller brains than people or whales. We have abundant data on the relationship of brain and body size in modern reptiles. Since we know that brains increase two-thirds as fast as bodies as we move from small to large living species, we can extrapolate this rate to dinosaurian sizes and ask whether dinosaur brains match what we would expect of living reptiles if they grew so large.

11   Harry Jerison studied the brain sizes of ten dinosaurs and found that they fell right on the extrapolated reptilian curve. Dinosaurs did not have small brains; they maintained just the right-sized brains for reptiles of their dimensions. So much for Ms. Parker's explanation of their demise.

12   Jerison made no attempt to distinguish among various kinds of dinosaurs; ten species distributed over six major groups scarcely provide

a proper basis for comparison. Recently, James A. Hopson of the University of Chicago gathered more data and made a remarkable and satisfying discovery.

13   Hopson needed a common scale for all dinosaurs. He therefore compared each dinosaur brain with the average reptilian brain we would expect at its body weight. If the dinosaur falls on the standard reptilian curve, its brain receives a value of 1.0 (called an encephalization quotient, or EQ—the ratio of actual brain to expected brain for a standard reptile of the same body weight). Dinosaurs lying above the curve (more brain than expected in a standard reptile of the same body weight) receive values in excess of 1.0, while those below the curve measure less than 1.0.

14   Hopson found that the major groups of dinosaurs can be ranked by increasing values of average EQ. This ranking corresponds perfectly with inferred speed, agility and behavioral complexity in feeding (or avoiding the prospect of becoming a meal). The giant sauropods, *Brontosaurus* and its allies, have the lowest EQ's—0.20 to 0.35. They must have moved fairly slowly and without great maneuverability. They probably escaped predation by virtue of their bulk alone, much as elephants do today. The armored ankylosaurs and stegosaurs come next with EQ's of 0.52 to 0.56. These animals, with their heavy armor, probably relied largely upon passive defense, but the clubbed tail of ankylosaurs and the spiked tail of stegosaurs imply some active fighting and increased behavioral complexity.

15   The ceratopsians rank next at about 0.7 to 0.9. Hopson remarks: "The larger ceratopsians, with their great horned heads, relied on active defensive strategies and presumably required somewhat greater agility than the tail-weaponed forms, both in fending off predators and in intraspecific combat bouts. The smaller ceratopsians, lacking true horns, would have relied on sensory acuity and speed to escape from predators." The ornithopods (duckbills and their allies) were the brainiest herbivores, with EQ's from 0.85 to 1.5. They relied upon "acute senses and relatively fast speeds" to elude carnivores. Flight seems to require more acuity and agility than standing defense. Among ceratopsians, small, hornless, and presumably fleeing *Protoceratops* had a higher EQ than great three-horned *Triceratops*.

16   Carnivores have higher EQ's than herbivores, as in modern vertebrates. Catching a rapidly moving or stoutly fighting prey demands a

good deal more upstairs than plucking the right kind of plant. The giant theropods (*Tyrannosaurus* and its allies) vary from 1.0 to nearly 2.0. Atop the heap, quite appropriately at its small size, rests the little coelurosaur *Stenonychosaurus* with an EQ well above 5.0. Its actively moving quarry, small mammals and birds perhaps, probably posed a greater challenge in discovery and capture than *Triceratops* afforded *Tyrannosaurus*.

17   I do not wish to make a naive claim that brain size equals intelligence or, in this case, behavioral range and agility (I don't know what intelligence means in humans, much less in a group of extinct reptiles). Variation in brain size within a species has precious little to do with brain power (humans do equally well with 900 or 2,500 cubic centimeters of brain). But comparison across species, when the differences are large, seems reasonable. I do not regard it as irrelevant to our achievements that we so greatly exceed koala bears—much as I love them—in EQ. The sensible ordering among dinosaurs also indicates that even so coarse a measure as brain size counts for something.

18   If behavioral complexity is one consequence of mental power, then we might expect to uncover among dinosaurs some signs of social behavior that demand coordination, cohesiveness, and recognition. Indeed we do, and it cannot be accidental that these signs were overlooked when dinosaurs labored under the burden of a falsely imposed obtuseness. Multiple trackways have been uncovered, with evidence for more than twenty animals traveling together in parallel movement. Did some dinosaurs live in herds? At the Davenport Ranch sauropod trackway, small footprints lie in the center and larger ones at the periphery. Could it be that some dinosaurs traveled much as some advanced herbivorous mammals do today, with large adults at the borders sheltering juveniles in the center?

19   In addition, the very structures that seemed most bizarre and useless to older paleontologists—the elaborate crests of hadrosaurs, the frills and horns of ceratopsians, and the nine inches of solid bone above the brain of *Pachycephalosaurus*—now appear to gain a coordinated explanation as devices for sexual display and combat. Pachycephalosaurs may have engaged in head-butting contests much as mountain sheep do today. The crests of some hadrosaurs are well designed as resonating chambers; did they engage in bellowing matches? The ceratopsian horn and frill may have acted as sword and shield in the battle

for mates. Since such behavior is not only intrinsically complex, but also implies an elaborate social system, we would scarcely expect to find it in a group of animals barely muddling through at a moronic level.

20   But the best illustration of dinosaurian capability may well be the fact most often cited against them—their demise. Extinction, for most people, carries many of the connotations attributed to sex not so long ago—a rather disreputable business, frequent in occurrence, but not to anyone's credit, and certainly not to be discussed in proper circles. But, like sex, extinction is an ineluctable part of life. It is the ultimate fate of all species, not the lot of unfortunate and ill-designed creatures. It is no sign of failure.

21   The remarkable thing about dinosaurs is not that they became extinct, but that they dominated the earth for so long. Dinosaurs held sway for 100 million years while mammals, all the while, lived as small animals in the interstices of their world. After 70 million years on top, we mammals have an excellent track record and good prospects for the future, but we have yet to display the staying power of dinosaurs.

22   People, on this criterion, are scarcely worth mentioning—5 million years perhaps since *Australopithecus,* a mere 50,000 for our own species, *Homo sapiens.* Try the ultimate test within our system of values: Do you know anyone who would wager a substantial sum, even at favorable odds, on the proposition that *Homo sapiens* will last longer than *Brontosaurus?*

The Patterns of Eating

Peter Farb
George Armelagos

1   Among the important societal rules that represent one component of cuisine are table manners. As a socially instilled form of conduct, they reveal the attitudes typical of a society. Changes in table manners through time, as they have been documented for western Europe, likewise reflect fundamental changes in human relationships. Medieval courtiers saw their table manners as distinguishing them from crude peasants; but by modern standards, the manners were not exactly refined. Feudal lords used their unwashed hands to scoop food from a common bowl and they passed around a single goblet from which all drank. A finger or two would be extended while eating, so as to be kept free of grease and thus available for the next course, or for dipping into spices and condiments—possibly accounting for today's "polite" custom of extending the finger while holding a spoon or small fork. Soups and sauces were commonly drunk by lifting the bowl to the mouth; several diners frequently ate from the same bread trencher. Even lords and nobles would toss gnawed bones back into the common dish, wolf down their food, spit onto the table (preferred conduct called for spitting under it), and blew their noses into the tablecloth.

2   By about the beginning of the sixteenth century, table manners began to move in the direction of today's standards. The importance attached to them is indicated by the phenomenal success of a treatise, *On Civility in Children,* by the philosopher Erasmus, which appeared in 1530; reprinted more than thirty times in the next six years, it also appeared in numerous translations. Erasmus' idea of good table manners was far from modern, but it did represent an advance. He believed, for example, that an upper class diner was distinguished by putting only three fingers of one hand into the bowl, instead of the entire hand in the manner of the lower class. Wait a few moments after being seated

before you dip into it, he advises. Do not poke around in your dish, but take the first piece you touch. Do not put chewed food from the mouth back on your plate; instead, throw it under the table or behind your chair.

3   By the time of Erasmus, the changing table manners reveal a fundamental shift in society. People no longer ate from the same dish or drank from the same goblet, but were divided from one another by a new wall of constraint. Once the spontaneous, direct, and informal manners of the Middle Ages had been repressed, people began to feel shame. Defecation and urination were now regarded as private activities; handkerchiefs came into use for blowing the nose; nightclothes were now worn, and bedrooms were set apart as private areas. Before the sixteenth century, even nobles ate in their vast kitchens; only then did a special room designated for eating come into use away from the bloody sides of meat, the animals about to be slaughtered, and the bustling servants. These new inhibitions became the essence of "civilized" behavior, distinguishing adults from children, the upper classes from the lower, and Europeans from the "savages" then being discovered around the world. Restraint in eating habits became more marked in the centuries that followed. By about 1800, napkins were in common use, and before long they were placed on the thighs rather than wrapped around the neck; coffee and tea were no longer slurped out of the saucer; bread was genteelly broken into small pieces with the fingers rather than cut into large chunks with a knife.

4   Numerous paintings that depict meals—with subjects such as the Last Supper, the wedding at Cana, or Herod's feast—show what dining tables looked like before the seventeenth century. Forks were not depicted until about 1600 (when Jacopo Bassano painted one in a Last Supper), and very few spoons were shown. At least one knife is always depicted—an especially large one when it is the only one available for all the guests—but small individual knives were often at each place. Tin disks or oval pieces of wood had already replaced the bread trenchers. This change in eating utensils typified the new table manners in Europe. (In many other parts of the world, no utensils at all were used. In the Near East, for example, it was traditional to bring food to the mouth with the fingers of the right hand, the left being unacceptable because it was reserved for wiping the buttocks.) Utensils were employed in part because of a change in the attitude toward meat. During the Middle Ages, whole sides of meat, or even an entire dead animal,

had been brought to the table and then carved in view of the diners. Beginning in the seventeenth century, at first in France but later elsewhere, the practice began to go out of fashion. One reason was that the family was ceasing to be a production unit that did its own slaughtering; as that function was transferred to specialists outside the home, the family became essentially a consumption unit. In addition, the size of the family was decreasing, and consequently whole animals, or even large parts of them, were uneconomical. The cuisines of Europe reflected these social and economic changes. The animal origin of meat dishes was concealed by the arts of preparation. Meat itself became distasteful to look upon, and carving was moved out of sight to the kitchen. Comparable changes had already taken place in Chinese cuisine, with meat being cut up beforehand, unobserved by the diners. England was an exception to the change in Europe, and in its former colonies—the United States, Canada, Australia, and South Africa—the custom has persisted of bringing a joint of meat to the table to be carved.

5   Once carving was no longer considered a necessary skill among the well-bred, changes inevitably took place in the use of the knife, unquestionably the earliest utensil used for manipulating food. (In fact, the earliest English cookbooks were not so much guides to recipes as guides to carving meat.) The attitude of diners toward the knife, going back to the Middle Ages and the Renaissance, had always been ambivalent. The knife served as a utensil, but it offered a potential threat because it was also a weapon. Thus taboos were increasingly placed upon its use: It was to be held by the point with the blunt handle presented; it was not to be placed anywhere near the face; and most important, the uses to which it was put were sharply restricted. It was not to be used for cutting soft foods such as boiled eggs or fish, or round ones such as potatoes, or to be lifted from the table for courses that did not need it. In short, good table manners in Europe gradually removed the threatening aspect of the knife from social occasions. A similar change had taken place much earlier in China when the warrior was supplanted by the scholar as a cultural model. The knife was banished completely from the table in favor of chopsticks, which is why the Chinese came to regard Europeans as barbarians at their table who "eat with swords."

6   The fork in particular enabled Europeans to separate themselves from the eating process, even avoiding manual contact with their food. When the fork first appeared in Europe, toward the end of the Middle

Ages, it was used solely as an instrument for lifting chunks from the common bowl. Beginning in the sixteenth century, the fork was increasingly used by members of the upper classes—first in Italy, then in France, and finally in Germany and England. By then, social relations in western Europe had so changed that a utensil was needed to spare diners from the "uncivilized" and distasteful necessity of picking up food and putting it into the mouth with the fingers. The addition of the fork to the table was once said to be for reasons of hygiene, but this cannot be true. By the sixteenth century people were no longer eating from a common bowl but from their own plates, and since they also washed their hands before meals, their fingers were now every bit as hygienic as a fork would have been. Nor can the reason for the adoption of the fork be connected with the wish not to soil the long ruff that was worn on the sleeve at the time, since the fork was also adopted in various countries where ruffs were not then in fashion.

7   Along with the appearance of the fork, all table utensils began to change and proliferate from the sixteenth century onward. Soup was no longer eaten directly from the dish, but each diner used an individual spoon for that purpose. When a diner wanted a second helping from the serving dish, a ladle or a fresh spoon was used. More and more special utensils were developed for each kind of food: soup spoons, oyster forks, salad forks, two-tined fondue forks, blunt butter knives, special utensils for various desserts and kinds of fruit, each one differently shaped, of a different size, with differently numbered prongs and with blunt or serrated edges. The present European pattern eventually emerged, in which each person is provided with a table setting of as many as a dozen utensils at a full-course meal. With that, the separation of the human body from the taking of food became virtually complete. Good table manners dictated that even the cobs of maize were to be held by prongs inserted in each end, and the bones of lamb chops covered by ruffled paper pantalettes. Only under special conditions—as when Western people consciously imitate an earlier stage in culture at a picnic, fish fry, cookout, or campfire—do they still tear food apart with their fingers and their teeth, in a nostalgic reenactment of eating behaviors long vanished.

8   Today's neighborhood barbecue recreates a world of sharing and hospitality that becomes rarer each year. We regard as a curiosity the behavior of hunters in exotic regions. But every year millions of North

Americans take to the woods and lakes to kill a wide variety of animals—with a difference, of course: What hunters do for survival we do for sport (and also for proof of masculinity, for male bonding, and for various psychological rewards). Like hunters, too, we stuff ourselves almost whenever food is available. Nibbling on a roasted ear of maize gives us, in addition to nutrients, the satisfaction of participating in culturally simpler ways. A festive meal, however, is still thought of in Victorian terms, with the dominant male officiating over the roast, the dominant female apportioning vegetables, the extended family gathered around the table, with everything in its proper place—a revered picture, as indeed it was so painted by Norman Rockwell, yet one that becomes less accurate with each year that passes.

Chapter Eight

Cause and Effect

The Chem 20 Factor

Ellen Goodman

1   When I was in college, there was an infamous course known as
Chem 20. Organic chemistry was the sieve into which was poured every
premedical student in the university. But only those who came through
it with an A or B could reasonably expect to get into medical school.

2   Chem 20, therefore, became a psychological laboratory of pre-
med anxiety. Every class was a combat mission. Each grade was a life-
or-death matter. It reeked of Olympian anguish and Olympic compet-
itiveness. It taught people whose goal in life was the relief of pain and
suffering that only the fittest, the most single-minded, would survive.

3   I remember Chem 20 whenever I read about President Carter's
outrage at the medical establishment, or when someone sardonically
points out yet another M.D. plate on yet another Mercedes Benz, or
when the National Council on Wage and Price Stability points out that
the median income of doctors—$63,000 in 1976—has risen faster than
any other group. In short, at times when other people talk about the
M.D. as a license to make money, I think of the Chem 20 factor.

4   I know that we regard doctors as altruistic when they are treating
us and avaricious when they are billing us. But I don't think we can
understand the end result—high fees—unless we understand the process
of selection and even self-selection by which people actually do become
doctors.

5   On the whole, doctors made a commitment to go into medicine
when they were eighteen or nineteen years old, with the full knowledge
that they wouldn't be "practicing" until they were thirty or older. In a
"Now Society," they would hold the record among their peers for de-
layed gratification. The sort of laid-back, non competitive person who
wants to "live in the Moment" would drop out of Chem 20 with an
acute case of culture shock in a week.

6   It is the dedicated or the narrow-minded (choose one from column
A) who go through college competing for medical school and go through

medical school competing for a good internship and go through internship competing for a good residency.

7   Today, residency is not the financial hardship it was when most practicing doctors in this country were young. The magazine *Hospital Physician* says that the average doctor in training earns $12,500 to $15,000. But it is still basically an emotionalized physical-endurance contest.

8   It is normal for a young doctor to work an eighty-hour week. It is normal to work every other night and every other weekend. It is normal to be cut off for ten years from anything approaching a rich personal life. It is normal to come to regard the world as a hierarchy and a ladder to be climbed. It is, after all, the Chem 20 factor.

9   While there are thousands of others who work long hours just to keep a toehold in solvency, there is no other professional training that is comparable in terms of sheer stress. So, many of the doctors are sustained through this training by one vision: the Big Payoff. In this society, the Big Payoff is traditionally translated into dollars.

10   The end result of the training process is doctors who are often as addicted to work as patients to morphine. And doctors who have come to genuinely believe that they are "worth" whatever fees they can charge because they "worked for it."

11   I suspect that they are searching—sometimes desperately, and often futilely—for a return on the real investment they have made: their twenties.

12   So, the government may be right when it says that medical fees are spiraling because there is no free-market economy in doctors. The law of supply and demand doesn't work very well in medicine.

13   But that is only half of the story. If they want to see the psychological side, they have to go deeper, further, back to where the system begins—back as far as Chem 20.

14   The course is still being given. Only these days, I hear, there are pre-med students who won't even share their notes.

The Nuclear Winter

Carl Sagan

Into the eternal darkness, into fire, into ice.

Dante,
The Inferno

1   Except for fools and madmen, everyone knows that nuclear war would be an unprecedented human catastrophe. A more or less typical strategic warhead has a yield of 2 megatons, the explosive equivalent of 2 million tons of TNT. But 2 million tons of TNT is about the same as all the bombs exploded in World War II—a single bomb with the explosive power of the entire Second World War but compressed into a few seconds of time and an area 30 or 40 miles across . . .

2   In a 2-megaton explosion over a fairly large city, buildings would be vaporized, people reduced to atoms and shadows, outlying structures blown down like matchsticks and raging fires ignited. And if the bomb were exploded on the ground, an enormous crater, like those that can be seen through a telescope on the surface of the Moon, would be all that remained where midtown once had been. There are now more than 50,000 nuclear weapons, more than 13,000 megatons of yield, deployed in the arsenals of the United States and the Soviet Union—enough to obliterate a million Hiroshimas.

3   But there are fewer than 3000 cities on the Earth with populations of 100,000 or more. You cannot find anything like a million Hiroshimas to obliterate. Prime military and industrial targets that are far from cities are comparatively rare. Thus, there are vastly more nuclear weapons than are needed for any plausible deterrence of a potential adversary.

4   Nobody knows, of course, how many megatons would be exploded in a real nuclear war. There are some who think that a nuclear war can be "contained," bottled up before it runs away to involve many

of the world's arsenals. But a number of detailed analyses, war games run by the U.S. Department of Defense and official Soviet pronouncements, all indicate that this containment may be too much to hope for: Once the bombs begin exploding, communications failures, disorganization, fear, the necessity of making in minutes decisions affecting the fates of millions and the immense psychological burden of knowing that your own loved ones may already have been destroyed are likely to result in a nuclear paroxysm. Many investigations, including a number of studies for the U.S. government, envision the explosion of 5000 to 10,000 megatons—the detonation of tens of thousands of nuclear weapons that now sit quietly, inconspicuously, in missile silos, submarines and long-range bombers, faithful servants awaiting orders.

5   The World Health Organization, in a recent detailed study chaired by Sune K. Bergstrom (the 1982 Nobel laureate in physiology and medicine), concludes that 1.1 billion people would be killed outright in such a nuclear war, mainly in the United States, the Soviet Union, Europe, China and Japan. An additional 1.1 billion people would suffer serious injuries and radiation sickness, for which medical help would be unavailable. It thus seems possible that more than 2 billion people—almost half of all the humans on Earth—would be destroyed in the immediate aftermath of a global thermonuclear war. This would represent by far the greatest disaster in the history of the human species and, with no other adverse effects, would probably be enough to reduce at least the Northern Hemisphere to a state of prolonged agony and barbarism. Unfortunately, the real situation would be much worse.

6   In technical studies of the consequences of nuclear weapons explosions, there has been a dangerous tendency to underestimate the results. This is partly due to a tradition of conservatism which generally works well in science but which is of more dubious applicability when the lives of billions of people are at stake. In the Bravo test of March 1, 1954, a 15-megaton thermonuclear bomb was exploded on Bikini Atoll. It had about double the yield expected, and there was an unanticipated last-minute shift in the wind direction. As a result, deadly radioactive fallout came down on Rongelap in the Marshall Islands, more than 200 kilometers away. Almost all the children on Rongelap subsequently developed thyroid nodules and lesions, and other long-term medical problems, due to the radioactive fallout.

7   Likewise, in 1973, it was discovered that high-yield airbursts will

chemically burn the nitrogen in the upper air, converting it into oxides of nitrogen; these, in turn, combine with and destroy the protective ozone in the Earth's stratosphere. The surface of the Earth is shielded from deadly solar ultraviolet radiation by a layer of ozone so tenuous that, were it brought down to sea level, it would be only 3 millimeters thick. Partial destruction of this ozone layer can have serious consequences for the biology of the entire planet.

8   These discoveries, and others like them, were made by chance. They were largely unexpected. And now another consequence—by far the most dire—has been uncovered, again more or less by accident.

9   The U.S. Mariner 9 spacecraft, the first vehicle to orbit another planet, arrived at Mars in late 1971. The planet was enveloped in a global dust storm. As the fine particles slowly fell out, we were able to measure temperature changes in the atmosphere and on the surface. Soon it became clear what had happened:

10   The dust, lofted by high winds off the desert into the upper Martian atmosphere, had absorbed the incoming sunlight and prevented much of it from reaching the ground. Heated by the sunlight, the dust warmed the adjacent air. But the surface, enveloped in partial darkness, became much chillier than usual. Months later, after the dust fell out of the atmosphere, the upper air cooled and the surface warmed, both returning to their normal conditions. We were able to calculate accurately, from how much dust there was in the atmosphere, how cool the Martian surface ought to have been.

11   Afterwards, I and my colleagues, James B. Pollack and Brian Toon of NASA's Ames Research Center, were eager to apply these insights to the Earth. In a volcanic explosion, dust aerosols are lofted into the high atmosphere. We calculated by how much the Earth's global temperature should decline after a major volcanic explosion and found that our results (generally a fraction of a degree) were in good accord with actual measurements. Joining forces with Richard Turco, who has studied the effects of nuclear weapons for many years, we then began to turn our attention to the climatic effects of nuclear war. [The scientific paper, "Global Atmospheric Consequences of Nuclear War," is written by R. P. Turco, O. B. Toon, T. P. Ackerman, J. B. Pollack and Carl Sagan. From the last names of the authors, this work is generally referred to as "TTAPS."]

12   We knew that nuclear explosions, particularly groundbursts, would

lift an enormous quantity of fine soil particles into the atmosphere (more than 100,000 tons of fine dust for every megaton exploded in a surface burst). Our work was further spurred by Paul Crutzen of the Max Planck Institute for Chemistry in Mainz, West Germany, and by John Birks of the University of Colorado, who pointed out that huge quantities of smoke would be generated in the burning of cities and forests following a nuclear war.

13   Groundbursts—at hardened missile silos, for example—generate fine dust. Airbursts—over cities and unhardened military installations—make fires and therefore smoke. The amount of dust and soot generated depends on the conduct of the war, the yields of the weapons employed and the ratio of groundbursts to airbursts. So we ran computer models for several dozen different nuclear war scenarios. Our baseline case, as in many other studies, was a 5000-megaton war with only a modest fraction of the yield (20 percent) expended on urban or industrial targets. Our job, for each case, was to follow the dust and smoke generated, see how much sunlight was absorbed and by how much the temperatures changed, figure out how the particles spread in longitude and latitude, and calculate how long before it all fell out of the air back onto the surface. Since the radioactivity would be attached to these same fine particles, our calculations also revealed the extent and timing of the subsequent radioactive fallout.

14   Some of what I am about to describe is horrifying. I know, because it horrifies me. There is a tendency—psychiatrists call it "denial"—to put it out of our minds, not to think about it. But if we are to deal intelligently, wisely, with the nuclear arms race, then we must steel ourselves to contemplate the horrors of nuclear war.

15   The results of our calculations astonished us. In the baseline case, the amount of sunlight at the ground was reduced to a few percent of normal—much darker, in daylight, than in a heavy overcast and too dark for plants to make a living from photosynthesis. At least in the Northern Hemisphere, where the great preponderance of strategic targets lies, an unbroken and deadly gloom would persist for weeks.

16   Even more unexpected were the temperatures calculated. In the baseline case, land temperatures, except for narrow strips of coastline, dropped to minus 25° Celsius (minus 13° Fahrenheit) and stayed below freezing for months—even for a summer war. (Because the atmospheric structure becomes much more stable as the upper atmosphere is heated

and the lower air is cooled, we may have severely *under*estimated how long the cold and the dark would last.) The oceans, a significant heat reservoir, would not freeze, however, and a major ice age would probably not be triggered. But because the temperatures would drop so catastrophically, virtually all crops and farm animals, at least in the Northern Hemisphere, would be destroyed, as would most varieties of uncultivated or undomesticated food supplies. Most of the human survivors would starve.

17   In addition, the amount of radioactive fallout is much more than expected. Many previous calculations simply ignored the intermediate time-scale fallout. That is, calculations were made for the prompt fallout—the plumes of radioactive debris blown downwind from each target—and for the long-term fallout, the fine radioactive particles lofted into the stratosphere that would descend about a year later, after most of the radioactivity had decayed. However, the radioactivity carried into the upper atmosphere (but not as high as the stratosphere) seems to have been largely forgotten. We found for the baseline case that roughly 30 percent of the land at northern midlatitudes could receive a radioactive dose greater than 250 rads, and that about 50 percent of northern midlatitudes could receive a dose greater than 100 rads. A 100-rad dose is the equivalent of about 1000 medical X-rays. A 400-rad dose will, more likely than not, kill you.

18   The cold, the dark and the intense radioactivity, together lasting for months, represent a severe assault on our civilization and our species. Civil and sanitary services would be wiped out. Medical facilities, drugs, the most rudimentary means for relieving the vast human suffering, would be unavailable. Any but the most elaborate shelters would be useless, quite apart from the question of what good it might be to emerge a few months later. Synthetics burned in the destruction of the cities would produce a wide variety of toxic gases, including carbon monoxide, cyanides, dioxins and furans. After the dust and soot settled out, the solar ultraviolet flux would be much larger than its present value. Immunity to disease would decline. Epidemics and pandemics would be rampant, especially after the billion or so unburied bodies began to thaw. Moreover, the combined influence of these severe and simultaneous stresses on life are likely to produce even more adverse consequences—biologists call them synergisms—that we are not yet wise enough to foresee.

19   So far, we have talked only of the Northern Hemisphere. But it now seems—unlike the case of a single nuclear weapons test—that in a real nuclear war, the heating of the vast quantities of atmospheric dust and soot in northern midlatitudes will transport these fine particles toward and across the Equator. We see just this happening in Martian dust storms. The Southern Hemisphere would experience effects that, while less severe than in the Northern Hemisphere, are nevertheless extremely ominous. The illusion with which some people in the Northern Hemisphere reassure themselves—catching an Air New Zealand flight in a time of serious international crisis, or the like—is now much less tenable, even on the narrow issue of personal survival for those with the price of a ticket.

20   But what if nuclear wars *can* be contained, and much less than 5000 megatons is detonated? Perhaps the greatest surprise in our work was that even small nuclear wars can have devastating climatic effects. We considered a war in which a mere 100 megatons were exploded, less than one percent of the world arsenals, and only in low-yield airbursts over cities. This scenario, we found, would ignite thousands of fires, and the smoke from these fires alone would be enough to generate an epoch of cold and dark almost as severe as in the 5000-megaton case. The threshold for what Richard Turco has called the Nuclear Winter is very low.

21   Could we have overlooked some important effect? The carrying of dust and soot from the Northern to the Southern Hemisphere (as well as more local atmospheric circulation) will certainly thin the clouds out over the Northern Hemisphere. But, in many cases, this thinning would be insufficient to render the climatic consequences tolerable—and every time it got better in the Northern Hemisphere, it would get worse in the Southern.

22   Our results have been carefully scrutinized by more than 100 scientists in the United States, Europe and the Soviet Union. There are still arguments on points of detail. But the overall conclusion seems to be agreed upon: There are severe and previously unanticipated global consequences of nuclear war—subfreezing temperatures in a twilit radioactive gloom lasting for months or longer.

23   Scientists initially underestimated the effects of fallout, were amazed that nuclear explosions in space disabled distant satellites, had no idea

that the fireballs from high-yield thermonuclear explosions could deplete the ozone layer and missed altogether the possible climatic effects of nuclear dust and smoke. What else have we overlooked?

24   Nuclear war is a problem that can be treated only theoretically. It is not amenable to experimentation. Conceivably, we have left something important out of our analysis, and the effects are more modest than we calculate. On the other hand, it is also possible—and, from previous experience, even likely—that there are further adverse effects that no one has yet been wise enough to recognize. With billions of lives at stake, where does conservatism lie—in assuming that the results will be better than we calculate, or worse?

25   Many biologists, considering the nuclear winter that these calculations describe, believe they carry somber implications for life on Earth. Many species of plants and animals would become extinct. Vast numbers of surviving humans would starve to death. The delicate ecological relations that bind together organisms on Earth in a fabric of mutual dependency would be torn, perhaps irreparably. There is little question that our global civilization would be destroyed. The human population would be reduced to prehistoric levels, or less. Life for any survivors would be extremely hard. And there seems to be a real possibility of the extinction of the human species.

26   It is now almost 40 years since the invention of nuclear weapons. We have not yet experienced a global thermonuclear war—although on more than one occasion we have come tremulously close. I do not think our luck can hold forever. Men and machines are fallible, as recent events remind us. Fools and madmen do exist, and sometimes rise to power. Concentrating always on the near future, we have ignored the long-term consequences of our actions. We have placed our civilization and our species in jeopardy.

27   Fortunately, it is not yet too late. We can safeguard the planetary civilization and the human family if we so choose. There is no more important or more urgent issue.

Pain Is Not the Ultimate Enemy

Norman Cousins

1   Americans are probably the most pain-conscious people on the face of the earth. For years we have had it drummed into us—in print, on radio, over television, in everyday conversation—that any hint of pain is to be banished as though it were the ultimate evil. As a result, we are becoming a nation of pill-grabbers and hypochondriacs, escalating the slightest ache into a searing ordeal.

2   We know very little about pain and what we don't know makes it hurt all the more. Indeed, no form of illiteracy in the United States is so widespread or costly as ignorance about pain—what it is, what causes it, how to deal with it without panic. Almost everyone can rattle off the names of at least a dozen drugs that can deaden pain from every conceivable cause—all the way from headaches to hemorrhoids. There is far less knowledge about the fact that about 90 percent of pain is self-limiting, that it is not always an indication of poor health, and that, most frequently, it is the result of tension, stress, worry, idleness, boredom, frustration, suppressed rage, insufficient sleep, overeating, poorly balanced diet, smoking, excessive drinking, inadequate exercise, stale air, or any of the other abuses encountered by the human body in modern society.

3   The most ignored fact of all about pain is that the best way to eliminate it is to eliminate the abuse. Instead, many people reach almost instinctively for the painkillers—aspirins, barbiturates, codeines, tranquilizers, sleeping pills, and dozens of other analgesics or desensitizing drugs.

4   Most doctors are profoundly troubled over the extent to which the medical profession today is taking on the trappings of a pain-killing industry. Their offices are overloaded with people who are morbidly but mistakenly convinced that something dreadful is about to happen to them. It is all too evident that the campaign to get people to run to a doctor at the first sign of pain has boomeranged. Physicians find it

difficult to give adequate attention to patients genuinely in need of expert diagnosis and treatment because their time is soaked up by people who have nothing wrong with them except a temporary indisposition or a psychogenic ache.

5   Patients tend to feel indignant and insulted if the physician tells them he can find no organic cause for the pain. They tend to interpret the term "psychogenic" to mean that they are complaining of nonexistent symptoms. They need to be educated about the fact that many forms of pain have no underlying physical cause but are the result, as mentioned earlier, of tension, stress, or hostile factors in the general environment. Sometimes a pain may be a manifestation of "conversion hysteria" . . . the name given by Jean Charcot to physical symptoms that have their origins in emotional disturbances.

6   Obviously, it is folly for an individual to ignore symptoms that could be a warning of a potentially serious illness. Some people are so terrified of getting bad news from a doctor that they allow their malaise to worsen, sometimes past the point of no return. Total neglect is not the answer to hypochondria. The only answer has to be increased education about the way the human body works, so that more people will be able to steer an intelligent course between promiscuous pill-popping and irresponsible disregard of genuine symptoms.

7   Of all forms of pain, none is more important for the individual to understand than the "threshold" variety. Almost everyone has a telltale ache that is triggered whenever tension or fatigue reaches a certain point. It can take the form of a migraine-type headache or a squeezing pain deep in the abdomen or cramps or a pain in the lower back or even pain in the joints. The individual who has learned how to make the correlation between such threshold pains and their cause doesn't panic when they occur; he or she does something about relieving the stress and tension. Then, if the pain persists despite the absence of apparent cause, the individual will telephone the doctor.

8   If ignorance about the nature of pain is widespread, ignorance about the way pain-killing drugs work is even more so. What is not generally understood is that many of the vaunted pain-killing drugs conceal the pain without correcting the underlying condition. They deaden the mechanism in the body that alerts the brain to the fact that something may be wrong. The body can pay a high price for suppression of pain without regard to its basic cause.

9   Professional athletes are sometimes severely disadvantaged by trainers whose job it is to keep them in action. The more famous the athlete, the greater the risk that he or she may be subjected to extreme medical measures when injury strikes. The star baseball pitcher whose arm is sore because of a torn muscle or tissue damage may need sustained rest more than anything else. But his team is battling for a place in the World Series; so the trainer or team doctor, called upon to work his magic, reaches for a strong dose of butazolidine or other powerful pain suppressants. Presto, the pain disappears! The pitcher takes his place on the mound and does superbly. That could be the last game, however, in which he is able to throw a ball with full strength. The drugs didn't repair the torn muscle or cause the damaged tissue to heal. What they did was to mask the pain, enabling the pitcher to throw hard, further damaging the torn muscle. Little wonder that so many star athletes are cut down in their prime, more the victims of overzealous treatment of their injuries than of the injuries themselves.

10   The king of all painkillers, of course, is aspirin. The U.S. Food and Drug Administration permits aspirin to be sold without prescription, but the drug, contrary to popular belief, can be dangerous and, in sustained doses, potentially lethal. Aspirin is self-administered by more people than any other drug in the world. Some people are aspirin-poppers, taking ten or more a day. What they don't know is that the smallest dose can cause internal bleeding. Even more serious perhaps is the fact that aspirin is antagonistic to collagen, which has a key role in the formation of connective tissue. Since many forms of arthritis involve disintegration of the connective tissue, the steady use of aspirin can actually intensify the underlying arthritic condition.

11   Aspirin is not the only pain-killing drug, of course, that is known to have dangerous side effects. Dr. Daphne A. Roe, of Cornell University, at a medical meeting in New York City in 1974, presented startling evidence of a wide range of hazards associated with sedatives and other pain suppressants. Some of these drugs seriously interfere with the ability of the body to metabolize food properly, producing malnutrition. In some instances, there is also the danger of bone-marrow depression, interfering with the ability of the body to replenish its blood supply.

12   Pain-killing drugs are among the greatest advances in the history of medicine. Properly used, they can be a boon in alleviating suffering

and in treating disease. But their indiscriminate and promiscuous use is making psychological cripples and chronic ailers out of millions of people. The unremitting barrage of advertising for pain-killing drugs, especially over television, has set the stage for a mass anxiety neurosis. Almost from the moment children are old enough to sit upright in front of a television screen, they are being indoctrinated into the hypochondriac's clamorous and morbid world. Little wonder so many people fear pain more than death itself.

13   It might be a good idea if concerned physicians and educators could get together to make knowledge about pain an important part of the regular school curriculum. As for the populace at large, perhaps some of the same techniques used by public-service agencies to make people cancer-conscious can be used to counteract the growing terror of pain and illness in general. People ought to know that nothing is more remarkable about the human body than its recuperative drive, given a modicum of respect. If our broadcasting stations cannot provide equal time for responses to the pain-killing advertisements, they might at least set aside a few minutes each day for common-sense remarks on the subject of pain. As for the Food and Drug Administration, it might be interesting to know why an agency that has energetically warned the American people against taking vitamins without prescriptions is doing so little to control over-the-counter sales each year of billions of pain-killing pills, some of which can do more harm than the pain they are supposed to suppress.

My Wood

E. M. Forster

1   A few years ago I wrote a book which dealt in part with the difficulties of the English in India. Feeling that they would have had no difficulties in India themselves, the Americans read the book freely. The more they read it the better it made them feel, and a cheque to the author was the result. I bought a wood with the cheque. It is not a large wood—it contains scarcely any trees, and it is intersected, blast it, by a public footpath. Still, it is the first property that I have owned, so it is right that other people should participate in my shame, and should ask themselves, in accents that will vary in horror, this very important question: What is the effect of property upon the character? Don't let's touch economics; the effect of private ownership upon the community as a whole is another question—a more important question, perhaps, but another one. Let's keep to psychology. If you own things, what's their effect on you? What's the effect on me of my wood?

2   In the first place, it makes me feel heavy. Property does have this effect. Property produces men of weight, and it was a man of weight who failed to get into the Kingdom of Heaven. He was not wicked, that unfortunate millionaire in the parable, he was only stout; he stuck out in front, not to mention behind, and as he wedged himself this way and that in the crystalline entrance and bruised his well-fed flanks, he saw beneath him a comparatively slim camel passing through the eye of a needle and being woven into the robe of God. The Gospels all through couple stoutness and slowness. They point out what is perfectly obvious, yet seldom realized: that if you have a lot of things you cannot move about a lot, that furniture requires dusting, dusters require servants, servants require insurance stamps, and the whole tangle of them makes you think twice before you accept an invitation to dinner or go for a bathe in the Jordan. Sometimes the Gospels proceed further and say with Tolstoy that property is sinful; they approach the difficult ground of asceticism here, where I cannot follow them. But as to the

immediate effects of property on people, they just show straightforward logic. It produces men of weight. Men of weight cannot, by definition, move like the lightning from the East unto the West, and the ascent of a fourteen-stone bishop into a pulpit is thus the exact antithesis of the coming of the Son of Man. My wood makes me feel heavy.

3   In the second place, it makes me feel it ought to be larger.

4   The other day I heard a twig snap in it. I was annoyed at first, for I thought that someone was blackberrying, and depreciating the value of the undergrowth. On coming nearer, I saw it was not a man who had trodden on the twig and snapped it, but a bird, and I felt pleased. My bird. The bird was not equally pleased. Ignoring the relation between us, it took fright as soon as it saw the shape of my face, and flew straight over the boundary hedge into a field, the property of Mrs. Henessy, where it sat down with a loud squawk. It had become Mrs. Henessy's bird. Something seemed grossly amiss here, something that would not have occurred had the wood been larger. I could not afford to buy Mrs. Henessy out, I dared not murder her, and limitations of this sort beset me on every side. Ahab did not want that vineyard—he only needed it to round off his property, preparatory to plotting a new curve—and all the land around my wood has become necessary to me in order to round off the wood. A boundary protects. But—poor little thing—the boundary ought in its turn to be protected. Noises on the edge of it. Children throw stones. A little more, and then a little more, until we reach the sea. Happy Canute! Happier Alexander! And after all, why should even the world be the limit of possession? A rocket containing a Union Jack, will, it is hoped, be shortly fired at the moon. Mars. Sirius. Beyond which . . . But these immensities ended by saddening me. I could not suppose that my wood was the destined nucleus of universal dominion—it is so very small and contains no mineral wealth beyond the blackberries. Nor was I comforted when Mrs. Henessy's bird took alarm for the second time and flew clean away from us all, under the belief that it belonged to itself.

5   In the third place, property makes its owner feel that he ought to do something to it. Yet he isn't sure what. A restlessness comes over him, a vague sense that he has a personality to express—the same sense which, without any vagueness, leads the artist to an act of creation. Sometimes I think I will cut down such trees as remain in the wood, at other times I want to fill up the gaps between them with new trees.

Both impulses are pretentious and empty. They are not honest movements towards money-making or beauty. They spring from a foolish desire to express myself and from an inability to enjoy what I have got. Creation, property, enjoyment form a sinister trinity in the human mind. Creation and enjoyment are both very very good, yet they are often unattainable without a material basis, and at such moments property pushes itself in as a substitute, saying, "Accept me instead—I'm good enough for all three." It is not enough. It is, as Shakespeare said of lust, "The expense of spirit in a waste of shame": it is "Before, a joy proposed; behind, a dream." Yet we don't know how to shun it. It is forced on us by our economic system as the alternative to starvation. It is also forced on us by an internal defect in the soul, by the feeling that in property may lie the germs of self-development and of exquisite or heroic deeds. Our life on earth is, and ought to be, material and carnal. But we have not yet learned to manage our materialism and carnality properly; they are still entangled with the desire for ownership, where (in the words of Dante) "Possession is one with loss."

6   And this brings us to our fourth and final point: the blackberries.

7   Blackberries are not plentiful in this meagre grove, but they are easily seen from the public footpath which traverses it, and all too easily gathered. Foxgloves, too—people will pull up the foxgloves, and ladies of an educational tendency even grub for toadstools to show them on the Monday in class. Other ladies, less educated, roll down the bracken in the arms of their gentlemen friends. There is paper, there are tins. Pray, does my wood belong to me or doesn't it? And, if it does, should I not own it best by allowing no one else to walk there? There is a wood near Lyme Regis, also cursed by a public footpath, where the owner has not hesitated on this point. He has built high stone walls each side of the path, and has spanned it by bridges, so that the public circulate like termites while he gorges on the blackberries unseen. He really does own his wood, this able chap. Dives in Hell did pretty well, but the gulf dividing him from Lazarus could be traversed by vision, and nothing traverses it here. And perhaps I shall come to this in time. I shall wall in and fence out until I really taste the sweets of property. Enormously stout, endlessly avaricious, pseudo-creative, intensely selfish, I shall weave upon my forehead the quadruple crown of possession until those nasty Bolshies come and take it off again and thrust me aside into the outer darkness.

Canadian Culture: A Brave New Spirit

Margaret Atwood

1   What does Canada have to offer besides Wayne Gretsky, the "Great White North," the first downhill gold medal won by a North American, fantastic restaurants, and cities where you can go for a walk at night without getting disemboweled, where murder is so rare that it makes the front pages, where people actually use the "Keep Our Cities Clean" bins, and where you can get twenty extra cents on your dollar? In the cultural line, for instance? Quite a lot nowadays, but it's all quite recent. Being a Canadian used to be like having a big wart on the end of your nose. Not a handicap that would put you completely out of the running; more on the order of a socially embarrassing disfigurement that for the sake of everybody, including yourself, you should have removed.

2   This was especially true for artists. When I was growing up in the late 'fifties, "Canadian" and "artist" were mutually exclusive terms, and everyone knew that to be an actor or a writer or a painter you had to go to London or New York, like Donald Sutherland, Mordecai Richler, Christopher Plummer, Margaret Laurence, and anyone else for whom cheap English china and good places to ski weren't good enough. Toronto was the place you left on the weekends for a culturally enriching trip to Buffalo, N.Y. Theater was the Earle Gray Players, who put on Shakespeare in high school auditoriums, with students supplying the crowd scenes (for *Julius Caesar* you brought your own sheet). There was no ballet or opera. A writer did well to sell a hundred copies of a book of poetry and five hundred copies of a novel, and you were lucky if you got one review and a tea put on by a local women's group. When anyone said "Canadian culture," about the only thing that came to mind was "Hockey Night in Canada." That was Toronto, and the other cities were worse.

3   Why was it like that? It wasn't that Canadians were illiterate or uninterested in matters cultural. They read lots of English and American

311

books, went to Hollywood and European movies in large numbers, flocked to imported plays and bought foreign paintings. Some blamed this state of affairs on size: Canada has an English-speaking population of a mere fourteen million or so, about the size of Australia's; and the French-speaking population is only slightly less than Sweden's. Some blamed it on the stifling Puritanism that made it impossible to import *Lady Chatterley's Lover* and divided "beer parlours" into Men Only and Ladies and Escorts sections. Some cited a deadening disease of the spirit known as "The Colonial Mentality": ex-colonies, such as New Zealand, Australia, and Canada, were doomed to see the great good place as being not where they were but back in the mystical motherland. Some noted the contempt for culture typical of frontier societies, the attitude that defined the arts as, at best, a frill and, at worst, pernicious and decadent. We still have that attitude; and at least once a year some member of Parliament causes a brief flurry by calling ballet a lot of creeps jumping around in long underwear, or asking why poets who use four-letter words should get grants. Some blamed it on the weather: how can you be creative, much less breathe, at fifty-below?

4   Despite these reasons, all of them true, all of them good, the whole picture changed suddenly in the mid-'sixties. Even Canadians—notoriously slow to recognize their own excellence, when they've managed to produce it—now realize that the country has undergone not a renaissance but a naissance over the past twenty years. Canadians still gobble up cultural imports at a great rate, just as they mainline international news and go through mountains of airplane tickets to foreign countries, but there's been an enormous shift.

5   In 1960, no one with any intellectual pretensions would have been caught reading a Canadian novel on the subway; this winter, Canadians held five of the ten slots on national bestseller lists. France has more than accepted Francophone writers such as Marie-Clair Blais from Quebec and Antonine Maillet from New Brunswick. Northrop Frye and Marshall McLuhan are, to say the least, well-known.

6   Arthur Erickson, the architect, is in considerable demand. The excellence of the National Ballet and the Royal Winnipeg Ballet are taken for granted, and no one is too surprised when Karen Kain gets rave reviews in Moscow. Toronto alone has gone from no theater companies twenty-five years ago to a present total of over forty (in North America, second only to New York); it's currently renovating the spec-

tacular Winter Garden Theatre, built in 1916 and unused for fifty years. Regional theaters are prospering from Newfoundland to British Columbia. Some of the plays they do are imports, but Canadian playwrights such as David Frenchy, Carol Bolt, James Reamay, and Rick Salutin are frequently performed as well. Toronto has fifteen or twenty dance companies ranging from tiny to huge.

7   Artists sell not only in their home towns but internationally (one thinks, for instance, of Riopelle, Jack Bush, and William Ronald). At a time when public galleries elsewhere are pulling in their horns, Ottawa is about to build a major national gallery to house its already extensive collection. Canadian studies programs are springing up all over the world, which is sometimes disconcerting to Canadians. We've been putting ourselves down for so long we can't quite believe it when places like France and Germany take us seriously.

8   Given the handicaps, why did this happen? It's a chicken-and-egg question: in this case, which came first, the excellence of the artists or audience appreciation and government support? I tend to think it was the artists, beginning with those in Quebec: but there's no doubt that the creation of the Canada Council, an arm's-length but government-funded arts granting agency, had a lot to do with the growth of the heavy money-swallowers, such as ballet companies, theater companies, and symphonies. The Council has also put money into publishing and has doled out grants to individual artists of every kind imaginable. For those who think such funding is only creeping socialism or smacks of ideological control, Canadians can only answer that, without it, we'd have to do without many of the arts.

9   This change was not without uproar. Canada, like any other country, has always been pulled two ways, inward and toward their own identity and the search for an indigenous art, outwards towards other countries and internationalism, sometimes called "internation standards." The United States has had its own episodes of conflict, notably in the 1840s, when the Anglophiles wanted American artists to do as the English did, and Young America was looking for a unique American genius. The results were Washington Irving for the Anglophiles and Melville for Young America, who didn't, however, find him American enough. The two categories are of course not mutually exclusive. International standards are appropriate for international forms, such as classical ballet and the Stratford Festival; but other kinds of creative

artists work from a locally entered vision, as they do everywhere. Is Faulkner provincial because he wrote about Mississippi instead of spies in Venice? Canadians love travel, vicarious and otherwise; but they like to look in the mirror, too.

10   The problems of being a small cold toad in a large empty puddle with a large warm toad just south of you are nowhere more evident than in the film industry. Should you make films about being a small cold toad ("Canadian Content") or should you try to appeal to the large warm toad ("Commercial Viability")? Very early on there were Canadian films (*Nanook of the North* was one of ours), but Hollywood competition and the takeover of most of the distribution left Canadian filmmakers filling an otherwise unwanted ecological niche: short shorts. The National Film Board specialized in tiny perfect films, with experimental genius Norman McLaren as its recognized leading light.

11   In the past decade there's been a film renaissance predicted at least every three years, and films have indeed been made, propped up by various forms of legislation and tax write-off; but Canada has yet to catch up with Australia in the small-budget honest-and-charming-but-with-guts category. It has too often either tried to be Hollywood and failed, or turned to moneymakers about giant leeches coming out of your armpits or whores with hearts of bankable bullion. But there are signs of a breakthrough, yet again: Ralph Thomas' *Ticket to Heaven,* about a man who gets his head vacuumed by a religious cult, played to critical shrugs in Canada but around-the-block lines in the U.S.; Don Shebib's *Heartaches,* with Margot Kidder, is doing nicely; Giles Carles' *Les Plouffes* is impressing France.

12   For the States, Canada has at the moment something else to offer. These are tough times for artists everywhere; and even in the States, land of proverbial plenty, the pinch is being felt. All the money given to the arts by the U.S. Government is sufficient to run the Pentagon for eight hours, and that was last year. Artists in the States are understandably gloomy. Under these circumstances Canada may turn out to be a new kind of role model: how to make something from nothing, against enormous odds, and survive while doing it. For the 1980s, it's a good trick to know.

The Great American Cooling Machine

Frank Trippett

1   "The greatest contribution to civilization in this century may well be air conditioning—and America leads the way." So wrote British Scholar-Politician S. F. Markham 32 years ago when a modern cooling system was still an exotic luxury. In a century that has yielded such treasures as the electric knife, spray-on deodorant and disposable diapers, anybody might question whether air conditioning is the supreme gift. There is not a whiff of doubt, however, that America is far out front in its use. As a matter of lopsided fact, the U.S. today, with a mere 5% of the population, consumes as much man-made coolness as the whole rest of the world put together.

2   Just as amazing is the speed with which this situation came to be. Air conditioning began to spread in industries as a production aid during World War II. Yet only a generation ago a chilled sanctuary during summer's stewing heat was a happy frill that ordinary people sampled only in movie houses. Today most Americans tend to take air conditioning for granted in homes, offices, factories, stores, theaters, shops, studios, schools, hotels and restaurants. They travel in chilled buses, trains, planes and private cars. Sporting events once associated with open sky and fresh air are increasingly boxed in and air cooled. Skiing still takes place outdoors, but such attractions as tennis, rodeos, football and, alas, even baseball are now often staged in synthetic climates like those of Houston's Astrodome and New Orleans' Superdome. A great many of the country's farming tractors are now, yup, air-conditioned.

3   It is thus no exaggeration to say that Americans have taken to mechanical cooling avidly and greedily. Many have become all but addicted, refusing to go places that are not air-conditioned. In Atlanta, shoppers in Lenox Square so resented having to endure natural heat while walking outdoors from chilled store to chilled store that the mall management enclosed and air-conditioned the whole sprawling shebang.

The widespread whining about Washington's raising of thermostats to a mandatory 78°F suggests that people no longer think of interior coolness as an amenity but consider it a necessity, almost a birthright, like suffrage. The existence of such a view was proved last month when a number of federal judges, sitting too high and mighty to suffer 78°, defied and denounced the Government's energy-saving order to cut back on cooling. Significantly, there was no popular outrage at this judicial insolence; many citizens probably wished that they could be so high-handed.   .

4   Everybody by now is aware that the cost of the American way is enormous, that air conditioning is an energy glutton. It uses some 9% of all electricity produced. Such an extravagance merely to provide comfort is peculiarly American and strikingly at odds with all the recent rhetoric about national sacrifice in a period of menacing energy shortages. Other modern industrial nations such as Japan, Germany and France have managed all along to thrive with mere fractions of the man-made coolness used in the U.S., and precious little of that in private dwellings. Here, so profligate has its use become that the air conditioner is almost as glaring a symptom as the automobile of the national tendency to overindulge in every technical possibility, to use every convenience to such excess that the country looks downright coddled.

5   But not everybody is aware that high cost and easy comfort are merely two of the effects of the vast cooling of America. In fact, air conditioning has substantially altered the country's character and folkways. With the dog days at hand and the thermostats ostensibly up, it is a good time to begin taking stock of what air conditioning has done besides lower the indoor temperature.

6   Many of its byproducts are so conspicuous that they are scarcely noticed. To begin with, air conditioning transformed the face of urban America by making possible those glassy, boxy, sealed-in skyscrapers on which the once humane geometrics of places like San Francisco, Boston and Manhattan have been impaled. It has been indispensable, no less, to the functioning of sensitive advanced computers, whose high operating temperatures require that they be constantly cooled. Thus, in a very real way, air conditioning has made possible the ascendancy of computerized civilization. Its cooling protection has given rise not only to moon landings, space shuttles and Skylabs but to the depersonalized punch-cardification of society that regularly gets people hot under the

collar even in swelter-proof environments. It has also reshaped the national economy and redistributed political power simply by encouraging the burgeoning of the sultry southerly swatch of the country, profoundly influencing major migration trends of people and industry. Sunbelt cities like Phoenix, Atlanta, Dallas and Houston (where shivering indoor frigidity became a mark of status) could never have mushroomed so prosperously without air conditioning; some communities—Las Vegas in the Nevada desert and Lake Havasu City on the Arizona-California border—would shrivel and die overnight if it were turned off.

7   It has, as well, seduced families into retreating into houses with closed doors and shut windows, reducing the commonalty of neighborhood life and all but obsoleting the front-porch society whose open casual folkways were an appealing hallmark of a sweatier America. Is it really surprising that the public's often noted withdrawal into self-pursuit and privatism has coincided with the epic spread of air conditioning? Though science has little studied how habitual air conditioning affects mind or body, some medical experts suggest that, like other technical avoidance of natural swings in climate, air conditioning may take a toll on the human capacity to adapt to stress. If so, air conditioning is only like many other greatly useful technical developments that liberate man from nature by increasing his productivity and power in some ways—while subtly weakening him in others.

8   Neither scholars nor pop sociologists have really got around to charting and diagnosing all the changes brought about by air conditioning. Professional observers have for years been preoccupied with the social implications of the automobile and television. Mere glancing analysis suggests that the car and TV, in their most decisive influences on American habits, have been powerfully aided and abetted by air conditioning. The car may have created all those shopping centers in the boondocks, but only air conditioning has made them attractive to mass clienteles. Similarly, the artificial cooling of the living room undoubtedly helped turn the typical American into a year-round TV addict. Without air conditioning, how many viewers would endure reruns (or even Johnny Carson) on one of those pestilential summer nights that used to send people out to collapse on the lawn or to sleep on the roof?

9   Many of the side effects of air conditioning are far from being fully pinned down. It is a reasonable suspicion, though, that controlled

climate, by inducing Congress to stay in Washington longer than it used to during the swelter season, thus presumably passing more laws, has contributed to bloated Government. One can only speculate that the advent of the supercooled bedroom may be linked to the carnal adventurism associated with the mid-century sexual revolution. Surely it is a fact—if restaurant complaints about raised thermostats are to be believed—that air conditioning induces at least expense-account diners to eat and drink more; if so, it must be credited with adding to the national fat problem.

10   Perhaps only a sophist might be tempted to tie the spread of air conditioning to the coincidentally rising divorce rate, but every attentive realist must have noticed that even a little window unit can instigate domestic tension and chronic bickering between couples composed of one who likes it on all the time and another who does not. In fact, perhaps surprisingly, not everybody likes air conditioning. The necessarily sealed rooms or buildings make some feel claustrophobic, cut off from the real world. The rush, whir and clatter of cooling units annoys others. There are even a few eccentrics who object to man-made cool simply because they like hot weather. Still, the overwhelming majority of Americans have taken to air conditioning like hogs to a wet wallow.

11   It might be tempting, and even fair, to chastise that vast majority for being spoiled rotten in their cool ascendancy. It would be more just, however, to observe that their great cooling machine carries with it a perpetual price tag that is going to provide continued and increasing chastisement during the energy crisis. Ultimately, the air conditioner, and the hermetic buildings it requires, may turn out to be a more pertinent technical symbol of the American personality than the car. While the car has been a fine sign of the American impulse to dart hither and yon about the world, the mechanical cooler more neatly suggests the maturing national compulsion to flee the natural world in favor of a technological cocoon.

12   Already architectural designers are toiling to find ways out of the technical trap represented by sealed buildings with immovable glass, ways that might let in some of the naturally cool air outside. Some have lately come up with a remarkable discovery: the openable window. Presumably, that represents progress.

Fashion and the Female Body

Anne Hollander

1   The strong appeal of female slimness in the twentieth century is usually accounted for by social and economic changes rather than through a purely aesthetic development of style. Feminine emancipation from many physical and moral restraints, the increasing popularity of sport for women, together with new possibilities for gainful employment and political power, all eventually contributed to the new physical ideal. Good sense and good health, mental and physical, were seen to be properly served by freedom and activity, and feminine clothing evolved so as to allow for these and (more importantly) for the look of these. What is meant by "modern" looks developed after the First World War with the aid of clothing that expressed (although it did not always provide) an ideal of comfort and the possibility of action.

2   The most important expressive element in this new visual conception of female dress was not the uncorseted torso but the shortened skirt. After women's skirts had risen off the ground, any given clothed woman was perceptibly smaller in scale than formerly. Hair was shortened, as well as skirts, and worn close to the head. Hats shrank. During most of the nineteenth century a fashionable woman's dress, including coiffure, headgear, and a possible muff, handbag, and parasol, had consisted of an extensive, complicated system with many different sections (sleeves, bodice, skirt, collar, train). These were all separately conceived and embellished and all tended to enlarge the total volume of the clothed body, partly by being difficult to perceive all at once. After the First World War a woman's dress came more and more to present a compact and unified visual image. This is what men's clothes had already succeeded in doing a century before. The new simplified and reduced clothes for women, although they were designed and made absolutely differently from men's clothes and out of different fabrics, nevertheless expressed the new sense of the equality of the sexes—an

equality, that is, with respect to the new character of their important differences.

3   Female sexual submissiveness, either meek or wanton, was no longer modish and no longer avowed by elements of dress. Feminine sexuality had to abandon the suggestion of plump, hidden softness and find expression in exposed, lean hardness. Women strove for the erotic appeal inherent in the racehorse and the sports car, which might be summed up as a mettlesome challenge: a vibrant, somewhat unaccountable readiness for action but only under expert guidance. This was naturally best offered in a self-contained, sleekly composed physical format: a thin body, with few layers of covering. Immanent sexuality, best expressed in a condition of stasis, was no longer the foundation of female allure. The look of possible movement became a necessary element in fashionable female beauty, and all women's clothing, whatever other messages it offered, consistently incorporated visible legs and feet into the total female image. Women, once thought to glide, were seen to walk. Even vain or fruitless or nervous activity, authorized by fashionable morbid aestheticism, came to seem preferable to immobility, idleness, passivity. The various dance crazes of the first quarter of the century undoubtedly were an expression of this restless spirit, but its most important vehicle was the movies.

4   The rapid advance of the movies as the chief popular art made the public increasingly aware of style in feminine physical movement. Movies taught everyone how ways of walking and dancing, of using the hands and moving the head and shoulders, could be incorporated into the conscious ways of wearing clothes. After about 1920 the fact that women's clothes showed such a reduction in overall volume was undoubtedly partly due to the visual need for the completely clothed body to be satisfactorily seen *in motion*. Perfect feminine beauty no longer formed a still image, ideally wrought by a Leonardo da Vinci or a Titian into an eternal icon. It had become transmuted into a photograph, a single instant that represented a sequence of instants—an ideally moving picture, even if it were momentarily still. For this kind of mobile beauty, thinness was a necessary condition.

5   The still body that is nevertheless perceived as ideally in motion seems to present a blurred image—a perpetual suggestion of all the other possible moments at which it might be seen. It seems to have a dynamic, expanding outline. The actual physical size of a human body

is made apparently larger by its movements, and if its movements are what constitute its essential visual reality, they must be what gives it its visual substance. Even if a body is perceived at a motionless instant, the possibility of enlargement by movement is implicit in the image. Before consciousness had been so much affected by photography, a body perceived as ideally still could be visually enlarged by layers of fat or clothing with aesthetic success, but a body that is perceived to be about to move must apparently replace those layers with layers of possible space to move in. The camera eye seems to fatten the figure; human eyes, trained by camera vision, demand that it be thin to start with, to allow for the same effect in direct perception. The thin female body, once considered visually meager and unsatisfying without the suggestive expansions of elaborate clothing (or of flesh, which artists sometimes had to provide), has become substantial, freighted with potential action.

6   It came about that all the varieties of female desirability conceived by the twentieth century seemed ideally housed in a thin, resilient, and bony body. Healthy innocence, sexual restlessness, creative zest, practical competence, even morbid but poetic obsessiveness and intelligence—all seemed appropriate in size ten. During the six decades following the First World War, styles in gesture, posture, and erotic emphasis have undergone many changes, but the basically slim female ideal has been maintained. Throughout all the shifting levels of bust and waist and the fluctuating taste in gluteal and mammary thrust, the bodies of women have been conceived as ideally slender, and clearly supported by bones.

The Great Person-Hole Cover Debate: A Modest Proposal for Anyone Who Thinks the Word "He" Is Just Plain Easier . . .

Lindsy Van Gelder

1   I wasn't looking for trouble. What I was looking for, actually, was a little tourist information to help me plan a camping trip to New England.

2   But there it was, on the first page of the 1979 edition of the State of Vermont *Digest of Fish and Game Laws and Regulations:* a special message of welcome from one Edward F. Kehoe, commissioner of the Vermont Fish and Game Department, to the reader and would-be camper, *i.e.,* me.

3   This person (*i.e.,* me) is called "the sportsman."

4   "We have no 'sportswomen, sportspersons, sportsboys, or sportsgirls,' " Commissioner Kehoe hastened to explain, obviously anticipating that some of us sportsfeminists might feel a bit overlooked. "But," he added, "we are pleased to report that we do have many great sportsmen who are women, as well as young people of both sexes."

5   It's just that the Fish and Game Department is trying to keep things "simple and forthright" and to respect "long-standing tradition." And anyway, we really ought to be flattered, "sportsman" being "a meaningful title being earned by a special kind of dedicated man, woman, or young person, as opposed to just any hunter, fisherman, or trapper."

6   I have heard this particular line of reasoning before. In fact, I've heard it so often that I've come to think of it as The Great Person-Hole Cover Debate, since gender-neutral manholes are invariably brought into the argument as evidence of the lengths to which humorless, Newspeak-spouting feminists will go to destroy their mother tongue.

7   Consternation about woman-handling the language comes from all sides. Sexual conservatives who see the feminist movement as a unisex plot and who long for the good olde days of *vive la différence,* when men were men and women were women, nonetheless do not rally behind the notion that the term "mankind" excludes women.

8   But most of the people who choke on expressions like "spokesperson" aren't right-wing misogynists, and this is what troubles me. Like the undoubtedly well-meaning folks at the Vermont Fish and Game Department, they tend to reassure you right up front that they're only trying to keep things "simple" and to follow "tradition," and that some of their best men are women, anyway.

9   Usually they wind up warning you, with great sincerity, that you're jeopardizing the worthy cause of women's rights by focusing on "trivial" side issues. I would like to know how anything that gets people so defensive and resistant can possibly be called "trivial," whatever else it might be.

10   The English language is alive and constantly changing. Progress—both scientific and social—is reflected in our language, or should be.

11   Not too long ago, there was a product called "flesh-colored" Band-Aids. The flesh in question was colored Caucasian. Once the civil rights movement pointed out the racism inherent in the name, it was dropped. I cannot imagine reading a thoughtful, well-intentioned company policy statement explaining that while the Band-Aids would continue to be called "flesh-colored" for old time's sake, black and brown people would now be considered honorary whites and were perfectly welcome to use them.

12   Most sensitive people manage to describe our national religious traditions as "Judeo-Christian," even though it takes a few seconds longer to say than "Christian." So why is it such a hardship to say "he or she" instead of "he"?

13   I have a modest proposal for anyone who maintains that "he" is just plain easier: since "he" has been the style for several centuries now—and since it really includes everybody anyway, right?—it seems only fair to give "she" a turn. Instead of having to ponder over the intricacies of, say, "Congressman" versus "Congress person" versus "Representative," we can simplify things by calling them all "Congresswoman."

14   Other clarifications will follow: "a woman's home is her castle. . . . " "a giant step for all womankind". . . . "all women are created
equal". . . . "Fisherwoman's Wharf." . . .

15   And don't be upset by the business letter that begins "Dear Madam,"
fellas. It means you, too.

Chapter Nine

Analogy

The Myth of the Cave

Plato

1   And now, I said, let me show in a figure how far our nature is enlightened or unenlightened:—Behold! human beings living in an underground den, which has a mouth open toward the light and reaching all along the den; here they have been from their childhood, and have their legs and necks chained so that they cannot move, and can only see before them, being prevented by the chains from turning round their heads. Above and behind them a fire is blazing at a distance, and between the fire and the and the prisoners there is a raised way; and you will see, if you look, a low wall built along the way, like the screen which marionette players have in front of them, over which they show the puppets.

2   I see.

3   And do you see, I said, men passing along the wall carrying all sorts of vessels, and statues and figures of animals made of wood and stone and various materials, which appear over the wall? Some of them are talking, others silent.

4   You have shown me a strange image, and they are strange prisoners.

5   Like ourselves, I replied; and they see only their own shadows, or the shadows of one another, which the fire throws on the opposite wall of the cave?

6   True, he said; how could they see anything but the shadows if they were never allowed to move their heads?

7   And of the objects which are being carried in like manner they would only see the shadows?

8   Yes, he said.

9   And if they were able to converse with one another, would they not suppose that they were naming what was actually before them?

10   Very true.

11 And suppose further that the prison had an echo which came from the other side, would they not be sure to fancy when one of the passers-by spoke that the voice which they heard came from the passing shadow?

12 No question, he replied.

13 To them, I said, the truth would be literally nothing but the shadows of the images.

14 That is certain.

15 And now look again, and see what will naturally follow if the prisoners are released and disabused of their error. At first, when any of them is liberated and compelled suddenly to stand up and turn his neck round and walk and look toward the light, he will suffer sharp pains; the glare will distress him, and he will be unable to see the realities of which in his former state he had seen the shadows; and then conceive some one saying to him, that what he saw before was an illusion, but that now, when he is approaching nearer to being and his eye is turned toward more real existence, he has a clearer vision—what will be his reply? And you may further imagine that his instructor is pointing to the objects as they pass and requiring him to name them— will he not be perplexed? Will he not fancy that the shadows which he formerly saw are truer than the objects which are now shown to him?

16 Far truer.

17 And if he is compelled to look straight at the light, will he not have a pain in his eyes which will make him turn away to take refuge in the objects of vision which he can see, and which he will conceive to be in reality clearer than the things which are now being shown to him?

18 True, he said.

19 And suppose once more, that he is reluctantly dragged up a steep and rugged ascent, and held fast until he is forced into the presence of the sun himself, is he not likely to be pained and irritated? When he approaches the light his eyes will be dazzled, and he will not be able to see anything at all of what are now called realities.

20 Not all in a moment, he said.

21 He will require to grow accustomed to the sight of the upper world. And first he will see the shadows best, next the reflections of men and other objects in the water, and then the objects themselves; then he will gaze upon the light of the moon and the stars and the

spangled heaven; and he will see the sky and the stars by night better than the sun or the light of the sun by day?

22   Certainly.

23   Last of all he will be able to see the sun, and not mere reflections of him in the water, but he will see him in his own proper place, and not in another; and he will contemplate him as he is.

24   Certainly.

25   He will then proceed to argue that this is he who gives the season and the years, and is the guardian of all that is in the visible world, and in a certain way the cause of all things which he and his fellows have been accustomed to behold?

26   Clearly, he said, he would first see the sun and then reason about him.

27   And when he remembered his old habitation, and the wisdom of the den and his fellow-prisoners, do you not suppose that he would felicitate himself on the change, and pity them?

28   Certainly, he would.

29   And if they were in the habit of conferring honors among themselves on those who were quickest to observe the passing shadows and to remark which of them went before, and which followed after, and which were together; and who were therefore best able to draw conclusions as to the future, do you think that he would care for such honors and glories, or envy the possessors of them? Would he not say with Homer,

> Better to be the poor servant of a poor master,

and to endure anything, rather than think as they do and live after their manner?

30   Yes, he said, I think that he would rather suffer anything than entertain these false notions and live in this miserable manner.

31   Imagine once more, I said, such an one coming suddenly out of the sun to be replaced in his old situation; would he not be certain to have his eyes full of darkness?

32   To be sure, he said.

33   And if there were a contest, and he had to compete in measuring the shadows with the prisoners who had never moved out of the den,

while his sight was still weak, and before his eyes had become steady (and the time which would be needed to acquire this new habit of sight might be very considerable), would he not be ridiculous? Men would say of him that up he went and down he came without his eyes; and that it was better not even to think of ascending; and if any one tried to loose another and lead him up to the light, let them only catch the offender, and they would put him to death.

34   No question, he said.

35   This entire allegory, I said, you may now append, dear Glaucon, to the previous argument; the prison-house is the world of sight, the light of the fire is the sun, and you will not misapprehend me if you interpret the journey upwards to be the ascent of the soul into the intellectual world according to my poor belief, which, at your desire, I have expressed—whether rightly or wrongly God knows. But, whether true or false, my opinion is that in the world of knowledge the idea of good appears last of all, and is seen only with an effort; and, when seen, is also inferred to be the universal author of all things beautiful and right, parent of light and of the lord of light in this visible world, and the immediate source of reason and truth in the intellectual; and that this is the power upon which he who would act rationally either in public or private life must have his eye fixed.

36   I agree, he said, as far as I am able to understand you.

37   Moreover, I said, you must not wonder that those who attain to this beatific vision are unwilling to descend to human affairs; for their souls are ever hastening into the upper world where they desire to dwell; which desire of theirs is very natural, if our allegory may be trusted.

38   Yes, very natural.

39   And is there anything surprising in one who passes from divine contemplations to the evil state of man, misbehaving himself in a ridiculous manner; if, while his eyes are blinking and before he has become accustomed to the surrounding darkness, he is compelled to fight in courts of law, or in other places, about the images or the shadows of images of justice, and is endeavoring to meet the conceptions of those who have never yet seen absolute justice?

40   Anything but surprising, he replied.

41   Any one who has common sense will remember that the bewilderments of the eyes are of two kinds, and arise from two causes, either from coming out of the light or from going into the light, which is true

of the mind's eye, quite as much as of the bodily eye; and he who remembers this when he sees any one whose vision is perplexed and weak, will not be too ready to laugh; he will first ask whether that soul of man has come out of the brighter life, and is unable to see because unaccustomed to the dark, or having turned from darkness to the day is dazzled by excess of light. And he will count the one happy in his condition and state of being, and he will pity the other; or, if he have a mind to laugh at the soul which comes from below into the light, there will be more reason in this than in the laugh which greets him who returns from above out of the light into the den.

42   That, he said, is a very just distinction.

The Battle of the Ants

Henry David Thoreau

1   One day when I went out to my wood-pile, or rather my pile of stumps, I observed two large ants, the one red, the other much larger, nearly half an inch long, and black, fiercely contending with one another. Having once got hold they never let go, but struggled and wrestled and rolled on the chips incessantly. Looking farther, I was surprised to find that the chips were covered with such combatants, that it was not a *duellum,* but a *bellum,* a war between two races of ants, the red always pitted against the black, and frequently two red ones to one black. The legions of these Myrmidons covered all the hills and vales in my wood-yard, and the ground was already strewn with the dead and dying, both red and black. It was the only battle which I have ever witnessed, the only battle-field I ever trod while the battle was raging; internecine war; the red republicans on the one hand, and the black imperialists on the other. On every side they were engaged in deadly combat, yet without any noise that I could hear, and human soldiers never fought so resolutely. I watched a couple that were fast locked in each other's embraces, in a little sunny valley amid the chips, now at noonday prepared to fight till the sun went down, or life went out. The smaller red champion had fastened himself like a vice to his adversary's front, and through all the tumblings on that field never for an instant ceased to gnaw at one of his feelers near the root, having already caused the other to go by the board; while the stronger black one dashed him from side to side, and, as I saw on looking nearer, had already divested him of several of his members. They fought with more pertinacity than bulldogs. Neither manifested the least disposition to retreat. It was evident that their battle-cry was "Conquer or die." In the meanwhile there came along a single red ant on the hillside of this valley, evidently full of excitement, who either had dispatched his foe, or had not yet taken part in the battle; probably the latter, for he had lost none of his limbs; whose mother had charged him to return with his shield or upon it. Or perchance he

was some Achilles, who had nourished his wrath apart, and had now come to avenge or rescue his Patroclus. He saw this unequal combat from afar—for the blacks were nearly twice the size of the red—he drew near with rapid pace till he stood on his guard within half an inch of the combatants; then, watching his opportunity, he sprang upon the black warrior, and commenced his operations near the root of his right foreleg, leaving the foe to select among his own members; and so there were three united for life, as if a new kind of attraction had been invented which put all other locks and cements to shame. I should not have wondered by this time to find that they had their respective musical bands stationed on some eminent chip, and playing their national airs the while, to excite the slow and cheer the dying combatants. I was myself excited somewhat even as if they had been men. The more you think of it, the less the difference. And certainly there is not the fight recorded in Concord history, at least, if in the history of America, that will bear a moment's comparison with this, whether for the numbers engaged in it, or for the patriotism and heroism displayed. For numbers and for carnage it was an Austerlitz or Dresden. Concord Fight! Two killed on the patriots' side, and Luther Blanchard wounded! Why here every ant was a Buttrick—"Fire! for God's sake fire!"—and thousands shared the fate of Davis and Hosmer. There was not one hireling there. I have no doubt that it was a principle they fought for, as much as our ancestors, and not to avoid a three-penny tax on their tea; and the results of this battle will be as important and memorable to those whom it concerns as those of the battle of Bunker Hill, at least.

2   I took up the chip on which the three I have particularly described were struggling, carried it into my house, and placed it under a tumbler on my window-sill, in order to see the issue. Holding a microscope to the first-mentioned red ant, I saw that, though he was assiduously gnawing at the near fore leg of his enemy, having severed his remaining feeler, his own breast was all torn away, exposing what vitals he had there to the jaws of the black warrior, whose breastplate was apparently too thick for him to pierce; and the dark carbuncles of the sufferer's eyes shone with ferocity such as war only could excite. They struggled half an hour longer under the tumbler, and when I looked again the black soldier had severed the heads of his foes from their bodies, and the still living heads were hanging on either side of him like ghastly trophies at his saddle-bow, still apparently as firmly fastened as ever,

and he was endeavoring with feeble struggles, being without feelers, and with only the remnant of a leg, and I know not how many other wounds, to divest himself of them, which at length, after half an hour more, he accomplished. I raised the glass, and he went off over the windowsill in that crippled state. Whether he finally survived that combat, and spent the remainder of his days in some Hôtel des Invalides, I do not know; but I thought that his industry would not be worth much thereafter. I never learned which party was victorious, nor the cause of the war, but I felt for the rest of that day as if I had my feelings excited and harrowed by witnessing the struggle, the ferocity and carnage, of a human battle before my door.

3   Kirby and Spence tell us that the battles of ants have long been celebrated and the date of them recorded, though they say that Huber is the only modern author who appears to have witnessed them. "Aeneas Sylvius," say they, "after giving a very circumstantial account of one contested with great obstinacy by a great and small species on the trunk of a pear tree," adds that "'this action was fought in the pontificate of Eugenius the Fourth, in the presence of Nicholas Pistoriensis, an eminent lawyer, who related the whole history of the battle with the greatest fidelity.' A similar engagement between great and small ants is recorded by Olaus Magnus, in which the small ones, being victorious, are said to have buried the bodies of their own soldiers, but left those of their giant enemies a prey to the birds. This event happened previous to the expulsion of the tyrant Christian the Second from Sweden." The battle which I witnessed took place in the Presidency of Polk, five years before the passage of Webster's Fugitive-Slave Bill.

Transfiguration

Annie Dillard

1   I live on northern Puget Sound, in Washington State, alone. I have a gold cat, who sleeps on my legs, named Small. In the morning I joke to her blank face, Do you remember last night? Do you remember? I throw her out before breakfast, so I can eat.

2   There is a spider, too, in the bathroom, with whom I keep a sort of company. Her little outfit always reminds me of a certain moth I helped to kill. The spider herself is of uncertain lineage, bulbous at the abdomen and drab. Her six-inch mess of a web works, works somehow, works miraculously, to keep her alive and me amazed. The web itself is in a corner behind the toilet, connecting tile wall to tile wall and floor, in a place where there is, I would have thought, scant traffic. Yet under the web are sixteen or so corpses she has tossed to the floor.

3   The corpses appear to be mostly sow bugs, those little armadillo creatures who live to travel flat out in houses, and die round. There is also a new shred of earwig, three old spider skins crinkled and clenched, and two moth bodies, wingless and huge and empty, moth bodies I drop to my knees to see.

4   Today the earwig shines darkly and gleams, what there is of him: a dorsal curve of thorax and abdomen, and a smooth pair of cerci by which I knew his name. Next week, if the other bodies are any indication, he will be shrunken and gray, webbed to the floor with dust. The sow bugs beside him are hollow and empty of color, fragile, a breath away from brittle fluff. The spider skins lie on their sides, translucent and ragged, their legs drying in knots. And the moths, the empty moths, stagger against each other, headless, in a confusion of arching strips of chitin like peeling varnish, like a jumble of buttresses for cathedral domes, like nothing resembling moths, so that I should hesitate to call them moths, except that I have had some experience with the figure Moth reduced to a nub.

5   Two summers ago I was camping alone in the Blue Ridge Mountains in Virginia. I had hauled myself and gear up there to read, among other things, James Ramsey Ullman's *The Day on Fire,* a novel about Rimbaud that had made me want to be a writer when I was sixteen; I was hoping it would do it again. So I read, lost, every day sitting under a tree by my tent, while warblers swung in the leaves overhead and bristle worms trailed their inches over the twiggy dirt at my feet; and I read every night by candlelight, while barred owls called in the forest and pale moths massed round my head in the clearing, where my light made a ring.

6   Moths kept flying into the candle. They would hiss and recoil, lost upside down in the shadows among my cooking pans. Or they would singe their wings and fall, and their hot wings, as if melted, would stick to the first thing they touched—a pan, a lid, a spoon—so that the snagged moths could flutter only in tiny arcs, unable to struggle free. These I could release by a quick flip with a stick; in the morning I would find my cooking stuff gilded with torn flecks of moth wings, triangles of shiny dust here and there on the aluminum. So I read, and boiled water, and replenished candles, and read on.

7   One night a moth flew into the candle, was caught, burnt dry, and held. I must have been staring at the candle, or maybe I looked up when a shadow crossed my page; at any rate, I saw it all. A golden female moth, a biggish one with a two-inch wingspan, flapped into the fire, dropped her abdomen into the wet wax, stuck, flamed, frazzled and fried in a second. Her moving wings ignited like tissue paper, enlarging the circle of light in the clearing and creating out of the darkness the sudden blue sleeves of my sweater, the green leaves of jewelweed by my side, the ragged red trunk of a pine. At once the light contracted again and the moth's wings vanished in a fine, foul smoke. At the same time her six legs clawed, curled, blackened, and ceased, disappearing utterly. And her head jerked in spasms, making a spattering noise; her antennae crisped and burned away and her heaving mouth parts crackled like pistol fire. When it was all over, her head was, so far as I could determine, gone, gone the long way of her wings and legs. Had she been new, or old? Had she mated and laid her eggs, had she done her work? All that was left was the glowing horn shell of her abdomen and thorax—a fraying, partially collapsed gold tube jammed upright in the candle's round pool.

8   And then this moth-essence, this spectacular skeleton, began to
act as a wick. She kept burning. The wax rose in the moth's body from
her soaking abdomen to her thorax to the jagged hole where her head
should be, and widened into flame, a saffron-yellow flame that robed
her to the ground like any immolating monk. That candle had two
wicks, two flames of identical height, side by side. The moth's head
was fire. She burned for two hours, until I blew her out.

9   She burned for two hours without changing, without bending or
leaning—only glowing within, like a building fire glimpsed through
silhouetted walls, like a hollow saint, like a flame-faced virgin gone to
God, while I read by her light, kindled, while Rimbaud in Paris burnt
out his brains in a thousand poems, while night pooled wetly at my
feet.

10   And that is why I believe those hollow crisps on the bathroom
floor are moths. I think I know moths, and fragments of moths, and
chips and tatters of utterly empty moths, in any state. How many of
you, I asked the people in my class, which of you want to give your
lives and be writers? I was trembling from coffee, or cigarettes, or the
closeness of faces all around me. (Is this what we live for? I thought;
is this the only final beauty: the color of any skin in any light, and
living, human eyes?) All hands rose to the question. (You, Nick? Will
you? Margaret? Randy? Why do I want them to mean it?) And then I
tried to tell them what the choice must mean: you can't be anything
else. You must go at your life with a broadax. . . . They had no idea
what I was saying. (I have two hands, don't I? And all this energy, for
as long as I can remember. I'll do it in the evenings, after skiing, or
on the way home from the bank, or after the children are asleep. . . .)
They thought I was raving again. It's just as well.

11   I have three candles here on the table which I disentangle from
the plants and light when visitors come. Small usually avoids them,
although once she came too close and her tail caught fire; I rubbed it
out before she noticed. The flames move light over everyone's skin,
draw light to the surface of the faces of my friends. When the people
leave I never blow the candles out, and after I'm asleep they flame and
burn.

"But a Watch in the Night": A Scientific Fable

James C. Rettie

1   Out beyond our solar system there is a planet called Copernicus. It came into existence some four or five billion years before the birth of our Earth. In due course of time it became inhabited by a race of intelligent men.

2   About 750 million years ago the Copernicans had developed the motion picture machine to a point well in advance of the stage that we have reached. Most of the cameras that we now use in motion picture work are geared to take twenty-four pictures per second on a continuous strip of film. When such film is run through a projector, it throws a series of images on the screen and these change with a rapidity that gives the visual impression of normal movement. If a motion is too swift for the human eye to see it in detail, it can be captured and artificially slowed down by means of the slow-motion camera. This one is geared to take many more shots per second—ninety-six or even more than that. When the slow motion film is projected at the normal speed of twenty-four pictures per second, we can see just how the jumping horse goes over a hurdle.

3   What about motion that is too slow to be seen by the human eye? That problem has been solved by the use of the time-lapse camera. In this one, the shutter is geared to take only one shot per second, or one per minute, or even one per hour—depending upon the kind of movement that is being photographed. When the time-lapse film is projected at the normal speed of twenty-four pictures per second, it is possible to see a bean sprout growing up out of the ground. Time-lapse films are useful in the study of many types of motion too slow to be observed by the unaided, human eye.

4   The Copernicans, it seems, had time-lapse cameras some 757 million years ago and they also had superpowered telescopes that gave

them a clear view of what was happening upon this Earth. They decided to make a film record of the life history of Earth and to make it on the scale of one picture per year. The photography has been in progress during the last 757 million years.

5   In the near future, a Copernican interstellar expedition will arrive upon our Earth and bring with it a copy of the time-lapse film. Arrangements will be made for showing the entire film in one continuous run. This will begin at midnight of New Year's Eve and continue day and night without a single stop until midnight of December 31. The rate of projection will be twenty-four pictures per second. Time on the screen will thus seem to move at the rate of twenty-four years per second; 1440 years per minute; 86,400 years per hour; approximately two million years per day; and sixty-two million years per month. The normal life-span of individual man will occupy about three seconds. The full period of earth history that will be unfolded on the screen (some 757 million years) will extend from what the geologists call Pre-Cambrian times up to the present. This will, by no means, cover the full time-span of the earth's geological history but it will embrace the period since the advent of living organisms.

6   During the months of January, February, and March the picture will be desolate and dreary. The shape of the land masses and the oceans will bear little or no resemblance to those that we know. The violence of geological erosion will be much in evidence. Rains will pour down on the land and promptly go booming down to the seas. There will be no clear streams anywhere except where the rains fall upon hard rock. Everywhere on the steeper ground the stream channels will be filled with boulders hurled down by rushing waters. Raging torrents and dry stream beds will keep alternating in quick succession. High mountains will seem to melt like so much butter in the sun. The shifting of land into the seas, later to be thrust up as new mountains, will be going on at a grand scale.

7   Early in April there will be some indication of the presence of single-celled living organisms in some of the warmer and sheltered coastal waters. By the end of the month it will be noticed that some of these organisms have become multicellular. A few of them, including the Trilobites, will be encased in hard shells.

8   Toward the end of May, the first vertebrates will appear, but they will still be aquatic creatures. In June about 60 per cent of the land area

that we know as North America will be under water. One broad channel will occupy the space where the Rocky Mountains now stand. Great deposits of limestone will be forming under some of the shallower seas. Oil and gas deposits will be in process of formation—also under shallow seas. On land there will still be no sign of vegetation. Erosion will be rampant, tearing loose particles and chunks of rock and grinding them into sand and silt to be spewed out by the streams into bays and estuaries.

9   About the middle of July the first land plants will appear and take up the tremendous job of soil building. Slowly, very slowly, the mat of vegetation will spread, always battling for its life against the power of erosion. Almost foot by foot, the plant life will advance, lacing down with its root structures whatever pulverized rock material it can find. Leaves and stems will be giving added protection against the loss of the soil foothold. The increasing vegetation will pave the way for the land animals that will live upon it.

10   Early in August the seas will be teeming with fish. This will be what geologists call the Devonian period. Some of the races of these fish will be breathing by means of lung tissue instead of through gill tissues. Before the month is over, some of the lung fish will go ashore and take on a crude lizard-like appearance. Here are the first amphibians.

11   In early September the insects will put in their appearance. Some will look like huge dragonflies and will have a wing spread of 24 inches. Large portions of the land masses will now be covered with heavy vegetation that will include the primitive spore-propagating trees. Layer upon layer of this plant growth will build up, later to appear as the coal deposits. About the middle of this month, there will be evidence of the first seed-bearing plants and the first reptiles. Heretofore, the land animals will have been amphibians that could reproduce their kind only by depositing a soft egg mass in quiet waters. The reptiles will be shown to be freed from the aquatic bond because they can reproduce by means of a shelled egg in which the embryo and its nurturing liquids are sealed and thus protected from destructive evaporation. Before September is over, the first dinosaurs will be seen—creatures destined to dominate the animal realm for about 140 million years and then to disappear.

12   In October there will be series of mountain uplifts along what is now the eastern coast of the United States. A creature with feathered limbs—half bird and half reptile in appearance—will take itself into the air. Some small and rather unpretentious animals will be seen to bring

forth their young in a form that is a miniature replica of the parents and to feed these young on milk secreted by mammary glands in the female parent. The emergence of this mammalian form of animal life will be recognized as one of the great events in geologic time. October will also witness the high water mark of the dinosaurs—creatures ranging in size from that of the modern goat to monsters like Brontosaurus that weighed some 40 tons. Most of them will be placid vegetarians, but a few will be hideous-looking carnivores, like Allosaurus and Tyranno-saurus. Some of the herbivorous dinosaurs will be clad in bony armor for protection against their flesh-eating comrades.

13   November will bring pictures of a sea extending from the Gulf of Mexico to the Arctic in space now occupied by the Rocky Mountains. A few of the reptiles will take to the air on bat-like wings. One of these, called Pteranodon, will have a wingspread of 15 feet. There will be a rapid development of the modern flowering plants, modern trees, and modern insects. The dinosaurs will disappear. Toward the end of the month there will be a tremendous land disturbance in which the Rocky Mountains will rise out of the sea to assume a dominating place in the North American landscape.

14   As the picture runs on into December it will show the mammals in command of the animal life. Seed-bearing trees and grasses will have covered most of the land with a heavy mantle of vegetation. Only the areas newly thrust up from the sea will be barren. Most of the streams will be crystal clear. The turmoil of geologic erosion will be confined to localized areas. About December 25 will begin the cutting of the Grand Canyon of the Colorado River. Grinding down through layer after layer of sedimentary strata, this stream will finally expose deposits laid down in Pre-Cambrian times. Thus in the walls of that canyon will appear geological formations dating from recent times to the period when the Earth had no living organisms upon it.

15   The picture will run on through the latter days of December and even up to its final day with still no sign of mankind. The spectators will become alarmed in the fear that man has somehow been left out. But not so; sometime about noon on December 31 (one million years ago) will appear a stooped, massive creature of man-like proportions. This will be Pithecanthropus, the Java ape man. For tools and weapons he will have nothing but crude stone and wooden clubs. His children will live a precarious existence threatened on the one side by hostile

animals and on the other by tremendous climatic changes. Ice sheets—in places 4000 feet deep—will form in the northern parts of North America and Eurasia. Four times this glacial ice will push southward to cover half the continents. With each advance the plant and animal life will be swept under or pushed southward. With each recession of the ice, life will struggle to reestablish itself in the wake of the retreating glaciers. The woolly mammoth, the musk ox, and the caribou all will fight to maintain themselves near the ice line. Sometimes they will be caught and put into cold storage—skin, flesh, blood, bones and all.

16   The picture will run on through supper time with still very little evidence of man's presence on the earth. It will be about 11 o'clock when Neanderthal man appears. Another half hour will go by before the appearance of Cro-Magnon man living in caves and painting crude animal pictures on the walls of his dwelling. Fifteen minutes more will bring Neolithic man, knowing how to chip stone and thus produce sharp cutting edges for spears and tools. In a few minutes more it will appear that man has domesticated the dog, the sheep and, possibly, other animals. He will then begin the use of milk. He will also learn the arts of basket weaving and the making of pottery and dugout canoes.

17   The dawn of civilization will not come until about five or six minutes before the end of the picture. The story of the Egyptians, the Babylonians, the Greeks, and the Romans will unroll during the fourth, the third, and the second minute before the end. At 58 minutes and 43 seconds past 11:00 PM (just 1 minute and 17 seconds before the end) will come the beginning of the Christian era. Columbus will discover the new world 20 seconds before the end. The Declaration of Independence will be signed just 7 seconds before the final curtain comes down.

18   In those few moments of geologic time will be the story of all that has happened since we became a nation. And what a story it will be! A human swarm will sweep across the face of the continent and take it away from the . . . red men. They will change it far more radically than it has ever been changed before in a comparable time. The great virgin forests will be seen going down before ax and fire. The soil, covered for eons by its protective mantle of trees and grasses, will be laid bare to the ravages of water and wind erosion. Streams that had been flowing clear will, once again, take up a load of silt and push it toward the seas. Humus and mineral salts, both vital elements of productive soil, will be seen to vanish at a terrifying rate. The railroads

and highways and cities that will spring up may divert attention, but they cannot cover up the blight of man's recent activities. In great sections of Asia, it will be seen that man must utilize cow dung and every scrap of available straw or grass for fuel to cook his food. The forests that once provided wood for this purpose will be gone without a trace. The use of these agricultural wastes for fuel, in place of returning them to the land, will be leading to increasing soil impoverishment. Here and there will be seen a dust storm darkening the landscape over an area a thousand miles across. Man-creatures will be shown counting their wealth in terms of bits of printed paper representing other bits of a scarce but comparatively useless yellow metal that is kept buried in strong vaults. Meanwhile, the soil, the only real wealth that can keep mankind alive on the face of this earth is savagely being cut loose from its ancient moorings and washed into the seven seas.

19   We have just arrived upon this earth. How long will we stay?

The Cosmic Prison

Loren Eiseley

1   "A name is a prison, God is free," once observed the Greek poet Nikos Kazantzakis. He meant, I think, that valuable though language is to man, it is by very necessity limiting, and creates for man an invisible prison. Language implies boundaries. A word spoken creates a dog, a rabbit, a man. It fixes their nature before our eyes; henceforth their shapes are, in a sense, our own creation. They are no longer part of the unnamed shifting architecture of the universe. They have been trans-fixed as if by sorcery, frozen into a concept, a word. Powerful though the spell of human language has proven itself to be, it has laid boundaries upon the cosmos.

2   No matter how far-ranging some of the mental probes that man has philosophically devised, by his own created nature he is forced to hold the specious and emerging present and transform it into words. The words are startling in their immediate effectiveness, but at the same time they are always finally imprisoning because man has constituted himself a prison keeper. He does so out of no conscious intention, but because for immediate purposes he has created an unnatural world of his own, which he calls the cultural world, and in which he feels at home. It defines his needs and allows him to lay a small immobilizing spell upon the nearer portions of his universe. Nevertheless, it transforms that universe into a cosmic prison house which is no sooner mapped than man feels its inadequacy and his own.

3   He seeks then to escape, and the theory of escape involves bodily flight. Scarcely had the first moon landing been achieved before one U.S. senator boldly announced: "We are the masters of the universe. We can go anywhere we choose." This statement was widely and ed-itorially acclaimed. It is a striking example of the comfort of words, also of the covert substitutions and mental projections to which they are subject. The cosmic prison is not made less so by a successful journey of some two hundred and forty thousand miles in a cramped and primitive vehicle.

4   To escape the cosmic prison man is poorly equipped. He has to drag portions of his environment with him, and his life span is that of a mayfly in terms of the distances he seeks to penetrate. There is no possible way to master such a universe by flight alone. Indeed such a dream is a dangerous illusion. This may seem a heretical statement, but its truth is self-evident if we try seriously to comprehend the nature of time and space that I sought to grasp when held up to view the fiery messenger that flared across the zenith in 1910. "Seventy-five years," my father had whispered in my ear, "seventy-five years and it will be racing homeward. Perhaps you will live to see it again. Try to remember."

5   And so I remembered. I had gained a faint glimpse of the size of our prison house. Somewhere out there beyond a billion miles in space, an entity known as a comet had rounded on its track in the black darkness of the void. It was surging homeward toward the sun because it was an eccentric satellite of this solar system. If I lived to see it it would be but barely, and with the dimmed eyes of age. Yet it, too, in its long traverse, was but a flitting mayfly in terms of the universe the night sky revealed.

6   So relative is the cosmos we inhabit that, as we gaze upon the outer galaxies available to the reach of our telescopes, we are placed in about the position that a single white blood cell in our bodies would occupy, if it were intelligently capable of seeking to understand the nature of its own universe, the body it inhabits. The cell would encounter rivers ramifying into miles of distance seemingly leading nowhere. It would pass through gigantic structures whose meaning it could never grasp—the brain, for example. It could never know there was an outside, a vast being on a scale it could not conceive of and of which it formed an infinitesimal part. It would know only the pouring tumult of the creation it inhabited, but of the nature of that great beast, or even indeed that it was a beast, it could have no conception whatever. It might examine the liquid in which it floated and decide, as in the case of the fall of Lucretius's atoms, that the pouring of obscure torrents had created its world.

7   It might discover that creatures other than itself swam in the torrent. But that its universe was alive, had been born and was destined to perish, its own ephemeral existence would never allow it to perceive. It would never know the sun; it would explore only through dim tactile sensations and react to chemical stimuli that were borne to it along the

mysterious conduits of the arteries and veins. Its universe would be centered upon a great arborescent tree of spouting blood. This, at best, generations of white blood cells by enormous labor and continuity might succeed, like astronomers, in charting.

8   They could never, by any conceivable stretch of the imagination, be aware that their so-called universe was, in actuality, the prowling body of a cat or the more time-enduring body of a philosopher, himself engaged upon the same quest in a more gigantic world and perhaps deceived proportionately by greater vistas. What if, for example, the far galaxies man observes make up, across void spaces of which even we are atomically composed, some kind of enormous creature or cosmic snowflake whose exterior we will never see? We will know more than the phagocyte in our bodies, but no more than that limited creature can we climb out of our universe, or successfully enhance our size or longevity sufficiently to thrust our heads through the confines of the universe that terminates our vision.

9   Some further "outside" will hover elusively in our thought, but upon its nature, or even its reality, we can do no more than speculate. The phagocyte might observe the salty turbulence of an eternal river system, Lucretius the fall of atoms creating momentary living shapes. We suspiciously sense, in the concept of the expanding universe derived from the primordial atom—the monobloc—some kind of oscillating universal heart. At the instant of its contraction we will vanish. It is not given us, nor can our science recapture, the state beyond the monobloc, nor whether we exist in the diastole of some inconceivable being. We know only a little more extended reality than the hypothetical creature below us. Above us may lie realms it is beyond our power to grasp.

My Horse

Barry Lopez

1   It is curious that Indian warriors on the northern plains in the nineteenth century, who were almost entirely dependent on the horse for mobility and status, never gave their horses names. If you borrowed a man's horse and went off raiding for other horses, however, or if you lost your mount in battle and then jumped on mine and counted coup on an enemy—well, those horses would have to be shared with the man whose horse you borrowed, and that coup would be mine, not yours. Because even if I gave him no name, he was my horse.

2   If you were a Crow warrior and I a young Teton Sioux out after a warrior's identity and we came over a small hill somewhere in the Montana prairie and surprised each other, I could tell a lot about you by looking at your horse.

3   Your horse might have feathers tied in his mane, or in his tail, or a medicine bag tied around his neck. If I knew enough about the Crow, and had looked at you closely, I might make some sense of the decoration, even guess who you were if you were well-known. If you had painted your horse I could tell even more, because we both decorated our horses with signs that meant the same things. Your white handprints high on his flanks would tell me you had killed an enemy in a hand-to-hand fight. Small horizontal lines stacked on your horse's foreleg, or across his nose, would tell me how many times you had counted coup. Horse hoof marks on your horse's rump, or three-sided boxes, would tell me how many times you had stolen horses. If there was a bright red square on your horse's neck I would know you were leading a war party and that there were probably others out there in the coulees behind you.

4   You might be painted all over as blue as the sky and covered with white dots, with your horse painted the same way. Maybe hailstorms were your power—or if I chased you a hailstorm might come down and hide you. There might be lightning bolts on the horse's legs and flanks,

and I would wonder if you had lightning power, or a slow horse. There might be white circles around your horse's eyes to help him see better.

5   Or you might be like Crazy Horse, with no decoration, no marks on your horse to tell me anything, only a small lightning bolt on your cheek, a piece of turquoise tied behind your ear.

6   You might have scalps dangling from your rein.

7   I could tell something about you by your horse. All this would come to me in a few seconds. I might decide this was my moment and shout my war cry—*Hoka hey!* Or I might decide you were like the grizzly bear: I would raise my weapon to you in salute and go my way, to see you again when I was older.

8   I do not own a horse. I am attached to a truck, however, and I have come to think of it in a similar way. It has no name; it never occurred to me to give it a name. It has little decoration; neither of us is partial to decoration. I have a piece of turquoise in the truck because I had heard once that some of the southwestern tribes tied a small piece of turquoise in a horse's hock to keep him from stumbling. I like the idea. I also hang sage in the truck when I go on a long trip. But inside, the truck doesn't look much different from others that look just like it on the outside. I like it that way. Because I like my privacy.

9   For two years in Wyoming I worked on a ranch wrangling horses. The horse I rode when I had to have a good horse was a quarter horse and his name was Coke High. The name came with him. At first I thought he'd been named for the soft drink. I'd known stranger names given to horses by whites. Years later I wondered if some deviate Wyoming cowboy wise to cocaine had not named him. Now I think he was probably named after a rancher, an historical figure of the region. I never asked the people who owned him for fear of spoiling the spirit of my inquiry.

10   We were running over a hundred horses on this ranch. They all had names. After a few weeks I knew all the horses and the names too. You had to. No one knew how to talk about the animals or put them in order or tell the wranglers what to do unless they were using the names—Princess, Big Red, Shoshone, Clay.

11   My truck is named Dodge. The name came with it. I don't know if it was named after the town or the verb or the man who invented it.

I like it for a name. Perfectly anonymous, like Rex for a dog, or Old Paint. You can't tell anything with a name like that.

12   The truck is a van. I call it a truck because it's not a car and because "van" is a suburban sort of consumer word, like "oxford loafer," and I don't like the sound of it. On the outside it looks like any other Dodge Sportsman 300. It's a dirty tan color. There are a few body dents, but it's never been in a wreck. I tore the antenna off against a tree on a pinched mountain road. A boy in Midland, Texas, rocked one of my rear view mirrors off. A logging truck in Oregon squeeze-fired a piece of debris off the road and shattered my windshield. The oil pan and gas tank are pug-faced from high-centering on bad roads. (I remember a horse I rode for a while named Targhee whose hocks were scarred from tangles in barbed wire when he was a colt and who spooked a lot in high grass, but these were not like "dents." They were more like bad tires.)

13   I like to travel. I go mostly in the winter and mostly on two-lane roads. I've driven the truck from Key West to Vancouver, British Columbia, and from Yuma to Long Island over the past four years. I used to ride Coke High only about five miles every morning when we were rounding up horses. Hard miles of twisting and turning. About six hundred miles a year. Then I'd turn him out and ride another horse for the rest of the day. That's what was nice about having a remuda. You could do all you had to do and not take it all out on your best horse. Three car family.

14   My truck came with a lot of seats in it and I've never really known what to do with them. Sometimes I put the seats in and go somewhere with a lot of people, but most of the time I leave them out. I like riding around with that empty cavern of space behind my head. I know it's something with a history to it, that there's truth in it, because I always rode a horse the same way—with empty saddle bags. In case I found something. The possibility of finding something is half the reason for being on the road.

15   The value of anything comes to me in its use. If I am not using something it is of no value to me and I give it away. I wasn't always that way. I used to keep everything I owned—just in case. I feel good about the truck because it gets used. A lot. To haul hay and firewood

and lumber and rocks and garbage and animals. Other people have used it to haul furniture and freezers and dirt and recycled newspapers. And to move from one house to another. When I lend it for things like that I don't look to get anything back but some gas (if we're going to be friends). But if you go way out in the country to a dump and pick up the things you can still find out there (once a load of cedar shingles we sold for $175 to an architect) I expect you to leave some of those things around my place when you come back—if I need them.

16   When I think back, maybe the nicest thing I ever put in that truck was timber wolves. It was a long night's drive from Oregon up into British Columbia. We were all very quiet about it; it was like moving clouds across the desert.

17   Sometimes something won't fit in the truck and I think about improving it—building a different door system, for example. I am forever going to add better gauges on the dash and a pair of driving lamps and a sunroof, but I never get around to doing any of it. I remember I wanted to improve Coke High once too, especially the way he bolted like a greyhound through patches of cottonwood on a river flat. But all I could do with him was to try to rein him out of it. Or hug his back.

18   Sometimes, road-stoned in a blur of country like southwestern Wyoming or North Dakota, I talk to the truck. It's like wandering on the high plains under a summer sun, on plains where, George Catlin wrote, you were "out of sight of land." I say what I am thinking out loud, or point at things along the road. It's a crazy, sun-stroked sort of activity, a sure sign it's time to pull over, to go for a walk, to make a fire and have some tea, to lie in the shade of the truck.

19   I've always wanted to pat the truck. It's basic to the relationship. But it never works.

20   I remember when I was on the ranch, just at sunrise, after I'd saddled Coke High, I'd be huddled down in my jacket smoking a cigarette and looking down into the valley, along the river where the other horses had spent the night. I'd turn to Coke and run my hand down his neck and slap-pat him on the shoulder to say I was coming up. It made a bond, an agreement we started the day with.

21   I've thought about that a lot with the truck, because we've gone out together at sunrise on so many mornings. I've even fumbled around trying to do it. But metal won't give.

22   The truck's personality is mostly an expression of two ideas: "with-you" and "alone." When Coke High was "with-you" he and I were the same animal. We could have cut a rooster out of a flock of chickens, we were so in tune. It's the same with the truck: rolling through Kentucky on a hilly two-lane road, three in the morning under a full moon and no traffic. Picture it. You roll like water.

23   There are other times when you are with each other but there's no connection at all. Coke got that way when he was bored and we'd fight each other about which way to go around a tree. When the truck gets like that—"alone"—it's because it feels its Detroit fat-ass design dragging at its heart and making a fool out of it.

24   I can think back over more than a hundred nights I've slept in the truck, sat in it with a lamp burning, bundled up in a parka, reading a book. It was always comfortable. A good place to wait out a storm. Like sleeping inside a buffalo.

25   The truck will go past 100,000 miles soon. I'll rebuild the engine and put a different transmission in it. I can tell from magazine advertisements that I'll never get another one like it. Because every year they take more of the heart out of them. One thing that makes a farmer or a rancher go sour is a truck that isn't worth a shit. The reason you see so many old pickups in ranch country is because these are the only ones with any heart. You can count on them. The weekend rancher runs around in a new pickup with too much engine and not enough transmission and with the wrong sort of tires because he can afford anything, even the worst. A lot of them have names for their pickups too.

26   My truck has broken down, in out of the way places at the worst of times. I've walked away and screamed the foulness out of my system and gotten the tools out. I had to fix a water pump in a blizzard in the Panamint Mountains in California once. It took all day with the Coleman stove burning under the engine block to keep my hands from freezing. We drifted into Beatty, Nevada, that night with it jury-rigged together with—I swear—baling wire, and we were melting snow as we went and pouring it in to compensate for the leaks.

27   There is a dent next to the door on the driver's side I put there one sweltering night in Miami. I had gone to the airport to meet my wife, whom I hadn't seen in a month. My hands were so swollen with poison ivy blisters I had to drive with my wrists. I had shut the door

and was locking it when the window fell off its runners and slid down inside the door. I couldn't leave the truck unlocked because I had too much inside I didn't want to lose. So I just kicked the truck a blow in the side and went to work on the window. I hate to admit kicking the truck. It's like kicking a dog, which I've never done.

28   Coke High and I had an accident once. We hit a badger hole at a full gallop. I landed on my back and blacked out. When I came to, Coke High was about a hundred yards away. He stayed a hundred yards away for six miles, all the way back to the ranch.

29   I want to tell you about carrying those wolves, because it was a fine thing. There were ten of them. We had four in the truck with us in crates and six in a trailer. It was a five hundred mile trip. We went at night for the cool air and because there wouldn't be as much traffic. I could feel from the way the truck rolled along that its heart was in the trip. It liked the wolves inside it, the sweet odor that came from the crates. I could feel that same tireless wolf-lope developing in its wheels; it was like you might never have to stop for gas, ever again.

30   The truck gets very self-focused when it works like this; its heart is strong and it's good to be around it. It's good to be *with* it. You get the same feeling when you pull someone out of a ditch. Coke High and I pulled a Volkswagen out of the mud once, but Coke didn't like doing it very much. Speed, not strength, was his center. When the guy who owned the car thanked us and tried to pat Coke, the horse snorted and swung away, trying to preserve his distance, which is something a horse spends a lot of time on.

31   So does the truck.

32   Being distant lets the truck get its heart up. The truck has been cold and alone in Montana at 38 below zero. It's climbed horrible, eroded roads in Idaho. It's been burdened beyond overloading, and made it anyway. I've asked it to do these things because they build heart, and without heart all you have is a machine. You have nothing. I don't think people in Detroit know anything at all about heart. That's why everything they build dies so young.

33   One time in Arizona the truck and I came through one of the worst storms I've ever been in, an outrageous, angry blizzard. But we went down the road, right through it. You couldn't explain our getting through by the sort of tires I had on the truck, or the fact that I had

chains on, or was a good driver, or had a lot of weight over my drive wheels or a good engine, because it was more than this. It was a contest between the truck and the blizzard—and the truck wouldn't quit. I could have gone to sleep and the truck would have just torn a road down Interstate 40 on its own. It scared the hell out of me; but it gave me heart, too.

34   We came off the Mogollon Rim that night and out of the storm and headed south for Phoenix. I pulled off the road to sleep for a few hours, but before I did I got out of the truck. It was raining. Warm rain. I tied a short piece of red avalanche cord into the grill. I left it there for a long time, like an eagle feather on a horse's tail. It flapped and spun in the wind. I could hear it ticking against the grill when I drove.

35   When I have to leave that truck I will just raise up my left arm— *Hoka hey!*—and walk away.

Is Canada Neurotic?

Robertson Davies

1 Canada's obvious troubles are not wholly her own; she simply has her share in them. Inflation, high rates of interest, widespread bankruptcy, unemployment, increasing Civil Service, burdensome taxation—these are common to all the Western world and are symptoms of a financial crisis that is even greater in the Communist countries. But these are external troubles; it is the way Canada takes them, and the neurotic spirit Canada has developed during the past twenty years, that gives them a special Canadian flavor. This neurotic spirit is our deepest trouble.

2 Canada neurotic? But its citizens present such an air of—well, perhaps not robust health, but at least of impassivity under stress. What do we mean by neurosis? The *Concise Oxford* says "inability to take a rationally objective view of life."

3 What are we unable to look at rationally? Ourselves, of course. It is the essence of a neurosis that it is personal. The psychiatrist knows that his conversation with the patient will focus on Number One. There is a type of neurosis, afflicting two people, called *folie à deux*. Canada's ailment is a *folie à 25,000,000*.

4 Like many a neurosis, it may be leading toward some substantial psychological advance. It is painful while it is going on, and may look ridiculous to outsiders, but it is far from ridiculous. Canada's neurosis is, I suggest, Canada's revolution.

5 Can you think of a country that has advanced toward world significance that has not at some time in its history endured the misery of a revolution? In retrospect, revolutions appear as glorious achievements, when some unendurable yoke was thrown off and a new spirit brought into being, but while they are going on, revolutions are painful, and some people suffer loss and ruin.

6 Canada has never had a revolution of the usual sort, though there have been minor risings against injustice. I think the nation is having

a painful revolution of a modern kind; it is a psychological revolution, a self-examination during which the country must come to terms with what other people think about it and what it may reasonably think about itself.

7   For two hundred and fifty years Canada has been treated with the indulgence proper to a child, and that is now over. The U.S. makes it clear that belonging to the North American block involves obligations, such as allowing the U.S. to use Canadian soil as a proving ground for weapons it does not wish to try at home. Britain, once heartily patronizing toward Canada, now shows signs of petulance and jealousy toward us, and misses no chance to let us know how lumpish and dull we are in comparison with their witty, resourceful selves. The European Parliament tells us that we are primitives who club baby seals to death, and Europe doesn't like it. When we reply that the U.S. might do something about the acid rain that is despoiling our woodlands, and that Britain is whistling while the ship sinks, and that we club the baby seals in the most caressing fashion in which one can beat anything to death, we are nevertheless coldly aware that Canada is no longer the popular, if minor, character she once was on the world stage.

8   Not that all trouble comes from abroad. Any Canadian now middle-aged was brought up in the belief that we were exemplary in our treatment of our native peoples. Our native peoples now assure us that we have been mistaken, and they want a bigger slice of the pie. Newfoundland presents itself as an Oliver Twist, pathetically asking for more. The Maritime Provinces have turned up the decibel strength of their cry that they have always had a raw deal. The West, once dependent and now rich in oil, declares with passion that it profoundly hates the East. British Columbia feels itself alienated. The central government at Ottawa sharply refuses to grant any new powers to the geographical region.

9   All of this makes for neurosis; but our prize neurotic exhibit is Quebec, a province profoundly schizophrenic. Urban Quebec talks of separation from the rest of the country, and the voices of university and media people are loud on this theme. The business community and rural Quebec say little, and aren't likely to budge. City Quebec likes to pretend that it is peopled by ebullient, laughter-loving Latins, artists with souls above trade; but rural Quebec knows that its ancestral stock is Norman, and that money is what makes the mare go.

10   As every neurosis must have its lightning rod which draws nervous energy away from the real cause of trouble, Canada finds its lightning rod in the Prime Minister, Pierre Trudeau.

11   Mr. Trudeau, who is sixty-two, is nevertheless regarded as an *enfant terrible;* and conventional people fear and dislike him, because he gives voice to unspeakable things.

12   He does not scruple, for instance, to say that Canada is a socialist country. Of course, Canada has been advancing further and further into state socialism of the Scandinavian order since the era of Mackenzie King (1921–48); but it keeps so quiet about it and calls a spade a delving tool so determinedly that many conservative Canadians still hope the clock might be turned back by a change in the government. Realists know that the clock will never be turned back, and that, whatever party rules in Canada, we are committed to more and more state interference and state subvention in every aspect of life. Party politics in Canada is ideologically and intellectually bankrupt because, though we have parties, we have only one policy—bigger and bigger handouts and more and more government control by a larger and larger Civil Service. This may or may not be a bad thing, though the U.S. might think it a bad thing if it were widely understood what Canada is doing. But Canada, with its broad, innocent face and its queer genius for politics, has kept this fact pretty much under its hat.

13   Mr. Trudeau may think—neither I nor anyone else knows what he really thinks—that a socialist North American country ought to be a republic and not a monarchy. This scares a lot of Canadians who are sentimentally inclined toward monarchy and who are deeply aware that the Crown is the last defense Canada has against ambitious politicians. Australia has recently shown this to be true. Whatever the truth may be, Mr. Trudeau created excitement by his determination to do something he calls bringing our Constitution home.

14   This is not the place to explain what that means save that it would make Canada totally independent of Britain in spirit; it has been politically independent since 1931. Mr. Trudeau has achieved his hope that the Queen will appear in Canada and personally deliver into his hands some document that will make this forever plain. He may be said to resemble that Old Man of Hong Kong—

   Who would frequently burst into song;
   It wasn't the words

That frightened the birds,

'Twas the horrible *dooble ongtong*.

The *double-entendre* in this case would be that Canada would find herself spiritually and psychologically naked and would have to decide who she was and what she stood for.

15   Plenty of fodder for neurosis here, I think you will agree. But neuroses assert themselves in the conscious mind when some problem in the unconscious demands solution, and it is from the unconscious that the solution eventually emerges. Our solution is near enough at hand for us to guess what it is: Canadians will have to stop playing innocent country jakes (which has been a disguise for at least fifty years) and admit that we are a special breed of North Americans, tough, resilient, and determined. That will not please our friends as did our earlier role, but it will be more honest and, in the long run, it will work better. We shall have achieved our revolution. We shall have found our own soul, whatever it may be, and what ever it may cost.

The Myth of Sisyphus

Albert Camus

1   The gods had condemned Sisyphus to ceaselessly rolling a rock to the top of a mountain, whence the stone would fall back of its own weight. They had thought with some reason that there is no more dreadful punishment than futile and hopeless labor.

2   If one believes Homer, Sisyphus was the wisest and most prudent of mortals. According to another tradition, however, he was disposed to practice the profession of highwayman. I see no contradiction in this. Opinions differ as to the reasons why he became the futile laborer of the underworld. To begin with, he is accused of a certain levity in regard to the gods. He stole their secrets. Aegina, the daughter of Aesopus, was carried off by Jupiter. The father was shocked by that disappearance and complained to Sisyphus. He, who knew of the abduction, offered to tell about it on condition that Aesopus would give water to the citadel of Corinth. To the celestial thunderbolts he preferred the benediction of water. He was punished for this in the underworld. Homer tells us also that Sisyphus had put Death in chains. Pluto could not endure the sight of his deserted, silent empire. He dispatched the god of war, who liberated Death from the hands of her conqueror.

3   It is said also that Sisyphus, being near to death, rashly wanted to test his wife's love. He ordered her to cast his unburied body into the middle of the public square. Sisyphus woke up in the underworld. And there, annoyed by an obedience so contrary to human love, he obtained from Pluto permission to return to earth in order to chastise his wife. But when he had seen again the face of this world, enjoyed water and sun, warm stones and the sea, he no longer wanted to go back to the infernal darkness. Recalls, signs of anger, warnings were of no avail. Many years more he lived facing the curve of the gulf, the sparkling sea, and the smiles of earth. A decree of the gods was necessary. Mercury came and seized the impudent man by the collar and, snatching him from his joys, led him forcibly back to the underworld, where his rock was ready for him.

4   You have already grasped that Sisyphus is the absurd hero. He *is*, as much through his passions as through his torture. His scorn of the gods, his hatred of death, and his passion for life won him that unspeakable penalty in which the whole being is exerted toward accomplishing nothing. This is the price that must be paid for the passions of this earth. Nothing is told us about Sisyphus in the underworld. Myths are made for the imagination to breathe life into them. As for this myth, one sees merely the whole effort of a body straining to raise the huge stone, to roll it and push it up a slope a hundred times over; one sees the face screwed up, the cheek tight against the stone, the shoulder bracing the clay-covered mass, the foot wedging it, the fresh start with arms outstretched, the wholly human security of two earth-clotted hands. At the very end of his long effort measured by skyless space and time without depth, the purpose is achieved. Then Sisyphus watches the stone rush down in a few moments toward that lower world whence he will have to push it up again toward the summit. He goes back down to the plain.

5   It is during that return, that pause, that Sisyphus interests me. A face that toils so close to stones is already stone itself! I see that man going back down with a heavy yet measured step toward the torment of which he will never know the end. That hour like a breathing-space which returns as surely as his suffering, that is the hour of consciousness. At each of those moments when he leaves the heights and gradually sinks toward the lairs of the gods, he is superior to his fate. He is stronger than his rock.

6   If this myth is tragic, that is because its hero is conscious. Where would his torture be, indeed, if at every step the hope of succeeding upheld him? The workman of today works every day in his life at the same tasks, and this fate is no less absurd. But it is tragic only at the rare moments when it becomes conscious. Sisyphus, proletarian of the gods, powerless and rebellious, knows the whole extent of his wretched condition: it is what he thinks of during his descent. The lucidity that was to constitute his torture at the same time crowns his victory. There is no fate that cannot be surmounted by scorn.

7   If the descent is thus sometimes performed in sorrow, it can also take place in joy. This word is not too much. Again I fancy Sisyphus returning toward his rock, and the sorrow was in the beginning. When the images of earth cling too tightly to memory, when the call of

happiness becomes too insistent, it happens that melancholy rises in man's heart: this is the rock's victory, this is the rock itself. The boundless grief is too heavy to bear. These are our nights of Gethsemane. But crushing truths perish from being acknowledged. Thus, Oedipus at the outset obeys fate without knowing it. But from the moment he knows, his tragedy begins. Yet at the same moment, blind and desperate, he realizes that the only bond linking him to the world is the cool hand of a girl. Then a tremendous remark rings out: "Despite so many ordeals, my advanced age and the nobility of my soul make me conclude that all is well." Sophocles' Oedipus, like Dostoevsky's Kirilov, thus gives the recipe for the absurd victory. Ancient wisdom confirms modern heroism.

8   One does not discover the absurd without being tempted to write a manual of happiness. "What! by such narrow ways—?" There is but one world, however. Happiness and the absurd are two sons of the same earth. They are inseparable. It would be a mistake to say that happiness necessarily springs from the absurd discovery. It happens as well that the feeling of the absurd springs from happiness. "I conclude that all is well," says Oedipus, and that remark is sacred. It echoes in the wild and limited universe of man. It teaches that all is not, has not been, exhausted. It drives out of this world a god who had come into it with dissatisfaction and a preference for futile sufferings. It makes of fate a human matter, which must be settled among men.

9   All Sisyphus' silent joy is contained therein. His fate belongs to him. His rock is his thing. Likewise, the absurd man, when he contemplates his torment, silences all the idols. In the universe suddenly restored to its silence, the myriad wondering little voices of the earth rise up. Unconscious, secret calls, invitations from all the faces, they are the necessary reverse and price of victory. There is no sun without shadow, and it is essential to know the night. The absurd man says yes and his effort will henceforth be unceasing. If there is a personal fate, there is no higher destiny, or at least there is but one which he concludes is inevitable and despicable. For the rest, he knows himself to be the master of his days. At that subtle moment when man glances backward over his life, Sisyphus returning toward his rock, in that slight pivoting he contemplates that series of unrelated actions which becomes his fate, created by him, combined under his memory's eye and soon sealed by his death. Thus, convinced of the wholly human origin of all that is

human, a blind man eager to see who knows that the night has no end, he is still on the go. The rock is still rolling.

10   I leave Sisyphus at the foot of the mountain! One always finds one's burden again. But Sisyphus teaches the higher fidelity that negates the gods and raises rocks. He too concludes that all is well. This universe henceforth without a master seems to him neither sterile nor futile. Each atom of that stone, each mineral flake of that night-filled mountain, in itself forms a world. The struggle itself toward the heights is enough to fill a man's heart. One must imagine Sisyphus happy.

Chapter Ten

Argument

A Modest Proposal

Jonathan Swift

1   It is a melancholy object to those who walk through this great town or travel in the country, when they see the streets, the roads, and cabin doors, crowded with beggars of the female sex, followed by three, four, or six children, all in rags and importuning every passenger for an alms. These mothers, instead of being able to work for their honest livelihood, are forced to employ all their time in strolling to beg sustenance for their helpless infants: who as they grow up either turn thieves for want of work, or leave their dear native country to fight for the pretender in Spain, or sell themselves to the Barbadoes.

2   I think it is agreed by all parties that this prodigious number of children in the arms, or on the backs, or at the heels of their mothers, and frequently of their fathers, is in the present deplorable state of the kingdom a very great additional grievance; and, therefore, whoever could find out a fair, cheap, and easy method of making these children sound, useful members of the commonwealth, would deserve so well of the public as to have his statue set up for a preserver of the nation.

3   But my intention is very far from being confined to provide only for the children of professed beggars; it is of a much greater extent, and shall take in the whole number of infants at a certain age who are born of parents in effect as little able to support them as those who demand our charity in the streets.

4   As to my own part, having turned my thoughts for many years upon this important subject, and maturely weighed the several schemes of our projectors, I have always found them grossly mistaken in their computation. It is true, a child just dropped from its dam may be supported by her milk for a solar year, with little other nourishment; at most not above the value of 2s., which the mother may certainly get, or the value in scraps, by her lawful occupation of begging; and it is exactly at one year old that I propose to provide for them in such a manner as instead of being a charge upon their parents or the parish,

or wanting food and raiment for the rest of their lives, they shall on the contrary contribute to the feeding, and partly to the clothing, of many thousands.

5   There is likewise another great advantage in my scheme, that it will prevent those voluntary abortions, and that horrid practice of women murdering their bastard children, alas! too frequent among us! sacrificing the poor innocent babes I doubt more to avoid the expense than the shame, which would move tears and pity in the most savage and inhuman breast.

6   The number of souls in this kingdom being usually reckoned one million and a half, of these I calculate there may be about 200,000 couple whose wives are breeders; from which number I subtract 30,000 couple who are able to maintain their own children (although I apprehend there cannot be so many, under the present distress of the kingdom); but this being granted, there will remain 170,000 breeders. I again subtract 50,000 for those women who miscarry, or whose children die by accident or disease within the year. There only remain 120,000 children of poor parents annually born. The question therefore is, how this number shall be reared and provided for? which, as I have already said, under the present situation of affairs, is utterly impossible by all the methods hitherto proposed. For we can neither employ them in handicraft or agriculture; we neither build houses (I mean in the country) nor cultivate land; they can very seldom pick up a livelihood by stealing, till they arrive at six years old, except where they are of towardly parts; although I confess they learn the rudiments much earlier; during which time they can, however, be properly looked upon only as probationers; as I have been informed by a principal gentleman in the county of Cavan, who protested to me that he never knew above one or two instances under the age of six, even in a part of the kingdom so renowned for the quickest proficiency in that art.

7   I am assured by our merchants, that a boy or a girl before twelve years old is no saleable commodity; and even when they come to this age they will not yield above 3l. or 3l. 2s. 6d. at most on the exchange; which cannot turn to account either to the parents or kingdom, the charge of nutriment and rags having been at least four times that value.

8   I shall now therefore humbly propose my own thoughts, which I hope will not be liable to the least objection.

9   I have been assured by a very knowing American of my acquaintance in London, that a young healthy child well nursed is at a year old a most delicious, nourishing, and wholesome food, whether stewed, roasted, baked, or broiled; and I make no doubt that it will equally serve in a fricassee or a ragout.

10   I do therefore humbly offer it to public consideration that of the 120,000 children already computed, 20,000 may be reserved for breed, whereof only one-fourth part to be males; which is more than we allow to sheep, black cattle, or swine; and my reason is, that these children are seldom the fruits of marriage, a circumstance not much regarded by our savages; therefore one male will be sufficient to serve four females. That the remaining 100,000 may, at a year old, be offered in sale to the persons of quality and fortune through the kingdom; always advising the mother to let them suck plentifully in the last month, so as to render them plump and fat for a good table. A child will make two dishes at an entertainment for friends; and when the family dines alone, the fore or hind quarter will make a reasonable dish, and seasoned with a little pepper or salt will be very good boiled on the fourth day, especially in winter.

11   I have reckoned upon a medium that a child just born will weigh 12 pounds, and in a solar year, if tolerably nursed, will increase to 28 pounds.

12   I grant this food will be somewhat dear, and therefore very proper for landlords, who, as they have already devoured most of the parents, seem to have the best title to the children.

13   Infant's flesh will be in season throughout the year, but more plentiful in March, and a little before and after: for we are told by a grave author, an eminent French physician, that fish being a prolific diet, there are more children born in Roman Catholic countries about nine months after Lent than at any other season; therefore, reckoning a year after Lent, the markets will be more glutted than usual, because the number of popish infants is at least three to one in this kingdom: and therefore it will have one other collateral advantage, by lessening the number of papists among us.

14   I have already computed the charge of nursing a beggar's child (in which list I reckon all cottagers, laborers, and four-fifths of the farmers) to be about 2s. per annum, rags included; and I believe no

gentleman would repine to give 10s. for the carcass of a good fat child, which, as I have said, will make four dishes of excellent nutritive meat, when he has only some particular friend or his own family to dine with him. Thus the squire will learn to be a good landlord, and grow popular among the tenants; the mother will have 8s. net profit, and be fit for work till she produces another child.

15   Those who are more thrifty (as I must confess the times require) may flay the carcass; the skin of which artificially dressed will make admirable gloves for ladies, and summer boots for fine gentlemen.

16   As to our city of Dublin, shambles may be appointed for this purpose in the most convenient parts of it, and butchers we may be assured will not be wanting: although I rather recommend buying the children alive, and dressing them hot from the knife as we do roasting pigs.

17   A very worthy person, a true lover of his country, and whose virtues I highly esteem, was lately pleased in discoursing on this matter to offer a refinement upon my scheme. He said that many gentlemen of this kingdom, having of late destroyed their deer, he conceived that the want of venison might be well supplied by the bodies of young lads and maidens, not exceeding fourteen years of age nor under twelve; so great a number of both sexes in every country being now ready to starve for want of work and service; and these to be disposed of by their parents, if alive, or otherwise by their nearest relations. But with due deference to so excellent a friend and so deserving a patriot, I cannot be altogether in his sentiments; for as to the males, my American acquaintance assured me from frequent experience that their flesh was generally tough and lean, like that of our schoolboys by continual exercise, and their taste disagreeable; and to fatten them would not answer the charge. Then as to the females, it would, I think, with humble submission be a loss to the public, because they soon would become breeders themselves: and besides, it is not improbable that some scrupulous people might be apt to censure such a practice (although indeed very unjustly), as a little bordering upon cruelty; which, I confess, has always been with me the strongest objection against any project, how well soever intended.

18   But in order to justify my friend, he confessed that this expedient was put into his head by the famous Psalmanazar, a native of the island Formosa, who came from thence to London about twenty years ago: and in conversation told my friend, that in his country when any young

person happened to be put to death, the executioner sold the carcass to persons of quality as a prime dainty; and that in his time the body of a plump girl of fifteen, who was crucified for an attempt to poison the emperor, was sold to his imperial majesty's prime minister of state, and other great mandarins of the court, in joints from the gibbet, at 400 crowns. Neither indeed can I deny, that if the same use were made of several plump young girls in this town, who without one single groat to their fortunes cannot stir without a chair, and appear at the playhouse and assemblies in foreign fineries which they never will pay for, the kingdom would not be the worse.

19   Some persons of a desponding spirit are in great concern about that vast number of poor people, who are aged, diseased, or maimed, and I have been desired to employ my thoughts what course may be taken to ease the nation of so grievous an encumbrance. But I am not in the least pain upon that matter, because it is very well known that they are every day dying and rotting by cold and famine, and filth and vermin, as fast as can be reasonably expected. And as to the young laborers, they are now in as hopeful a condition: they cannot get work, and consequently pine away for want of nourishment, to a degree that if at any time they are accidentally hired to common labor, they have not strength to perform it; and thus the country and themselves are happily delivered from the evils to come.

20   I have too long digressed, and therefore shall return to my subject. I think the advantages by the proposal which I have made are obvious and many, as well as of the highest importance.

21   For first, as I have already observed, it would greatly lessen the number of papists, with whom we are yearly overrun, being the principal breeders of the nation as well as our most dangerous enemies; and who stay at home on purpose to deliver the kingdom to the Pretender, hoping to take their advantage by the absence of so many good Protestants, who have chosen rather to leave their country than stay at home and pay tithes against their conscience to an Episcopal curate.

22   Secondly, The poor tenants will have something valuable of their own, which by law may be made liable to distress and help to pay their landlord's rent, their corn and cattle being already seized, and money a thing unknown.

23   Thirdly, Whereas the maintenance of 100,000 children from two years old and upward, cannot be computed at less than 10s. a-piece per annum, the nation's stock will be thereby increased £50,000 per annum,

beside the profit of a new dish introduced to the tables of all gentlemen of fortune in the kingdom who have any refinement in taste. And the money will circulate among ourselves, the goods being entirely of our own growth and manufacture.

24   Fourthly, The constant breeders beside the gain of 8s. sterling per annum by the sale of their children, will be rid of the charge of maintaining them after the first year.

25   Fifthly, This food would likewise bring great custom to taverns, where the vintners will certainly be so prudent as to procure the best receipts for dressing it to perfection, and consequently have their houses frequented by all the fine gentlemen, who justly value themselves upon their knowledge in good eating; and a skilful cook who understands how to oblige his guests, will contrive to make it as expensive as they please.

26   Sixthly, This would be a great inducement to marriage, which all wise nations have either encouraged by rewards or enforced by laws and penalties. It would increase the care and tenderness of mothers toward their children, when they were sure of a settlement for life to the poor babes, provided in some sort by the public, to their annual profit instead of expense. We should see an honest emulation among the married women, which of them would bring the fattest child to the market. Men would become as fond of their wives during the time of their pregnancy as they are now of their mares in foal, their cows in calf, their sows when they are ready to farrow; nor offer to beat or kick them (as is too frequent a practice) for fear of a miscarriage.

27   Many other advantages might be enumerated. For instance, the addition of some thousand carcasses in our exportation of barreled beef, the propagation of swine's flesh, and improvement in the art of making good bacon, so much wanted among us by the great destruction of pigs, too frequent at our table; which are no way comparable in taste or magnificence to a well-grown, fat, yearling child, which roasted whole will make a considerable figure at a lord mayor's feast or any other public entertainment. But this and many others I omit, being studious of brevity.

28   Supposing that 1,000 families in this city would be constant customers for infants' flesh, besides others who might have it at merry-meetings, particularly at weddings and christenings, I compute that Dublin would take off annually about 20,000 carcasses; and the rest of

the kingdom (where probably they will be sold somewhat cheaper) the remaining 80,000.

29   1 can think of no one objection that will possibly be raised against this proposal, unless it should be urged that the number of people will be thereby much lessened in the kingdom. This I freely own, and it was indeed one principal design in offering it to the world. I desire the reader will observe, that I calculate my remedy for this one individual kingdom of Ireland and for no other that ever was, is, or I think ever can be upon earth. Therefore let no man talk to me of other expedients: of taxing our absentees at 5s. a pound: of using neither clothes nor household furniture except what is of our own growth and manufacture: of utterly rejecting the materials and instruments that promote foreign luxury: of curing the expensiveness of pride, vanity, idleness, and gaming in our women: of introducing a vein of parsimony, prudence, and temperance: of learning to love our country, in the want of which we differ even from Laplanders and the inhabitants of Topinamboo: of quitting our animosities and factions, nor acting any longer like the Jews, who were murdering one another at the very moment their city was taken: of being a little cautious not to sell our country and conscience for nothing: of teaching landlords to have at least one degree of mercy toward their tenants: lastly, of putting a spirit of honesty, industry, and skill into our shopkeepers; who, if a resolution could now be taken to buy only our native goods, would immediately unite to cheat and exact upon us in the price, the measure, and the goodness, nor could ever yet be brought to make one fair proposal of just dealing, though often and earnestly invited to it.

30   Therefore I repeat, let no man talk to me of these and the like expedients, till he has at least some glimpse of hope that there will be ever some hearty and sincere attempt to put them in practice.

31   But as to myself, having been wearied out for many years with offering vain, idle, visionary thoughts, and at length utterly despairing of success, I fortunately fell upon this proposal; which, as it is wholly new, so it has something solid and real, of no expense and little trouble, full in our own power, and whereby we can incur no danger in disobliging England. For this kind of commodity will not bear exportation, the flesh being of too tender a consistence to admit a long continuance in salt, although perhaps I could name a country which would be glad to eat up our whole nation without it.

32   After all, I am not so violently bent upon my own opinion as to reject any offer proposed by wise men, which shall be found equally innocent, cheap, easy, and effectual. But before something of that kind shall be advanced in contradiction to my scheme, and offering a better, I desire the author or authors will be pleased maturely to consider two points. First, as things now stand, how they will be able to find food and raiment for 100,000 useless mouths and backs. And secondly, there being a round million of creatures in human figure throughout this kingdom, whose subsistence put into a common stock would leave them in debt 2,000,000*l*. sterling, adding those who are beggars by profession to the bulk of farmers, cottagers, and laborers, with the wives and children who are beggars in effect; I desire those politicians who dislike my overture, and may perhaps be so bold as to attempt an answer, that they will first ask the parents of these mortals, whether they would not at this day think it a great happiness to have been sold for food at a year old in the manner I prescribe, and thereby have avoided such a perpetual scene of misfortunes as they have since gone through by the oppression of landlords, the impossibility of paying rent without money or trade, the want of common sustenance, with neither house nor clothes to cover them from the inclemencies of the weather, and the most inevitable prospect of entailing the like or greater miseries upon their breed for ever.

33   I profess, in the sincerity of my heart, that I have not the least personal interest in endeavoring to promote this necessary work, having no other motive than the public good of my country, by advancing our trade, providing for infants, relieving the poor, and giving some pleasure to the rich. I have no children by which I can propose to get a single penny; the youngest being nine years old, and my wife past child-bearing.

Universal Military Motion

Russell Baker

1   The idea behind the MX missile system is sound enough. Place bomb-bearing missiles on wheels and keep them moving constantly through thousands of miles of desert so enemy bombers will not have a fixed target. To confuse things further, move decoy missiles over the same routes so the enemy cannot distinguish between false missiles and the real thing.

2   As my strategic thinkers immediately pointed out, however, the MX missile system makes very little sense unless matched by an MX Pentagon system. What is the point, they asked, of installing a highly mobile missile system if its command center, the Pentagon, remains anchored like a moose with four broken legs on the bank of the Potomac River?

3   This is why we propose building 250 moveable structures so precisely like the Pentagon that no one can tell our fake Pentagons from the real thing and to keep all of them, plus the real Pentagon, in constant motion through the country.

4   Our first plan was to move only the real Pentagon, which would be placed on a large flat-bottom truck bed and driven about the countryside on the existing highway system. We immediately realized, however, that this would not provide sufficient protection against nuclear attack. The Pentagon is very big and easily noticeable. When it is driven along at 55 miles per hour, people can see it coming from miles away. It attracts attention. In short, it is a fat, easily detected target.

5   With 250 fake Pentagons constantly cruising the roads, the problem is solved. Now, trying to distinguish the real Pentagon from the fake Pentagons, enemy attackers will face the maddening problem of finding a needle in a haystack. With 251 Pentagons in circulation, the sight of a Pentagon on the highway will attract no more attention than a politician's indictment. Thus we foil the spies.

6   Still, to add another margin of security we will confuse matters further by building 1,500 Pentagon-shaped fast-food restaurants along the nation's highways.

7   Each will be an exact replica of the real Pentagon, at least as seen from the outside. Inside, of course, they will be equipped to provide all the necessities for producing acute indigestion, thus providing the wherewithal of highway travel and, in the process, earning the Government a little return on its investment.

8   Occasionally, when generals and admirals tire of touring and yearn for a little stability, the real Pentagon will be parked alongside the road to masquerade as a fast-food Pentagon. The danger of highway travelers wandering in for a quick hot dog and making trouble while the authentic Pentagon is in the "parked" or "fast-food" mode has also been considered.

9   These interlopers will simply be told by receptionists that hot dogs are in the back of the building and directed to walk the long route around the Pentagon's outer ring. As they drop from exhaustion they will be removed by military police, carried to their cars, given free hot dogs and advised that next time they should enter their Pentagon fast-food dispensary through the rear door.

10   There are problems to be ironed out in the MX Pentagon, but we are too busy at the moment perfecting our MX Congress system to trifle with details. With 850 United States Capitols on the highway, we have an extremely touchy problem in deciding whether a Capitol or a Pentagon should have the right of way when they meet at an intersection.

Four-Letter Words Can Hurt You

Barbara Lawrence

1   Why should any words be called obscene? Don't they all describe natural human functions? Am I trying to tell them, my students demand, that the "strong, earthy, gut-honest"—or, if they are fans of Norman Mailer, the "rich, liberating, existential"—language they use to describe sexual activity isn't preferable to "phony-sounding, middle-class words like 'intercourse' and 'copulate'?" "Cop You Late!" they say with fancy inflections and gagging grimaces. "Now, what is *that* supposed to mean?"

2   Well, what is it supposed to mean? And why indeed should one group of words describing human functions and human organs be acceptable in ordinary conversation and another, describing presumably the same organs and functions, be tabooed—so much so, in fact, that some of these words still cannot appear in print in many parts of the English-speaking world?

3   The argument that these taboos exist only because of "sexual hangups" (middle-class, middle-age, feminist), or even that they are a result of class oppression (the contempt of the Norman conquerors for the language of their Anglo-Saxon serfs), ignores a much more likely explanation, it seems to me, and that is the sources and functions of the words themselves.

4   The best known of the tabooed sexual verbs, for example, comes from the German *ficken,* meaning "to strike"; combined, according to Partridge's etymological dictionary *Origins,* with the Latin sexual verb *futuere;* associated in turn with the Latin *fustis,* "a staff or cudgel"; the Celtic *buc,* "a point, hence to pierce"; the Irish *bot,* "the male member"; the Latin *battuere,* "to beat"; the Gaelic *batair,* "a cudgeller"; the Early Irish *bualaim,* "I strike"; and so forth. It is one of what etymologists sometimes call "the sadistic group of words for the man's part in copulation."

5   The brutality of this word, then, and its equivalents ("screw," "bang," etc.), is not an illusion of the middle class or a crotchet of

Women's Liberation. In their origins and imagery these words carry undeniably painful, if not sadistic, implications, the object of which is almost always female. Consider, for example, what a "screw" actually does to the wood it penetrates; what a painful, even mutilating, activity this kind of analogy suggests. "Screw" is particularly interesting in this context, since the noun, according to Partridge, comes from words meaning "groove," "nut," "ditch," "breeding sow," "scrofula" and "swelling," while the verb, besides its explicit imagery, has antecedent associations to "write on," "scratch," "scarify," and so forth—a revealing fusion of a mechanical or painful action with an obviously denigrated object.

6   Not all obscene words, of course, are as implicitly sadistic or denigrating to women as these, but all that I know seem to serve a similar purpose: to reduce the human organism (especially the female organism) and human functions (especially sexual and procreative) to their least organic, most mechanical dimension; to substitute a trivializing or deforming resemblance for the complex human reality of what is being described.

7   Tabooed male descriptives, when they are not openly denigrating to women, often serve to divorce a male organ or function from any significant interaction with the female. Take the word "testes," for example, suggesting "witnesses" (from the Latin *testis*) to the sexual and procreative strengths of the male organ; and the obscene counterpart of this word, which suggests little more than a mechanical shape. Or compare almost any of the "rich," "liberating" sexual verbs, so fashionable today among male writers, with that much-derided Latin word "copulate" ("to bind or join together") or even that Anglo-Saxon phrase (which seems to have had no trouble surviving the Norman Conquest) "make love."

8   How arrogantly self-involved the tabooed words seem in comparison to either of the other terms, and how contemptuous of the female partner. Understandably so, of course, if she is only a "skirt," a "broad," a "chick," a "pussycat" or a "piece." If she is, in other words, no more than her skirt, or what her skirt conceals; no more than a breeder, or the broadest part of her; no more than a piece of a human being or a "piece of tail."

9   The most severely tabooed of all the female descriptives, incidentally, are those like a "piece of tail," which suggest (either explicitly

or through antecedents) that there is no significant difference between the female channel through which we are all conceived and born and the anal outlet common to both sexes—a distinction that pornographers have always enjoyed obscuring.

10   This effort to deny women their biological identity, their individuality, their humanness, is such an important aspect of obscene language that one can only marvel at how seldom, in an era preoccupied with definitions of obscenity, this fact is brought to our attention. One problem, of course, is that many of the people in the best position to do this (critics, teachers, writers) are so reluctant today to admit that they are angered or shocked by obscenity. Bored, maybe, unimpressed, aesthetically displeased, but—no matter how brutal or denigrating the material—never angered, never shocked.

11   And yet how eloquently angered, how piously shocked many of these same people become if denigrating language is used about any minority group other than women; if the obscenities are racial or ethnic, that is, rather than sexual. Words like "coon," "kike," "spic," "wop," after all, deform identity, deny individuality and humanness in almost exactly the same way that sexual vulgarisms and obscenities do.

12   No one that I know, least of all my students, would fail to question the values of a society whose literature and entertainment rested heavily on racial or ethnic pejoratives. Are the values of a society whose literature and entertainment rest as heavily as ours on sexual pejoratives any less questionable?

Why I Want a Wife

Judy Syfers

1   I belong to that classification of people known as wives. I am A Wife. And, not altogether incidentally, I am a mother.

2   Not too long ago a male friend of mine appeared on the scene fresh from a recent divorce. He had one child, who is, of course, with his ex-wife. He is looking for another wife. As I thought about him while I was ironing one evening, it suddenly occurred to me that I, too, would like to have a wife. Why do I want a wife?

3   I would like to go back to school so that I can become economically independent, support myself, and, if need be, support those dependent upon me. I want a wife who will work and send me to school. And while I am going to school I want a wife to take care of my children. I want a wife to keep track of the children's doctor and dentist appointments. And to keep track of mine, too. I want a wife to make sure my children eat properly and are kept clean. I want a wife who will wash the children's clothes and keep them mended. I want a wife who is a good nurturant attendant to my children, who arranges for their schooling, makes sure that they have an adequate social life with their peers, takes them to the park, the zoo, etc. I want a wife who takes care of the children when they are sick, a wife who arranges to be around when the children need special care, because, of course, I cannot miss classes at school. My wife must arrange to lose time at work and not lose the job. It may mean a small cut in my wife's income from time to time, but I guess I can tolerate that. Needless to say, my wife will arrange and pay for the care of the children while my wife is working.

4   I want a wife who will take care of *my* physical needs. I want a wife who will keep my house clean. A wife who will pick up after my children, a wife who will pick up after me. I want a wife who will keep my clothes clean, ironed, mended, replaced when need be, and who will see to it that my personal things are kept in their proper place so

that I can find what I need the minute I need it. I want a wife who cooks the meals, a wife who is a *good* cook. I want a wife who will plan the menus, do the necessary grocery shopping, prepare the meals, serve them pleasantly, and then do the cleaning up while I do my studying. I want a wife who will care for me when I am sick and sympathize with my pain and loss of time from school. I want a wife to go along when our family takes a vacation so that someone can continue to care for me and my children when I need a rest and change of scene.

5   I want a wife who will not bother me with rambling complaints about a wife's duties. But I want a wife who will listen to me when I feel the need to explain a rather difficult point I have come across in my course of studies. And I want a wife who will type my papers for me when I have written them.

6   I want a wife who will take care of the details of my social life. When my wife and I are invited out by my friends, I want a wife who will take care of the babysitting arrangements. When I meet people at school that I like and want to entertain, I want a wife who will have the house clean, will prepare a special meal, serve it to me and my friends, and not interrupt when I talk about things that interest me and my friends. I want a wife who will have arranged that the children are fed and ready for bed before my guests arrive so that the children do not bother us. I want a wife who takes care of the needs of my guests so that they feel comfortable, who makes sure that they have an ashtray, that they are passed the hors d'oeuvres, that they are offered a second helping of the food, that their wine glasses are replenished when necessary, that their coffee is served to them as they like it. And I want a wife who knows that sometimes I need a night out by myself.

7   I want a wife who is sensitive to my sexual needs, a wife who makes love passionately and eagerly when I feel like it, a wife who makes sure that I am satisfied. And, of course, I want a wife who will not demand sexual attention when I am not in the mood for it. I want a wife who assumes the complete responsibility for birth control, because I do not want more children. I want a wife who will remain sexually faithful to me so that I do not have to clutter up my intellectual life with jealousies. And I want a wife who understands that *my* sexual needs may entail more than strict adherence to monogamy. I must, after all, be able to relate to people as fully as possible.

8   If, by chance, I find another person more suitable as a wife than the wife I already have, I want the liberty to replace my present wife with another one. Naturally, I will expect a fresh, new life; my wife will take the children and be solely responsible for them so that I am left free.

9   When I am through with school and have a job, I want my wife to quit working and remain at home so that my wife can more fully and completely take care of a wife's duties.

10   My God, who *wouldn't* want a wife?

The Declaration of Independence

Thomas Jefferson

In CONGRESS, July 4, 1776.
The Unanimous Declaration of the Thirteen United States of America.

1   When in the Course of human events, it becomes necessary for one people to dissolve the political bands which have connected them with another, and to assume among the powers of the earth, the separate and equal station to which the Laws of Nature and of Nature's God entitle them, a decent respect to the opinions of mankind requires that they should declare the causes which impel them to the separation.

2   We hold these truths to be self-evident, that all men are created equal, that they are endowed by their Creator with certain unalienable Rights, that among these are Life, Liberty and the pursuit of Happiness.

3   That to secure these rights, Governments are instituted among Men, deriving their just powers from the consent of the governed.

4   That whenever any Form of Government becomes destructive of these ends, it is the Right of the People to alter or to abolish it, and to institute new Government, laying its foundation on such principles and organizing its powers in such form, as to them shall seem most likely to effect their Safety and Happiness. Prudence, indeed, will dictate that Governments long established should not be changed for light and transient causes; and accordingly all experience hath shewn, that mankind are more disposed to suffer, while evils are sufferable, than to right themselves by abolishing the forms to which they are accustomed. But when a long train of abuses and usurpations, pursuing invariably the same Object evinces a design to reduce them under absolute Despotism, it is their right, it is their duty, to throw off such Government, and to provide new Guards for their future security.

5   Such has been the patient sufferance of these Colonies; and such is now the necessity which constrains them to alter their former Systems

of Government. The history of the present King of Great Britain is a history of repeated injuries and usurpations, all having in direct object the establishment of an absolute Tyranny over these States. To prove this, let Facts be submitted to a candid world.

6   He has refused his Assent to Laws, the most wholesome and necessary for the public good.

7   He has forbidden his Governors to pass Laws of immediate and pressing importance, unless suspended in their operation till his Assent should be obtained; and when so suspended, he has utterly neglected to attend to them.

8   He has refused to pass other Laws for the accommodation of large districts of people, unless those people would relinquish the right of Representation in the Legislature, a right inestimable to them and formidable to tyrants only.

9   He has called together legislative bodies at places unusual, uncomfortable, and distant from the depository of their public Records, for the sole purpose of fatiguing them into compliance with his measures.

10   He has dissolved Representative Houses repeatedly, for opposing with manly firmness his invasions on the rights of people.

11   He has refused for a long time, after such dissolutions, to cause others to be elected; whereby the Legislative powers, incapable of Annihilation, have returned to the People at large for their exercise; the State remaining in the mean time exposed to all the dangers of invasion from without, and convulsions within.

12   He has endeavoured to prevent the population of these States; for that purpose obstructing the Laws for Naturalization of Foreigners; refusing to pass others to encourage their migrations hither, and raising the conditions of new Appropriations of Lands.

13   He has obstructed the Administration of Justice, by refusing his Assent to Laws for establishing Judiciary powers.

14   He has made Judges dependent on his Will alone, for the tenure of their offices, and the amount and payment of their salaries.

15   He has erected a multitude of New Offices, and sent hither swarms of Officers to harass our people, and eat out their substance.

16   He has kept among us, in times of peace, Standing Armies without the Consent of our legislatures.

17   He has affected to render the Military independent of and superior to the Civil power.

18   He has combined with others to subject us to a jurisdiction foreign to our constitution, and unacknowledged by our laws; giving his Assent to their Acts of pretended Legislation:

19   For Quartering large bodies of armed troops among us:

20   For Protecting them, by a mock Trial, from punishment for any Murders which they should commit on the Inhabitants of these States:

21   For cutting off our Trade with all parts of the world:

22   For imposing Taxes on us without our Consent:

23   For depriving us in many cases, of the benefits of Trial by Jury:

24   For transporting us beyond Seas to be tried for pretended offenses:

25   For abolishing the free System of English Laws in a neighbouring Province, establishing therein an Arbitrary government, and enlarging its Boundaries so as to render it at once an example and fit instrument for introducing the same absolute rule into these Colonies:

26   For taking away our Charters, abolishing our most valuable Laws, and altering fundamentally the Forms of our Governments:

27   For suspending our own Legislatures, and declaring themselves invested with power to legislate for us in all cases whatsoever.

28   He has abdicated Government here, by declaring us out of his Protection and waging War against us:

29   He has plundered our seas, ravaged our Coasts, burnt our towns, and destroyed the lives of our people.

30   He is at this time transporting large Armies of foreign Mercenaries to compleat the works of death, desolation and tyranny, already begun with circumstances of Cruelty & perfidy scarcely paralleled in the most barbarous ages, and totally unworthy the Head of a civilized nation.

31   He has constrained our fellow Citizens taken Captive on the high Seas to bear Arms against their Country, to become the executioners of their friends and Brethren, or to fall themselves by their Hands.

32   He has excited domestic insurrections amongst us, and has endeavoured to bring on the inhabitants of our frontiers, the merciless Indian Savages, whose known rule of warfare, is an undistinguished destruction of all ages, sexes and conditions. In every stage of these Oppressions We have Petitioned for Redress in the most humble terms: Our repeated Petitions have been answered only by repeated injury. A

Prince, whose character is thus marked by every act which may define a Tyrant, is unfit to be the ruler of a free people. Nor have We been wanting in attentions to our British brethren. We have warned them from time to time of attempts by their legislature to extend an unwarrantable jurisdiction over us. We have reminded them of the circumstances of our emigration and settlement here. We have appealed to their native justice and magnanimity, and we have conjured them by the ties of our common kindred to disavow these usurpations, which, would inevitably interrupt our connections and correspondence. They too have been deaf to the voice of justice and of consanguinity. We must, therefore, acquiesce in the necessity, which denounces our Separation, and hold them, as we hold the rest of mankind, Enemies in War, in Peace Friends.

33   We, THEREFORE the Representatives of the UNITED STATES OF AMERICA, in General Congress Assembled, appealing to the Supreme Judge of the world for the rectitude of our intentions, do, in the Name and by Authority of the good People of these Colonies, solemnly publish and declare, That these United Colonies are, and of Right ought to be FREE AND INDEPENDENT STATES: that they are Absolved from all Allegiance to the British Crown, and that all political connection between them and the State of Great Britain, is and ought to be totally dissolved; and that as Free and Independent States, they have full Power to levy War, conclude Peace, contract Alliances, establish Commerce, and to do all other Acts and Things which Independent States may of right do.

34   And for the support of this Declaration, with a firm reliance on the protection of divine Providence, we mutually pledge to each other our Lives, our Fortunes and our sacred Honor.

I Have a Dream

Martin Luther King, Jr.

1   Five score years ago, a great American, in whose symbolic shadow we stand, signed the Emancipation Proclamation. This momentous decree came as a great beacon light of hope to millions of Negro slaves who had been seared in the flames of withering injustice. It came as a joyous daybreak to end the long night of captivity.

2   But one hundred years later, we must face the tragic fact that the Negro is still not free. One hundred years later, the life of the Negro is still sadly crippled by the manacles of segregation and the chains of discrimination. One hundred years later, the Negro lives on a lonely island of poverty in the midst of a vast ocean of material prosperity. One hundred years later, the Negro is still languishing in the corners of American society and finds himself an exile in his own land. So we have come here today to dramatize an appalling condition.

3   In a sense we have come to our nation's capital to cash a check. When the architects of our republic wrote the magnificent words of the Constitution and the Declaration of Independence, they were signing a promissory note to which every American was to fall heir. This note was a promise that all men would be guaranteed the unalienable rights of life, liberty, and the pursuit of happiness.

4   It is obvious today that America has defaulted on this promissory note insofar as her citizens of color are concerned. Instead of honoring this sacred obligation, America has given the Negro people a bad check; a check which has come back marked "insufficient funds." But we refuse to believe that the bank of justice is bankrupt. We refuse to believe that there are insufficient funds in the great vaults of opportunity of this nation. So we have come to cash this check—a check that will give us upon demand the riches of freedom and the security of justice. We have also come to this hallowed spot to remind America of the fierce urgency of *now*. This is no time to engage in the luxury of cooling off or to take the tranquilizing drugs of gradualism. *Now* is the time to

make real the promises of Democracy. *Now* is the time to rise from the dark and desolate valley of segregation to the sunlit path of racial justice. *Now* is the time to open the doors of opportunity to all of God's children. *Now* is the time to lift our nation from the quicksands of racial injustice to the solid rock of brotherhood.

5   It would be fatal for the nation to overlook the urgency of the moment and to underestimate the determination of the Negro. This sweltering summer of the Negro's legitimate discontent will not pass until there is an invigorating autumn of freedom and equality. 1963 is not an end, but a beginning. Those who hope that the Negro needed to blow off steam and will now be content will have a rude awakening if the nation returns to business as usual. There will be neither rest nor tranquillity in America until the Negro is granted his citizenship rights. The whirlwinds of revolt will continue to shake the foundations of our nation until the bright day of justice emerges.

6   But there is something that I must say to my people who stand on the warm threshold which leads into the palace of justice. In the process of gaining our rightful place we must not be guilty of wrongful deeds. Let us not seek to satisfy our thirst for freedom by drinking from the cup of bitterness and hatred. We must forever conduct our struggle on the high plane of dignity and discipline. We must not allow our creative protest to degenerate into physical violence. Again and again we must rise to the majestic heights of meeting physical force with soul force. The marvelous new militancy which has engulfed the Negro community must not lead us to a distrust of all white people, for many of our white brothers, as evidenced by their presence here today, have come to realize that their destiny is tied up with our destiny and their freedom is inextricably bound to our freedom. We cannot walk alone.

7   And as we walk, we must make the pledge that we shall march ahead. We cannot turn back. There are those who are asking the devotees of civil rights, "When will you be satisfied?" We can never be satisfied as long as the Negro is the victim of the unspeakable horrors of police brutality. We can never be satisfied as long as our bodies, heavy with the fatigue of travel, cannot gain lodging in the motels of the highways and the hotels of the cities. We cannot be satisfied as long as the Negro's basic mobility is from a smaller ghetto to a larger one. We can never be satisfied as long as a Negro in Mississippi cannot vote and a Negro in New York believes he has nothing for which to vote. No, no, we

are not satisfied, and we will not be satisfied until justice rolls down like waters and righteousness like a mighty stream.

8   I am not unmindful that some of you have come here out of great trials and tribulations. Some of you have come fresh from narrow jail cells. Some of you have come from areas where your quest for freedom left you battered by the storms of persecution and staggered by the winds of police brutality. You have been the veterans of creative suffering. Continue to work with the faith that unearned suffering is redemptive.

9   Go back to Mississippi, go back to Alabama, go back to South Carolina, go back to Georgia, go back to Louisiana, go back to the slums and ghettos of our northern cities, knowing that somehow this situation can and will be changed. Let us not wallow in the valley of despair.

10   I say to you today, my friends, that in spite of the difficulties and frustrations of the moment I still have a dream. It is a dream deeply rooted in the American dream.

11   I have a dream that one day this nation will rise up and live out the true meaning of its creed: "We hold these truths to be self-evident; that all men are created equal."

12   I have a dream that one day on the red hills of Georgia the sons of former slaves and the sons of former slaveowners will be able to sit down together at the table of brotherhood.

13   I have a dream that one day even the state of Mississippi, a desert state sweltering with the heat of injustice and oppression, will be transformed into an oasis of freedom and justice.

14   I have a dream that my four little children will one day live in a nation where they will not be judged by the color of their skin but by the content of their character.

15   I have a dream today.

16   I have a dream that one day the state of Alabama, whose governor's lips are presently dripping with the words of interposition and nullification, will be transformed into a situation where little black boys and black girls will be able to join hands with little white boys and white girls and walk together as sisters and brothers.

17   I have a dream today.

18   I have a dream that one day every valley shall be exalted, every hill and mountain shall be made low, the rough places will be made

plain, and the crooked places will be made straight, and the glory of the Lord shall be revealed, and all flesh shall see it together.

19   This is our hope. This is the faith with which I return to the South. With this faith we will be able to hew out of the mountain of despair a stone of hope. With this faith we will be able to transform the jangling discords of our nation into a beautiful symphony of brotherhood. With this faith we will be able to work together, to pray together, to struggle together, to go to jail together, to stand up for freedom together, knowing that we will be free one day.

20   This will be the day when all of God's children will be able to sing with new meaning

> My country, 'tis of 'thee,
> Sweet land of liberty,
>   Of thee I sing:
> Land where my fathers died,
> Land of the pilgrims' pride,
> From every mountain-side
>   Let freedom ring.

21   And if America is to be a great nation this must become true. So let freedom ring from the prodigious hilltops of New Hampshire. Let freedom ring from the mighty mountains of New York. Let freedom ring from the heightening Alleghenies of Pennsylvania!

22   Let freedom ring from the snowcapped Rockies of Colorado!

23   Let freedom ring from the curvaceous peaks of California!

24   But not only that; let freedom ring from Stone Mountain of Georgia!

25   Let freedom ring from Lookout Mountain of Tennessee!

26   Let freedom ring from every hill and molehill of Mississippi. From every mountainside, let freedom ring.

27   When we let freedom ring, when we let it ring from every village and every hamlet, from every state and every city, we will be able to speed up that day when all of God's children, black men and white men, Jews and Gentiles, Protestants and Catholics, will be able to join hands and sing in the words of the old Negro spiritual, "Free at last! free at last! thank God almighty, we are free at last!"

Eight Signposts to Salvation

Alan Paton

1   Does a ruling group change towards those it rules because of considerations of justice? The answer is, almost certainly, no. Does it change because of internal and external pressures? Possibly, yes.

2   This second answer is not wholly encouraging. If the internal and external pressures become really dangerous, it may be too late to change. The people exerting the pressures may no longer care if you change. The time has come to destroy you. But the answer is not wholly discouraging. A ruling group may consent to change while it can still influence the situation. It may realise that the way to survival no longer lies in resistance to change. It may see the clouds on the horizon and know what they mean.

3   There is a not very nice picture that comes often to my mind. A man lives in a house full of possessions. The poor and the angry and the dispossessed keep knocking at the door. Inside some members of his family urge him to open the door and others tell him that he must never open the door. Then comes the final imperious knock, and he knows at last that he must open. And when he opens, it is Death who is waiting for him.

4   And the man is me, my wife, our children; he is the White man; above all he is the Afrikaner.

5   But I am not writing to spread gloom. I am writing especially for those inside the house who are telling the man to open the door. I am writing for White students and priests and newspapermen and trade unionists, for the young people of the United Party and the National Party and the Progressive Party, for all those who are working for change in this implacable land.

6   Why on earth do they do it?

7   They do it because of those strange unweighable and immeasurable things like hope and faith. And I admire them for it in this faithless world where for many nothing exists that cannot be weighed and measured, a world that believes in so little.

8   What a strange thing, to have been away from South Africa for some months, from its threats and bannings and denial of passports, and its implacability, and then to want to get back to it again!

9   Some people would say: Of course, you want to get back to your White comforts and privileges. Whatever truth there is in this it's not true enough. You want to get back because it's there that your life has meaning. You want to get back to those stubborn things which are the very stuff of your life. You want to get back to the students and the priests and the newspapermen. They make you feel you are alive more than all the sights of Paris and London and even Copenhagen.

10   These young White people, the Young Turks,[1] the young UPs and Progs and Nats, what do they want?

11   Well, at least it is clear what a great many of them want. They want nothing less than a new country. They have realised that White leadership and Anglo-Afrikaner solidarity and Afrikaner supremacy don't mean anything anymore. Nothing means anything at all if its architects and planners are all White.

12   I am no longer a party man, and I must confess my impatience with those who think that any existing political party can possibly hold the best, wisest, most practicable solution for our problems, or can possibly know the best, wisest, most practicable way towards such a solution. Some of the computer-like arguments between party and party are exasperating. The house is burning down and the would-be saviours are arguing about what colour to choose for the buckets.

13   I don't expect younger White people to rush into a new party. But I do expect them to drop these useless recriminations. They must not shun one another. One thing binds them together that is greater than any loyalty to any party, and that is loyalty to their country and all its people.

14   Are there any things they might all agree about? I believe so and here they are. But I do not dogmatise about them.

15   1. The days of White domination are over.

16   2. The days of unilateral White political decisions are over.

17   3. The progress of the homelands to political independence—however much may be left to be desired—is irreversible.

18   4. The possibility that all or most of the homelands will eventually form a Black Federation must be recognised.

---

[1]Verligte, or enlightened, members of the United Party.

19   5. The possibility that the Black Federation may itself offer to federate with 'White' South Africa must be recognised.

20   6. If it does not make this offer, or if the offer is refused, then the final extinction of 'White' South Africa will be assured.

21   7. The offer will not be made if 'White' South Africa is not prepared to begin the dismantling of the machinery of apartheid.

22   8. It is the political constitution of the future 'White' South Africa that is the supreme political question facing all White people, especially young White people. When I say 'young', I don't mean only students. I mean all who are young enough to know that we must change or die.

23   The problem of 'White' South Africa is that there are:

24   Some four million Whites.

25   Some two million Coloured people.

26   Some 750,000 Asians.

27   Some eight million Africans.

28   According to Nationalist theory these eight million Africans are 'temporary sojourners'. They really belong somewhere else. But at least six million are permanent residents, *except for the fact that no urban African has any real sense of permanence:*

29   Four million Whites therefore constitute a third of the population of 'White' South Africa. The days of their domination are over. They are faced with the problem—the magnitude of which cannot be exaggerated—of constructing a social order in which justice will be done to all. And they cannot construct it unilaterally. Better wages, the quality of education, the quality of housing, the preservation of family life, all are important. But they are no longer gifts to be given by Whites to Blacks.

30   I beg to close with three questions to all White people who understand that we change or die. Is there any future for apartheid in 'White' South Africa? Is Afrikaner-English co-operation good enough, and is Afrikaner-English-Coloured-Asian co-operation not only unattainable, but downright dangerous? Is there any place for the qualified franchise in 'White' South Africa, or is it only another of these unilateral gifts?

31   Change is in the air. It will come whether we White people like it or not. It won't—it cannot—be completely safe, completely sure, completely satisfying. But it will be safer and surer and more satisfying if we take our share in bringing it about in the company of all our fellow South Africans.

On Rabbits, Morality, Etc.

Walter Murdoch

1   I hope the compositor will be especially careful over the title of this essay, and that the linotype will play no unseemly tricks. To guard against any accident, I must ask you to take notice that the word 'rabbits' is, or ought to be, followed by a comma, not an apostrophe. It would be most distressing if any innocent person were cheated into reading the article in the hope of learning something about rabbits' morality— a subject on which my ignorance is profound. . . . When you come to think of it, it would not be a bad subject. The rabbit might be taken as a fine example of what we call race patriotism. His supreme ethical motive is the expansion of the race. He dreams of the day when the rabbit family shall inherit the earth from pole to pole. If we could imagine a rabbit singing, we may suppose his song would be something like 'Rule, Britannia', or 'Deutschland uber Alles'. He is careless of the single life; the individual is nothing to him, the race is all. 'Do what you will with me,' he says; 'trap me, poison me, skin me, pack me tight in tins, make my fur into a hat and my carcass into a pie—what does it matter so long as my race endures and spreads and burrows its way across kingdoms until all the earth is one huge rabbit-warren?' He is the perfect Imperialist—that, however, is not my subject today; nor any other day. It deserves to be treated, not in my halting prose, but in Homeric verse. It is a matter for an epic. Mine is a humbler theme.

2   A little while ago you may have noticed on the cable page of your morning paper the following item: 'The death is reported from London of Mr John R. Collison of Maidstone, Kent, who claimed to be the first person to introduce rabbits into Australia. He was 85 years of age.' A few days later the cables informed us that Mr Collison's claim to this distinction was disputed. 'Mr C. J. Thatcher contends that his father was responsible for having introduced rabbits into Australia.'

3   Now, to begin with, this conflict of claims is surely a somewhat curious and diverting spectacle. The idea of two men each 'claiming'

to have been the first to introduce a deadly pest into a country hitherto free from it, has the charm of novelty. Mr C. J. Thatcher, ready to die in the last ditch defending his father's claim to have done more harm to Australia than anybody else, presents a singular example of filial devotion. It is as if a man went about boasting that one of his ancestors had the honour of bringing malaria into Europe. It is as if a man gave himself airs because his Uncle Henry, and nobody else, had started the recent bush-fires in Victoria. It is as if a statesman were to write a large book to prove that he, and he alone, had had the honour of starting the Great War.

4   As to the historic fact, I have no doubt that Mr C. J. Thatcher is in the right. In 1863, or thereabout, some Victoria sportsmen, sighing like Alexander for more worlds to conquer, bethought them that the coursing of hares and rabbits was a luxury no civilized country ought to be without. So they applied to the Acclimatization Society; and the Society, thinking it rather a bright idea, wrote to its travelling agent in Great Britain, Mr Manning Thatcher, who soon got together a sufficient herd of rabbits and started for Australia in the sailing-ship *Relief*. Ship life seems to have disagreed with the rabbits; when Mr Thatcher reached Australia, not a single one of his rabbits was alive. But he, indomitable man, went straight back to England to get some more rabbits. His next attempt was again unsuccessful; and the next. Three times he started for Australia with a cargo of rabbits; three times he failed to bring a rabbit alive to port. Three times the gods strove to save Australia; but against determination like Mr Thatcher's the very gods do battle in vain. On his third journey he had kept a close watch on his charges and found out the cause of their extraordinary death-rate; he provided a remedy, and his fourth voyage was entirely successful. It was as if the gods had given up the struggle in disgust; Mr Thatcher landed without the loss of a rabbit.

5   Meanwhile, owing to the long delay, the aforesaid sportsmen seem to have lost interest. Mr Thatcher found that nobody wanted his rabbits. With a companion, he went about the country offering baskets of live rabbits for sale, but he did not sell enough to pay expenses. His stock of rabbits increased faster than he could sell them. One hot summer afternoon the two men decided that they had had enough of the tedious and unprofitable business; so they took all their rabbits out into the bush—and opened the baskets.

6   I happen to have in my possession an old newspaper containing
a portrait of Mr Thatcher—and a thoroughly benevolent old gentleman
he looks—also a picture of the medal presented by the Acclimatization
Society to Mr Thatcher in recognition of his splendid achievement in
the matter of rabbits. I presume Mr C. J. Thatcher possesses the original
medal; probably it hangs in a conspicuous place in his drawing-room.
It is a perfect example of the irony of history.

7   Why have I kept that old newspaper? Well, primarily, I suppose,
because I am interested in ethics, as we all are whether we know it or
not. Every one of us, every day, is passing moral judgments, though
not in the technical terms of the moralist. We do not, in our daily
conversation, talk much about virtue, or the *summum bonum,* or the
moral sense, or the categorical imperative, or the hedonistic calculus,
or our ethical ideals; at least, we do talk about them continually, but
not under those names. We don't say of a man that he is a highly
virtuous character; we say he's a pretty decent sort of chap. We don't
say that certain conduct is ethically indefensible; we say it's a bit over
the fence. We mean just the same. We are passing moral judgments.

8   And our underlying assumption is that it is quite easy to tell a
good action from a bad one, right conduct from wrong conduct. And
this common assumption is favoured by popular preachers and writers,
who tell us that we ought not to split straws about a plain question, and
that it is a simple thing to obey conscience, that divinely-given faculty
which tells us, infallibly, what we ought to do and what we ought not
to do. They speak as if this conscience were a kind of moral sense of
smell, by which we can tell a good action from a bad one just as certainly
as we can, in the dark, tell a violet from a polecat. Well, I want to ask
those who hold such a comfortable doctrine a question which puzzles
me. Was Mr Thatcher's action, in introducing the rabbit into Australia,
a good action or a bad one?

9   Mere common sense will not give us the answer. It would be hard
to persuade common sense that an action which ruined thousands of
innocent people and made desolate vast tracts of country, which struck
a terrific blow at the agricultural and pastoral industries of a continent,
can be described as a good action. Neither will common sense blame
Mr Thatcher for obeying orders. He is unquestionably to be praised for
his zeal, his enthusiasm, his unconquerable persistence in what he though
to be an admirable project. We have only to look at his portrait to see

that he was a man of high character, a man actuated by the best intentions. If intentions, as common sense tells us, are what really distinguish
right conduct from wrong, Mr Thatcher beyond doubt acted rightly.
What then?—will common sense admit that a man may act rightly in
doing a bad action? It sounds like a paradox. It is certainly a puzzle;
and if you never, in the course of your practical life, feel that you are
puzzled by it, that can only be because you never think.

10   We make a mistake, of course, when we think of 'an action' as
if it were a simple separate whole. Merely to open a basket, as Mr
Thatcher did, is a thing neither right nor wrong in itself; all depends
on what is inside the basket—depends, that is, on the *consequence* of
the basket's being opened. The immediate consequence, in this instance,
was that the rabbits jumped out, happy in their freedom; so far, the act
had added to the sum of happiness in the sentient world; so far, it was
a good action. Ten years later, it began to be of a darker colour, for
its consequences had begun to develop.

11   Surely there never was a more fallacious saying than Tennyson's:

> And, because right is right, to follow right
> Were wisdom in the scorn of consequence.

Half the disasters endured by the long-suffering human race have been
produced by good men who acted in the scorn of consequence. To do
a thing without considering what the result of your action will be is
mere imbecility. The truth is with that other poet who tells us that

> . . . Of waves
> Our life is, and our deeds are pregnant graves
> Blown rolling from the sunset to the dawn.

12   An action must be considered with its consequences; with the
sum-total of its consequences. And as no human being will live long
enough to see the sum-total of the consequences of any of his actions—
for the ultimate consequence cannot be known until time comes to an
end—we can never say that a given action is absolutely good or absolutely bad.

13   How then are we to choose between right and wrong conduct? Choose we must, somehow; 'life's business', as Browning says, 'being just the terrible choice.' Some years ago, certain persons wished to introduce into Western Australia a certain kind of deer. It was pointed out, however, that this very species had been introduced into South Africa, had eaten farmers out of house and home, and had been in fact a greater plague than ever the rabbit was in Australia. The persons who were preparing to do this thing without inquiry into the consequence of similar procedure in other countries would have been guilty, had they had their way, not merely of a bad action, but of a wrong action. It would be of no use to plead that their intentions were good—we know what road is paved with good intentions. It would be of no use to tell us that their consciences had commended the act; it is a common and deadly fallacy, that a mysterious faculty called the conscience absolves us from the duty of finding out, to the best of our ability, the probable consequences of our action. . . . Consideration of Mr Thatcher and his basket of rabbits thus brings us round to the conclusion reached so many centuries ago by Socrates. Virtue is knowledge.

Acknowledgments

Woody Allen, "Slang Origins." From *Without Feathers*, by Woody Allen. Copyright © 1975 by Woody Allen. Reprinted by permission of Random House, Inc.

Maya Angelou, "Grandmother's Victory." From *I Know Why the Caged Bird Sings*, by Maya Angelou. Copyright © 1969 by Maya Angelou. Reprinted by permission of Random House, Inc.

Isaac Asimov, "Anatomy of a Martian." Original title: "Is Anyone There?" Copyright 1964 by Isaac Asimov. Reprinted by permission of the author.

Margaret Atwood, "Canadian Culture: A Brave New Spirit." First appeared in *Vogue*, June 1982. Copyright © 1982 by The Condé Nast Publications Inc. Reprinted by permission of the author.

Russell Baker, "Universal Military Motion." Copyright © 1981 by The New York Times Company. Reprinted by permission.

James David Barber, "Presidential Character and How To Foresee It." From *The Presidential Character*, by James David Barber. Copyright 1972 by James David Barber. Reprinted by permission of Prentice-Hall, Inc., Englewood Cliffs, NJ 07632.

Bruno Bettelheim, "The Holocaust." From *Surviving and Other Essays,* by
Bruno Bettelheim. Copyright © 1979 by Bruno Bettelheim and Trude
Bettelheim as Trustees. Reprinted by permission of Alfred A. Knopf,
Inc.

Robert Brustein, "Reflections on Horror Movies." Copyright © 1958 by Robert
Brustein. Adapted by permission of Alfred A. Knopf, Inc. from *The
Third Theatre,* by Robert Brustein.

William F. Buckley, Jr., "Why Don't We Complain?" First appeared in
Esquire. Copyright © 1960 by William F. Buckley, Jr. Reprinted by
permission of Wallace & Sheil Agency, Inc.

Morley Callaghan, "Hemingway and Fitzgerald." From *That Summer in Paris.*
Copyright Morley Callaghan 1963. Reprinted by permission of Mac-
millan of Canada, A Division of Canada Publishing Corporation; and by
Don Congdon Associates, Inc.

Albert Camus, "The Myth of Sisyphus." From *The Myth of Sisyphus and Other
Essays,* by Albert Camus, translated by Justin O'Brien. Copyright ©
1955 by Alfred A. Knopf, Inc. Reprinted by permission of the publisher.

Rachel Carson, "The Grey Beginnings." From *The Sea Around Us,* Revised
Edition, by Rachel L. Carson. Copyright © 1950, 1951, 1961 by Rachel
L. Carson; renewed 1979 by Roger Christie. Reprinted by permission of
Oxford University Press, Inc.

Bruce Catton, "Grant and Lee: A Study in Contrasts." From *The American
Story.* Reprinted by permission of the U.S. Capitol Historical Society.

Norman Cousins, "Pain Is Not the Ultimate Enemy." From *Anatomy of an
Illness,* by Norman Cousins, by permission of W. W. Norton & Company, Inc. Copyright © 1979 by W. W. Norton & Company, Inc.

Robertson Davies, "Is Canada Neurotic?" First appeared in *Vogue,* Sept. 1982.
Copyright © 1982 by Robertson Davies. Reprinted by permission of
Curtis Brown, Ltd.

Simone de Beauvoir, "The Discovery and Assumption of Old Age." Reprinted
by permission of the Putnam Publishing Group from *The Coming of Age,*
by Simone de Beauvoir. Copyright © 1972 by Andre Deutsch; Weiden-
feld and Nicolson; and G. P. Putnam's Sons.

Joan Didion, "On Going Home." From *Slouching Towards Bethlehem.* Copyright © 1966, 1968 by Joan Didion. Reprinted by permission of Farrar,
Straus, & Giroux, Inc.

Annie Dillard, "Transfiguration." From *Holy the Firm.* Copyright © 1977 by
Annie Dillard. Reprinted by permission of Harper & Row, Publishers,
Inc.

Loren Eiseley, "The Cosmic Prison." From *Pyramid.* Copyright © 1970 by
Loren Eiseley. Reprinted by permission of Simon & Schuster, Inc.

Peter Elbow, "Desperation Writing." From *Writing Without Teachers,* by Peter Elbow. Copyright © 1973 by Oxford University Press, Inc. Reprinted with permission.

Peter Farb and George Armelagos, "The Patterns of Eating." From *Consuming Passions,* by Peter Farb and George Armelagos. Copyright © 1980 by the Estate of Peter Farb. Reprinted by permission of Houghton Mifflin Company.

E. M. Forster, "My Wood." From *Abinger Harvest.* Copyright 1936; renewed 1964 by Edward Morgan Forster. Reprinted by permission of Harcourt Brace Jovanovich, Inc. and by Edward Arnold Publishers Ltd.

Erich Fromm, "Three Kinds of Symbols." Excerpt from "Symbolic Language of Dreams" from *Language: An Inquiry into its Meaning and Function,* edited by Ruth Nanda Anshen. Copyright 1957 by Erich Fromm. Reprinted by permission of Harper & Row, Publishers, Inc.

William Golding, "Thinking as a Hobby." From *Holiday.* Copyright © 1961 by William Golding. Reprinted by permission of Curtis Brown, Ltd.

Ellen Goodman, "The Chem 20 Factor." From *Close to Home.* Copyright © 1979 by The Washington Post Company. Reprinted by permission of Simon & Schuster, Inc.

Stephen Jay Gould, "Were Dinosaurs Dumb?" From *The Panda's Thumb: More Reflections in Natural History,* by Stephen Jay Gould, by permission of W. W. Norton & Company, Inc. Copyright © 1980 by Stephen Jay Gould.

Jeff Greenfield, "The Black and White Truth About Basketball." Copyright © 1980 by Jeff Greenfield. Reprinted by permission of The Sterling Lord Agency, Inc.

Gilbert Highet, "Kitsch." From *The Clerk of Oxenford.* Copyright © 1954 by Gilbert Highet. Reprinted by permission of Curtis Brown, Ltd.

Edward Hoagland, "In the Toils of the Law." Copyright © 1972 by Edward Hoagland. Reprinted from *Walking the Dead Diamond River,* by Edward Hoagland, by permission of Random House, Inc.

Anne Hollander, "Fashion and the Female Body." From *Seeing Through Clothes,* by Anne Hollander. Copyright © 1975, 1976, 1978 by Anne L. Hollander. Reprinted by permission of Viking Penguin Inc.

Richard Howey, "How To Write a Rotten Poem with Almost No Effort." First appeared in *The Plain Dealer.* Reprinted by permission of the author.

Langston Hughes, "Salvation." From *The Big Sea,* by Langston Hughes. Copyright 1940 by Langston Hughes. Reprinted by permission of Farrar, Straus & Giroux, Inc.

Martin Luther King, Jr., "I Have a Dream." Copyright © 1963 by Martin Luther King, Jr. Reprinted by permission of Joan Daves.

Maxine Hong Kingston, "The Wild Man of the Green Swamp." From *China Men,* by Maxine Hong Kingston. Copyright © 1980 by Maxine Hong Kingston. Reprinted by permission of Alfred A. Knopf, Inc.

Margaret Laurence, "Where the World Began." From *Heart of a Stranger.* Copyright © 1976 by Margaret Laurence. Reprinted by permission of McClelland & Stewart, Ltd.

Barbara Lawrence. "Four-Letter Words Can Hurt You." Copyright © 1973 by The New York Times Company. Reprinted by permission.

Stephen Leacock, "Roughing It in the Bush." From *The Bodley Head Leacock.* Reprinted by permission of Barbara Nimmo.

Fran Lebowitz, "The Sound of Music: Enough Already." From *Metropolitan Life,* by Fran Lebowitz. Copyright © 1974, 1975, 1976, 1977, 1978 by Fran Lebowitz. Reprinted by permission of the publisher, E. P. Dutton, a division of New American Library.

Dorothy Livesay, "All Aboa-r-rd!" First appeared in *Canadian Literature,* Spring 1984. Reprinted by permission of the author.

Barry Lopez, "My Horse." First appeared in *The North American Review,* Summer 1975. Reprinted by permission of *The North American Review* and by the author.

Joyce Maynard, "I Remember. . . ." This article first appeared in *TV Guide.* Copyright © 1975 by Joyce Maynard. Reprinted by permission of Robert Cornfield Literary Agency.

H. L. Mencken, "The Libido for the Ugly." Copyright 1927 by Alfred A. Knopf, Inc. and renewed 1955 by H. L. Mencken. Reprinted from *A Mencken Chrestomathy,* edited by H. L. Mencken, by permission of the publisher.

Jessica Mitford, "Behind the Formaldehyde Curtain." From *The American Way of Death.* Copyright © 1963, 1978 by Jessica Mitford. Reprinted by permission of Simon & Schuster, Inc.

Desmond Morris, "Territorial Behavior." From *Manwatching.* Copyright © 1977 by Desmond Morris. Reprinted by permission of Harry N. Abrams, Inc.

Walter Murdoch, "On Rabbits, Morality, Etc." From *The Best of Walter Murdoch: 72 Essays.* Reprinted by permission of Angus & Robertson Publishers, Sydney, Australia.

Donald M. Murray, "The Maker's Eye: Revising Your Own Manuscripts." First appeared in *The Writer.* Copyright © 1973 by Donald M. Murray. Reprinted by permission of Roberta Pryor, Inc.

George Orwell, "Shooting an Elephant." From *Shooting an Elephant and Other Essays,* by George Orwell. Copyright 1950 by Sonia Orwell; renewed 1978 by Sonia Brownell Orwell. Reprinted by permission of Harcourt Brace Jovanovich, Inc.; A. M. Heath & Company Ltd.; the estate of the late Sonia Brownell Orwell; and Secker & Warburg, Ltd.

Jo Goodwin Parker, "What Is Poverty?" From *America's Other Children: Public Schools Outside Suburbs,* by George Henderson. Copyright 1971 by the University of Oklahoma Press. Reprinted by permission of George Henderson.

Alan Paton, "Eight Signposts to Salvation." From *Knocking on the Door: Shorter Writings,* edited by Colin Gardner. Copyright © 1975 by Alan Paton. Reprinted by permission of Simon & Schuster, Inc.

Alexander Petrunkevitch, "The Spider and the Wasp." First appeared in *Scientific American,* August 1952. Copyright © 1952 by Scientific American, Inc. All rights reserved. Reprinted with permission.

James C. Rettie, "'But a Watch in the Night': A Scientific Fable." From *Forever the Land,* edited by Russell and Kate Lord. Copyright 1950 by James Rettie. Reprinted by permission of Harper & Row, Publishers, Inc.

Mordecai Richler, "Main Street." From *The Street: A Memoir.* Copyright © 1969 by Mordecai Richler. Reprinted by permission of International Creative Management. First published in *The New Republic.*

Richard Rodriguez, "Does America Still Exist?" First appeared in *Harper's,* March 1984. Copyright © 1984 by Richard Rodriguez. Reprinted by permission of Georges Borchardt, Inc.

Murray Ross, "Football Red and Baseball Green." First appeared in *Chicago Review,* 1971. Copyright © 1971 by Murray Ross. Reprinted by permission of the author.

Carl Sagan, "The Nuclear Winter." Reprinted by permission of the author and the author's agents, Scott Meredith Literary Agency, Inc., 845 Third Avenue, New York, New York 10022.

Richard Selzer, "The Discus Thrower." First appeared in *Harper's,* 1977. Copyright © 1977 by Richard Selzer. Reprinted by permission of Georges Borchardt, Inc.

Susan Sontag, "Beauty." Original title: "Women's Beauty: Put Down or Power Source." Copyright © 1975 by Susan Sontag. Reprinted by permission of Farrar, Straus & Giroux, Inc.

Judy Syfers, "Why I Want a Wife." Copyright 1970 by Judy Syfers. Reprinted by permission of the author.

Lewis Thomas, "Notes on Punctuation." From *The Medusa and the Snail,* by Lewis Thomas. Copyright © 1979 by Lewis Thomas. Reprinted by permission of Viking Penguin Inc.

James Thurber, "University Days." Copyright © 1933, 1961 James Thurber from *My Life and Hard Times,* published by Harper & Row. Reprinted by permission of Mrs. James Thurber.

Frank Trippett, "The Great American Cooling Machine." Copyright © 1979 Time Inc. All rights reserved. Reprinted by permission from *Time.*

Barbara Tuchman, "The Decline of Quality." Copyright © 1980 by The New York Times Company. Reprinted by permission.

John Updike, "Venezuela for Visitors." From *Hugging the Shore,* by John Updike. Copyright © 1983 by John Updike. Reprinted by permission of Alfred A. Knopf, Inc.

Lindsay Van Gelder, "The Great Person-Hole Cover Debate: A Modest Proposal for Anyone Who Thinks the Word 'He' Is Just Plain Easier . . ." First appeared in *Ms. Magazine,* April 1980. Reprinted by permission of the author.

E. B. White, "Once More to the Lake." From *The Essays of E. B. White.* Copyright 1939, 1967 by E. B. White. Reprinted by permission of Harper & Row, Publishers, Inc.

Marie Winn, "Viewing Vs. Reading." From *The Plug-in Drug,* by Marie Winn. Copyright © 1977, 1985 by Marie Winn Miller. By permission of Viking Penguin Inc.

Tom Wolfe, "Pornoviolence." From *Mauve Gloves and Madmen, Clutter and Vine.* Copyright © 1967 by Tom Wolfe. Reprinted by permission of Farrar, Straus & Giroux, Inc.

Virginia Woolf, "The Death of the Moth." From *The Death of the Moth and Other Essays.* Copyright 1942 by Harcourt Brace Jovanovich, Inc.; renewed 1970 by Marjorie T. Parsons, Executrix. Reprinted by permission of the publisher, and by The Hogarth Press Ltd.

William Zinsser, "The Transaction." From *On Writing Well, Second Edition.* Copyright © 1980 by William K. Zinsser. Reprinted by permission of the author.